NEW PERSPECTIVES ON THE SOUTH

Charles P. Roland, General Editor

Cotton Fields No More

Southern Agriculture 1865-1980

GILBERT C. FITE

THE UNIVERSITY PRESS OF KENTUCKY

Scholarly publisher for the Commonwealth,
serving Bellarmine College, Berea College, Centre
College of Kentucky, Eastern Kentucky University,
The Filson Club, Georgetown College, Kentucky
Historical Society, Kentucky State University,
Morehead State University, Murray State University,
Northern Kentucky University, Transylvania University,
University of Kentucky, University of Louisville,
and Western Kentucky University.

Editorial and Sales Offices: Lexington, Kentucky 40506-0024

Library of Congress Cataloging in Publication Data

Fite, Gilbert Courtland, 1918
  Cotton fields no more.

  (New perspectives on the South)
  Bibliography: p.
  Includes index.
  1. Agriculture-Economic aspects-Southern States
History. I. Title. II. Series.
HD1773.A5F58 1984   338.1'0975   84-7439
ISBN 0-8131-0306-1
ISBN 0-8131-0160-3 (pbk.)

For my grandchildren
Nicolas, Sonny, Ryan, Matthew, Olivia, and Michael
all of whom were born too late to experience the joys
and agonies of farm life

Contents

Illustrations follow page 114

Tables

Editor's Preface

The South throughout most of its history has been a predominantly rural and agricultural society. For more than two centuries the plantation and slave labor were the most distinguishing features of southern agriculture, though the overwhelming majority of the region's farmers were neither planters, in the traditional meaning, nor slaveowners. Then came the Civil War and emancipation, followed by almost a century and a quarter of change. Today the southern population has virtually ceased to be rural, and to a significant extent the economy has become industrial, yet the area continues to be one of the major agricultural producers of the world.

Mr. Fite brings to the present study a distinguished career in scholarship on American agriculture and farm life. Here he describes splendidly the vast changes that have taken place in southern agriculture since the Civil War. He pays special attention to the problems of cotton monoculture, tenantry, the crop-lien credit system, and soil erosion—factors that affected the southern farmer from the Civil War to the New Deal of the 1930s. He also emphasizes the stunning developments of the post-World War II decades, including the spread of large-scale commercial farming, mechanization, and crop diversification. Nor does he lose sight of the human dimension, the farmers and workers who remain on the land after most of their fellows have been displaced by machines, and whose numbers have now diminished to fewer than 3 percent of the total southern population.

In telling the story of southern agriculture and farm life since the Civil War, and in demonstrating their critical roles in the larger experience of the region, the author makes this volume eminently suitable for inclusion in "New Perspectives on the South." The series is designed to give a fresh and comprehensive view of the South's history, as seen in the light of the many occurrences since World War II. Each volume is expected to be a complete essay representing both a synthesis of the best scholarship on the subject and an interpretive analysis derived from the author's own research and reflections. More than twenty volumes are in prospect.

CHARLES P. ROLAND

Preface

Despite the economic importance of agriculture in the post-Civil War South, no general history of southern farming since the end of slavery has been written. Numerous book-length studies have been published on particular aspects of southern agriculture, such as sharecropping and tenancy, and on the problems southern farmers faced during the Great Depression. Some excellent interpretative articles also have appeared. But the many pieces that make up commercial agricultural development in the South since the Civil War have not been put together into a meaningful whole. That is the purpose of this book.

There is, of course, no single agricultural South. The variations in climate, rainfall, landforms, and quality of soil are enormous. It is a region where many larger and smaller geographic subregions exist which have historically provided the basis for great differences in productivity, the kinds of crops raised, and farm organization. Besides such major subregions as the Piedmont, the Coastal Plains, and the Mississippi River alluvial valley, there are numerous smaller subregions, such as the central highlands of Florida, where citrus came to predominate. The South is a land of infinite geographical and agricultural variety. Because of this, exceptions can be made to nearly every generalization about the history of southern farming. Nevertheless, there have been some common denominators, and these I have sought to identify and explain.

For purposes of my study I have arbitrarily defined the South as the eleven former Confederate States stretching from Virginia to Texas. It might be argued that other states or parts of states, such as Oklahoma and Kentucky or Southern Missouri, should be included in any book on southern agriculture. However, the principal elements of southern farming are found in the old Confederacy. Thus, unless otherwise indicated, when I write about the South I am referring to the eleven-state region. Occasionally, to present a broader picture, I may mention the census South, which includes sixteen states, but this is rare.

This study deals mainly with commercial farmers, the problems they faced, and their long struggle to modernize and to earn a decent standard of living. Unfortunately most farmers never achieved economic success, and through the 1930s poverty was the most common condition among farmers throughout the South. Because of the persistence of rural poverty from the 1870s to World War II, reference to living conditions on southern farms is made at several points through the book. While this results in some repetition, it shows more clearly that time did not heal the situation for millions of farm people in the region. Moreover, in order to document fully the developments in southern agriculture, I have relied heavily on statistics.

The main economic problem confronting southern farmers for three generations after 1865 was an excess of rural population in relation to developed land resources. The change to a more favorable man-land ratio was thwarted by the lack of off-farm jobs to siphon away surplus farm workers. The pressure of people on land was heavy from the 1880s to the 1940s. Not until the 1930s did events begin to merge in such a way as to destroy the old patterns of small, nonproductive, and poverty-ridden farms throughout the South. The New Deal's acreage restriction and price support programs, federal credit agencies, and support for soil conservation, combined with agricultural science and technology, finally produced a new and modernized agriculture. Within one generation, from the late 1930s to the 1960s, a revolution occurred on southern commercial farms. The fewer and larger farms became mechanized, capital intensive, and labor efficient. My intent is to explain why agricultural change was so slow in the South and to show how the agents of change worked throughout the region after 1933 to destroy the old and produce a modernized agriculture.

Many people have generously assisted me in this work. Since my graduate school days in the 1940s, Lewis E. Atherton has been a constant inspiration. My colleague Numan V. Bartley has been most helpful in sharing with me his incisive insights about recent southern history. Paul C. Nagel and Lester D. Stephens, heads of the History Department at the University of Georgia since I began working on this project, have provided time and support for research and writing. The University of Georgia librarians have also provided valuable assistance. Several farmers and agricultural scientists shared their knowledge and experience with me; these include Burnell Gaskins, Fred B. Collins, Luther Spooner, Glenn W. Burton, J. Guy Woodroof, B. L. Southwell, Frank P. King, and D. W. Brooks. During the course of this project four research assistants, William Cawthon, Michael Hammett, Beverly Williams, and Randall Patton were most helpful. Most of all however, I am indebted to the University of Georgia, especially to President Fred C. Davison and to Dean W. J. Payne, for providing an environment conducive to scholarly work.

I could not have completed this book without the hard and efficient work of my secretary, Mrs. Edna Fisher. To her I am grateful. Finally, despite her aversion to agricultural history, my wife June has provided support and inspiration for this, and all my work, extending over more than forty years.

1

Descent into Poverty, 1865-1900

When southern soldiers trudged back to their farms and plantations in the spring of 1865, they found agriculture in serious disarray. In many areas of the defeated Confederacy houses and farm buildings had been burned, fences torn down, and livestock stolen or killed, while fields were overgrown with weeds. One planter wrote: "I had the misfortune to be in the line of Sherman's march, and lost everything-Devon cows, Merino sheep, Chester hogs, Shanghai chickens, and in fact everything but my land, my wife and children and the clothing we had at that time." In some areas land prices had dropped to about one-fourth of what they had been in 1860. Moreover, the slaves who had provided much of the farm labor in the South before the Civil War had suddenly become freedmen, and the planters were without workers. A young Georgia girl wrote: "A settled gloom, deep and heavy, hangs over the whole land."[1]

Farmers and planters all the way from the hills and valleys of Virginia to the prairies of central Texas confronted new and perplexing problems. Besides having to restore declining production caused by the war, farmers faced the difficult matters of soil erosion, poor markets and transportation, and credit costs. The small white farmers who owned their land and provided their own labor were able to recover most rapidly. They returned to raise a few head of livestock, to grow some cotton and corn, and, at least for a while, to operate much as they had before the war. Being relatively self-sufficient and independent, this group of farmers quickly overcame most adverse economic effects of the fighting.

In contrast, cotton, rice, and sugar planters with large acreages faced major adjustments, as did the recently freed slaves. The freedmen wanted their own land. This desire, according to General Davis Tillson of the Freedmen's Bureau, resembled "an instinct and it is almost uncontrollable."[2] Many victorious northerners believed they should have it. There was much discussion about granting blacks land acquired through the confiscation of southern estates. The Freedmen's Bureau, set up in 1865, proposed to give any abandoned and confiscated rebel lands to blacks in 40-acre farms. The idea of becoming an independent farmer by acquiring 40 acres and a mule was an exciting prospect for many freedmen. But such hopes were soon dashed. The federal government did not confiscate much land held by former confederates and authorities had little or nothing to distribute.

Another possibility of land ownership for freedmen was to carve out farms from the millions of acres of public land in five southern states. In 1866 Congress passed the Southern Homestead Act with the express purpose of providing land for blacks. As Senator Samuel C. Pomeroy, chairman of the Senate Committee on Public Lands, said, the main idea behind the law was to give preference to former slaves who were seeking farms. Despite these good intentions, only about 4,000 blacks filed entries for land under the law up to late 1869, and Congress repealed the measure in 1876.[3]

Why did so few freedmen succeed in establishing farms on public lands in the South? The answers are clear enough. Much of the available land was of relatively poor quality, covered with pines and fairly far removed from where most blacks lived. Furthermore, the great majority of freedmen had no property or capital. They did not have money for transportation, housing, equipment, seed, or even food and clothes to sustain themselves until they made the first crop. There was also opposition by white southerners who did not want blacks to acquire land.

It is important to remember that the great majority of blacks moved from slavery to freedom with no money or capital, and with nothing marketable except strong backs and hard-working hands. The only work most of them knew was farming. Moreover, they had been kept illiterate by their former masters and for the most part had been denied managerial and supervisory experience. Their entire lives had been spent taking orders from their owners and living in an environment of restrictions and controls. For many blacks, to become independent farmers immediately after freedom would have required drastic federal intervention in the southern economy and a fundamental change in race relations. The federal government would have had to give the freedmen land, provide capital for a minimum amount of equipment and for operating and living expenses for at least a year, and, finally, supply temporary business advice. Such an extension of power and assistance by the federal government was so far ahead of popularly accepted political principles that nothing can be gained by speculating on what the progress of rural blacks would have been if such actions had been taken in the late 1860s. The problem of adjusting to a free labor system was left largely to landowners and individual freedmen with some help from the Freedmen's Bureau and the Union army.

However strong traditions of dependence and paternalism may have been, blacks wanted economic freedom, and their emancipation did give them more bargaining power in the economy than they had experienced as slaves. In celebrating their freedom immediately after the war, many former slaves rejected work and drifted around the countryside and cities enjoying their new-found independence. Whether they refused to work or could not find employment, many were kept from starving in 1866 and 1867 only by relief from the Freedmen's Bureau. Thousands from the Southeast were attracted westward to Mississippi, Arkansas, and Texas, where wages were higher. A notice in the *Report of the Commissioner of Agriculture* in 1866 estimated that about 1,000 black Georgians a day were passing through Atlanta on their way west.[4]

The scarcity, independence, and unreliability of labor created severe problems for many planters. They had land and some equipment, but unless they could make satisfactory arrangements with the former slaves, their fields would lie idle and unproductive. Governor James L. Orr of South Carolina declared in 1866 that Negroes were invaluable "to the productive resources of the state, and if their labor be lost by removal to other sections, it will convert thousands of acres of productive land into a dreary wilderness."[5] Cotton production, especially, was highly labor intensive and required cheap workers. As the price of cotton soared right after the war, southern farmers had "cotton on the brain," experiencing a kind of "insanity," according to one observer.[6] To get in on the high prices, planters had to recruit sufficient workers to cultivate their lands.

Landowners at first tried to hire their former slaves for wages, but they found the system unsatisfactory. In the first place, many planters did not have ready cash with which to pay wages before harvest, and blacks wanted to be paid at regular intervals. "They are more willing to work when they can be paid by the week or month as they thus obtain ready money," wrote a Georgian in 1866.[7] Planters also complained that the wage system gave them insufficient control over their workers. Accusing black freedmen of being indolent, careless, and lazy, landowners initiated highly restrictive employment contracts. Blacks resented these contracts, interpreting them as constraints on their freedom. Thousands of blacks refused to sign work contracts at all in 1866 and 1867, and tensions and unrest prevailed in many communities.[8] Somehow arrangements had to be worked out that would bring the planters' land and capital and the freedmen's labor into a satisfactory and productive economic unit. After considerable trial and error, the sharecropping and tenant systems fell into place. They were really not

fully satisfactory to either landowners or workers, but the arrangements did bring land and labor together to restore agricultural production in the plantation areas.

Under the sharecropping arrangement, a landowner made an
agreement with a worker, including the worker's entire family, to farm
some 20 to 40 acres of cultivated land. This was about the size cotton
farm that one family could work. Besides land, the owner provided a
house, tools, seed, and sometimes a mule for plowing. The farmer
supplied only his labor and that of his family. The crop was then
divided equally. In reality sharecroppers were laborers whose wages
were paid with a share of the crop. For example, in 1872 the Georgia
Supreme Court asserted that "the cropper is rather a mode of paying
wages than a tenancy. The title to the crop subject to the wages is in the
owner of the land."[9] Describing the situation in 1916, two Mississippi
observers wrote: "The landlords exercise careful supervision over the
sharecroppers, who are locally not considered tenants at all, but as
laborers hired to do work in return for half the crop and the use of a
cabin."[10]

Since recently freed blacks and many whites had no money, they
had to borrow for living expenses until the crop was harvested. A
system developed under which the landowner, who was often also a
merchant, advanced around $6 to $10 a month in cash or supplies to
each sharecropper. The farmer was then obligated by contract to deliver
his crop to the landowner, who sold it and settled up the accounts.
Often, however, the crop did not cover the advances made by the
planter, and the sharecropper dropped into perpetual debt and poverty. By controlling the land and food supply, landowners gained a high
degree of control over their labor. In addition the legal system in the
southern states was designed to protect the economic interests of
landlords and merchants.[11]

Other kinds of tenancy also developed. Farmers who were somewhat better off and owned some capital equipment rented land for
cash, usually stated as a specific quantity of cotton, while others
arranged to give the landlord some specified share of whatever crop
was raised. Where the tenant furnished the mules, equipment, and
other means of production, he usually received two-thirds of the crop
and the landlord one-third. But there were many different arrangements between landowner and renter which changed over time in
various parts of the South. One observer told the Industrial Commission in 1899 that "the details of these variations in dealings of landlord
and tenant are practically endless." The fundamental difference between the sharecropper and other types of tenancy was that, as Harold
D. Woodman has explained, the wages of a sharecropper were "paid *to*

him *by* the landlord" from the worker's production. Other tenants were renters "who paid rent *to* the landlord for use of the land."[12]

The crop-lien system was another arrangement which developed throughout the South. Under this plan merchants loaned farmers money for operating and living expenses and took a mortgage or lien on the crop as security. The lender also commonly took a chattel mortgage on any other property owned by the farmer, such as a mule. One critic said that the only restriction on the lien laws was that a farmer could not "give a mortgage on his wife and children."[13]

Unable to make enough to buy a farm, and in some cases even losing land they once owned, an increasing number of southern farmers, both black and white, fell into one of the varieties of tenancy. Some planters paid wages and worked their laborers in gangs much as had been done under slavery, but by the 1880s most landowners, at least those outside of the Louisiana sugar parishes, relied mainly on share-croppers and tenants. Even Louisiana planters depended more on tenants to produce cane for their mills after 1880. A Georgia cotton planter reported that he abandoned the wage system in 1885 because "hired labor became too sorry and unreliable." Another landowner wrote that he quit paying wages "because of more profit in share system to landlord."[14] Despite the increase in sharecropping and other forms of tenancy, many southern farmers and planters continued to use some wage labor.

By the 1880s tenancy and sharecropping had fastened an inescapable grip on hundreds of thousands of southern famers. While the total number of farm owners increased throughout the South after 1880, the number of tenants grew much faster. In the eleven southern states, farms operated by tenants and sharecroppers rose from 37.9 to 48.4 percent of the total between 1880 and 1900. The highest rates of tenancy were in pre-Civil War plantation areas. Tenancy was extremely high in the so-called "black belt" extending from South Carolina, through central Georgia and central Alabama, across north-central Mississippi, and farther west into parts of Arkansas, Louisiana, and eastern Texas. In counties with the heaviest black population and where cotton was the main crop, tenancy rose to as much as 70 to 80 percent of the farms. In contrast, the percentage of farm owners was much higher in parts of northern Alabama and Mississippi, the uplands of Arkansas, and sections of the western Carolinas, northern Georgia, and central Tennessee, where a high percentage of whites carried on more generalized farming operations.[15]

Sharecropping and tenancy were more than economic systems. In many areas these economic arrangements were the basis for social control of blacks and poor whites. Landlords and merchants not only controlled what was grown but how business and social relations were carried on. For example, a black sharecropper dared not question the figures of the landlord at settlement time. To do so would mark him as a "trouble-making nigger" who might find himself unable to get any farmland the next year. Within a generation or less after the Civil War, relations between poor blacks and whites in the rural South had become institutionalized in a way that was to change little until after World War II. Looking back at the situation from the vantage point of 1943, Frank J. Welch, an agricultural expert from Mississippi State College, wrote that plantation tenancy had been the "partially accepted solution to a race problem. . . . Elaborate codes, now largely receded from consciousness, have grown up to rural relations between the white and negro races."[16]

While the growing sharecropping and other tenant systems were most closely associated with the larger landholders and planters, many middle-level farmers also employed sharecroppers and tenants. Farmers who had 200 to 300 acres of cropland did not usually try to farm all of that acreage themselves, as was the case in the Midwest. Midwestern farmers usually had four to eight head of horses and machinery, including harvesting equipment, which permitted them to handle much more acreage. In the South, where cotton was the main commercial crop, most labor was performed by one or two mules and by human hands. Since cotton was a very labor-intensive crop, the larger family farmer commonly arranged with two or three sharecroppers or tenants to farm 40 to 50 acres of his land each, while reserving 50 to 100 acres for his own farming operations. He then employed wage labor, sometimes hiring one or more of his sharecroppers part-time, to do much of the cotton planting, hoeing, weeding, and picking. In many cases the larger family farmer in the South became a manager rather than providing his own labor. This helped give rise to the charge that many southern farmers were lazy.

After 1880 there was a significant change in the tenant mix. Share tenants increased 4 percent in ten southern states between 1880 and 1900, while cash tenancy rose about 8 percent, or twice as fast, in the same period. While in some cases this represented a degree of economic progress by workers and tenants, according to the census of 1900 the rise in cash tenancy was "due largely to the transfer of ownership of lands from the farmer to local merchants or cotton factors, whose policy is to lease their lands for a fixed money rental."[17]

High cotton prices for nearly a decade after the Civil War encouraged planters and farmers to grow cotton at the expense of other crops. In 1866 cotton brought as much as 43 cents a pound, and it continued high in 1867 and 1868. There was, as some contemporaries observed, a kind of "epidemic cotton fever" among farmers.[18] As the labor situation stabilized, production rose steadily and prices declined. By 1876 cotton fell to less than 10 cents a pound. Nevertheless, heavy production continued and in 1879 the South could boast an output that exceeded the 5.4 million bales grown in 1859.

Although farm prices for cotton averaged less than 10 cents a pound throughout the 1880s, producers devoted more and more land and labor to the white lint. By 1890 production exceeded 8 million bales for the first time. Despite depression prices of 5 to 7 cents a pound during and following the Panic of 1893, southern farmers chalked up a record-breaking crop of 11.5 million bales in 1898. That forced another sharp drop in prices. A traveler who observed 5-cent cotton in 1898 found poverty and despair everywhere he went.[19]

By 1899 there were 1,034,777 farms in the nine states where cotton provided the main source of income. This was about 54 percent of the farms in those states. Of the 824,069 farms in Mississippi, Alabama, Georgia, and South Carolina, slightly over 70 percent depended mainly on cotton as a source of income.[20] As Clarence H. Poe, editor of the *Progressive Farmer*, wrote in 1904, "When southern cotton prices drop every southern man feels the blow; when cotton prices advance, every industry throbs with vigor."[21] One of the worst features of cotton growing was that it was a feast and famine proposition. While growers might suffer from low prices and hard times for several years, high prices usually brought a stampede to increase production and enjoy prosperity for a year or two, only to slip back into poverty again when prices declined.

As cotton production rose, the planting of corn and other food crops, as well as the raising of livestock, showed a relative decline in many areas. Before the Civil War farmers and planters tended to produce much of their own food and used cotton as the supplementary cash crop. Southern farmers also raised large numbers of hogs and cattle in the prewar years. Corn eaten in many forms, vegetables such as peas, cabbage, and sweet potatoes, and plenty of lean meat gave prewar southern farmers a fairly adequate diet. Even in the 1850s, however, southern planters began to produce cotton at the expense of other crops. During that decade cotton acreage grew by more than 100 percent compared to only 17 percent for corn. The fixation on cotton after Appomattox became even stronger as planters and farmers diverted their attention away from the production of corn and other grains and livestock. By 1909 southern farmers produced only 25 percent of the nation's corn crop compared to 43 percent in 1859. In some of the heavy cotton regions acreage in corn actually dropped well below that planted to cotton. In the fifty-five counties of middle Georgia, farmers grew 1,363,539 acres of cotton and only 1,109,047 acres of corn in 1879. In Sharkey County, located in the Mississippi-Yazoo Delta, farmers raised 17,041 acres of cotton compared to only 7,540 acres of corn.[22]

In the five southeastern states of the Carolinas, Georgia, Alabama, and Mississippi, livestock also lost out to cotton. In 1860 South Carolina had 506,776 cattle, but the number dropped to only 268,293 by 1900. There was also a loss in Georgia. While there was a small increase in cattle numbers throughout the entire South, especially in Texas, the growth in the late nineteenth century lagged far behind that in the Midwest or West. There was an actual decline in many of the counties that concentrated so heavily on cotton. The number of milk cows dropped in the 1870s and then rose by 1900 to a figure slightly above that of 1860. But the number of farmers in the five southeastern cotton states jumped from 268,345 to 1,048,706 in the same period. This meant that there was an average of less than one milk cow per farm in 1900, compared to 4.4 in 1860. Only 45.6 percent of the black and 80 percent of the white farmers reported milk cows in the census of 1900. There were also fewer hogs on farms in those same southeastern states in 1900 than there had been four decades earlier, although for the region as a whole the number was about the same at the end as at the beginning of the period. The central fact was, however, that too many southern farmers were raising cotton at the expense of food crops and livestock. Many sharecroppers and tenants had no livestock at all, while others had only a few chickens and two or three hogs.[23]

Not only did livestock numbers decline throughout much of the South in the late nineteenth century, but the quality was low. Large areas of the South were still in open range in the 1880s and 1890s and on into the twentieth century. Cattle and hogs ran wild, making it difficult if not impossible to improve the breeds. Most cattle were small and scrawny, while hogs were lanky and lean. In areas such as the Great Pine Barrens, which stretched along the Atlantic and Gulf coastal plain from the Carolinas to Louisiana, farmers and ranchers resisted laws that would require them to fence their livestock.

As crop farming expanded and livestock production experienced a relative decline, political pressure arose to enact laws requiring that livestock be fenced. A resident of Carroll County in western Georgia wrote in 1887 that when livestock became a "smaller interest" to farmers than in earlier years, it was more economical to fence livestock than to "fence our farms."[24] Southern states began passing fencing laws in the 1860s, but these statutes usually provided only for some specific limitations or for local option, rather than a statewide requirement for confining livestock. Alabama and Mississippi, for example, passed laws in 1866 placing some restrictions on the open range, and in 1872 Georgia enacted a law permitting county elections on the issue. But effective statewide laws were not passed until well into the twentieth century.

The question of fencing became a lively political issue in many communities during the 1870s and 1880s. Many of those who opposed fencing joined the Farmers Alliance movement. A degree of class conflict also was involved. Poorer people who owned no land but had a few head of livestock wanted to let their animals run at large. Moreover, many farm owners who did not cultivate much of their land and relied on stock raising favored the open range. On the other hand, the large landholders who rented land to sharecroppers and tenants, and who concentrated on crop farming, were the strongest advocates of fencing livestock. When this issue was being debated at a meeting of the Georgia Agricultural Society in 1878, one member who opposed fence laws asked: "Shall we pass a law that will press upon nine-tenths of the people for the sake of a few nabobs of the country?" Another person declared that a fence law would "oppress the poor and induce the planting of more cotton." Over time, however, the interests of crop farmers prevailed, but the persistence of the open range made it difficult to introduce better animals and improve the breeds, and the intermingling of herds contributed to losses from livestock diseases.[25]

When farmers failed to produce their own meat or enough food crops, tens of thousands of cotton producers had to buy corn and other supplies from landlords and merchants. In the late nineteenth century millions of dollars worth of corn, meat, and other supplies were imported from the Midwest through Memphis, Louisville, St. Louis, and other cities. Many observers believed that the root of poverty on southern farms was the failure of farmers to grow most of their own food. The cost of buying provisions on credit at high rates of interest, provisions that could be raised at home, seemed senseless to these critics. A resident of Mississippi wrote the Senate committee studying the cotton situation in 1893 that the "financial distress" of cotton growers arose because of "the neglect of food crops."[26]

What led southern farmers to devote so much of their land and labor to cotton production? Why did the large landowners and so many of the smaller commercial operators seek to make a living from one main crop? One obvious answer to these questions is the fact that the soils and climate of much of the region were especially well suited to cotton. Furthermore, cotton was the traditional crop in many areas of the South and one which blacks and many white farmers knew best how to raise. Of greater importance, however, was the fact that cotton's cash return per acre was higher than that of any other major field crop. Speaking before the Georgia State Agricultural Society in 1878, J. R. Respass of Schley County declared that "Cotton was the most money-making crop . . . in the world." "I tell you," he added, "it is the best friend the Southern farmer has got now."[27] Another Georgian said that "cotton affords the greatest profits to farmers."[28]

Statistics confirmed what the ordinary dirt farmer already knew—that cotton was the best cash crop. For example, in the 1880s the per acre value of cotton production was about twice that for corn in North Carolina, South Carolina, Georgia, Alabama, and Mississippi.[29] Cotton was also a product that would always produce cash for the farm owner or cash tenant, as well as for sharecroppers and landlords. Commenting to census officials in 1880 on why so many farmers in his community raised cotton, a Louisiana resident explained that it was the only crop on which producers could "depend for money."[30]

Moreover, sharecropping, other kinds of tenancy, and the crop-lien system helped to fasten cotton culture on the postwar South. Cotton was an ideal crop for absentee landowners and creditors, who usually insisted that cotton be grown by those to whom they rented land and extended credit for supplies. Besides always having a cash market and being good security for credit, cotton, unlike corn or livestock, could not be eaten or pilfered for food by those actually raising the crop, and there was little chance that it would be stolen. There were widespread complaints of thievery of crops in the 1870s and 1880s. The commissioner of agriculture in Georgia wrote in 1875 that "the stealage of field crops has been a source of much annoyance, irritation and discouragement," and farmers in some counties had met to discuss the situation. He added that thefts of hogs by Negroes had to be stopped before farmers could successfully raise home supplies.[31] In 1880 a report from two counties in Louisiana said that farmers were raising fewer commodities for home consumption because "of the practice among the Negroes of stealing swine." Writing in 1907, two agricultural authorities declared that "a dishonest tenant can dispose of eggs, butter, grain, pork, hay, or truck without the knowledge of the creditor, but a cotton bale is too large to escape undetected."[32] Even if white farmers exaggerated the pilfering of edible crops and livestock, many held that view. Furthermore, cotton could not be sold until it was ginned. This gave the landowner or creditor another point of control. The cost of supervising sharecroppers and crop-lien tenants who raised cotton was minimal, usually less than that required for day labor to raise other crops or handle livestock.

The result of all this was strong pressure on farmers to grow cotton. Quoting Henry Grady, Charles H. Otken wrote in 1894 that if farmers tried to raise other crops and reduce cotton acreage, merchants would cut their "line of credit." "The debts of the farmer," Otken continued, "bound him to cotton." Otken quoted a merchant-landlord who frankly admitted that his sharecroppers were not free to do as they pleased: "If I say 'plant cotton' they plant cotton."[33]

Although cotton came to dominate agriculture throughout much of the south after the Civil War, tobacco, sugar, and rice were important commercial crops. Farmers in Kentucky, Virginia, and Tennessee continued to be heavy producers of the leaf, with Kentucky maintaining its lead in acreage and production. After about 1890, however, with the increased demand for bright flue-cured tobacco by the growing cigarette industry, there was a great surge of tobacco growing in North Carolina. The soil and climate in the eastern part of the state were ideal for the crop. By 1900 about 51,000 North Carolina farmers were cultivating some 203,000 acres of tobacco, or an average of about 4 acres each.[34] A few farmers in southern Georgia and northern Florida also raised small quantities of tobacco by the turn of the century.

Tobacco was a very labor-intensive crop. A seedbed had to be carefully prepared and seed planted. After working the soil, the tobacco plants were set out by hand in rows about two feet apart. Hoeing and weeding followed. The plants subsequently had to be cut off at the top, a process called topping, suckers or extra shoots had to be removed, and tobacco worms had to be picked off the leaves. At harvest time each leaf was removed by hand and hung on sticks in a tobacco barn to cure before it was sold at auction. One of the characters in Guy Owen's *Journey for Joedel* remarks: "By God, it takes thirteen months to the year to raise that infernal crop."[35] As a result of the labor demands, tobacco farms were customarily very small, with two to six acres of tobacco, plus a few additional acres for corn and other food crops, and often some cotton.

Rice production, which had centered in the South Carolina and Georgia coastal lowlands before the Civil War, shifted westward after 1865, though some South Carolina and Georgia planters continued to grow rice until about 1900. It was in the prairie lands of southwestern Louisiana and southeastern Texas that a "rice revolution" occurred between 1880 and 1910. When the railroad reached southwestern Louisiana in 1881, land speculators and farmers from the Midwest began moving into the region and turned to wheat technology to produce a rice crop. The new rice farms were not the one- or two-mule operations so characteristic of farming in most of the South. With larger acreages, the Louisiana and Texas growers adopted gang plows, seeders, discs, the twine binder for harvesting, and steam engines to power their threshing machines. In the 1890s irrigation practices were perfected. Also better breeds of rice and improved milling technology increased the efficiency of rice growers. By the early twentieth century rice farmers in Louisiana and Texas, joined by growers in Arkansas after about 1904, were the most modernized farm operators in the South. In 1909, for example, only 7,293 rice growers in Louisiana and Texas produced some 90 percent of the 21.8 million bushel crop.[36]

Sugar planters suffered severely during the Civil War and it was several years before production was restored to prewar levels. Louisiana planters returned home in 1865 to find their mills destroyed, implements broken, irrigation ditches overgrown, and an unsettled labor force. One sugarcane grower said: "All is dark and dreary in the future, and the present is not better." Some were so discouraged they left the country for Cuba or Brazil.[37]

Sugar planters who had relied on slave labor before 1860 did not find the sharecropping or tenant system of employing freedmen very satisfactory. They tried both systems, but the problem of how to divide the cane caused most planters to resort to wage labor by the 1870s. While credit was expensive, most planters were able to borrow money for operating expenses and capital outlays. Many large landowners had their own sugar mills and in the 1870s they processed sugarcane from their own fields, worked by wage hands, and purchased additional cane from small farmers who had no processing facilities. In some cases planters rented out land to small farmers who in turn promised to deliver all of their cane to the planter's mill. After about 1880 there was a growing division between producing sugarcane and processing the crop. The central sugar mills became larger, fewer, and more expensive. This meant that they had to branch out and obtain the sugarcane of more and more farmers if they were to operate at capacity during harvest. By 1910 Louisiana sugar factories produced about 58 percent of the cane they processed, mostly with wage labor, and bought the rest from several hundred small farmers.[38]

By the early 1900s a kind of three-class labor and production system had developed in the Louisiana sugarcane business. There was the large plantation of at least several hundred acres where cane was produced by hired workers under the supervision of a company manager. Land owned by the plantation but which could not be economically incorporated in the central operating unit was rented to tenants or sharecroppers, who delivered a portion of the crop to the plantation mill. These farmers operated under close supervision of the landowner. A third group of producers were those independent farmers— owners or renters of land not owned by the plantation—who grew cane and sold it to the nearest mill. While these small farmers were independent, they had a close relationship with the mill owner who provided their market. Indeed, the mill owner and small farmer were to some extent interdependent. The farmer got most of his advice on improved varieties of cane, better farming practices, and even some financial aid from the mill owner. The processor depended on these small farmers to provide enough cane to assure an efficient mill operation.[39]

Few farmers outside Louisiana grew sugarcane for commercial sale. Thousands of farmers in the South, however, raised cane for syrup, which was a prominent part of the diet of rural southerners. Individual farmers often had one-fourth to one acre of cane from which they made enough syrup for their families.[40]

Besides corn, which occupied more acreage than any other crop in the post-Civil War south, farmers did not raise much grain. Small amounts of oats and wheat were grown, usually during times of lowest cotton prices. Some farmers, mainly in Virginia, Georgia, and Alabama cultivated peanuts. Pecans, walnuts, and other nuts were also grown. In 1887 J.B. Wight, Sr., established the Wight Pecan Grove Farm at Cairo in southern Georgia. This farm developed into one of the largest nurseries in the South and initially did a great deal to foster the raising of pecans. By 1900 farmers in southwestern Georgia and in parts of Texas and Alabama found that pecans were a good cash crop. Southern farmers also raised fruit. Apples, pears, peaches and plums, as well as many smaller fruits and berries, did well in parts of the South. Georgia, which became known as the Peach State, was shipping peaches to northern markets as early as the 1870s, and in 1898 producers in the state shipped 3,000 carloads to distant buyers.[41]

Many kinds of vegetables also did well in the South. Farmers raised potatoes, sweet potatoes, peas, beans, and other garden vegetables. Most of the output was consumed at home. Sweet potatoes were an especially important item in the southern diet and were raised on many farms.

As a year-round demand for fresh vegetables developed, truck gardens were established from Norfolk southward into the Carolinas, southern Georgia, Florida, and westward to Mobile. Farmers who were relatively close to market towns, or who were near a railroad or along a river on which fresh produce could be shipped without damaging it by bumping along on rough roads, found occasional profits in strawberries, watermelons, stringbeans, tomatoes, asparagus, and other produce. Some cotton farmers tried to get into truck farming, but usually with what one observer called "disastrous results." To succeed in truck farming or fruit growing the operator had to give close attention to proper crating and shipping, as well as to marketing. This required better management and more knowledge than most farmers could muster. One southern farmer shipped 30 crates of apples to market in 1884 "because his hogs wouldn't eat them." Such inattention to quality assured failure. Producers also suffered from sharp price fluctuations, bad weather, and even dishonest commission merchants. But in some cases farmers did well. In 1882 a truck farmer near Savannah netted $600 from only one and one-half acres of eggplants. In 1884 some $178,532 worth of vegetables were shipped from the single port of Mobile.[42]

Marketing was a major problem for producers of specialized crops, many of which were perishable. Even after the railroads penetrated most areas of the rural South in the 1880s and 1890s, the markets for fresh fruit, vegetables, and dairy products were uncertain and sometimes chaotic. W.J. Spillman, a knowledgeable economist, wrote in 1905 that for a farmer to switch out of cotton to grow peaches or vegetables would be dangerous. There were no reliable markets for perishable crops, he wrote.[43] Except for small quantities sold locally, farmers had to depend on commission merchants to sell their produce in distant cities where fluctuating consumer demand rather than profitable prices for farmers governed the situation. Farmers never knew how much they could sell or at what price. Moreover, a year of good prices sometimes encouraged additional producers to go into fruit or vegetable production, resulting in price-depressing surpluses. In some cases farmers could find no market at all and left their fruit or vegetables on the ground to rot.

The marketing system that had been developed to handle cotton did not exist for other crops and livestock in the late nineteenth-century South. As a Georgia farmer stated in 1886, crops other than cotton would perhaps pay "much better if there was any market for them," while another Georgian declared that "owing to the distance to market, we grow but little for market except cotton." As farmers considered raising other crops and becoming less dependent upon cotton, they constantly complained about the problems associated with unsuitable and undependable markets. Farm spokesmen continually called for better rural roads to make markets more available. S.P. Sanford told the Georgia Agricultural Society in 1878 that good roads would provide "cheap and easy transportation to market" and make the producer "independent."[44]

In the case of livestock, local markets were often flooded and prices depressed. After the first cold snap in the fall, a farmer would sometimes butcher eight or ten hogs and try to sell them to dealers or merchants in the local town or village, but the demand might be limited to only two or three head. This oversupply drastically depressed prices. Where no packing plants existed, farmers had to depend on dealer-shippers to sell the animals that could not be sold locally. The shippers bought enough for a train carload, but the farmer had to accept whatever price was offered. Some communities had no livestock dealers and were cut off from any distant urban markets.[45]

It is clear that natural conditions in the south were favorable to the production of a wide variety of crops. It is equally clear that throughout most of the region cotton and corn occupied a great majority of the cultivated acreage. In 1899 farmers in the nine leading cotton states grew 25 million acres of corn and 23.3 million acres of cotton. Cotton occupied much more acreage than any other crop in Alabama, Georgia,

Louisiana, Mississippi, South Carolina, and Texas.[46] Corn was raised for food and feed for the mules, while cotton was the principal cash crop. In hundreds of communities from North Carolina to Texas, cotton became the central fact of life. It was the basis of credit and rent for land and the source of cash. Cotton was King.

By 1880 the eleven southern states had 1,252,249 farms, up from 549,109 in 1860. Much of this rapid increase in numbers did not represent genuinely new farms such as those being created in states like Iowa or Kansas. Rather, the increase was the result of statistical methods used by the Census Bureau. Census officials counted as separate farms all of those small plots farmed by sharecroppers and tenants. If one landowner held 1,000 acres, for instance, and had twenty sharecroppers farming 50 acres each, that was counted as 20 farms. As the United States commissioner of agriculture wrote in 1883, in the Midwest and West new farms were being created, while in the South the increase resulted from dividing "the old plantations."[47] In addition, however, many genuinely new farms were established, particularly outside the plantation areas.

The average size of farms dropped dramatically after 1870. Between 1860 and 1900 the average farm throughout the eleven states of the Deep South declined from 390 to 122 acres. In the main cotton states the drop was much greater. In Alabama, for example, the average farm contained 346 acres in 1860 and only 93 in 1900. The story was the same in Mississippi, the Carolinas, Georgia, Louisiana, and Arkansas. By 1900 farms averaged less than 100 acres in several southern states. In South Carolina the figure was only 91 acres. The average cropland harvested in the seven southeastern states averaged a mere 29 acres per farm by 1900. In Iowa, by comparison, farmers harvested an average of 96 acres, and in Kansas, 104. Although there were wide variations, the South had become a land of predominantly small farms populated by poor people.[48]

An examination of the manuscript census of 1880 indicates the pattern of southern agriculture as it was developing in the postwar generation. Ten farmers picked at random in different sections of Georgia but listed consecutively in the manuscript census show the types of farm organization and operation common throughout much of the South.

Of the ten farmers examined in Harris County in western Georgia, five were sharecroppers, four black and one white, and five were white owners. There was little basic difference between the farming operations of the sharecroppers and those of the small owners in that particular area. All of them had small farms with 13 to 45 acres under cultivation. Three of the white owners had only 20 acres in crops, while the other two cultivated 40 and 45 acres. Except for the single white sharecropper, who farmed only 13 acres, the four black sharecroppers cultivated 25, 35, and 40 acres each. All of the farmers had some unimproved land, except the white sharecropper.

Each of the ten farmers raised cotton as the main crop, and all except one raised a few acres of corn. Three of the ten raised oats and four grew a little wheat. Of the four wheat growers, two were share-croppers and two were owners. In 1879 the cotton production of these ten farmers varied from three to seven bales, usually making one-third to one-fourth of a bale to the acre. The largest cotton grower had 30 acres and produced seven bales. Most farmers raised three, four, or five bales. All of the owners but none of the sharecroppers raised sweet potatoes, and none of the ten grew any Irish potatoes in 1879.

These farmers had very little livestock in 1880. Sharecroppers and owners alike had one mule or horse apiece except for one owner who had two horses. Three of the black sharecroppers, the white sharecrop-per, and one white owner had no milk cows. Four of the other farmers had one milk cow, and a single owner had two. Of those who had milk cows, four claimed to have produced 50 pounds of butter in 1879, and one reported 100 pounds. One owner and one sharecropper had no swine, and the other eight farmers had from two to eight head each. Seven of the ten farmers had from five to twenty-five chickens which produced a few eggs. Three of the sharecroppers owned no poultry.

The estimated value of farm production for sale and use at home by these farmers in 1879 varied from a low of $160 to a high of $650. Most of the sharecroppers and owners alike produced $200 to $300 worth of commodities. A comparison of the value of production of one of the better-off black sharecroppers with one of the white farm owners is revealing. Tony Brooks, a sixty-year old black cropper with seven children, cultivated a total of 35 acres, and the farm had an additional 115 acres of woodland. He owned $5 worth of implements and ma-chinery, probably hoes and an axe. He had one mule, no milk cow, no chickens, and two swine. Brooks grew 1 acre of corn on which he raised 20 bushels, and 30 acres of cotton which produced seven bales. He had no garden, bees, or fruit trees. The value of his production for sale and home use totaled $260. Out of that he had to give the landlord half of the cotton, which represented virtually all of his cash income, leaving the Brooks family $125 to $130 for the year's work. That was hardly enough to buy the food and clothing needed, to say nothing of other consumer goods.

Bill Cook was a thirty-seven-year-old white owner with a wife and six children. He cultivated 40 acres, five more than Brooks, and had 240 acres of unimproved woodland. He had $20 worth of implements and grew 10 acres of corn which produced 50 bushels, and 20 acres of cotton on which he raised six bales. He farmed with one mule and had one milk cow but no other cattle. Cook also owned ten hogs and ten chickens. He raised cowpeas and 30 bushels of sweet potatoes, and his bees produced 20 pounds of honey. The value of his annual production in 1879 was $300. As an owner, the value of Cook's production exceeded that of Brooks, the sharecropper, by only $40 a year, part of which consisted of a greater variety of items raised for the family living. However, he received all of the income that he produced, minus any operating expenses.

Moving over to Laurens County in central Georgia, one can examine a district where sharecropping was the established pattern of operation. Considering ten farmers listed consecutively in the manuscript census of agriculture, eight black sharecroppers and two white farm owners appear on the record. The large landholder not only provided land for sharecroppers, but owned 4,500 acres of forest and woodland and farmed 40 acres himself. The small white farm owner in the community farmed 98 acres.

Six of the eight black sharecroppers farmed 40 acres each, in most cases 20 acres of corn and 20 acres of cotton. Two sharecroppers cultivated 35 and 80 acres each. None of the black sharecroppers raised any grain or vegetable crops. Two of the eight sharecroppers had one milk cow each, while another had two head. All of the sharecroppers except one had hogs, the number varying from four to eight. The farmer without any hogs was single and was listed as a laborer. He probably lived and boarded with another family. The white landowners had much more livestock. The large owner had 11 milk cows and sold 700 gallons of milk in 1879, and he also owned 200 hogs. The smaller landowner had 4 milk cows and 23 hogs. Besides his milk cows, the biggest operator had 30 other cattle, and the other owner held an additional eight head. Although sweet potatoes were important in the southern diet, of the ten farmers studied only the large landowner raised any. He may have sold both sweet potatoes and milk to some or all of his sharecroppers.

What about production and income? Those who had 20 acres of corn reported a crop of 200 bushels, or a little above or below that figure. Of the sharecroppers with 20 acres of cotton, 4 raised 6 bales, or a little less than one-third bale to the acre; one had 5 bales, while two other croppers reported 9 and 10 bales respectively. The large landowner raised eight bales on 16 acres, while the small white owner produced six bales on 22 acres. Only one sharecropper raised less cotton per acre than the small landowner, and six did better. One black sharecropper, Ned Horner, raised more on his 80-acre farm than owner Alfred Morgan did on 98 acres. Horner produced 160 pounds of seed cotton to the acre in 1879 compared to 132 pounds for Morgan. Sharecroppers often farmed better land than small owners, but Horner's record indicates that he could be quite productive by the standards of the time.

Except for the large landholder, the value of products sold and used at home generally ranged from $400 to $500. Three of the share-croppers actually produced a greater value of commodities than Morgan, the white owner. From his 80 acres, Ned Horner raised $900 worth of products. In the case of the sharecroppers, the landlord would get half the cotton and half the corn, leaving most of the black families with $200 to $300 worth of production, less any expenses.

There were areas in the South where all, or nearly all, of the farmers owned their land in 1880. They typified that Jeffersonian ideal of a landowning yeomanry which would be economically and politically independent. Such an area was part of Jackson County in the Upper Piedmont of northern Georgia. Looking at one randomly selected district in that county, the manuscript census reveals that in some communities every farmer was a landowner. In the community studied all were also white, except for one black widow, who evidently retained ownership of land after her husband's death. Most of these owners cultivated from 40 to 60 acres and had some additional forest and other land. One white widow and her son had the smallest farm, with only 15 acres under cultivation.

These white landowning farmers were much more diversified than those in the Black Belt of central or southwestern Georgia. They all had at least one horse or mule, and most had two horses or one horse and one mule. They all owned milk cows, but usually not more than one or two head. Every farm wife churned butter. Six of the ten had other cattle, and all of them owned hogs, varying from one to twelve, and a few chickens. Besides corn, all but one produced a little oats and seven of the ten grew some wheat. Cotton was the main cash crop, although all but two produced less than 5 bales.

Although these farmers varied their production, the value of their output was small. Half of the ten farm owners produced only $300 worth of products for sale or home use in 1879, while the two highest had $650 and $700 worth. All of these owners had expenses and taxes to deduct from the value of their marketed commodities. For example, Rice Turner, whose products were worth $700, had spent $100 for fertilizer that had to be deducted from any cash income. These owners were independent and probably had a better diet than the black and white sharecroppers, but their cash income was no greater and in many cases was less than that earned by a sharecropper on good land.[49]

Any detailed investigation of local communities in different parts of the South indicates the existence of small and nonproductive farms, emphasis upon staple crops, absence of much equipment and machinery, a scarcity of livestock and poultry, a high rate of tenancy in much of the region, and general poverty. By looking at the published censuses after 1880 it is clear that conditions did not improve for most farmers. Examination of a few sample counties will illustrate the situation.

In Greene County, North Carolina, located in the eastern part of the state in the bright flue-cured tobacco belt, only 28 percent of the farmers tilled their own farms in 1910. The great majority of operators were sharecroppers and tenants, of whom 774 were white and 806 were black. Tenancy was no respecter of color. The farms averaged 33 acres of improved land each, on which producers raised an average of 11 acres of corn, 8.3 acres of cotton and 4 acres of tobacco. There were only 1,786 cattle in the county, or less than one head per farm, while the 859 milk cows meant that a majority of the 2,193 farmers produced no milk. Some farmers had a few chickens and hogs, but most of their labor was directed toward producing cotton and tobacco.

The situation in Laurens County in central Georgia was little different, except that farmers concentrated even more heavily on cotton, with corn as a secondary food crop. By 1909 slightly over 100,000 acres of cotton were planted by the county's 4,923 farmers, compared with only 72,000 acres of cereals, mostly corn. Whites operated 53 percent of the farms and blacks 47 percent. While farms were a little larger than in Greene County, North Carolina, more than half of them were less than 50 acres. Tenancy was high, and climbing. In 1900 about 50 percent of the white operators owned their own farms; for blacks it was only 14 percent. By 1910, despite a decade of supposed prosperity, white ownership in Laurens County dropped to 48 percent and to only 9 percent for blacks. For all farmers in the county, tenancy had risen to about 73 percent.[50] Most farmers had a few domestic animals, but hundreds of small operators raised nothing more than a few chickens or two or three hogs, if that.

Some counties in the Mississippi-Yazoo Delta were typical of concentrated land ownership and an extraordinarily large number of black tenants. There were 8,253 farms in Yazoo County in 1910, of which 1,539 were operated by whites and 6,714 by blacks. Only about 14 percent of the farmers owned their own farms. The rest, consisting of 804 white and 6,239 black tenants, farmed most of the land for large operators. More than one-fourth of the farmers had less than 20 acres, and slightly over half were in the 20- to 49-acre category. Cotton was all-encompassing. The county had 120,000 acres of cotton, twice the amount of land planted to corn. Cotton accounted for nearly 80 percent of the value of all crops. As was true elsewhere, some farmers had livestock, but the numbers were few.[51]

Farmers in Rutherford County in central Tennessee followed a somewhat different pattern. In a region ideal for general farming, the average amount of improved land per farm was 45 acres. About 75 percent of the county's farmers were white, and over half of these white farmers owned their farms in 1910. While cotton was raised as a cash crop, the 19,313 acres were only about a fourth of the acreage devoted to corn and other cereals. Rutherford County farmers had more livestock than those in Greene and Laurens. They averaged nearly five head of cattle per farm, including two milk cows. They also had more hogs, sheep, and poultry. Central Tennessee farmers, then, were more diversified, more self-sufficient, and less dependent on a single cash crop.[52]

There were thousands of farmers in parts of the South who were only minimally involved in commercial agriculture. In the "piney woods" of southern Georgia, Alabama, and Mississippi, and in the southern Appalachians extending from southern Virginia to northeastern Alabama, many farmers were nearly self-sufficient.[53] They raised a few acres of stunted corn, grew some vegetables, let their livestock run at large in the woods, killed game, and lived isolated lives. In the 1880s commercial agriculture began penetrating the southern Georgia wiregrass region and other areas of self-sufficiency in the Coastal Plain, but in the southern Appalachians farms continued small and unproductive. Appalachian farmers began taking jobs in the mines and mills on a full- or part-time basis and by the early twentieth century some of them were getting much of their cash income from nonfarm work.

What was the condition among black farmers who had sought to bridge the gap between slavery and freedom? How much economic progress had they made by 1900? As was true of the total farm population, the situation among black farmers varied a great deal. But the central fact was that the great majority were unable to move to a position of farm ownership and economic independence. There were even fewer rungs on the agricultural ladder leading upward for blacks than for whites.

By 1900 there were 707,364 black farmers in the South. Of these, 162,000, or about 23 percent, were owners or part owners. Except for a few managers, the rest were divided about equally between share and cash tenants. Most black farmers, even the owners, had very small farms, averaging only 52 acres in 1900. The average cropland harvested on black farms was 29 acres, compared to a little over 50 acres for southern whites. The improved land on farms operated by black owners and tenants was virtually the same.[54]

Blacks acquired land in a variety of ways. In some cases landowners gave favorite former slaves a small quantity of land. In other instances blacks were able to save enough money to buy a few acres. Because of racial discrimination in the southern communities, a black usually had to have some white man's support before he could acquire land. A few blacks worked hard enough, were shrewd enough in business and personal relations, and good enough managers to gain substantial acreages. For example, William David Flowers, who lived in Crawford County in central Georgia, acquired about 900 acres, most of which he held until his death in 1931. Deal Jackson of Albany, Georgia, was another large black landowner. Nearly 500 blacks operated farms of over 1,000 acres in 1899, while about 92,000 had enterprises exceeding 100 acres.[55]

By 1900 black farmers in the South owned 13.5 million acres of land, compared to more than 100 million for whites. During the next decade the number of black operators rose by some 140,000, to a total of 847,907, of whom 195,432 were farm owners. They, along with a few thousand black farmers outside the eleven-state region, owned 15.7 million acres by 1910, up more than 2 million acres since 1900. This was the height of black land ownership. While substantial numbers of blacks began losing their land during World War I, the record of black ownership by the early twentieth century was remarkable. When it is considered that blacks started out without capital or independent business experience and faced severe racial discrimination, it is not surprising that so few became landowners. The surprise is that so many blacks acquired even small amounts of land and became independent operators.[56]

Cotton was the main source of income for about 71 percent of the South's black farmers. The remainder made a living from grain, tobacco, rice, dairying, livestock, and other types of farming. Incomes produced on these mostly small farms were low for the vast majority. In 1899, 134,000 black farm families produced agricultural products valued at less than $100 each. Another 247,000 farmers raised between $100 and $250 worth of commodities. About half of the South's black farmers produced less than $250 worth of products, and in many cases they did not receive more than half of their output.[57]

For the great majority of both black and white farmers in the South during the late nineteenth century, the most distinct characteristic was poverty. While blacks generally operated smaller farms and were the poorest among the poor, low farm incomes were the order of the day. This was confirmed both by contemporary observation and by state and federal statistics. The special study done on cotton farmers by the Census Bureau in 1880 recorded abundant evidence of a hand-to-mouth existence for very large numbers of southern farmers. Many sharecroppers and tenants had cash incomes of less than $100 a year, while thousands more existed year in and year out on between $100 and $200 annually. Describing the situation among black farmers in parts of Georgia in 1880, reporters for the Census Bureau used such phrases as "sometimes without bread for their families," "in a destitute condition," and "many are in a worse [economic] condition than they were during slavery." A northern minister who visited the South in 1901 declared that he found the comforts of Atlanta comparable to those of any northern city, but "as soon as one gets away from the towns, and ventures himself into the barren wastes of the unredeemed country about, the wretchedness is pathetic and the poverty colossal."[58]

Such conditions, of course, were not universal. Other observers wrote that in some Louisiana parishes farmers had "good clothes, cabins and food." In parts of Mississippi farmers were able "to pay their merchants and have some money besides," but "in many other counties," according to a reporter, "they [cotton farmers] are in a rather destitute condition due to improvidence and indolence." There were exceptions to rural poverty, but it was the norm for most southern farmers.

While some observers may have tried to place the blame for so much rural poverty in the South on lazy and unmotivated workers, the basic difficulties were much more fundamental. Southern farms lacked what modern economists call an adequate resource base. The fundamental cause of poverty in the southern countryside was small farms and low production. The most common operation was the one- or two-mule farm. As a South Carolina reporter wrote the Senate Agriculture and Forestry Committee in 1893: "There is . . . a tendency on the part of landowners to subdivide their lands into such small farms that the tenant often does not have a sufficient quantity of land to raise both cotton and abundant food crops."[59] To put it another way, the farm population was too large in relation to the developed land resources. This meant that most small cotton farms did not require full-time, year-round work and that farmers were simply underemployed.

Many farmers in the South did not work more than six or seven months a year and were idle or engaged in nonproductive activity the rest of the time. "The average laborer [in cotton production] of the county makes a support by working half his time," wrote an observer in northern Georgia in 1880. Referring to Natchitoches Parish in Louisiana at about the same time, a correspondent said that sharecropping kept the worker "busy for only half his time." Reporting from Bossier Parish one resident wrote that three hands, the farmer, his wife, and two "half-hands," or children, produced 4 bales of cotton on 8 acres. This, he added, was "what one good slave formerly did."[60] Writing in the *Annals of the American Academy of Political and Social Science* in 1893, George K. Holmes clearly saw this problem. Referring mainly to black tenants, Holmes explained that the farmer "operates on so small a scale on his one-mule or two-mule holding that his net product of wealth gives him no more than a poor subsistence."[61] A correspondent for the

American Agriculturist wrote in November 1885 that southern farmers spent too much time in nonproductive activities. "There is more leisure taken by one farmer in the South than by twenty farmers in the North and West," he insisted.[62]

One need only analyze a typical small cotton farm to see the problem. Assume that a sharecropper cultivated 20 acres of cotton. In 1879 production per acre in South Carolina, Georgia, and Alabama was only about one-third of a bale, or 160 pounds, per acre. During the 1880s the average production per acre in those three states was 148 pounds. With a farm price of generally 8 to 9 cents in the 1880s, the value of the farmer's gross output would be about $13.40 per acre (148 pounds per acre at 9 cents a pound). With 20 acres that would total $266. The sharecropper, however, would receive only half the amount, minus any expenses for marketing the crop, which left around $125 for a year's work by him and his family. This was the situation when the cotton crop was average and the price was reasonable. In poor years, when drought or pests reduced production for particular farmers, income was much below the average. Occasionally, in years of better prices and good production, cotton produced a much better income. From 1880 to 1900, however, cotton prices moved downward.

Even if the sharecropper or tenant had cotton valued at $125 for his share of the crop at year end, he did not actually receive that much money. Indeed, he may have received no money at all. During the year, the sharecropper had borrowed money from the landlord or merchant, or had been advanced food and supplies under the "furnish" system. This was a kind of line of credit provided by landowners and merchants to families who did not have enough home-produced food or money to buy clothing and other needed supplies. Many southern farmers began with little or nothing. That was true of nearly all of the black farmers who were less than a generation from slavery. One landlord in northern Georgia wrote that "all the hands I employ come to me poverty stricken" and had to be provided all supplies. "I never yet," he added, "since the negroes were freed, had a negro or white man I employed that ever came to me with anything but the clothes they had on their back."[63] Thousands of sharecropper families had no milk cows or enough other livestock to provide meat. They bought their meat, cornmeal, and other provisions from the local merchant. The advances for supplies, varying from $6 to $10 and sometimes up to $12 a month for at least six or eight months, left the sharecropper with a debt of $75 to $150 at settlement time.

Merchants had two prices, one for credit and one for cash customers. Those who bought on credit usually paid from 30 to 60 percent more than those who offered cash. The Georgia Commissioner of Agriculture reported in 1875 that farmers were paying 44 percent interest on advanced supplies.[64] Farmers, in other words, were paying exorbitant rates of interest on their daily expenses—mainly food and clothing, to say nothing of any operating costs. Thus at the end of the year when the sharecropper or tenant settled up with the merchant or landlord, he often found that his share of the small crop would hardly pay his debts, and many times fell short. Once in debt there was little opportunity to escape the demands of credit. As Clarence H. Poe, editor of the *Progressive Farmer*, wrote: "The pathos of the lien-farmer is that he is always only 12 months from freedom."[65] To make matters worse, planters kept the books, and sharecroppers and tenants, especially illiterate and intimidated blacks, were sometimes cheated. Their main problem, however, was lack of enough output to produce an adequate income for a decent living, to pay debts, or to accumulate any capital. As George K. Holmes stated it so well, they "owed more than they owned."[66]

If lack of full-time productive work and inadequate output were the underlying problems facing so many southern farmers, what could be done? One approach was to operate larger acreages which would occupy the farmers full-time. Many farmers in the South who had enough land followed this practice. As mentioned earlier, in Rutherford County, Tennessee, a general farming area, farmers had enough cultivated land on which to grow a variety of cereal crops and also to raise livestock. In addition they grew cotton for cash sale. But in the main cotton areas where land ownership was concentrated and where there were large numbers of sharecroppers and tenants, landlords insisted on cotton production. Since one family could raise 15 to 30 acres of cotton, farms were kept at between 20 and 50 acres. But cotton only required six to eight months of labor, leaving many sharecroppers and tenants idle the rest of the year. If they had grown feed crops and hay and raised livestock during the idle months, they would have been more productively employed and could have added to their earnings. But individual sharecroppers and tenants had little or no chance to buy a farm, to enlarge their operation, to obtain machinery, or to change the crop pattern.

If a farmer could not enlarge his farm, one alternative was to increase production per acre. Surely one reason for southern rural poverty was low productivity associated with eroded, worn-out soil. Cotton lands east of the Mississippi had been greatly impoverished even before the Civil War. One authority wrote that "the post-bellum farmer received as an inheritance, large areas of worn-out and generally unproductive soils."[67] In general, western lands in Mississippi, Louisiana, and Texas were more productive than those in the Southeast. For example, in the 1880s cotton production in Louisiana averaged

232 pounds per acre compared to only 157 pounds in South Carolina and 146 in Georgia. Thousands of farmers in the Southeast grew what was sometimes referred to as bumble bee cotton. It was reportedly so short and poor that a bumble bee could sit on its hind legs and sip nectar from the flowering plant.[68] While there were still millions of acres of unsettled virgin land throughout the South in the 1870s and 1880s, most farmers stayed with the old fields because of the expense of clearing off the timber and getting the land ready for crops. Thus southern farmers cultivated millions of acres of land from which the topsoil and nutrients had been washed away by heavy rains, reducing yields and requiring the expense of commercial fertilizer. Soil conservation practices found few adherents on southern farms. For years cotton seed was "thrown out to rot," or burned rather than being returned to the soil. Animals were penned up in unsheltered lots, and the manure washed away into creeks and rivers instead of being placed on the fields. As early as 1866, a Georgia correspondent for the United States Department of Agriculture wrote that middle Georgia, once a rich, productive farm region, had been "scourged by bad cultivation, and worn and gullied to a deplorable degree."[69] In 1880 a reporter wrote that restoration of soil fertility was one of the most pressing problems facing farmers in Mississippi's uplands.[70]

While it could be argued that soil conservation would ultimately pay good dividends in greater productivity per acre, it initially cost money that most farmers did not have. Effective conservation meant rotation of crops, raising more livestock, and adopting better methods of cultivation which required knowledge, motivation, and capital, all of which were lacking. Small acreages and declining soil fertility almost assured poverty among a great majority of southern farmers.

To make matters even worse most farmers in the South had poor and inadequate equipment and machinery. Improved machinery such as cotton-seed planters, fertilizer spreaders, stalk cutters, and better plows and harrows did become available, but most farmers lacked money to buy the new equipment. Except for plowing, which was done with mule and horse power, cotton growing was mainly a hand operation. Some farmers used mechanical, mule-drawn cotton planters, but much cotton was also planted by hand as the farmer walked behind the plow dropping seed in the furrow. Thinning and weeding the crop were also hand operations. The hoe was the most widely used tool in the cotton fields. Picking was, of course, also done by hand. Only a few progressive farmers used the newer plows, discs, harrows, and planters, and little change occurred in cotton technology before 1915. The best machinery was seen on very few farms in the South. Writing in 1880, a reporter from northern Georgia said that "our people are slow to adopt modern improvements." He estimated that only 14 out of 2,003 farms in the county had adopted efficient methods of production.[71]

The man-hours required to produce an acre of cotton stayed high compared to those required for corn and wheat. The number of man-hours necessary to grow an acre of cotton throughout the main cotton belt, averaging about 160 pounds, dropped less than one-third, from 148 to 102 hours, between 1841 and 1895. For most of the South this meant that farmers exchanged 102 hours of labor for $13 to $16, or about 13 cents an hour. And this was for the entire family, not just a single worker. On the other hand, man-hours for producing an acre of wheat, or some 20 bushels, declined from 57.7 to 8.8 in the same period, and for an acre of corn, averaging about 40 bushels in the Midwest, from 33.6 to 15.1 hours.[72] While the value per acre of cotton was higher than that of corn or wheat in either the corn belt or the wheat belt in the 1880s, less labor and larger acreages gave corn and wheat farmers a distinct advantage.

So long as cheap labor was available and there was no machine to pick cotton, little economic incentive existed to adopt modern machinery. Workers had to be kept available for chopping, weeding, and picking, and they might as well be maintained to do the other hand work as well. Moreover, such small acreages would not have justified the investment in machinery in most cases. When a farmer and his family were already underemployed on a small farm, it did not make economic sense to buy machinery which would increase the efficiency of their labor. Even among farmers who would have benefited by having more and better machinery, most did not have the money to buy it. Thus productivity on thousands of southern farms was low because so much of the work was done with human hands. While midwestern farmers were turning to the latest horse-drawn machines to prepare the soil, plant, cultivate, and harvest their crops of corn and small grains, southerners plodded along trying to produce a living by methods little advanced over those used in the eighteenth century. By failing to substitute animal power and machines for hand labor, the productivity of most southern farmers remained low, as in all under-developed economies where hand labor prevails.

To utilize the available machinery effectively, tens of thousands of southern farms would have had to be enlarged. The fundamental problem facing farmers who might have profited from increased acreages and machinery was the lack of funds for capital investment. There were two practical ways to acquire capital—saving and borrowing. One way that farmers had always accumulated capital was through savings from current production. Rather than consume their entire production or spend on consumer goods all of the money realized from the sale of crops and livestock, farmers invested part of the value of their output in income-producing items such as more land, machinery, fertilizer, and livestock. Since farming throughout most of the United States in the nineteenth century paid only small returns on labor and investment, in order to accumulate money to invest, farmers postponed their consumption. Many farmers in the Midwest, for example, reduced or postponed the purchase of store goods in order to have something left over for investment.

Farmers in the South, however, were too poor and unproductive to save anything for investment in capital goods. Thousands were in debt just for their day-to-day and month-to-month living. Unable to produce a surplus above their consumption and debts, capital accumulation was impossible. To reduce consumption further as a way to save would have threatened the very existence of many farm families, sharecroppers and owners alike.

Moreover, most of them had little or no borrowing ability for capital expansion. The South's banking system in the late nineteenth century was entirely inadequate to meet rural needs. But even if better and more widespread bank credit had been available, most southern farmers would not have been able to borrow money for land purchases or capital equipment. Lenders would not loan money without sufficient security or the prospect of a productive farming operation. To extend credit beyond the minimal needs of a farmer to grow a cotton crop was not only risky but foolish from a lender's viewpoint. A farmer cultivating only 20 or 30 acres of someone else's land and producing from $200 to $400 worth of cotton that had to be divided with the landlord was, indeed, a poor credit risk.

Southern farmers, then, became "trapped" in a cotton economy. Without land or equipment the newly freed blacks, and many whites as well, sold their labor in exchange for a share of the crop which they produced on credit. This system increased the cost of nearly everything they consumed and fastened a yoke of permanent and oppressive debt upon hundreds of thousands of farmers, both white and black. The meager production from small farms was insufficient to pull them out of poverty or ever permit them to buy a farm. The alternative of becoming a larger, more efficient farm operator, or a more intensive and productive producer, was simply not available to most southern farmers in the late nineteenth century.

Furthermore, southern farmers, like those nationwide, faced new economic problems as agriculture became more commercialized in the post-Civil War years. American farmers had always raised some products for sale, but in the pre-Civil War era they were considerably more self-sufficient than during the late nineteenth and early twentieth centuries. As southern farmers became less self-sufficient and more market oriented, their welfare depended heavily on the relationship between the prices of their products and those of the nonfarm commodities which they purchased. So long as farmers consumed their own commodities, the price of those products was not so important. But when they sold their cotton, tobacco, livestock, or grain and bought industrial goods, the relationship between farm and nonfarm prices was crucial. It made a great deal of difference whether it took 200, 300, or 400 pounds of cotton to buy a plow, or 1,000 or 2,000 pounds to purchase a mule. Low prices for farm products and high prices for industrial commodities, interest, or transportation placed farmers in a cost-price squeeze that kept their purchasing power low.

The long decline in farm prices from the 1870s to around 1900, a time when farmers were buying more and more nonfarm inputs for their operations and trying to increase their living standards, placed them in a difficult position. From 1872 to 1894, for example, the price of cotton dropped 70 percent while that of general commodities declined only 50 percent. Moreover, with no control over the price of what they sold or bought, they were in a weak bargaining position with other elements in the economy. In short, the terms of trade for farmers were highly unfavorable. As one scholar summed up the situation, farmers were "regulated by a market over which they had little or no control, a market subordinating countryside to town, agriculture to industry."[73]

As industrialization advanced, more consumer goods were offered by the growing number of merchants in southern towns and villages. Farmers wanted sewing machines, pianos, store-bought shoes and clothes, furniture, curtains, household utensils, and scores of other items that filled storekeepers' shelves. To most southern farmers in the 1880s and 1890s, cotton seemed to provide the best, and perhaps the only, means of acquiring such goods. So farmers produced cotton, even though increased production periodically depressed prices and encouraged them to raise even more cotton in hopes of gaining needed cash or credit.[74] The result was low net incomes and low standards of living.

Leaving agriculture and seeking employment in industry was not a viable option. Employment in factories, transportation, banking, trade, and the services was extremely limited in the South before World War I. While some people found work in lumbering, turpentining, textiles, and other developing industries, the opportunities were far short of the need to siphon off the surplus farm population. Thus year after year and decade after decade, a majority of southern farmers eked out a poor living on increasingly small farms with little hope of improvement. There was no meaningful labor mobility for the great majority of sharecroppers and tenants, either to better agricultural opportunities or to nonfarm jobs. Sharecroppers and tenants frequently moved from farm to farm, but they found conditions about the same everywhere, and these moves seldom brought any major improvements in their condition. Even higher prices for cotton in the early twentieth century did not bring any permanent relief to the South's producers of the white lint.

2

Down on the Farm before World War I

Most southern farm families in the late nineteenth and early twentieth centuries experienced a narrow, isolated, and restricted existence. Millions of men, women, and children were born, lived, and died without ever being exposed to the influences of growing urbanization. The South was a region made up predominantly of farms and small towns. Many families never traveled out of their home county or beyond the nearby village. In most communities roads were poor or nonexistent, and when farmers did venture from home they generally traveled by foot, horseback, or wagon. In an urban age it is difficult to realize how rural the South actually was.

As late as 1900 one could travel for hundreds of miles throughout much of the region and never encounter a place of 8,000 or more population, the census definition of an urban center. On the nearly 300-mile trip from Memphis, Tennessee, across the entire state of Arkansas to Fort Smith, a traveler would pass through only Little Rock, with its 39,000 people, that resembled a city. Or leaving Atlanta, one might travel seventy-five miles or more in any direction before coming to another town of any consequence. There were only forty towns with as many as 8,000 persons in the eight states of the Carolinas, Tennessee, Georgia, Alabama, Mississippi, Arkansas, and Louisiana. New Orleans was the single southern city with a population exceeding 100,000. While there were hundreds of towns throughout the South, most of them were very small. Many were only crossroads villages with a store, a blacksmith shop, a cotton gin, and a few other businesses. These small towns were dependent almost entirely on the surrounding farms.[1] In Alabama, for instance, 141 of the state's 203 towns contained fewer than 1,000 residents each in 1900, and many had only 200 to 500 people. Prior to the census of 1920 there was no count of persons who actually resided on farms, but in 1900 some 82 percent of the total population in the South was considered rural, most of which consisted of farmers and their families.[2]

Population statistics, however, cannot fully portray the real sense of ruralness in the late nineteenth-century South. Town and village people, as well as farmers, depended almost entirely on agriculture. The welfare of merchants, cotton ginners, and other small-town businessmen was firmly linked to the farm trade. Indeed, many merchants were also landowners and had a direct stake in farming. Because of the overriding importance of agriculture, about everyone in a community was interested in the same things—the condition of the crops, the weather, the prices of farm commodities, and other matters relating to farming. Interest in farming was nearly universal. If farmers did well the merchants prospered; if farmers fell on hard times, business profits declined. As one observer wrote, "Agriculture . . . supplied a topic of conversation, an economic bond of union, and set the tone and tempo of society in and around the village."[3]

Much of the rural South was not fully integrated into the rest of American society. Poor roads and primitive mail service contributed to the continued isolation of thousands of farmers throughout the region into the first years of the twentieth century. While roads existed between the towns and villages, foot paths and wagon trails were the main links connecting many farm homes. Speaking before the Georgia Agricultural Society in 1876, D.W. Lewis, a former president of the society, explained that the state's "retrogression" could be accredited to *"the want of first class dirt roads . . .* graded and culverted with stone." Such roads, he insisted, should connect "every court house to the railroad and . . . every court house to the next court house." A writer in the *Progressive Farmer* declared in 1886 that "the country roads in North Carolina are in a disgustingly wretched condition," while a correspondent for the *Southern Cultivator & Dixie Farmer* wrote in 1890 that better roads would be one of the greatest benefits that could befall southern farmers. But two decades later only 17,700 of the total 502,057 miles of road in ten southern states were improved with gravel or stone surfaces.[4] It was not until after passage of the Federal Highway Act in 1916 that much progress occurred. Georgia, for example, established a highway commission in that year to promote road building, but in most of the rural South farmers were still "in the mud," as they referred to their condition, into the 1920s and beyond. There was much discussion about the importance of roads to farmers, but few results were achieved. Railroad mileage expanded substantially in the South in the 1870s and 1880s, but many farmers were not near a rail line.

Southern farmers were also among the last to get rural free delivery of mail. In 1890 farm families got their mail from fourth-class post offices located in the villages and towns, often several miles away. Star route carriers brought the mail to these post offices. The farmers commonly picked up their mail on a trip to town for some other purpose, which meant that most received mail only once or possibly twice a week, and probably less often. South Carolina Congressman James Ellerbe said in 1910 that as a boy he had to travel eleven miles to a post office, and Senator John Sharp Williams of Mississippi estimated in 1894 that 50 percent of the people in his home area had to go at least six miles to obtain their mail. Moreover, service at the fourth-class post offices was generally poor and limited.

Under these conditions it is not surprising that southern congressmen and senators fought hard for rural free delivery of mail. In the 1890s Congressman Tom Watson of Georgia and Senator Marion Butler of North Carolina were among those who campaigned vigorously to get mail delivered to their farm constituents. But when Congress finally began to experiment with rural free delivery in the 1890s, southerners found themselves gaining relatively little. Republicans controlled Congress and the Post Office Department after McKinley's election in 1896, and most of the new rural routes were established in Republican states, particularly in the Midwest. In 1900 Ohio had 225 rural free delivery routes, while Mississippi had none and Alabama only eight. By 1906 twelve southern states had 9,126 rural mail routes compared to 11,794 in only five midwestern states.[5] Besides the political factors that held up establishment of rural mail routes in the South, post office officials hesitated to organize routes where illiteracy was as high as it was in much of the rural South.

While agriculture was predominant in the South, there were many different kinds of farms and farmers scattered across that vast rural landscape from southern Virginia to central Texas. Farms differed in size, productivity, quality of land, crops and livestock raised, tenure, and the standard of living they provided. As was true of agriculture throughout the United States, there was no typical southern farm.

In 1900 there were about 2.1 million farms in the eleven southern states. At the top of the economic pyramid were the relatively small number of around 50,000 large farmers and planters whose holdings varied from a few hundred to several thousand acres. At the other extreme were the sharecroppers and poorer tenants who farmed 20 to 50 acres, most of them barely earning enough to support their minimum needs. Among commercial farmers these families had the lowest standard of living in the region. Between the extremes of large planters and poor sharecroppers were 750,000 to one million family farmers who had 100 to 200 acres of land which they owned or rented. These farmers usually had greater and more varied production than sharecroppers and raised a larger proportion of their living. Nevertheless, they had a relatively low standard of living and found it difficult to hold their own in the generation between 1870 and 1900. Although conditions improved with rising cotton prices after 1898, the situation did not basically change for most producers.

While southern farmers may be divided into at least three major groups, there were variations of income and standard of living within each group. Conditions among sharecroppers differed considerably, depending on the size of the farm tilled, the quality of the soil, the attitude of the landlord, the number of workers in the family, and other factors. When the U.S. Department of Agriculture (USDA) studied 878 sharecroppers, share tenants, and cash tenants in the Mississippi-Yazoo Delta during 1913, researchers found that major differences in labor income resulted from different sizes of operations. Those with less than 15 acres of cotton averaged only $293 in labor income a year; those with 15 to 19 acres had an average of $332, and farmers with 20 to 24 acres of cotton averaged $387. Tenants who had 25 or more acres of cotton had average incomes of $622. In other studies variations were found because of greater productivity per acre and varying crop and livestock mixes.[6]

At the other extreme, not all planters did equally well. While some prospered, others lost their land through debt and foreclosure. There were also substantial differences among the middle-class family farmers who owned their farms. The fertility of the land, the size of their holdings, and managerial abilities made a great difference in how they fared. In brief, income and living standards varied greatly on southern farms between major classes and within each class.

In 1909 and 1910 the Census Bureau made a special study of large landholders in 325 counties throughout the South, most of whom were located in the black belt. They found 39,073 plantations in those counties which had five or more tenants. The largest number of planters surveyed had between five and nine tenants, but a few had more than fifty. Landholding in the main plantation areas had become concentrated before the Civil War and this situation continued into the postwar years. These and the other large planters outside the regions surveyed made up the South's agricultural upper class.[7]

Most large planters enjoyed a good standard of living for the time. They generally lived in spacious homes, often located in town, and had an abundance and good variety of food. Their tables contained various kinds of meat, vegetables, milk, eggs, bread made out of corn and wheat flour, and fruits. Coffee and tea were common mealtime drinks. They had sufficient income to send their children to school, to subscribe to farm magazines, and to engage in some travel. If they lived on their plantations they drove to town in buggies pulled by handsome teams of horses, dressed their wives and daughters in the latest fashions, and enjoyed occasional parties and community affairs. On the larger plantations most of the work in the house and fields was done by servants and laborers who worked long hours for only a few dollars a year. Eight to twelve dollars a month was a common wage for field hands. Managers supervised most of the actual production operations on the large plantations. Smaller planters with five to ten tenants devoted more time to personal management and usually lived much more modestly.

While the larger planters usually insisted that their sharecroppers or tenants plant cotton or some other cash crop, they commonly diversified production on that part of their land that was under their direct operation, referred to as "landlord farms." More of the land in landlord farms was in woodland and other land not under cultivation, and those farms generally had more livestock. A few planters took the lead in the late nineteenth century in experimenting with improved breeds of livestock and crops and in adopting better farming methods. While southern planters and the larger farmers were relatively well off, they were not without problems. They had to worry about weather, prices, credit, and dealings with their sharecroppers and tenants, either directly or through their managers. Debts often harried planters, who sometimes suffered from foreclosure or became so discouraged they sold out. But compared to other farmers they produced enough income to provide a reasonably good living and to maintain and even expand their estates.

If the 40,000 to 50,000 large farmers and planters, making up only between 2 and 3 percent of all farmers in the South, enjoyed a fairly comfortable existence in the late nineteenth and early twentieth centuries, most of the others faced extremely hard times. Life was dull and difficult for the great majority of people on American farms, but nowhere was this more evident than among southern farmers. Their low incomes were reflected in poor housing, inadequate diets, lack of education and health care, and a hopelessness that permeated so much of farm life. After studying the position of cotton farmers throughout the South in 1893, a Senate committee reported that hard times debarred "farmers from any enjoyment of the luxuries and elegancies of life, and prevents the education of their children. Leisure essential for the mental cultivation and social enjoyment accorded to the prosperous is wholly wanting." The living standard of so many farmers in the South was not a relative matter but one of absolute poverty.[8]

The prospects of owning one's own farm deteriorated as sharecropping and tenancy grew decade after decade. The percentage of all kinds of tenancy throughout the South rose from 36 to 49 percent in the generation between 1880 and 1910. While black farmers made some gains in land ownership up to about 1910, when some 25 percent of them were owners, acreage and production remained small and un-profitable for most of the 218,467 blacks who were full or part owners. Off-farm employment opportunities were so limited that the rapidly increasing rural population placed ever greater demands upon the land. In the two generations between the end of the Civil War and World War I, many southern farmers lost ground, barely held their own, or at best made modest gains. Their lives and living standards remained distressingly the same.

D.W. Brooks, who as a boy observed life on poor northeastern Georgia farms and who later became head of Gold Kist, a large farmer cooperative, once said that many Georgia farmers were both astrono-mers and agronomists. They could, Brooks declared, observe the stars through the roofs of their leaky shacks and study the soil through holes in the floor. The southern landscape was thickly dotted with houses that conformed to the Brooks description.

Only about half of the southern farmers owned their own farms in 1900.[9] The larger landowners customarily provided some kind of house on each small acreage rented to sharecroppers and tenants. These houses were generally drab and unpainted one- or two-room cabins or shacks. Constructed of logs or rough lumber with a fireplace at one end, the houses usually sat up on posts a foot or so above the ground. Spaces between the logs or boards let in the cold winter winds, and the roofs often leaked profusely during rain storms. Sometimes the walls were covered with pages from old newspapers or magazines. Many cabins were without glass windows, and the wooden shutters were left open in summer to admit air and light. The same opening that let in light also admitted flies, mosquitoes, and other insects. In 1895, when one black woman who lived in a shack near Tuskegee, Alabama, was asked if the snakes did not crawl through the cracks in the floor, she replied, "Oh, yes, they gets in sometimes, but I just bresh 'em out."[10]

In the one-room cabins which dotted hundreds of southern planta-tions, the family cooked, ate, and slept in the single room. These houses sometimes had a porch where the family sat in the evening, and occasionally there was a lean-to or small outbuilding in which cooking was done. When the cabin had two rooms one was used for cooking and eating and one for sleeping. It was common for three or four children, sometimes more, to sleep in one bed. In a study done in the 1920s of preschool children in 359 white and 111 black families in South Carolina, investigators found that 16 percent of the small children in white families and 8 percent in black families slept with five other children.

These farm families had little that resembled furniture. There was usually a pine table, two or three chairs, often partly broken, and sometimes a rickety cupboard which held a miscellany of dishes and pans. More likely dishes were simply placed on board shelves nailed to the wall. The bedroom contained one or two beds with rope supports on which rested a mattress filled with corn shucks. A trunk or chest might sit in the bedroom to hold clothing and bedding. It was customary to cook over the fireplace, which also served for heat in the winter. Iron pots and skillets were the main cooking utensils. If the farmer had a milk cow, his wife probably owned a churn to make butter. Few of the amenities of life were evident. A clock, a Bible, and perhaps a few pictures were about all that challenged the stark existence. Some cabins were graced by growing flowers in the summer, but in many instances on the large plantations cotton came to within a few feet of the cabin door. Between the cotton field and the house, the earth was beaten hard and became dust in dry weather and mud when it rained. Atticus G. Haygood hit the mark when he told the ladies of the Philadelphia Woman's Home Missionary Society of the Methodist Episcopal Church in 1885: "Compared with the houses you good women know they [black sharecroppers] lack all things."[11]

The family water supply generally came from a shallow, dug well, a spring, or a stream. Water was obtained by lowering a bucket on a rope into the well or by using a hand pump. While most of the wells were cased with boards, stones, or perhaps brick, they were seldom tight enough around the top to keep out bugs, snakes, dirt, and other foreign materials. The outdoor privy was the most common toilet facility and often was found not far from the well, further contaminating the family's drinking water. Many of the toilet facilities were extremely unsanitary, but they were better than nothing. Investigators found that in some communities there were farm homes that had no toilet whatever and family members used a barn, the yard, or nearby woods.[12]

The farmstead of poor farmers sometimes included one or two dilapidated outbuildings in which to house a few head of livestock. But most sharecroppers and many tenants had very few cows, mules, hogs, or chickens. Although the farmer often kept a mule belonging to the landlord, many had no livestock of their own. In surveying some black farmers in Alabama in 1895 and 1896, the investigators made such reports as, "A mule, an ox, and a pig made up the livestock" or "The livestock consisted of a mule, two cows, and some hens," while other families were described as having "one mule and a pig" or "two hogs, three hens and a turkey." Many farmers also had small gardens. In 1899, Census Bureau officials found that in eight southern states around 70 percent of the farms reported vegetable gardens. The value of these gardens varied from $13.36 a year in South Carolina to $16.74 in Mississippi. In the plantation areas the number and value of farm gardens were less.[13]

Middle-class farmers usually had better homes than sharecroppers and poorer tenants. Frame houses of five and six rooms were common for farm owners and better-off tenants. These farmsteads also had more outbuildings to house livestock and poultry. Fences were generally better. While heat might be derived from fireplaces, cooking was more likely to be done on a cook stove. The interiors of these farm homes were more pleasant because of better furnishings and more amenities. Dishes were more likely to be kept in cupboards, beds had improved mattresses, and chairs and tables were of better quality. Sometimes there were such luxuries as a piano or organ.

Great variations existed not only in housing but also in the food eaten by southern farm families. As mentioned earlier, planters had an abundance and fair variety of food. Middle-class farmers, both owners and tenants, tended to be diversified and had different kinds of food and enough of it. Their tables had vegetables and fruit in season, and pork, beef, and poultry. They also consumed butter, milk, and eggs.

Tens of thousands of poor farmers, however, existed year in and year out on a limited and unhealthy diet. The worst of it was that there was little change in the diets of poorer farmers from the 1870s to the World War I period. There were times when abnormally high cotton prices might provide a little more money and slightly better food, but for the most part diets were pitifully inadequate. The standard fare for much of the year in the poorer farm homes consisted of salt pork, cornmeal, and syrup or molasses. Many farmers made their own syrup from some variety of sorghum or cane raised on the farm. In thousands of poor farm homes cornmeal was mixed with water and cooked in a skillet or on a griddle over the open fire in the fireplace. Corn was also eaten as grits, roasting ears, and hominy. The salt pork, almost entirely fat, was sliced thin and fried until it became brown and freed from much of the grease. Syrup would be mixed with the grease to make what many called "sap," which was poured over or mixed with the corn bread. A beverage was made by mixing syrup with hot water. "This is the bill of fare," wrote on investigator from Tuskegee Institute in 1895, "of most of the cabins on the plantations of the 'black belt' three times a day during the year." One black farmer recalled years later that in his youth during the early twentieth century he crumbled up dry corn bread, soaked it with water, and sprinkled salt over it for his evening meal. Only two meals a day were eaten on many southern farms.[14]

There were, of course, some variations in this monotonous and unhealthful diet. Collards and turnip greens provided leafy vegetables part of the year, and sweet potatoes were eaten by farm families. Those who did have gardens had such vegetables as beans, okra, field peas, and cabbage in the summer months. To vary the steady diet of salted fat pork, families killed and cooked wild animals such as rabbits, squirrels, or opossums. One black who grew up in Georgia before World War I recalled that "Ma would rub the possum's skin with salt, red pepper and black pepper and boil him up to one and half hours if he was a tough one. Then she would bake him just like a turkey to a light brown all over" and serve with sweet potatoes.[15] Many of the poorer farmers had no milk cows, but those who did ate butter and drank buttermilk, which was popular on southern farms. Fresh milk, commonly known as "sweet milk," was also consumed. Eggs were scarce because of the lack of chickens.

The diet of many southern farmers, then, was not very tasty, but more important it was nutritionally unbalanced. It was high in fat and carbohydrates and low in minerals, protein, and vitamins. In dietary studies done among black sharecroppers in Macon County, Alabama, over a fifteen-day period in February 1896, it was found that a family of nine on a forty-acre cotton farm consumed 41,270 grams of food, of which 26,000 grams consisted of carbohydrates and fats.

Inadequate diets among large numbers of southern farmers, both black and white, became clear as social scientists studied the matter in the early twentieth century. Researchers from the U.S. Department of Agriculture, the agricultural experiment stations, and the Department of Labor made a number of revealing studies on the quality and quantity of food consumed by farm families. A study in four rural counties of South Carolina in the 1920s found that 41 percent of the white children from one to five years old, and 71 percent of the blacks, existed on deficient diets. With shortages of minerals and vitamins, large numbers of southern farm children suffered from pellagra, rickets, and other diseases related to unbalanced diets.[16]

Most poor southern farmers spent a high percentage of their meager income on food and clothing. These farmers did not earn enough even to provide those essentials. The stark fact was that relatively few families on southern farms had much of anything left after expenditures for food and clothing to spend for furniture, reading materials, travel, education, and other amenities. The situation for large numbers of southern farmers was not unlike that of the peasants of India and other underdeveloped countries where the bulk of the earnings go for a few absolute essentials.

Inadequate housing, unbalanced diets, impure water, and unsanitary living conditions all contributed to poor health among many southern farmers. Both children and adults were subject to dysentery, various kinds of stomach trouble, malaria, typhoid, hookworms, and pellagra. Children acquired hookworms by going without shoes in unsanitary places. The rural school was a place where many youngsters got hookworms. These parasites fastened themselves on the intestinal tract and sapped the child's strength. While hookworms seldom caused death, they weakened and dulled their victims.

Pellagra, identified as an American problem by an Atlanta physician in 1902, remained a somewhat mysterious disease until its causes were finally diagnosed some years later. Long known in Europe, pellagra caused scaly skin and digestive troubles and affected the nervous system. Thousands of southerners suffered from the disease in the early twentieth century as doctors and researchers sought to isolate the reasons so many people contracted the malady. In 1914 Dr. Joseph Goldberger discovered that pellagra stemmed from diets that lacked milk, eggs, vegetables, fruits, lean meat, and other foods containing proteins and vitamins. It was a case of poor southerners eating too much fat meat, meal, and molasses, which caused a niacin deficiency. Although a person with pellagra often died, more frequently victims lost weight and had no energy or vitality. Hookworms, pellagra, and malaria were the three worst scourges affecting the health of generally poor southern farmers. Yellow fever also took its toll from time to time.[17]

Farm families received very little professional medical attention. Babies were generally delivered by midwives, and a visit from the doctor was an uncommon event. One usually had to be near death before a doctor could justifiably be called. Poor farmers seldom had enough money to afford a doctor. "A farmer only gets money twice a year, and if the children get sick between seasons," said a Mississippi mother, "they have to get along." Even if people had the money there were too few doctors to treat all of the farm patients. Families in the country relied on patent medicines and home remedies. For various illnesses people took castor oil, calomel, paregoric, salts, quinine, and tea made from herbs. Sheer endurance was a major factor in meeting health problems.[18] Just how much poor health among thousands of southern farmers contributed to their poverty is uncertain. It seems fair to assume, however, that the ever-present maladies that weakened and sapped people's strength played some part in their low productivity and subsistence standard of living.

One great lack in the rural South was education. The percentage of illiteracy was high and the level of educational attainments extremely low in most farm communities. In 1870 the illiterate white population over ten years of age varied from 17 percent in Mississippi to 33 percent in North Carolina; for the newly freed blacks it was more than 80 percent in most southern states. While by 1890 the figure for whites had dropped to below 20 percent and for blacks to between 50 and 60 percent, the number of illiterates was still extremely high. And many people who were not illiterate by definition, especially in predominantly black communities, were functionally illiterate. Lack of education was certainly one factor contributing to rural poverty in the South. People who could not read or write or who could not do simple arithmetic were at a distinct disadvantage in a competitive economy. Indeed, it could be argued that poor education was both a result and a cause of rural poverty. Low incomes and a diminished tax base perpetuated poor schools, which in turn contributed to continued poverty.

Inadequate education, however, did not result from an absence of interest among farmers. After gaining their freedom, blacks had an insatiable desire for schooling, and many whites also saw the values of education as a way to improve their condition. As the state commissioner of education in Georgia wrote in 1875, there was growing sentiment in favor of public schools, and he believed at least half of the white population and "nearly the entire mass of the colored" wanted such institutions.[19]

During the generation following the Civil War, the southern states struggled to establish statewide, tax-supported public school systems. Progress, however, was slow because of the region's general poverty and considerable opposition to the principle of public education. An additional and highly important problem was the insistence by whites that separate schools be maintained for white and black students. Nevertheless, by the late nineteenth century the foundations had been laid for public school systems throughout the South.

While most public education in the South was poor, farm children had the poorest facilities, the most limited curriculum, and the weakest instruction. Until late in the nineteenth century most rural schools were ungraded, terms were short, and attendance was skimpy. Some whites opposed educating blacks at all, believing that, as one North Carolina editor said, "Nothing is so surely ruining Negroes of the South as the accursed free schools." A farmer from that state declared that educating blacks would ruin the South's labor system.[20] To many, education of blacks was a threat to white supremacy. Moreover, town people tended to give rural education a low priority. They did not consider a good education necessary for country boys and girls whose job was to plant, hoe, and harvest cotton.

Schoolhouses in the rural South were usually nothing more than frame shacks or log houses. The board structures were commonly about 14 by 20 feet in size with a door on one end and three unshaded windows on each side. Children hung their wraps on pegs or nails on the wall and sat on straight board seats. Many schools did not have any kind of desks. These structures were crowded and uncomfortable. The school commissioner in Georgia wrote in 1895 that he had recently received information on sixty country schools and only four or five were fit for use. The schoolhouses, he wrote, were in "such wretched condition that the schools can not be conducted during the winter at all." When school was held in the summer because of cold school-houses in the winter, children were denied any education because then they were kept at home to work in the fields. In 111 counties in Georgia, the schoolhouses were of less value than the jails. Such figures, the commissioner said, "tell an appalling story." Some districts in North Carolina had no schoolhouses at all and instruction was attempted in whatever makeshift building could be found.[21]

Teachers in the rural schools had little preparation and were often not far ahead of their pupils. The worst situation was in the black schools. Salaries were low, usually varying from $15 to $30 a month in the 1890s. There were not enough institutions to train teachers, so many communities simply ignored the standards required for certification and permitted teachers to teach on temporary certificates. In 1895 it was reported that in South Carolina there was one teacher for every twenty-nine white children and one for every thirty-three blacks.[22]

The curriculum in country schools was confined mainly to reading, writing, spelling, and arithmetic. Patrons and educational reformers talked about providing what they considered a more practical type of education for farm youth, but nothing much changed before World War I. The land-grant colleges established for training students in agriculture and other practical subjects were of little value to southern farm youth, either black or white, prior to World War I because so few of them ever went to high school, to say nothing of college. And there was little overall administrative supervision of the public schools. As late as 1913 an Alabama supervisor wrote that "nearly 50 percent of the county superintendents . . . did not visit a single negro school."[23]

Until at least the end of the nineteenth century most rural schools in the South had only three- or four-month terms. In 1895 the state superintendent in South Carolina referred to "short-termed country schools." Georgia raised the school term to five months in 1891, but most schools continued to meet only three or four months a year. Not only were the terms short, but thousands of students who were enrolled simply did not attend. Compulsory attendance laws were not passed in the southern states until after 1905, and then they were only indifferently enforced. The average daily attendance in the late 1890s was usually not more than 50 to 70 percent of the enrollment. While a much smaller percentage of black than white students between the ages of five and eighteen were enrolled in school in the 1890s, the percentage of black enrollees who actually attended school was about the same as that for whites. In some states the percentage of black attendance was even higher, indicating the strong desire among blacks for education. A major deterrent to school attendance for both whites and blacks was the widespread practice of parents' keeping children out of class to work on the farm. During cotton picking season, for example, almost all hands were pressed into service. To meet this problem school terms were actually built around the periods of peak labor demands.[24]

Most black schools were extremely inferior. One observer recalled that the Negro schoolhouses in the Carolinas looked "more like a refuge for bats and owls than a place of learning."[25] This resulted from the unwillingness of whites to spend anywhere near as much on the education of black youth as they spent on their own sons and daughters. They argued that since whites paid most of the local taxes, more of that money should be spent on the white schools. In 1888 in Wilkes County, Georgia, there were thirty-seven schools for 1,403 white students and only ten for 2,507 black youth. White teachers commonly received higher pay, although this was not universally the case. In Wilkes County, Georgia, black teachers received about $6 a month less than their white counterparts; in some counties the discrepancy was as high as $10 or $12 a month, or 30 to 40 percent. But according to official reports there were counties in Georgia that provided equal pay for white and black teachers.[26]

As a result of poor schools, illiteracy continued high among rural youth. Investigators found in 1893 that illiteracy of country boys and girls in Georgia between the ages of ten and eighteen was 29 percent for blacks and 13 percent for whites. For all young people in that age bracket on farms the figure was 21 percent, or twice as high as for city youth. According to some observers, one of the main factors drawing people away from the farms was the poor country schools. The Georgia school commissioner reported in 1894 that he had traveled over ninety counties in the state and found that people were "fast leaving the country and moving to town" in order to obtain better education for their children. If that trend continued, the commissioner remarked later, "we shall soon bring all of the wealth and intelligence to city centers, and we shall inevitably have an ignorant peasant population in the rural districts." This would, he said, bring great harm to country life. But improved education came slowly to most rural communities in the South. The United States commissioner of education reported in 1899 that the average annual expenditure per pupil was only $3.59 in Alabama, $7.70 in Louisiana, and $7.30 in Georgia, compared to $18.99 for the United States as a whole.[27]

The lack of progress in the economic development of the rural South was certainly associated with low educational levels. The diffusion of knowledge has been widely recognized as a major factor in the development of modern economic life. Failure of southern farmers to participate in the educational advancements and knowledge explosion in the late nineteenth and early twentieth centuries provided a strong barrier to economic progress.[28]

Religion provided comfort and solace for many poor and disheart-ened southern farm families. If life was hard in the cotton and tobacco fields, faithful followers of God might expect a better life in that distant place where the streets were reportedly paved with pure gold. By the 1880s and 1890s hundreds of churches, mostly Baptist and Methodist, dotted the rural landscape and occupied a central place in small towns. The country church was as much a social as a spiritual institution, and in many parts of the South it became, along with the school, the center of community activities and one of the region's most influential institu-tions. Churches were racially segregated. Black congregations affiliated with the Colored Methodist Episcopal Church, the African Methodist Episcopal Church, the National Baptist Convention, and other Negro denominations.

Church membership grew rapidly among farm people in the late nineteenth and early twentieth centuries. Between 1890 and 1916, for example, the number of church organizations in North Carolina rose from 6,824 to 9,135, and membership from 685,660 to 1,080,723, most of whom were in the Baptist, Methodist, and African Methodist Episco-pal groups. Alamance County in North Carolina's Piedmont had thirty churches for white worshippers in 1872, or one for every 274 persons. By 1890 there were forty-seven churches in the county. As was true elsewhere, more women than men participated in church life.[29]

The Sunday school became an increasingly important part of church activities in most denominations. Of the 9,402 religious organi-zations in Alabama in 1916, 7,847 reported operating Sunday schools. Writing about the Baptists in Alabama, one authority observed that by the 1880s the Sunday school had "become a preeminent feature" of church life. Until well into the twentieth century, many country churches suspended Sunday school in the winter because of cold weather and inability to heat the churches.[30]

Throughout much of the rural South, church buildings were primi-tive structures. Until the 1880s they were commonly built of logs. As one Baptist explained, log churches were retained "partly out of regard for sacred memories, and partly because of the indifference of the people to provide better places of worship." In some cases country churches were in utter disrepair. Open doors and glassless windows provided entry for bats and owls and sometimes a retreat for stray hogs and goats. Whatever the condition of church structures, they were usually located in a grove of trees with enough land around them to provide space for a cemetery and for the horses and wagons by which the parishioners arrived at Sunday school and church. By the late nineteenth and early twentieth centuries the old log churches were being replaced by frame buildings and an occasional brick structure. Sunday school could now be held year around, and the new structures built by Baptists and other denominations which immersed new converts had baptisteries and other conveniences unknown in earlier churches throughout the countryside.[31]

Country churches had a hard time obtaining ministers. Most preachers in southern farm communities devoted only part time to church work. They often farmed in the area or had other employment. Sometimes one minister served several congregations, which meant that many churches had services only once or twice a month. Preachers generally lacked formal education and they preached a simple faith uncluttered by theology. It was an old-fashioned gospel of personal salvation and morality that tired southern farmers heard when they gathered on Sunday morning or afternoon. The average congregation was small, usually less than 100 members, and they supported the church by free will offerings. In 1916 the black congregations in Mississippi that reported said they paid their pastors an average annual salary of $270. But even this was a better income than that earned by most sharecroppers. Besides, the minister was a recognized leader in the community.[32]

Revival meetings were an important part of the religious life of southern farm families, both white and black. These so-called "protracted meetings" usually lasted at least a week. They were commonly held in late July or August after the crops were "laid by" and just before cotton picking began. Farm families and others gathered from miles around, arriving on foot, by horseback, or in buggies and wagons. The meetings were generally held in the open air or under a large tent. Led by some famous evangelist and assisted by local preachers, these were highly emotional gatherings with much singing, praying, and preaching. Describing a revival meeting in Marengo County, Alabama, in 1910, one observer declared that preachers "pounded the pulpit, lashed the air and ranted about sins." Dancing, card playing, swearing, drinking, gossip, and "petting" were among the sins that people were urged to forsake. It was expected that the mourners' bench would be filled with repentent sinners at both afternoon and evening services. Baptism in a nearby creek or pond awaited the newly converted.[33] The Ball's Creek campground in Catawba County, North Carolina, was the scene of a revival meeting every year, except two, after 1853.

The revival meetings, as well as the regular church services, were social as well as spiritual occasions. People often pooled their food and ate together after church. It was a time for visiting and fellowship with neighbors and friends. Farmers exchanged gossip and talked about the weather, prices, and condition of the crops, while the women discussed their children, cooking, and home life. The young people socialized and courted.

While much social life centered around the church in most southern rural communities, farmers also found other ways to socialize. Fraternal orders such as the Masons, Woodmen of the World, and Odd Fellows had many farmer members. There were also military companies, county fairs, Grange meetings, picnics, and political gatherings that brought farm people together. The Fourth of July, Thanksgiving, Christmas, and New Year's were all celebrated with family and friends. Sometimes large landowners would prepare a huge barbecue for all their sharecroppers on the Fourth of July. After feasting on barbecued pork and beef, potato salad, cake, pie, and lemonade, the people played cards, had a ball game, or engaged in some other social or recreational activity. For many farm people just going to town once a week, usually on Saturday afternoon, was a significant social experience.[34]

Southern farmers spent a good deal of time hunting and fishing. To critics who believed that southerners were shiftless and lazy, farmers were perceived as spending far too much time in such activities. John Dent, a northern Georgia planter, once complained that among both his white and his black farm hands, "fish is the paramount idea with them."[35] In any event, farmers dropped their hooks in the streams and rivers for whatever fish would bite, and followed their dogs through the forests and fields hunting for rabbits, squirrels, opossums, raccoons, and other animals. These activities were both recreational and practical. The results of the hunt or the fishing trip ended up on farm tables.

Life was hardest for southern farm women. They worked longer and harder than other members of the family and enjoyed the least recreation and social life. While larger farmers and planters hired household help for their wives, the great majority of lower- and middle-class women had a host of tasks which wore them out before their time. The manuscript census reveals that women also operated a substantial number of farms on their own, usually after the death of a husband. Many farm women looked old by the age of forty or before. Since families were large, the younger farm women were pregnant much of the time. Besides rearing the children, they had to cook, keep house, wash clothes, sew, and care for the garden. Women also worked in the fields, hoeing and picking cotton, picking worms off tobacco plants, or performing other work. Social activities were confined mainly to neighborly visiting and occasional trips to town or to church. Even at church affairs they were often expected to serve meals. Practically every activity on the farm involved some work for the women. There was little money to improve and brighten their homes. At cotton and tobacco planting time a farm wife might hope and plan for some new curtains, dishes, or an added piece of furniture to be purchased when the crop was sold in the fall, but too often her hopes were shattered by a short crop or low prices. Nothing remained but to hope for better things next year. But again the hope was usually unrealized.

Besides poverty, frequent moves by the tenant classes discouraged the development of a more rewarding social and community life. Sharecroppers and tenants were continually looking for a better situation. In some localities as many as half the farmers changed farms every year or two in search of a more generous landlord or a place with a more livable house. Most farmers did not move very far, usually not outside the county, but these frequent moves required adjustments in regard to neighbors, social life, schools, and churches. There was an old saying that "three moves were equal to a fire." That was an exaggeration, but movement from place to place by poor farmers tended to weaken community relationships and the growth of a satisfying social life.

One overriding fact of southern society was racial segregation and the desire by whites to maintain social dominance over blacks. While white and black farmers might live in the same community in general peace and harmony, that situation existed only so long as the blacks did not insist on equality. Keeping the black "in his place" was not only a goal in the plantation areas, where blacks outnumbered whites, but in the larger farm society as well. Black and white children might play or frequent the old swimming hole together up to a certain age, but as they went into their teens a division and separation developed. Blacks used the back door at a white home, and a white scarcely ever ate with a black family. That was not a part of the accepted social mores.

Since most blacks were among the poorest farmers who worked land owned by others, they had little choice but to be subservient. At settlement time in the fall they were in no position to argue over the accounts. One bit of doggerel went:

A naught is a naught,
A figger is a figger;
All for the white man,
None for the nigger.

Many white landowners preferred black tenants over poor whites because they were more tractable and would settle for lower standards of living. Blacks resented their powerless position and felt mistreated. This was especially true of younger blacks who had never known the controls of slavery, but tradition, custom, paternalism, and, if necessary, such violent actions as lynching, kept blacks in line.[36]

In 1915 and 1916 the *Progressive Farmer,* which was published in Raleigh, North Carolina, but which circulated widely throughout the South, launched a campaign to get legislation which would permit the segregation of the ownership of farmland. Editor Clarence Poe advocated permitting whites by majority vote to deny blacks the right to buy land in white communities. He argued that when blacks moved into white farm neighborhoods land values dropped. This, he said, was unfair to white farmers. Poe's proposal was resisted by large landowners who rented to black sharecroppers. While it never gained majority support, it reflected the deep racism prevalent in the rural South.[37]

At the turn of the twentieth century more than a million black and white southern farmers were mired in what seemed to be inescapable poverty. These farm families lived out their lives in a hand-to-mouth existence. Their homes, their diets, their clothes, and their meager expenditures for items other than food, fuel, and shelter all testified to perpetual hard times. Hundreds of thousands of farmers were unable to accumulate enough capital to own a farm, to earn sufficient money to provide a decent house and furnishings, or to buy the amenities that might make life a little more pleasant. In an economy where money was essential to acquire the industrial products being turned out by the nation's expanding factories, poor southern farmers were left in the economic and social backwash. Although both white and black farm families developed institutions which met some of their social and cultural needs, life was too often dull and monotonous.

The New South, touted so loudly by Henry Grady and others, had produced little that was new or beneficial to the mass of southern farmers. The growth of industry, especially textiles, had provided some off-farm jobs for white farmers or members of their families, but industrial growth had not been sufficient to reduce the poverty-ridden surplus farm population. Southern farmers lived little differently in 1900 than they had in 1880; most of their children in the 1930s were still mired in static communities separated from, or touched only lightly by, modern cultural and economic life. How could poor farmers increase their incomes and improve their living conditions? That was the basic but unanswered question in the late nineteenth and early twentieth centuries throughout the rural South.

3

Salvation through Organization and Politics

Southern farmers knew well enough that something was wrong with the system that kept them in such a state of poverty. For most of them the American dream of "getting ahead" economically and of perhaps being able to leave some inheritance to their children remained just that—a dream. At an interstate convention of farmers in Atlanta in August 1887, the delegates concluded that "the agricultural interests of the South are languishing and depressed to a distressing degree." They insisted that farmers were currently hurting, "have been suffering for twenty years," and concluded that "the outlook is not favorable."[1] Indeed, conditions were about to get worse. Cotton prices had turned downward in the 1870s and reached as much as 10 cents a pound in only two years, 1879 and 1881, between 1876 and 1900. In the 1890s cotton dropped to around 5 cents a pound in most interior markets.

Producers saw their enemies not in small, inefficient operations or in overproduction, but in the money lenders, the supply merchants, and the cotton buyers who were tied to the country's large financial, transportation, and industrial corporations. Monopolies, farmers said, were bleeding them of their rightful rewards. Despite their vast numerical majority in the South, farmers saw themselves being controlled and exploited by others. Whatever profits existed in farming were being siphoned off by a privileged few.

While southern farmers complained about lack of credit, high interest charges, unfair railroad rates and real estate taxes, and profits by supply merchants, they faced some even more basic problems that were fundamental to the entire agricultural industry. Because of weather, insects, and a variety of other factors, farmers, even if they wanted to, could not regulate their production of cotton, tobacco, and other commercial crops to the demands of the market. Moreover, they could not control their costs. When asked in 1874 about how much it cost him to produce cotton, David Dickson, a prominent Georgia planter, replied that he could not answer the question because, among other things, it depended on "sun and rain, time and quantity; worms, caterpillars, storms, frost, and land."[2] Farmers often grew more than the market could absorb at prices profitable to producers. Widely scattered and independent, farmers could not get together to regulate production and avoid price-depressing surpluses. They usually argued that there should be no real surpluses so long as people in the world were hungry and naked. But so long as the needy had no money with which to buy, production frequently outran effective demand. Indeed, it was not uncommon for large crops to bring less money than smaller ones. The farm value of the 9 million bales of cotton grown in 1891 was about $65 million less than that of the 8.6 million bales grown in 1890.[3]

If farmers could not control their production, they could not determine the price of their commodities. If cotton farmers, for example, had been able to produce only what the market would take, and organize one great sales pool, they could have bargained over price with the textile manufacturers. If they had had bargaining power, presumably they could have sought a price that would have given them a fair return on their labor and capital. But this was not the case.

Farmers dealt as individuals. When they took their cotton to market they were in no position to bargain. They had to take what the cotton buyer offered since there was little or no competition among buyers. The price of cotton was set in New York or Liverpool, and on any given date cotton would be about the same price in Atlanta, Birmingham, or Jackson, Mississippi, as well as in the hundreds of markets in small towns. Tobacco growers were in the same unenviable position. They had no choice but to take what the buyers bid at the tobacco auctions. There was no place else to sell it.

The welfare of farmers was, of course, only partially determined by the prices they received for their products. As the economy modernized and industrialized in the late nineteenth century, and as farming became more commercialized and less self-sufficient, the prices of commodities that farmers had to purchase became increasingly important. As mentioned in chapter 1, when farmers sold their products and bought nonfarm goods, the exchange value between farm and nonfarm commodities became crucial. The price of cotton, for example, was not really very significant if a farmer spun and wove his own crop into cloth for clothing and blankets for his family. It was when he sold his cotton and bought his clothing that the price relationship affected his income and standard of living. The basic question for a farmer was the quantity and quality of nonfarm goods a bale of cotton or 100 pounds of tobacco would buy.

But farmers were in a weak bargaining position to improve the relationship between farm and nonfarm prices. In the first place, business and industry were becoming increasingly better organized and even monopolistic, while farmers remained scattered and individualistic. Furthermore, farmers were exchanging cheap raw materials—cotton, tobacco, grain, and livestock—for expensive manufactured goods. In this situation the terms of trade were fundamentally unfavorable to the farmers except in a few unusual periods. While the issue of farm price parity did not become a major political question until the early twentieth century, farmers were acutely aware of the problem much earlier.

Farm prices were also very important in relation to debt. If a southern farmer borrowed $100 when cotton was 10 cents a pound, he would need 1,000 pounds, or two bales, to repay the principal amount. If, on the other hand, cotton fell to five cents, it would take four bales, or twice as much, to settle the debt. Falling farm prices in the late nineteenth century created serious problems for farmers with debts.

To many farmers, inflation of the currency seemed to be a solution to this problem. Holding to the quantity theory of money, farmers urged the government to inflate the currency by issuing more greenbacks or increasing the amount of silver money in circulation. They believed such policies would raise agricultural prices and make it easier for them to pay their debts.

Strongest support for inflationary policies in the 1870s came from western farmers, but some southerners also backed inflation as a means of relieving farm distress. The Panic of 1873 and the subsequent drop in farm prices did much to encourage inflationary sentiment. Senator John B. Gordon of Georgia was a strong advocate of monetary inflation. But Greenbackism did not become a popular political issue in the South during the 1870s. When the Greenbackers ran presidential candidates in 1876 and 1880, the party polled very few votes in the South outside of Texas. Thus while there were individual southerners, including farmers, who favored inflation in the 1870s, there was no mass movement or organized effort to adopt so-called cheap money policies.[4]

As southern farmers viewed their problems after the Civil War, many of them concluded that some kind of organization was essential for their welfare. Looking about, they saw that other major economic groups were organizing. Businessmen and industrialists were forming pools, trusts, and combines of various types, while workers were joining unions. How could the individual farmer protect his interests in an economy where other groups were setting prices, wages, and levels of service through organized effort. As southern farmers were mulling over this question, they suddenly found the means to organize at hand. It was the Grange, or Patrons of Husbandry.

The Grange was founded in 1867 by Oliver H. Kelley of Minnesota, a government clerk in Washington. It had been Kelley's trip through the South for the Department of Agriculture in 1867 that caused him to see the need for some kind of organization that would help improve the social and economic life of people on farms. The objectives of the Grange were to enhance the comforts of farm homes and to improve rural social life, to oppose monopoly, to get better transportation facilities, to obtain improved education, to encourage crop diversification, and to establish business cooperatives as a means of eliminating middlemen and commission merchants.[5] It was a secret organization and admitted women on an equal basis with men.

Initially the Grange made slow progress, and what growth it did show was mainly in the Midwest. By the early 1870s, however, it began to spread rapidly throughout the South. By the end of 1873 locals, known as subordinate Granges, existed in all of the southern states from Virginia to Texas.[6] State organizations also had been formed. Grange leadership in the South frequently came from the larger farmers and even from the planter class, but most of the members were small, white farmers. As one Louisiana official declared, "The small farmers of Eastern, Northern and Western Louisiana are the best fields to work in. The large planters of Southern Louisiana have never taken any interest in our organization."[7] While no rules or policies denied black farmers membership in the local Grange, with few exceptions racial views precluded blacks' joining their white brethren in the local organization. The Grange reached its height in late 1875, when there were 6,392 locals with 210,590 members in the eleven southern states.[8] Tennessee and Texas had the largest memberships, with more than 37,000 in each state.

Southern Grangers, like those elsewhere, were vitally interested in reducing the role and economic power of merchants and commission agents. Grange principles stated that members had no ill feeling against middlemen, but insisted that they were unnecessary and "their exactions diminish our profits." Grangers declared that they wanted "to bring producers and consumers, farmers and manufacturers into the most direct and friendly relations possible."[9] In practical terms this meant giving farmers greater control over the process of selling their products and buying their supplies. One way to do this was through the establishment of purchasing and marketing cooperatives.

There were several means by which farmers could join together in cooperative enterprise. Under the Rochdale system imported from England, persons bought stock in the cooperative but had only one vote regardless of the number of shares held. By restricting all stock-holders to a single vote each, it was believed that democratic control would be assured. If, for example, a cooperative store was established under the Rochdale system, regular competitive prices would be charged for goods and then any profits would be distributed to patrons at the end of the year on the basis of the amount of business done. Another approach was to engage an agent to take orders from farmers, combine the orders into a single large purchase, and buy directly from the manufacturer, presumably at a cheaper price. Marketing cooperatives combined the cotton or other produce of several farmers and cut out the local commission man by selling directly to processors or manufacturers. Sometimes the marketing cooperatives tried to hold cotton for a better price rather than dump it on the market at harvest time.

Under various forms southern Grangers organized scores of cooperatives in the 1870s as a means of reducing their costs of operation and getting better prices for their products. A Grange agency at Louisville, Kentucky, bought agricultural implements for farmers in Kentucky and Tennessee at reported savings of from 10 to 37 percent. In South Carolina the Grange bought fertilizer, cotton bagging, and flour at wholesale and sold the supplies to members at prices well below those charged by local merchants. One of the most successful Grange cooperatives was the Texas Cooperative Association, which was chartered in 1878. It acted as a wholesale company and by 1887 was serving some 155 cooperative stores in the state. In that year it did over $500,000 worth of business and paid nearly $20,000 in dividends. The association had around 6,000 members.[10]

In some cases state Granges arranged with regular commercial firms to act as their agents. The Alabama and Mississippi Granges both followed this approach. The Mississippi Grange even had an agent in Liverpool, England, to handle consignments of cotton.[11] Keenly interested in getting better cotton prices, some cooperatives tried to force markets higher by withholding sales until prices rose. But these efforts were too small to affect prices. In 1875 Louisiana and South Carolina cooperatives held an insignificant 4,797 bales, which could not influence the market.[12]

Some Grangers wanted to organize cooperatives that would engage in manufacturing. In 1875 a committee of the Georgia State Grange recommended setting up Grange-owned cotton mills. This, in theory at least, would give farmers control of their cotton from production through processing.[13] But these plans never materialized.

The most popular farmer cooperative in the 1870s was the retail store, and hundreds were established to supply the farm trade. These associations were generally organized on Rochdale principles and were viewed as an important means of helping producers. Some states set up so-called exchanges, which acted as wholesale houses to provide goods for the cooperative stores. The Texas Cooperative Association was the most successful of these enterprises.

The Grange also undertook other businesses which it hoped would assist farmers. Mutual insurance societies were established in Arkansas, Tennessee, and the Carolinas. Grange members in Texas could get fire insurance through the Texas Cooperative Association. In 1874 the Grange chartered the Direct Trade Union in Georgia. This was a cooperative designed to market cotton overseas. It handled some cotton for Grangers in 1874 and 1875, but then went out of business.[14]

In contrast to Grangers in the Midwest, southerners did not make railroad regulation a major issue. They were not immune to the high and discriminatory rates that stirred midwestern Grangers to action, but credit and marketing abuses were more pressing problems for southern farmers. Believing that they would be helped by completion of the Texas and Pacific, some southern Grangers supported federal aid for that line.[15]

After rising to a high point in the mid-1870s, the Grange in the South, as well as elsewhere, declined with equal rapidity. By 1880 most of the locals had ceased to exist. Those still operating were little more than social and cultural clubs for rural residents. A few cooperatives, such as the Texas Cooperative Association, continued active into the 1880s, but this was the exception. Indeed, the most important factor in the demise of the southern Granges was the failure of their cooperatives.

There were many reasons for the failure of cooperative enterprise. One of the most important factors was the lack of capital to establish an adequately funded business. Groups of poor farmers without access to major sources of credit could not fund a solid cooperative. Too many of the Grange business ventures operated on a hand-to-mouth basis. A poor management decision, price fluctuations, or any one of a number of other developments could spell disaster. In addition to insufficient capital, many cooperatives failed because of poor management. Too often farmers without business experience were placed in charge of cooperatives and either individually or under pressure from neighbors and friends made bad business decisions, such as extending credit to poor risks. In some cases fraud as well as mismanagement were involved in cooperative failure. Also, of course, local merchants and businessmen who saw the cooperatives as harmful competition did everything they could to destroy these upstart enterprises. Sometimes the regular merchants would lower prices temporarily in an effort to draw business away from the cooperative, and then after the cooperative failed they would raise prices to where they had been or perhaps higher. One of the biggest problems in getting farmers to work together was the absence of a truly cooperative spirit. The traditional independence and individualism of farmers created a basic difficulty that cooperative leaders and promoters simply could not overcome. This was the case not only in the late nineteenth century but also in the twentieth.

Despite its seeming failure, the Grange exerted a number of positive influences in southern rural communities in the 1870s. It promoted improved education for farm children and in some states strongly supported the new agricultural and mechanical colleges. In North Carolina the Grange waslargely responsible for establishing the state's Department of Agriculture.[16] While most of the Grange cooperatives failed, they did give farmers some experience in business and organizational techniques. Moreover, there were some cases where farmers saved money through their cooperatives. Surely farmers gained a fuller awareness of their problems as they met and talked together. Finally, the Grange provided important social benefits. The meetings, picnics, and programs brightened and enlivened the dull existences common to so many southern farmers and their wives.

Failure of the Grange did not mean that southern farmers had lost interest in organization. Even as the Grange declined, a new farmers' movement was arising in the Southwest. While historians do not agree on the exact date, in 1874 or 1875 farmers in Lampasas County, Texas, were organizing to deal with horse thieves and land monopolists. During the next few years discontented farmers formed clubs in nearby counties and in 1878 combined to organize the Texas Farmers' Alliance. By 1882, after more failures than successes, the organization had only 120 suballiances in twelve north-central counties. As yet the precise objectives of the Alliance were unclear. The leaders talked vaguely about developing "a better state mentally, morally, socially and financially" among farmers. In order to help develop a sense of unity and solidarity, the Alliances maintained secrecy and were also social in nature. Membership was restricted to genuine dirt farmers or those, such as rural ministers or small-town residents, who acknowledged the importance of agriculture. Merchants, bankers, stockholders in corporations, and lawyers were among those excluded.

The growth of the Texas Farmers' Alliance in 1884 and 1885 centered around the formation of purchasing and marketing cooperatives. As had been true a decade earlier, when the Grange was at its height, farmers recognized that one of their main problems was dealing with those from whom they bought supplies and to whom they sold their products. Farmers believed they should control those economic functions as a means of easing the cost-price squeeze and eliminating exploitation by other economic groups. During the middle 1880s, as scores of cooperatives were formed, the Texas Farmers' Alliance swept across northern Texas. Some 600 farmers gathered at the statewide Farmers' Alliance meeting in August 1885. Many of the farmers were obviously aroused and ready for some kind of action that would alleviate their ills.

Farmers were becoming increasingly critical of monopolies and corporate power. As they discussed their condition, some basic objectives emerged. By 1886 farmers were demanding higher taxes on land held for speculation, as well as heavier levies on railroads. They wanted a law that would regulate interstate commerce and outlaw dealing in futures of farm products. They also called for inflation of the currency. Texas Alliancemen were emphasizing the issues that were becoming of increasing concern to farmers throughout the West and South—land, transportation, and money.[17]

Divisions over whether the organization should enter directly into politics to achieve its goals nearly wrecked the organization. It was C.W. Macune who held factionalism at bay. Macune, a native of Wisconsin, had settled in Milan County, Texas, after living in Kansas and California. A self-trained doctor, he joined the Alliance in 1886 and became chairman of the executive committee. At a meeting in January 1887, Macune convinced delegates that the Texas Farmers' Alliance should avoid conflict over political action and concentrate on the important goals of organizing farmer cooperatives and spreading the Alliance throughout the South.[18] One of the first steps in strengthening the movement was the consolidation of the Texas Alliance and the Louisiana Farmers Union, which occurred in 1887. The new organization was called the National Farmers' Alliance and Co-operative Union. In 1888 the Agricultural Wheel, a farm organization that had begun in Arkansas in 1882, joined the new National Farmers' Alliance. This brought together the three leading farm organizations in the South. They took the name Farmers' and Laborers' Union of America, but the organization was commonly called the Southern Farmers' Alliance.

Meanwhile, organizers from Texas fanned out over the southern states to form local and state alliances. The organizers used lectures, picnics, barbecues, and dinners to spread the Alliance gospel. When they got as far east as North Carolina, they found that Colonel Leonidas L. Polk, editor of the *Progressive Farmer*, had already organized more than 40,000 farmers, who were pressing farm demands in that state. During 1887 and 1888, thousands of farmers from Texas to North Carolina joined the agricultural uprising. S.O. Daws, one of the original Alliance organizers in Texas, went to Mississippi, his home state, and helped a team of workers enroll thousands of members. By the fall of 1887, the master of Mississippi's State Grange declared that "the Alliance has swept the state like a cyclone. They have more than 70,000 members and are still organizing."[19]

A full-fledged agrarian revolt was under way across the South. When the National Farmers Alliance met in Meridian, Mississippi, in December 1888, the organization claimed 400,000 members.[20] This figure was a little higher than that given in the best scholarly estimates, but there is no doubt that rapid expansion was occurring. The best calculation on Southern Alliance membership is that by 1889 it reached 654,000 and by 1890, 857,000.[21] Most of the expansion came among white farmers. While there were discussions about uniting white and black producers, racism was too deep to permit such unity and cooperation. In 1886 a separate organization for blacks, the Colored Alliance, was started for black farmers in Texas. As the Alliance spread among blacks, a Colored Farmers' National Alliance was organized in March 1888.[22] While whites helped to organize black Alliances, there was little contact between the two groups.

As Lawrence Goodwyn has emphasized, cooperatives provided the inspiration and means by which farmers were organized. The idea of taking control of their own business and freeing themselves from the furnishing merchants and landlords was a compelling prospect. The Georgia Allianceman who wrote that "we are going to get out of debt and be free and independent people once more" represented the thinking of multitudes of southern farmers.[23] Hundreds of local cooperatives were formed to sell goods to farmers, and several states organized statewide exchanges to market cotton and to handle fertilizer and other farm supplies. Some state Alliances set up agencies to deal in supplies and farm produce. Whatever the cooperative type, farmers were enthusiastic about any development that could free them from the credit merchant. The kinds of cooperative enterprises were not unlike those organized by the Grange. Macune headed the Texas State Exchange, which did not operate on Rochdale principles but which sold goods to the local cooperatives at prices only slightly above wholesale costs. The exchange also marketed cotton for local Alliances and reduced selling costs. State exchanges were organized also in Georgia, Alabama, and elsewhere to do a wholesale-type business with local cooperatives and to market crops.

The temporary success of some cooperatives and the hope placed in them as a means of solving agricultural problems brought enthusiasm and commitment to the farmers' movement. But successes were generally short-lived. The Texas State Exchange went broke by December 1889, and Macune resigned as manager. Elsewhere local cooperatives, state exchanges, and commission agencies failed or were in financial trouble. Alliancemen learned what Grangers had discovered earlier—farmers faced very difficult problems in performing all of the functions of producer, merchant, and banker. Strong opposition from local merchants, lack of credit and capital to establish soundly operated businesses, extension of credit to farm customers by the cooperatives, poor management, and a weak cooperative spirit among farmers were the familiar problems that doomed most of the cooperatives to failure. While in some cases cooperatives had provided temporary help to farmers, most of their problems remained unsolved.

As the cooperatives and exchanges failed, southern farmers and their leaders became convinced that they could not pull themselves up by their own bootstraps. The mass of poor southern producers simply could not generate the credit and capital needed to make their cooperatives successful self-owned businesses. Farmers needed outside assistance, which, as Macune and many others concluded, could only be provided by the federal government. Macune's answer to the problem was the subtreasury system.

This plan called for establishing subtreasuries in each county where large amounts of farm commodities were grown. At these points warehouses would be set up in which farmers could store their products. The principal southern crops that qualified for storage were cotton, tobacco, sugar, and rice. When a farmer brought his crop to the warehouse, according to Macune's original suggestion, he could borrow up to 80 percent of its value from the subtreasury at an annual interest rate of a mere 1 percent. Farmers could redeem their commodities within a year by repaying the amount of the certificate of deposit which represented the value of their loan, plus interest and other small charges. The idea was that if prices rose while commodities were in storage, farmers would redeem the products at the loan value and sell them on the regular market. If the loan was not repaid within a year, the subtreasury would sell the commodities and pay off the obligation, or as much of it as the income would cover. Here was a method for farmers to borrow money directly from the federal government by using their crops as security.

The subtreasury had tremendously important implications for staple crop producers, such as those growing cotton and tobacco. In the first place, it would break the credit monopoly of the merchants and landowners throughout the South. If the plan was adopted farmers would no longer be dependent upon local moneylenders for their operating credit. Secondly, farmers would not have to dump their crops on the market at harvest time when prices were generally lowest. A government loan would give them money to live on while they held their crops for better prices. There was an element of what later became known as "orderly marketing" in the scheme. Farmers who believed in monetary inflation and the need for a more flexible currency also saw another great advantage in the plan. The issuing of certificates, or paper money, to farmers against farm crops would, supporters claimed, expand the currency to meet the particular needs of agriculture. Indeed, the currency would expand and contract in proportion to the amount of business being done. Furthermore, the subtreasury plan might reduce price and income instability, a major problem facing farmers and contributing to their discontent.[24]

Macune presented the subtreasury plan near the end of a meeting of the Southern Alliance held in St. Louis in December 1889. This meeting was important also because there was an effort to unite the southern and northern Alliances. While the Southern Alliance had been expanding in 1887 and 1888, a smaller movement of farmers was taking place in the Upper Midwest and plains states. Representatives of the Northern Alliance too were also demanding some fundamental reforms to help farmers. They had gone beyond government regulation of railroads and called for government ownership and operation of the lines. They also demanded abolition of the national banking system, greater control over interstate commerce, a federal income tax, revised patent laws, and the free and unlimited coinage of silver.[25] While southerners also favored government ownership of railroads and free silver, there were several issues that kept the two groups from merging into a single, national organization. There was jealousy over the relative strength of the two Alliances, and northerners disagreed with southerners on the question of excluding black farmers. There was also economic conflict over the demands of northern dairy producers for federal regulation to control butter substitutes made from cottonseed oil. So while southern and northern farmers had some mutual interests, their differences precluded any organizational unity at St. Louis. The Southern Alliance did take a new name, the National Farmers' Alliance and Industrial Union, at that meeting.[26]

The question of whether farmers should organize politically as a means of winning their objectives had been a matter of controversy and division in southern farm ranks since the early days of the Texas Alliance. By 1890, however, the logic of the situation pushed farmers toward political action. There was no way to achieve farmers' goals except by influencing government. Establishment of the subtreasury, monetary inflation, and government ownership of the railroads could be achieved only if Congress enacted appropriate legislation and it was approved by the president. As events unfolded in 1890, the National Farmers' Alliance gradually shifted from a strictly farm organization to an agrarian political movement. The question was whether farmers had the will, unity, and organizational skills necessary to gain successful political power. As the situation emerged in 1890, they had to act through the ballot box or see their demands go unachieved.

While neither of the old parties had shown much concern over a possible farm revolt, the National Farmers' Alliance and Industrial Union could no longer be ignored. Leonidas L. Polk, who had been elected president of the organization at the St. Louis meeting, moved to Washington in January 1890 to press the demands of farmers. During the summer and fall he traveled widely to Alliance meetings throughout the West, enunciating Alliance principles and arousing the masses to action.[27] Macune, who edited the *National Economist* in Washington, and who probably had more influence than Polk, pushed hard for the subtreasury plan. In February 1890 subtreasury bills were introduced in Congress, although no action was taken in either the House or the Senate. At the grassroots, both southern and northern farmers were organizing for the 1890 elections.

By 1890 farm speakers and writers were attacking big business and monopoly with special intensity. In speeches filled with emotion, Alliance leaders declared that farmers were being exploited by corporate giants and Wall Street bankers. Stressing the important role of farmers as producers, they argued that the plutocrats and monopolists were robbing farmers of the fruits of their labor. Besides appealing to anitmonopolist sentiments, farm orators drew on the agrarian tradition for strength and support. Millions of Americans in both town and country believed that there was something special about farmers. They were, as Thomas Jefferson had said, "God's chosen people." According to some agrarians, farmers worked hand in hand with the Creator in producing food and fiber. Moreover, the farmer was supposed to be more independent, self-reliant, virtuous, honest, and democratic, and a greater defender of freedom than other people, and to possess other admirable qualities. To weaken agriculture and to hurt farmers was, for some, a big step toward destroying the nation's political and economic fabric. Farm spokesmen objected to the big gap between the yeoman ideal and actual conditions, and they appealed for change.

As the agrarian movement swept through the southern states and the Upper Midwest and Great Plains, sharp sectional differences emerged. The Kansas Alliancemen and others in that region wanted to form an independent or farmers' party, while most members of the Southern Alliance favored working within the Democratic party. As a practical matter, many Southern Alliancemen believed they could take over the Democratic party. One Georgian declared of his state: "The Farmers' Alliance *is* the Democratic Party."[28] Moreover, the issue of race could not be separated from farm politics. To form an independent party in the southern states would split the Democratic ranks and possibly open the way for Republicans, with black support, to return to power. Southern whites were frightened and angered when Senator Henry Cabot Lodge introduced a bill in June 1890 which would have permitted supervision of federal elections. Everyone knew that the law was directed against the South.[29] This brought visions of post-Civil War Reconstruction to the minds of many whites, who closed ranks in the Democratic party. Thus, as the elections of 1890 approached, Southern Alliancemen sought to take over the white man's Democratic party and commit the candidates to Alliance principles, especially to the subtreasury plan.

The campaign of 1890 found southern farmers engaged in heated and emotional campaigns. The election of scores of local, state, and national officials who had Alliance backing clearly showed the farmers' political strength. Thomas A. Watson, a vigorous, outspoken lawyer-farmer from Thomson, Georgia, overwhelmed the three-term incumbent, George T. Barnes, in every county in the Tenth Congressional District except one. In Tennessee, John P. Buchanan, president of the State Alliance, was elected governor, as was James Hogg in Texas. Overall, however, political victories for the Southern Alliance turned out to be more image than reality. Some of those elected with Alliance support did not really subscribe to the organization's main principles. Senator Zebulon B. Vance of North Carolina, for example, had introduced a subtreasury bill in the United States Senate in 1890 and, while he later repudiated the measure, he was reelected with farmer support. Ben Tillman was elected governor of South Carolina with farm votes but, despite his radical oratory, he brought little change to traditional Democratic politics. In Texas, Hogg won the governorship with Alliance backing but he did not favor the subtreasury or several other Alliance principles.[30] In their euphoria in 1890, farmers had not grasped a major fact of American political life. Although they had numbers on their side, they did not have the political experience, unity, and skill of their opponents.

In December 1890, the Supreme Council of the National Farmers' Alliance and Industrial Union met at Ocala, Florida, to discuss its next steps. The recent elections seemed to be pushing farmers toward third-party political action. Most of those attending the Ocala meeting were from the South, however, and they opposed fastening the Alliance to a third party. Rather, they adopted the Ocala Platform, which reiterated farmer demands for a subtreasury. But southerners could not prevent a call going out for a meeting at Cincinnati in May 1891, where the organization of a third party would be discussed.

Most of the farm delegates who gathered at Cincinnati were from the Upper Midwest and plains states. They were definitely committed to independent political action and arranged for a meeting in St. Louis the following February to launch a People's party. The St. Louis meeting attracted a wide variety of reformers, but only about one-third of those attending were from the South. Yet some southerners were in the forefront of the move toward organizing a third party. Foremost among these was L.L. Polk. In a welcoming address, Polk declared: "The time has arrived for the great West, the great South and the great Northwest, to link their hands and hearts together and march to the ballot box and take possession of the government . . . and run it in the interests of the people."[31]

The St. Louis platform called, among other things, for the subtreasury, free and unlimited coinage of silver, a federal income tax, and government ownership and operation of the railroads, telegraph, and telephone lines. When it was read, the delegates went wild. The farmers and other critics of the old parties were only a step away from organizing a national third party. That occurred at Omaha on July 4, 1892. Polk would have been the presidential nominee of the People's party if he had not died in June. The convention then turned to James B. Weaver of Iowa, an old Greenbacker, as its standardbearer.

Meanwhile, many Southern Alliancemen were resisting the organization of a third party. Shortly before his death, at a meeting in Birmingham, Polk had sought to convince leaders of the Alliances in eleven southern states that they should support the People's party. Despite a public statement that they intended to stand by their northern brothers who were seeking "to redeem this country from the clutches of organized capital," these leaders voted 21 to 16 against endorsing the People's party. A majority of southern farmers could not be wooed into a third party. As Goodwyn has written, racism was stronger among southern white farmers than the desire for economic reform.[32] Furthermore, some southern Democrats used every tactic imaginable, including violence, to maintain political power.

By 1892 the Farmers' Alliance was all but dead. Without strong appeal in the South, Weaver received only a few votes in that region. During the next four years farmers continued to look for political solutions to their problems, but they were fooled at every turn. Some of the southern leaders used the rhetoric of radical reform, but the Democratic party remained under conservative control in most southern states. In 1896 the Democrats swallowed the People's party and that aspect of the independent farmers' revolt was nearly over. Some farmers took hope in William Jennings Bryan, who wrested the presidential nomination from the conservatives and campaigned on one of the major farm planks, free and unlimited coinage of silver, but he was defeated. William McKinley effectively rallied support from industrialists, bankers and other businessmen, as well as better-off midwestern farmers and many industrial workers. Not only southern farmers but all of the nation's farmers had been shown where the true political power lay. It did not rest with poor, depression-ridden farmers, regardless of how numerous they were, but in the board rooms of banks and corporations, among the small-town merchants and profes-sional men, and with those who controlled the country's communica-tions.[33] Some local and state Populist organizations continued for several years in some of the southern states, but they were no real threat to the Democratic party in the South. The Alliances and Popu-lists helped bring about some reforms, but the main influence of the farmers' revolt at the national level came to fruition in the Progressive movement and later in the New Deal.

In the middle 1890s southern farmers could look back over two decades of sporadic effort to improve their condition through organiza-tion, and could see nothing encouraging. After studying the condition of cotton farmers in 1893, the Senate Committee on Agriculture and Forestry reported that "generally the financial condition of the farmers is bad, a very large percentage insolvent, and . . . very few indeed are substantially increasing in the possession of property."[34] The previous twenty years were strewn with the failures of Grange and Alliance cooperatives. While farmers had learned that cooperatives could be potentially helpful, they also discovered that the mass of agri-culturalists in the South were too poor to provide enough capital and operating credit to establish successful cooperative enterprises. More-over, they saw that farmers were too weak and disorganized to combat those merchants and businessmen who resented farmers trying to take control of their own buying and selling. And their own lack of experience and business judgment had not helped.

When farmers turned to political action to get help from the federal government, they found themselves divided on the issues and lacking the skills of political organization. So, while farmers were more numer-ous than any other group, they were unable to translate their numbers into political power. Furthermore, they were not successful in teaming up with labor. While the Alliances cooperated with the Knights of Labor from time to time, they failed to form a farmer-labor political coalition. Part of the reason for this failure was the difference in self-interest among farmers and workers. Higher agricultural prices that benefited farmers meant rising food costs for urban laborers. McKinley presented this conflict very successfully to the detriment of farmers in the campaign of 1896. Finally, southern farmers were divided by a heavy burden of racism, which kept whites and blacks from working together. White upper-class conservatives effectively used the race issue to divide and control poor white and black southern farmers before, during, and after the 1890s.

Despite the Grange and Alliance failures, southern farmers did not give up their search for economic relief through organization. In Au-gust 1902, Newton Gresham formed the first local of the Farmers' Educational and Cooperative Union of America in Rains County, a few miles east of Dallas, Texas. A native of Alabama, Gresham had migrated to Texas some years before. He had been an organizer for the Farmers' Alliance and later edited a small newspaper at Point, Texas. The importance of the need for organizing farmers can be seen in the preamble of the Farmers' Union declaration of principles: "Speculators and those engaged in distribution of farm products," the statement said, "have organized and operate to the great detriment of the farming class." The implication was clear—farmers must meet organized economic power with their own organization.[35]

The objectives of the Farmers' Union were to discourage "the credit and mortgage system," "to assist members in buying and selling," to promote scientific farming, to eliminate gambling in farm products, and "to systematize methods of production and distribution."[36]

The Farmers' Union spread rapidly into other southern states. Many of the promoters had been active in organizing farmers for the Grange and Alliances, and received a small fee for their work.[37] The Farmers' Union was a secret organization until 1914, and also provided a social outlet for farmers, as had the Grange and Alliances earlier. By 1906 locals were active all the way from Texas to North Carolina, and state unions existed in seven southern states. Meanwhile, the National Farmers' Union was officially organized at a meeting in December 1905. By that time considerable dissension prevailed within the organization between the Texas leaders and those from the Southeast. In 1906, Charles S. Barrett, a middle-Georgian with strong rural ties, became national president. He continued to hold that post until 1928, long after the Farmers' Union had lost its influence in the South.

As had been true in the Grange and the Alliance, blacks were excluded from the Farmers' Union. Some whites argued that southern farmers could not get control of cotton marketing unless black farmers were brought into the effort, but deeply held racist views among most whites would not permit unity and cooperation by white and black farmers. Consequently, in 1908 blacks formed the Negro Farmers' and Laborers' Educational Cooperative Union of America.

The major objective of the Farmers' Union in the early years was to gain control of cotton marketing. The local and state unions established farmer-owned cooperative warehouses where producers could store their cotton and receive certificates of deposit, a type of warehouse receipt, which could be used as security for loans. The idea was to cut out middlemen and commission merchants and also to market cotton in a more orderly fashion. When farmers could borrow against their warehouse receipts, they could hold their crop instead of selling it at the usual low harvest-time prices.

In some cases the Farmers' Union tried to set minimum prices for cotton. Here was an idea taken from business. In the fall of 1904 the

Texas Farmers' Union recommended that farmers hold their crop for a minimum price of 10 cents a pound. But farmers did not join in this crusade, and by January 1905 cotton was bringing only 7 cents. In 1906, as cotton prices began to climb, farmers again talked about holding their crops off the market to force prices up to as much as 10 or even 15 cents a pound. Indeed, just before the Panic of 1907, cotton brought as much as 12 and 13 cents, and farmers erroneously concluded that their demand for a 15-cent minimum price was becoming effective. But they soon learned that they had not influenced the price by engaging in a feeble withholding action. Following the Panic, prices began to drop, and by early 1908 cotton brought only 8 cents a pound. This fairly well destroyed any idea that farmers could control cotton prices through their Farmers' Union warehouses.[38] It was clear that members of the Farmers' Union did not control enough cotton to make a withholding action succeed.

By 1908 the Farmers Union had reached its height in the South, with 111,022 families belonging to the organization. Membership then began to decline rapidly, and by 1916 only 44,280 families claimed affiliation with the Farmers' Union. The largest number was in North Carolina.[39] The organization's strength was shifting to the Midwest and plains states. By that time many of the cooperatively-owned cotton warehouses had gone broke, as had farmer cooperatives established to deal in fertilizer, groceries, and other commodities. They had failed for much the same reasons as the Grange and Alliance cooperatives— inadequate capitalization, poor management, and lack of a cooperative spirit among farmers, along with opposition from the regular business community.

In the tradition of the Grange, Alliances, and Populists, Farmers' Union spokesmen attacked the business and banking interests who they believed were exploiting the agricultural producers. Leaders were especially critical of the commodity exchanges. In 1908 one critic declared that the New York Cotton Exchange had "dictated the price of cotton for almost forty years . . . and held the South in practical slavery, and will not, if possible, permit the Southern farmer anything more than a bare living." Charles Barrett referred to speculators in farm products as "bloodsuckers" who had grown fat off the labor of farmers.[40]

While the Farmers' Union emphasized the importance of strengthening the bargaining position of farmers through cooperatives, it also advocated other reforms. Some of these included better education for rural youth, improved country roads, diversified production, better farm management, and in general programs that would enhance the quality of farm life. The organization also demanded banking and currency reform. Although the Farmers' Union achieved national recognition and President Barrett became known as "a friend of presidents," its influence on improving conditions among southern farmers was minimal.

Some southern farmers in the 1890s and the early years of the twentieth century approached the problem of low prices from another angle. Rather than stressing marketing controls after the cotton crop was produced, they advocated trying to restrict production to estimated market demands, that is, to create a scarcity and force prices upward by restricting output. This idea had surfaced periodically ever since the 1630s, when Virginia tobacco growers attempted to raise prices by cutting tobacco plantings. In the 1890s some farm spokesmen believed the proposal's time had finally come. In 1895, for instance, there was considerable discussion throughout the cotton belt of limiting acreage the following year.

Three years later a member of the South Carolina Cotton Growers Union remarked that cotton farmers must create an "efficient organization which would control the volume of production and regulate its marketing." When every cotton farmer, he continued, sought to increase his own acreage at the expense of his neighbor, all cotton growers became the "prey of the usurer, the speculator and the manufacturer." What farmers needed to do was to imitate the manufacturers—"form trusts, cooperate and fix minimum prices." Were farmers so devoid "of manhood [and] intelligence that . . . the welfare of their section and the maintenance of their families cannot induce them to unite," he asked. This observer recommended a reduction of 50 percent in cotton acreage in 1899.[41] Taking their cue from business, other farm spokesmen repeated the call for production control. But farmers ignored such advice. Under the influence of rising prices, production gradually continued upward until it reached 30 million acres and a record-breaking crop of 13.7 million bales in 1904. This expansion produced a sharp break in prices and caused many farmers to reconsider various plans to bring production and demand into better balance.

When cotton prices dropped to between 6 and 7 cents a pound late in 1904, a decline of about 40 percent over a brief three months, some farmers became desperate. It was suggested that 2 million bales be destroyed to bring production and consumption into better balance and to restore prices. On December 28, 1904, farmers at Fort Gaines in southwestern Georgia, joined by merchants facing bankruptcy, rolled 3,000 bales of cotton into the Court House square, marched around the huge pile singing hymns, and then set the cotton on fire. This dramatic action, the Georgians said, was only the first of such burnings across the entire cotton belt. There were a few other incidents of burning cotton, but the proposal to destroy 2 million bales never materialized.[42]

To deal with the problem of price-depressing surpluses, representatives from the cotton states met in New Orleans in January 1905. Out of those deliberations came a demand that cotton growers cut their acreage by 25 percent in the coming season. The program was endorsed by the Southern Bankers' Association, politicians, and farm leaders. While farmers planted about 18 percent fewer acres in 1905, the decline was more a response to low prices than to any acreage-reduction campaign. When cotton prices rose in 1906 and 1907, farmers again expanded their acreage. But 8-cent cotton in the spring of 1908 brought calls to plow up growing cotton to reduce future surpluses. President Barrett of the Farmers' Union urged locals to call meetings and urge growers "to plow up a given amount of cotton" and plant other crops.[43] When this failed, extralegal attempts were made to force producers to withhold cotton from market. Night riders rode through rural communities in Texas, Arkansas, Mississippi, and Georgia threatening violence to farmers who did not hold their cotton for at least 10 cents a pound. These acts by hard-pressed farmers soon subsided, but they reflected deep anger and frustration at their economic plight.

The cotton belt night riders may well have taken their example from the tobacco growers in Tennessee and Kentucky. Like their brethren raising cotton, tobacco farmers were the victims of lack of control over the price of their product. They saw monopoly, especially the Tobacco Trust, headed by the American Tobacco Company, as their main enemy. In order to deal with their problem, growers began to organize in 1903 and 1904. Farmers were urged to pledge their crops to a marketing pool which would bargain over price with the American Tobacco Company. While thousands of farmers committed their tobacco to the pool in 1907, many refused. The same old problem emerged. Farmers would or could not cooperate among themselves effectively. Consequently, some of the more militant organizers turned to intimidation and violence to bring noncooperators into line. In 1907, "night riders" took the law into their own hands in sections of Kentucky and Tennessee and destroyed tobacco warehouses, tore up plant beds, burned tobacco barns, and whipped and beat some farmers who sold tobacco outside the association. Night riding was soon brought under control by state troops and court action. Physical violence was no way to build farmer cooperatives. The result was rather to alienate the public's support for the plight of farmers.[44]

In the generation between the 1870s and the eve of World War I, southern farmers sought to improve their lot through economic and political organization. The Grange, Alliances, and Farmers' Union formed hundreds of cooperatives to strengthen their position in the marketplace. By 1890 farmers recognized the need for outside help if their cooperatives were to succeed. Between 1890 and 1896 southern farmers campaigned for economic and political reforms, such as the subtreasury, which they believed would bring them the needed assistance and improve their condition.

Although some of the economic and political goals advanced by southern farmers, as well as by farmers elsewhere, were later achieved through state and national legislation, they were never able to do anything about controlling the price of their products or the prices they paid for nonfarm goods. Moreover, they failed to solve their credit problems.

Despite some intense but periodic efforts, farmers had simply been unable to enhance their power through organization. Many factors accounted for this failure. Besides being isolated and scattered, southern farmers represented many different kinds of producers and varying economic interests. And their vaunted individualism kept many from joining friends and neighbors and presenting a solid front to the nonfarm interests. Southern farmers, especially the poorer sharecroppers and tenants, lacked the economic resources to take independent action. They were too dependent upon the merchants and landlords. The divisions between white and black farmers based on racism made any solidarity among southern farmers impossible. The small white farmer was among those giving strongest support to disfranchising and controlling the black in the 1890s and the early years of the twentieth century.[45] The poor of whatever color had similar economic problems, but failure to overcome historic racial feelings precluded cooperation between whites and blacks.

If neither economic organization nor politics was a proven route to economic salvation, what alternative remained? One approach was scientific farming and diversification. That is, a farmer might solve his problems through improved efficiency. This was the clarion call to southern farmers by farm journal editors, some progressive farmers, educators, newspaper editors, agricultural scientists, politicians, and many others.

4

The Gospel of Diversification, Science, and Efficiency, 1870-1914

If southern commercial farmers could have cashed in the advice they received on the merits of diversified agriculture, the virtues of scientific farming, and the benefits of farm efficiency, they would all have been rich. As cotton production expanded and as farmers were drawn increasingly into the market economy, the call for diversification intensified. By the early twentieth century it had become little short of a religion. Proponents preached the doctrines of diversification, science, and efficiency with all the fervor of evangelists appealing to fallen sinners. If there was any southern farmer outside of southern Appalachia and other self-sufficient subregions of the South who was unaware of the principles of diversified farming and improved agricultural practices, it was only because he refused to listen or was unable to read.

Diversified farming in the South involved a number of interrelated principles. First and most simply it meant reducing farmers' dependence on cotton and raising a greater variety of other crops and livestock. The main purpose of growing other products was to provide much of the farmer's own food. Thus farmers should raise more corn, small grain, vegetables, fruit, grass, legumes, livestock, and poultry. Such balanced production, it was said, would provide almost all of a farm family's dietary needs.

The advocates of diversified farming argued that it was bad business for a farmer to concentrate on raising cotton and then buy his pork, meal, molasses, and other commodities at the store. Even when cotton was 10 cents a pound, a farmer was usually at a disadvantage in such an exchange. It was this system, the reformers argued, that placed southern farmers in debt to merchants and landlords and kept them in a position of peonage. As early as 1866 a writer declared that a thrifty farmer in southwestern Georgia "need buy very little to eat or wear," as he could raise practically everything his family needed. At about the same time United States Commissioner of Agriculture Isaac Newton said that concentrating on a single agricultural crop "points unerringly the way to national proverty and individual bankruptcy." Years later, in 1902, George Washington Carver, the black scientist at Tuskegee, wrote that "it is not unusual to see so-called farmers drive to town weekly with their wagons empty and return with them full of various kinds of produce that should have been raised on the farm."[1]

Most agricultural reformers agreed that farmers should continue to raise cotton as a cash crop. It was widely recognized that throughout much of the South no other field crop could compare with cotton as a producer of cash income. But farmers were advised to reduce cotton acreage and use part of their land for other crops and livestock. Always produce the products for family living first, said the diversifiers, and then the cash derived from cotton would supply the other family needs and desires. Moreover, the risk associated with one-crop farming could be reduced by raising a variety of commodities. Diversified farming, then, would bring a higher standard of living by making the farmer independent. It might also encourage higher cotton prices by reducing the size of that crop.

Furthermore, diversified farming would contribute to rebuilding the eroded and depleted southern soils. The constant production of cotton and corn, both commonly referred to as "bare ground" crops, had led to destructive erosion throughout much of the South. As mentioned earlier, productivity per acre on many farms was extremely low. Corn often made only 8 to 12 bushels and cotton less than 150 pounds to the acre. To get more than minimum production, commer-cial fertilizer had become an essential part of operating costs on south-ern farms by the 1870s and 1880s. Indeed, much southern land was worn out even before the Civil War. Under diversified agriculture, farmers would plant grass and legumes, especially cowpeas, which would serve at least two purposes—these crops would reduce soil erosion and provide feed for livestock. As the United States commis-sioner of agriculture wrote in 1873, it was folly for a farmer to spend the summer killing grass in his cotton field and then ship in hay from the West. Moreover, manure produced by livestock feeding off the grass and hay would supply at least part of the fertilizer needed for the cotton and corn crops.[2]

The row crops of corn and cotton, reformers argued, should be confined as much as possible to level land in order to reduce erosion. "Corn has been our 'king'—and tyrant—no less than cotton," said a member of the Georgia State Agricultural Society in 1876. "Both had laid a tribute upon us, almost to our life blood." While corn and cotton should not be abandoned, farmers were advised to rotate them with small grain and legumes. One of the greatest values of cowpeas was said to be as green manure when they were plowed under. In summary, diversified farming was presented as a way to become economically independent, largely self-sufficient, and liberated from the furnishing merchants. Farmers should first provide themselves "an anchor of safety" by producing their own food, and then produce some other crop, mainly cotton, for cash.[3] A further advantage of diversifying production would be to free farmers from unfavorable market fluctuations.[4]

Diversification alone, of course, was not considered a complete cure for the ills of southern farmers. They must also improve their farming methods. The old system of farming in which the soil was "scratched and washed away," must change, wrote a Georgian in 1870.[5] Farmers needed to plow deep and cultivate effectively. They were told to use more and better machinery, to plant the best seeds, and to follow the most advanced cultural practices. When a farmer applied commercial fertilizer, he should know the kind and amount that would stimulate the best production of specific crops on his particular land. One of the strongest messages to farmers in the late nineteenth century was that they should cultivate fewer acres but make them more productive.

Much of the argument in favor of reforming southern agriculture rested on the proposition that science and technology must be substituted for labor. An inordinate amount of work on southern farms was done with hand tools or with primitive machines pulled by one mule or a horse. Plows often scraped the soil no more than one to three inches deep, and the subsoil was never touched by plow or disc. Cotton was commonly planted by hand as a worker followed the plow and dropped seeds in the furrow. The soil needed to be worked better and fertilized properly in order to get more output from a particular amount of labor. "To be successful, and to pay dividends," David Dickson, a progressive Georgia farmer wrote, "you must do the greatest quantity of work with the least labor."[6]

Southern farmers had relatively little machinery and equipment to help extend a worker's productivity. As a member of the South Carolina Agricultural and Mechanical Society said at a meeting in 1869, farmers needed "improved mechanical appliances" and "more perfect and powerful implements" to do a better job of farming. The manuscript census of 1880 showed that many southern farmers had no more than $5 to $10 worth of implements and machinery. This meant that their implements consisted only of a few hand tools, such as a hoe. By 1900 the Census Bureau found that the average investment in implements and machinery was still extremely low. On Alabama farms the figure was only $39, while it was $40 in North Carolina and $44 in

Georgia. In Kansas, Nebraska, and Iowa the average investment by farmers in implements and machinery was $170, $205, and $253 respectively, or four to six times as much. In six southeastern states sharecroppers and tenants commonly had only from $17 to $30 invested in farm implements. Investments by farm owners were higher, but the figures as late as 1900 showed that the average was usually only between $50 and $75. Without good equipment or adequate horsepower, most southern farmers were neither efficient nor productive.[7]

"The chief enemy of progressive agriculture in the Southern States is the 'one horse farm,' " wrote J.S. Newman in a South Carolina Experiment Station bulletin in 1904. "The equipment of the one horse farm is generally a cheap mule, too weak, as usually fed, to do good work, a boy Dixie [a one-horse turning plow] and a scooter plow provided with shovel, scooter and half shovel." Newman added that such "primitive equipment in the hands of one ignorant of the very fundamental principles underlying successful agriculture is a guarantee of not only failure in production, but of the deterioration of the soil."

Newman urged farmers to obtain two mules and to get better machinery. With additional power the farmer could prepare his land more thoroughly and get greater utilization from the fertilizer applied. Then, by rotating his crops, a farmer could increase "the productive capacity of his land." By using the best labor-saving implements, "the wages of one man can be saved and this will buy the extra mule," Newman insisted, "while the improvement of the land and increased crops will pay for the implements." He also emphasized the important connection between better machinery and more horsepower and timeliness in farm operations. With a full team the farmer could work faster and take advantage of weather conditions. "By using wide scrapes and cultivators the two mules will be able to cultivate the corn and cotton promptly after each rain and thus dispense with much of the hoe work." Finally, he argued that "one man with two mules can do more and better work in preparing land than two men with one horse plows. One man riding a mowing machine can do more work and do it better than five men with grass scythes."[8]

The overall purpose of many of the changes and reforms urged upon farmers was to make them more efficient. Improved efficiency was a major theme in American economic and political life in the late nineteenth and early twentieth centuries, and farmers were urged to join the ranks of efficient and profitable producers. The idea was to produce more per acre and per worker. Greater and more varied production at less cost, it was argued, would increase agricultural efficiency and presumably lift farmers out of the mire of poverty. In this connection, farmers would also have to become better managers. As the editor of the *Southern Cultivator* wrote in 1902, the "cost of making the [cotton] crop can be greatly lessened by better management. Labor bills have been too high. So we must use better tools and cover more ground with hand and horse. Guano bills have been too high."[9] In short, the editor was telling farmers to manage better and increase their efficiency.

"The fact is," wrote J. Dickson Smith of Houston County, Georgia, in January 1869, "we are on the very verge of a total revolution in agriculture." After referring to David Dickson's scientific work as leading the way, Smith continued: "The day of reform is clearly dawning, and the sun-light of science will soon brighten with exuberant harvests, every cultivated field of the South." A year later another Georgian wrote that farmers needed book learning and science. Such statements were common among southern agricultural reformers in the post-Civil War years, but they proved to be hopelessly optimistic. Despite the urgings and pleadings of a wide variety of farm and political leaders, scientists, and educators, the old methods of farming in the South persisted with stubborn tenacity far into the twentieth century.[10]

While unprogressive and uneconomic agricultural practices characterized most of southern agriculture up to World War II, strong efforts were made to produce the changes advocated by reformers from the 1870s onward. The problem was how to influence or educate farmers in the best known methods of husbandry. The answer to this problem was sought by a few individual farmers, by the farm journals, colleges of agriculture, the United States Department of Agriculture and agricultural societies, the state-federal experiment stations, and other groups and agencies.

Scattered through the South were a number of farmers and planters who set the pace for agricultural change. Among the most important of these were two Georgians, David Dickson and Farish Furman. Raised on a farm in the pre-Civil War years, Dickson concluded as a young man that there must be an easier and more productive way to farm than what he had experienced as a youth. After making some money in merchandising, he bought 260 acres of land in 1845 near Sparta, Georgia. He also acquired some slaves, livestock, and machinery. From the beginning of his farming operations he sought to use the most advanced methods then known and to develop new practices out of his own experiences. In 1846 he began to use guano fertilizer and to study carefully the most appropriate applications for his soils and crops. Besides using heavy amounts of guano, he plowed deep and was careful to cultivate shallowly enough so as not to harm the roots of growing cotton or corn plants. He acquired the best machinery available and increased the productivity of labor. Dickson also emphasized producing as many of the needed supplies as possible on his own plantation. On the eve of the Civil War, Dickson owned 20,000 acres of land in Georgia and 10,000 acres in Texas, along with 230 slaves.

Dickson suffered heavy losses during the Civil War, but he did not lose his land. He still owned 30,000 acres in 1870. In that year many of his ideas on improved farming were published as *A Practical Treatise on Agriculture*. So widely known had Dickson become as a progressive farmer that people came from far and wide to observe his operations. He spent about half of his time with visitors. Despite the wide publicity given to Dickson's farming methods, his practical influence among farmers and planters was minimal. As the editor of *A Practical Treatise on Agriculture* wrote, "many old planters are still obstinate, and will not depart from old habits. They are joined to their idols and cannot be moved by any argument."[11]

Farish Furman, a middle Georgia planter, attained even greater notoriety as an agricultural reformer. A graduate of the University of South Carolina and a lawyer, Furman began farming part of his land in 1878. He believed that farmers could profit only if they could produce more per acre. His emphasis was on intensive farming. Furman stressed that eroded and exhausted soil must be improved if productivity was to rise. This meant restoring both humus and nutrients to the land. Working with Professor of Chemistry H.C. White at the University of Georgia, Furman determined the elements needed to maintain and build up soil fertility. Besides applying phosphoric acid, potash, lime, and some other minerals, he wanted to restore humus to the soil. Thus he developed a "formula" consisting of livestock manure, cottonseed, acid phosphate, and potash, which he mixed in a compost heap. He then applied this mixture to his cotton fields. By spreading this "compound" to 60 acres of cotton, he increased production from 8 to 47 bales between 1878 and 1881. One visitor to Furman's plantation in the fall of 1882 said: "I literally saw a wilderness of cotton," while the secretary of the Georgia State Agricultural Society reported that he had never seen "sixty acres of such cotton in my life, and I'm an old farmer."

The so-called "Furman's formula" received wide publicity through farm journals, newspapers, and agricultural society meetings. Henry W. Grady of the *Atlanta Constitution* praised Furman's approach to increased efficiency, as did other writers across the South. Through publications and lectures, especially in Georgia, South Carolina, and Alabama, Furman popularized aspects of scientific farming and was instrumental in stimulating the growing movement for agricultural reform throughout the South.[12]

Although the example and admonitions of individual agriculturalists might have some effect in getting ordinary farmers to diversify their operations and to adopt better practices, others believed that cooperative efforts would be more effective. Progressive farmers, politicians, businessmen, and publicists were among the leaders who organized agricultural societies. As early as 1785 the South Carolina Society for Promoting and Improving Agriculture was established, and subsequently similar groups were organized. By the 1870s and 1880s agricultural societies were active in all southern states. At their annual or semiannual meetings members were informed of improved farming methods and exchanged ideas as to how agriculture might be made more profitable.

Diversification of production, use of better machinery, soil conservation, fertilization, improved farm management, and the role of science in agriculture were among the topics discussed at society meetings. Sometimes lively arguments occurred among members of these societies on the best agricultural practices. At a meeting of the Georgia State Agricultural Society in 1878 a discussion took place on the subject "Have commercial fertilizers on cotton paid?" One planter insisted that he had increased production and reduced costs by applying fertilizer. As an example, he reported that after one of his tenants had spread one and a half tons of fertilizer, he had raised more than twice as much cotton on the same land. "The fourteen bales," the planter added, cost the tenant "no more labor than the six bales" which had been raised prior to the fertilization program. But another member of the society was applauded when he argued that only the fertilizer companies benefited from its use. "We will be better off if we never have another ton imported into Georgia," he said. When asked why he continued to use fertilizer if it did not pay, the critic replied that he was influenced by his neighbors who bought it. Moreover, he said, he had kept hoping that he would find a brand that would improve his profitability—a hope that so far had proven in vain.[13]

Besides urging their members to try new approaches, the agricultural societies offered prizes for the best livestock and crops exhibited. This was part of the campaign to show farmers what could be achieved with better methods. There was no substitute for first-hand observation. Yet the impact of the societies was very limited. Membership was small and most of the farmer and planter members were already converts to production of home supplies, diversification, good fertilizer programs, and other improvements. Nevertheless, the societies had some impact on increasing farmer awareness of how old methods contributed to farm poverty.

The farm organizations also urged farmers to diversify and to become independent of the furnishing merchants. Two of the basic principles of the Grange enunciated in 1874 were "to diversify our crops, and crop no more than we can cultivate," and "to buy less and produce more, in order to make our farms self-sustaining." Leonidas

L. Polk, a leader in the North Carolina Farmers' Association, was a vigorous proponent of diversified farming. He told farmers that they should raise their own bread and meat before growing cotton or tobacco. One of the original objectives of the Farmers' Union was "to educate the agricultural class in scientific farming." The Georgia Farmers' Union urged members to raise their own supplies, and claimed that only if farmers first "made a living at home" could they have any influence over the marketing or price of their cotton.[14]

Agricultural journals were in the vanguard of those urging southern farmers to diversify and adopt improved practices. The *Texas Farm and Ranch*, the *Southern Cultivator* in Atlanta, and the *Progressive Farmer*, edited by such prominent farm leaders as Polk and Clarence H. Poe in North Carolina, were among the South's most important agricultural papers. While these and scores of other journals, many of which had a short publication life, carried a wide variety of news and general advice to farmers, they emphasized diversification and lessening dependence on cotton.

In October 1890, for instance, the *Southern Cultivator* agreed that, while farmers should not abandon cotton, they should not import "one pound of beef, bacon, lard, butter or cheese, or a pound of hay or a single horse or mule." Speaking to Georgia farmers, the editor said that these supplies could be raised profitably at home. He particularly stressed the importance of raising livestock. Diversification, the editor claimed, would lead to farmer independence. Under the system in which they raised cotton and exchanged it for products of the North and West, he continued, southern farmers simply invited exploitation by the "trusts and pools." With the passage of time these themes received even greater emphasis. In his New Year's greeting to readers on January 1, 1902, the *Southern Cultivator's* editor observed that changes were beginning to occur in the countryside. "Those who have adhered, blindly, to the old idea of shallow scratching and all cotton, have not made money. Those who made their soil deep and fine have reaped a rich reward for their labors. Those who have raised home supplies and food crops for sale are prosperous." Daily, he continued, more and more farmers were trying "new and better methods of farming."[15]

Clarence H. Poe, who had escaped his father's poverty-ridden farm in North Carolina, joined the staff of the *Progressive Farmer* in 1897. Late in 1903 he bought the publication and through hard work and acquisition of other agricultural publications, he ultimately made it the leading farm paper in the South. Poe became one of the nation's strongest voices for the improvement of southern agriculture. By the eve of World War I the *Progressive Farmer* reached about 150,000 homes.[16]

Even before Poe took over the editorship and ownership of the journal, the editors had been crusading for diversification. Writing in early 1897, the editor declared that "so much has been said about diversified farming" that it seemed nothing new could be added. But, he wrote, it must continually be emphasized that "what is needed . . . is greater diversity in farm products as applied to individual farmers and a more intense system of cultivation." Some nine months later a correspondent to the *Progressive Farmer* argued that a farm could become a factory by turning grain into meat. "We can use the hen, the cow, the pig [and] the sheep," he said, "for that purpose." To be successful a farmer must read and study "the minutest details of his particular line." If a farmer was to succeed, he needed "thorough business training."[17] And so the word went out, week after week, month after month, and year after year. J.C. Hardy, president of Mississippi Agricultural and Mechanical College, estimated that by 1903 agricultural journals had a circulation of some 278,000 in the South; by 1911 the figure had jumped to 636,000.[18]

Much of the advice directed to southern farmers was too general and vague to be of much practical value. By the 1870s and 1880s an increasing number of people interested in diversification, soil conservation, higher productivity, and greater efficiency of labor saw the need for a better body of scientific knowledge and a more effective way to get the information to farmers. Farm journals often carried stories on what a particular producer had done to increase output, and members of agricultural societies sometimes reported on how they had benefited from improved practices. The mass of farmers, however, even if they read about those experiences, did not respond to examples of success. They tended to dismiss such illustrations as not being comparable to their own situation. Some kind of successful demonstrations in a farmer's own community seemed to be the great need to convert skeptics to improved agricultural practices.

First, however, information derived from basic scientific research and practical applications had to be provided. It was here that the newly founded agricultural colleges began to make notable contributions. Professorships in agriculture, soil science, chemistry, and other scientific subjects were established in a number of the land-grant colleges in the South. But for years these institutions were criticized and scorned by farmers who believed that the professors were too impractical. "What are they [the agriculture professors] going to do about hog cholera?" asked one disgruntled farmer.[19]

To meet the demand for new knowledge and education through demonstration, several southern states, beginning in the 1870s, established agricultural experiment stations. The North Carolina legislature provided for such a station or "farm," as it was called, in 1877, and Texas legislators set up what they called "a practical working laboratory" the following year in connection with Texas Agricultural and Mechanical College.[20] The Alabama State Experiment Station had published thirty-two bulletins on the results of practical research before the Hatch Act was enacted by Congress in 1887. Under that law Congress began to appropriate funds for agricultural experiment stations which gave support to those institutions already established, and helped to fund additional stations. With both state and federal money, the agricultural experiment stations throughout the southern states began to carry out a wide range of scientific and practical experiments designed to benefit farmers.[21]

By the early 1890s hundreds of bulletins were reporting on a great variety of agricultural experiments. Much of the early work at the experiment stations dealt with analyzing the content of commercial fertilizers and showing how certain kinds of soil and crops responded to particular chemical combinations. Because of the importance of cotton on southern farms, a great deal of research was directed toward increasing the production of that crop. For example, in 1891 the Mississippi Experiment Station at Starkville experimented with different varieties of cotton, the best methods of cultivation, and the application of particular kinds of fertilizer which would result in a higher yield.

Much of the work of agricultural researchers, however, was directed toward removing the barriers to diversification by showing farmers how they could raise something besides cotton. Georgia Agricultural Experiment Station scientists published a bulletin in 1893 on "Practical Dairying," and argued that "to divert our energies and efforts from the past policies of Southern farmers" was a most worthy goal. In South Carolina there were also studies of dairying in the mid-1890s, with emphasis upon breeding better cows and informing farmers on how to care for dairy cattle, as well as how to handle the milk after it was produced. Scientists also carried on experiments with livestock disease, crop rotation, how to fight damaging insects such as the boll weevil, the values of fruit and vegetable growing, soil analysis, grass and forage crops, and many other important and practical subjects. These studies were published in separate bulletins and were available free to anyone who requested a copy.[22]

In some cases the experiment station administrators made every effort to educate and inform farmers in language so plain that it could be understood by all who could read. As the country expression went, they tried to pitch the hay down to where the calves were. In 1891, for instance, the North Carolina Experiment Station published "Facts for Farmers: A Bulletin of Information on Scientific Matters, in Plain Language for Unscientific Readers." The author explained in simple terms how plants got food from the soil, and then defined "humus" and other terms commonly used in discussions of soil conservation and improvement. He argued that the common practice of "resting" the soil, that is, leaving land idle for a year or more as a means of restoring fertility, was foolish. All this did, the writer said, was to encourage erosion and the growth of weeds and brush. A farmer could not "rest" land, he said; land was not "tired," it was "starved." Then he advised farmers to grow crops that would add food value to the soil. He also explained how rotation of crops and plowing under legumes would keep soil productive. This was clear, plain language that almost any farmer could understand.

By the late 1890s and the early twentieth century the experiment stations in the southern states were carrying on more sophisticated research and making studies that had the potential for great economic and social impact among southern farmers. The weaknesses of the one-horse farm with its inadequate equipment and machinery were reported by the South Carolina Experiment Station in April 1904, and a month later a bulletin was published giving advice on how to improve sanitary conditions on South Carolina farms. In 1906 a Mississippi Experiment Station bulletin reported on the credit problems of farmers. Research on the boll weevil and its impact was undertaken at most of the experiment stations, and studies were made on other insects and diseases. Indeed, by the early twentieth century there were few aspects of southern agriculture that were not being studied by researchers and scientists at one or more of the southern experiment stations.

Meanwhile, the United States Department of Agriculture, often in conjunction with the state experiment stations, was also conducting studies and experiments on ways and means to improve the output and profitability of southern farming. Much emphasis was placed on planting grasses and forage plants. One USDA official referred to cowpeas as "the poorman's bank" because they increased soil fertility and fostered greater productivity. The result of the studies by USDA scientists were made available through the publication of a series of farmers' bulletins and other publications. The *Report of the Commissioner of Agriculture* in the 1870s and 1880s carried a wide variety of useful information. Beginning in 1894 the *Yearbook of Agriculture* appeared annually with numerous articles and studies which often included material on problems connected with southern farming.

In 1906, for example, the Louisiana Agricultural Experiment Station and the USDA made a rather extensive study on *Diversified Farming under the Plantation System,* which was published as a Farmers' Bulletin. Working with tenants on the Rosalie Plantation of William Polk at Moreland, Louisiana, the researchers got tenants to set aside two acres each on which they planted potatoes, sweet corn, cabbage, and watermelons. While the results varied from sharecropper to sharecropper because of drought, marketing problems and individual abilities, the overall results were favorable and the farmers' income increased. The study concluded that "it was possible to establish a system of diversification on plantations and that tenants were eager to raise other things than cotton." There was a catch, however. The landlord must be cooperative and supportive, and the tenants must be given instruction on how to care for the new and different crops.[23]

While there was a growing body of scientific data and information available on improved agricultural practices from the 1880s onward, most of it was not getting to the masses of southern farmers. Not many farmers wrote for experiment station bulletins, even though they were free. The very act of acquiring a bulletin required the ability to write, to read, and to understand, and implied a willingness at least to consider new methods. These criteria were absent among most southern farmers. The high rate of illiteracy, especially among rural blacks, added to the problem of educating farmers through the written word.

One way to get information to the grassroots was the development of farmers' institutes. This involved sending lecturers and scientists into communities to discuss with groups of farmers crop rotation, animal and plant diseases, soil conservation, dairy and livestock farming, and other practical topics. The institutes usually lasted two or three days. Besides the lectures, there was time for questions and discussion. Here was a kind of early adult education designed to make farmers aware of new methods and convince them to adopt improved practices.

By the 1880s the institute movement had become well established in the Midwest and had begun to penetrate the South. A farmers' institute was held at Mississippi State Agricultural and Mechanical College as early as 1884, but relatively few were conducted throughout Mississippi or elsewhere in the South until after 1900. Usually sponsored by the experiment stations or the colleges of agriculture, hundreds of institutes were held in the southern states before World War I. In the sixteen southern and border states, the number increased from 364 in 1901-1902 to 1,843 in 1909-1910, and rose even further later. Black farmers attended institutes which were usually conducted by personnel from the new Negro land-grant colleges. Tuskegee Institute was a leader in working for agricultural change among blacks in eastern Alabama. In 1906 Thomas M. Campbell was appointed by the USDA as the first black to go among black farmers and show them how to improve their farming practices.[24]

Although thousands of farmers attended institutes before World War I, the response to lectures and verbal advice was disappointing. This method of education fell short of providing that practical instruction through demonstration that might convince farmers to change their methods. For most farmers, to see was to believe; merely to hear or read was usually to ignore the advice. To overcome the skepticism of farmers to so-called "book farming" and to encourage producers to change their ways, the USDA and the agricultural experiment stations turned to demonstration plots or farms.

It was Seaman H. Knapp who was given the responsibility for showing southern farmers how to increase their income by adopting better methods. A New Yorker who went to Iowa, where he taught and was president of Iowa State College for a time, Knapp began his practical agricultural work among Louisiana rice growers. In the 1880s he helped an English syndicate by showing rice farmers on company land how to increase their production. His method was to place a farmer, with company support, in each community and to see that the producer followed a set of principles and practices. This proved to be a most successful method of teaching farmers in a locality because they could actually see the results of improved practices on the nearby demonstration farm. Knapp's work resulted in a substantial increase in rice production in Louisiana.[25]

Knapp began working for the USDA in 1898, and in 1902 he was selected to head a campaign to promote agricultural change and reform in the South. He began near Terrell, Texas, where he arranged to use 70 acres of depleted land on the farm of Walter C. Porter. Knapp advised Porter on the best methods of plowing, cultivating, and fertilizing his land. Porter reported such good success in increasing production on those 70 acres that he said he would apply the practices to his entire farm the following year. The favorable results were observed at first hand by his admiring neighbors.

The demonstration farms were not operated or worked by USDA personnel. Knapp and his agents just provided advice and practical instruction to the farmers who agreed to participate in the demonstration efforts. To spread the program, Knapp hired agents to go into farm communities throughout the South and select in each a cooperating farmer who would provide 10 acres or so of land for demonstration purposes. On those plots the farmer-cooperator showed his neighbors how improved seed, proper use of fertilizer, rotation of crops, production of livestock, better machinery and raising more feed on the farm could improve a family's income. Farmers had to be shown that different methods of production would actually pay on their farms. By 1912 there were around 100,000 farmers cooperating with the program as demonstrators.[26]

The demonstration farm program got a boost from an unexpected source—the boll weevil. In the early 1890s boll weevils from Mexico invaded a few Texas cotton counties. By 1901 the damaging insect had migrated nearly as far north as Waco and provided a serious threat to cotton growers. Continuing to move north and east, the weevil made its way to Louisiana and posed a threat to all growers in the cotton belt. Late in 1903 Congress appropriated $250,000 for boll weevil control and Knapp was given $40,000 of that amount to promote his community demonstration farms. The justification for the expenditure was that farmers must be taught the importance of burning the cotton stalks after picking, fall plowing, and other cultural practices which would reduce boll weevil propagation. But at the same time Knapp saw this as an opportunity to teach farmers much more.[27]

Some spokesmen believed that the boll weevil would force southern farmers to diversify and improve their farming methods. W.J. Spillman of the USDA said in 1904 that "the boll weevil is really a blessing in disguise." S.M. Tracy, writing in the *Annals of the American Academy of Political and Social Science* in 1910, declared that "the coming of the boll weevil has broken up the old system of agriculture, but a better system is being developed." An advocate of change on southern farms in Louisiana later recalled that "the boll weevil became a more potent school master in teaching the farmer the folly of pinning his faith on the 'single-crop system' than all the theorists who had yet inveighed against the practice." However, the leading authority on the history of the boll weevil has conclusively shown that, except in parts of Louisiana and a few other areas, the boll weevil did not force diversified farming in the southern cotton belt before 1910.[28]

Others also joined state and national agencies to help influence desirable changes in southern agriculture. The railroads were especially active in promoting agricultural change, as were some of the farm machine companies and other businesses. The educational trains organized by the railroads distributed literature to farmers, hauled speakers free or at reduced rates, and displayed the products of improved farm practices. They also established some demonstration farms. Boys' and girls' clubs were organized in many communities with the hope that if young people could be convinced of the advantages of diversification and better methods, true change would come in the next generation of farmers. There were also corn clubs and pig clubs in which youngsters emphasized increasing efficiency and productivity.

The wide variety of efforts to educate farmers to better methods and improved organization of their farming operations finally culminated in passage of the Smith-Lever Act of 1914. Senator Hoke Smith of Georgia and Congressman A.F. Lever of South Carolina, both important southern political figures, were among those who saw the need for some systematic federal support for practical agricultural education through extension. The Smith-Lever Act provided for establishing extension departments in the nation's agricultural colleges. These departments were directed to give "instruction and practical demonstrations in agriculture and home economics . . . through field demonstrations, publications, and otherwise."[29]

Despite more than a generation of agitation and education to get southern farmers to diversify, to adopt scientific methods, and to become more efficient, relatively little had been achieved. To be sure, a few farmers had shown some remarkable results when they followed better practices. In 1909 a representative of the USDA reported working with 509 farmers in Alabama who produced an average of 33¼ bushels of corn to the acre on their experimental plots, compared to the state average of only 13½ bushels. In South Carolina 658 cooperating farmers greatly increased their production of both cotton and corn. But in reporting on these experiments, W.J. Spillman wrote that, while soil conservation was appreciated by "agriculturalists and progressive farmers," it was "not understood by the great majority of farmers." They must be taught by "precept and example," he concluded.[30]

And so it was on the eve of World War I. The southern rural landscape looked little different than it had a generation earlier. Despite all of the talk and optimistic predictions about changes on the farm—about soil conservation, planting grasses and legumes, raising more livestock, increasing productivity per acre, and other aspects of agricultural reform—cotton was still king. M.W. Richards, the land and industrial agent of the Southern Railway, said in 1904 that all the South needed for abundance was "intelligent husbandry." The region could be the garden spot of America, he wrote, but "it is now little else than its [the nation's] cotton patch." Those like the writer in the *Independent* who said in 1907 that "progressive farming" was growing so rapidly in the South that it was "revolutionary," simply did not know what they were talking about.[31] Some foundations had been laid in agricultural science and education, but practical applications by the masses of southern farmers remained far in the future.

One had only to look at the agricultural census of 1910 to see how little southern farming had changed during the previous ten to twenty years during which intense efforts had been made to bring about agricultural reform. The pleas to grow less cotton had been totally ignored by most farmers. Between 1899 and 1909 the number of farmers raising cotton had grown from 1.4 to 1.7 million, and the total land devoted to the crop had risen some 6 million acres. Only Louisiana among the eight main cotton states reduced its acreage, and that was because of the boll weevil infestation rather than any planned crop shifts by farmers. Cotton was actually more important in Mississippi, the Carolinas, Georgia, Alabama, Arkansas, and Texas in 1909 than a decade earlier. In several southern states cotton occupied an increasing amount of the improved acreage after 1900, reaching between 35 and 40 percent by 1909. Cereals, on the other hand dropped as a percentage of the improved acreage. For example, in 1899 cereal crops were raised on 35 percent of the improved land in Alabama, but a decade later it was only 29 percent. Instead of diversifying, reducing cotton plantings, and turning to other crops and livestock, southern farmers were becoming ever more dependent upon the white lint. In South Carolina, Georgia, Alabama, and Mississippi, cotton accounted for about 55 percent of the value of all crops in 1909.[32]

All of the appeals to farmers to plant grass and legumes had met with little response. Hay and forage acreage did rise after 1900, but in the southeastern cotton states only between 2 and 4 percent of the improved cropland was in hay and forage at the end of the decade. Nevertheless, southern farmers did increase their livestock, especially milk cows and other cattle. The percentage rise was quite dramatic, but the total numbers remained small. In Georgia, for example, the number of dairy cows rose from 276,000 to 407,000, and in Alabama from 279,000 to 391,000 during the decade. But even with this increase, only 71.5 and 78 percent of the farmers in the South Atlantic and East South Central states respectively had milk cows in 1910. This meant that 22 to 29 percent of the farmers did not have a single milk cow. The picture of swine production shows no consistent pattern. Farmers in North Carolina, Alabama, Tennessee, and Texas actually had fewer hogs in 1910 than in 1900, but swine numbers grew in Georgia and Louisiana. Poultry production also followed an irregular pattern. There were gains in some southern states and losses in others. In summary, there is no evidence to suggest that farmers in the South were reducing cotton and moving significantly into forage crops and livestock, or cereals, as preached by the diversifiers.

Neither were producers acquiring farm units of a more economic size. Indeed, the amount of cultivated acreage per farm family was declining. In Louisiana, Arkansas, Mississippi, Alabama, Georgia, and the Carolinas farms averaged only about 37 improved acres. Many farms were even smaller, with sharecroppers and tenants commonly farming 20 to 30 acres. Farms of such size usually could not produce enough to provide an adequate family living. Little was changing for the better.

That romantic ideal of a rural society dominated by self-sufficient, independent landowning farmers was further from reality in 1910 than it had ever been in the history of the South. Tenancy of all kinds held 49.6 percent of southern farmers in its grip, up from 47 percent a decade before. In South Carolina 63 percent of the farmers were tenants, and in Mississippi and Georgia it was about 66 percent. The chance of getting their own farms, tilling their own land, and becoming independent was not even a distant hope for most farmers.[33] While about 24 percent of the South's black farmers owned their farms in 1910, more than three-fourths were sharecroppers or tenants, most of whom eked out an existence on less than 40 acres.[34]

General agricultural conditions improved considerably between 1900 and World War I. But this so-called Golden Era in American agriculture bypassed most southern farmers. Both white and black sharecropper and tenant families continued to live in dire poverty. Only occasionally did they get a respite as a result of higher cotton prices. In 1903, 1905, and 1907, cotton brought more than 10 cents a pound. But big crops following those higher prices depressed the market. Cotton farmers just could not seem to get good crops and high prices at the same time. As they moved into the twentieth century there was little to bring them encouragement.

Why did southern farmers cling so tenaciously to the old ways and patterns of farming? Why did they ignore the advice and warnings of those calling for diversification and greater efficiency? Professors at the agricultural colleges and demonstration specialists could prove beyond a doubt that soil conservation, livestock production, and growing feed and food crops, in addition to cotton, paid better returns to producers. What kept southern farmers from modernizing and following the example of their counterparts in the Midwest?

There are many answers to these questions. In the first place, there was widespread resistance to "book farming." This situation was, of course, not confined to the South. But habit and tradition were stronger in the South, where farmers tended to be more isolated and cut off from the mainstream of the nation's economic development. Farmers who planted their crops or castrated their hogs by the positon of the moon and held other superstitions were not easily convinced that science had much to offer. The president of the Georgia State Agricultural Society told the assembled members in 1876 that the society had begun "under popular derision." Those trying to reform agriculture, he continued, had been faced with sarcastic statements and ridiculed for talking about book farming and scientific agriculture. Scornfully referring to the ideas of a college professor, one Louisiana farmer remarked: "Why, I've worn out two farms; you can't tell *me* how to farm."[35] Prerequisite to any reform, then, were changes in attitude and the abandonment of old habits and customs.

More important in resisting change was the reluctance of planters to let their sharecroppers and tenants grow any commercial crop other than cotton. Most planters continued to find cotton their most valuable cash crop. Cotton was also the best money crop for small farm owners. Furthermore, diversification required different kinds of tasks and decision making by farm laborers, sharecroppers, and small independent operators. There was a vast difference between growing cotton and operating a dairy or livestock farm. Indeed, many believed that most southern farmers, especially black sharecroppers and tenants, were, as W.J. Spillman of the USDA wrote, "incapable of the proper management of dairy cows or other classes of livestock." Spillman said that it would be "necessary to train the available labor in entirely new channels and to give it a sense of responsibility not heretofore necessary." Many planters simply had no interest in change or reform. J.C. Hardy of Mississippi State Agricultural and Mechanical College observed that Delta planters were only interested in the "negro and mule" and saw little relation between that combination and scientific farming. Large farmers did not favor increased economic independence for blacks because it would threaten their labor supply. Finally, the sharecropper operations, the "furnish" plan, and the paternalistic system of labor were, as two southern authorities wrote years later, "the very heart and soul of an economic and social institutional system" that had become "a distinctive symbol and traditional way of life in the Cotton Belt South."[36]

Since most landowners believed that sharecroppers and tenants could not successfully manage more diversified and complicated agricultural operations, the switch away from cotton would have greatly increased the cost of supervision to planters in the black belt. Moreover, the entire credit structure had been built on the production of cotton. Money was advanced to growers on the crop, and it was the only collateral accepted by most merchants and landowners. They might demand additional security in the form of chattels, but cotton was the principal basis for credit. To obtain a loan from a furnishing merchant to buy cows or hogs was almost unthinkable. The lender reasoned that his security might die or be eaten and he would be left holding a worthless note. Therefore, when he advanced credit the borrower had to promise to grow cotton.[37]

One of the major goals of the diversifiers was to develop an efficient agriculture based on a mix of crops and livestock. The problems connected with raising more livestock, however, were much greater than were commonly recognized. A major factor, of course, was the lack of capital or credit needed to purchase breeding stock. But beyond this obstacle was the fact that the natural grasses and forage in much of the South were less nutritious than those found in the Midwest. To get satisfactory pastures and hay in the Deep South the soil had to be plowed, planted, and fertilized at considerable expense. When cattle were left to find their own food, they often perished. The United States commissioner of agriculture reported in 1884 that 2,000 cattle had died in Winston County, Mississippi, because of "want of proper pasturage."[38]

In addition, southern livestock was subject to diseases that caused heavy losses. Swine and fowl cholera were common, and Texas fever became so widespread that in the early 1880s it was being referred to by a veterinarian in the USDA as "Southern cattle fever." Cattle imported from the North for the purpose of improving southern breeds were the very ones most subject to the disease.[39] In the early years of the twentieth century as many as 60 percent of the cattle imported from the North died. Native cattle also succumbed. It was not until 1906 that a concentrated effort to eradicate Texas fever began. Georgia farmers who tried to diversify in the 1870s and 1880s stood by helplessly as their cattle died by the thousands. In 1879 some 21 percent of the hogs in Georgia died compared to only 6 percent for the United States as a whole. In addition to diseases, livestock also suffered from a large number of insects and parasites common in the South. Sheep raisers, in addition, constantly faced losses from marauding dogs.[40]

To develop a viable diversified farm based on a mix of livestock and crops required more land than most southern farms contained. The 20- to 50-acre farms that became so common in the cotton belt were too small to provide the pasture and feed crops needed for cattle and also leave enough acres for cotton, corn, and other cereals. Diversification, beyond simply producing some home supplies, could not be successfully implemented on such small acreages. Farm size in much of the region developed around cotton growing after 1870, and once the small-farm pattern was established it could not be changed easily under normal economic conditions.

A further factor that retarded diversification was the absence of satisfactory markets. As mentioned earlier, cotton was the only commercial crop for which a well developed marketing system existed. Using fruit growing as an example, an authority in the USDA wrote in 1905 that "there is no use in growing apples, oranges, or peaches commerically without an efficient system of safe and rapid distribution." At about the same time, W.J. Spillman argued that it would actually be dangerous for a farmer to switch to commercial fruit or vegetable growing because perishable crops had no dependable market. Another agricultural expert said that, while good profits might sometimes be made in truck farming, it involved maximum risk. Staple products, he added, offered much more security for the producer.[41]

Some critics blamed the lack of general agricultural progress in the South on the blacks. They were pictured as being unable to implement improved practices, not because of the system but because of their ignorance and need for close supervision. A correspondent for the federal census in 1880 argued that a wage system should be substituted for sharecropping "at least so far as the negro laborer is concerned." Otherwise, he added, there was no chance of introducing a "rational" system of agriculture because Negroes required close direction and control. While admitting that white farmers did not appreciate the

advantages of what he called a "rational agriculture," the writer declared that they were more "accessible to the influence of progress than
the negro race."[42] Professor D. Wallace of Wofford College in South
Carolina called Negro labor "inefficient, expensive, and unprogressive" and suited only to a few staple crops.[43]

Clarence Poe referred to the black as a great economic burden to the
South who mistreated the land and made it "unfruitful." Poe said that
"we must either have the Negro trained or we must not have him at
all."[44] A few years later an Alabamian wrote that "the average negro
seeking a farm is looking for a place to get supplies, not caring whether
he pays for them or not." He added that if a black lived on a farm for
several years "the land goes to gullies and grows up in pines and
broom straw, the houses go down, the barns fall, the fences disappear
and the cropper must move or perish."[45] While there were many
indifferent black farmers, whites farmed in much the same manner.
Only faintly disguised racism was behind much of the criticism of
blacks. The manuscript census of 1880 actually shows that black farmers often outproduced whites.

Other contemporary observers of farming in the South believed
that little change could be achieved without modifying the basic structure of southern agriculture. They argued that by their very nature, the
sharecrop and tenant systems militated against reform. Actually, they
said, the "system" encouraged the status quo by discouraging self-
reliance, initiative, and the development of management and business
skills. Southern sharecroppers and tenants had little if any motivation
to improve. If the landlord or merchant took everything produced
above mere subsistence, as was the case under most forms of tenancy,
there was no incentive to produce more, to conserve the soil, or to
maintain the buildings and fences.

Frequent moving, prompted by an effort to get a better deal or
perhaps to escape debt, was a further factor in causing sharecroppers
and tenants to ignore improved methods of farming. Farmers could not
possibly benefit by investing time or money on a farm from which they
would likely move at year end. In some communities as many as a third
to a half of the farmers moved each year. The lack of interest by tenants
in maintaining land and buildings in turn caused the landowners to
hold expenditures on their property to a minimum. They reasoned that
the tenants would not "keep up the place," so any outlays would be
wasted. Landowners and tenants blamed one another for the situation.
Owners said the renters were lazy and shiftless and let the land and
buildings deteriorate; the tenants replied that they received nothing in
return for trying to maintain the property so would do as little as
possible. The result was that neither tenants nor landowners showed
much interest in eroded soil and crumbling shacks. An Alabama

correspondent writing to the *Progressive Farmer* observed that no country could prosper under such a type of farm organization. He was right. While some theorists have suggested that sharecropping provided a "continuing incentive for both landlord and tenant to maximize the efficiency of agricultural production," it did not work that way out on the farm.[46]

While there were many actual and perceived factors working against modernizing southern farming, one of the most important was lack of capital or credit to initiate the desired changes. However motivated, hardworking, and diligent many farmers may have been, they could not change their methods of farming and break out of their poverty without funds for investment. Everything suggested to farmers by the reformers to improve their agriculture cost money. It could be shown, for example, that planting legumes to improve soil quality would pay off in greater production, but it was a future, not an immediate, benefit. Meanwhile, there were costs to be borne. To purchase equipment and machines to farm better, or to move from a one-mule to a two-mule operation, or to get into livestock production—all required capital. If a sharecropper or tenant was to enter the ranks of farm ownership, or if an owner wanted to increase his acreage, it demanded investment.

Prior to World War I, southern farmers had no adequate credit facilities either for capital or for operational loans. Merchants and landlords provided most of the farmer's operating funds at extremely high rates of interest; there simply was no source of long-term credit available to most farmers to buy land, to invest in machinery, or to make fixed improvements. The South as a region was deficient in capital and credit. And, most southern farmers did not produce enough above bare subsistence to accumulate savings that could be invested in land, equipment, livestock, and other needs for more efficient farming. It was silly to expect the poor farmer who earned $150 to $300 a year or less to save. As Harold Woodman has stated so cogently, diversification was a "fantasy" for poverty-ridden farmers who did not have capital or credit to take the first step. "A tenant who owned nothing," Woodman wrote, "was being asked to grow a food crop for which he had neither seed nor land. And, presumably, the landlord was expected to supply land to a tenant who was cutting back on his cash crop [cotton], the only means he had to pay his rent."[47]

Lack of capital in the form of long-term credit was a major deterrent to agricultural change in the South, but investment funds by no means assured ownership and independence of small farmers. In 1900 a group of northern investors established the Southern Improvement Company and bought 4,500 acres of land in Macon County, Alabama, for resale to black farmers on long-term contracts. The company usually sold about 40 acres to landless black farmers for $7 to $8 an acre at 8 percent interest. In addition to money for land, the company advanced each family about $350 for food, housing, workstock, and other operating expenses. By 1905 some sixty families were living on SIC lands and struggling to make land payments.

This experiment by the SIC made money for the stockholders, but very few of the farmers ever became independent landowners. Intermittent poor crops, lack of enough production to pay the debts, poor management, and other factors caused most of the tenants to fail. They were bound to the company through lease contracts in such a way that there was little difference between being in debt to the SIC or to the local merchant. William V. Chambliss, the only black stockholder in the company, who became superintendent of the operations, gradually gained control of much of the land by making loans to the farmers in exchange for a real estate mortgage. Chambliss finally bought out the company in 1919 and ended up as a large landowner. The black farmers, however, found no relief from their peasantry. The founders of the company initially tried to make the landlord-tenant relations more humane, but the structure of the relationship was never threatened. This experiment of funding small southern farmers in the black belt had failed.[48]

There were many factors, then, that prohibited major changes in southern farming before World War I. Habit and tradition were strong, many landowners insisted that their sharecroppers and tenants grow cotton, farmers were suspicious of "book farming," and management abilities were low among the relatively high number of illiterate farmers. The soils and climate of the South made it difficult to change crop and livestock patterns before the day of pesticides, fungicides, and scientific health care for livestock. The absence of markets for some commodities was also a deterrent to diversification of commercial crops. Finally, the lack of capital and long-term credit at reasonable costs precluded farmers' reorganizing their operations into more profitable enterprises. The majority of farms remained too small and the methods of production too primitive to produce a decent family living.

In the late nineteenth- and early twentieth-century South there was much rhetoric about the virtues of the small farm, diverse production, and self-sufficiency. But as Seaman A. Knapp wisely pointed out in 1908, any farm needed to be big enough and have sufficient output to produce sufficient income "to improve the farm, educate the family, assist in starting its members in ways of independent support, and provide a reserve for old age."[49] Few of the small southern farmers could ever hope to find such a happy lot in life. Surely, diversification—which to most people implied self-sufficiency—could never achieve such economic and social goals. While growing more food might have improved the family diet for many sharecroppers and poorer tenants, it would not have added much to the family's cash needs. Farm owners and better-off tenants were already producing much of their own food supply in the form of cornmeal, vegetables, meat, milk, and eggs. What southern farmers needed more than anything else was to produce commerical surpluses which could provide capital, operating expenses, and money for a rising standard of living. The critical problem of how to help southern farmers to become successful commercial operators was largely ignored by the diversifiers. Until farmers could produce a sufficient marketable surplus, they would never be able to earn a modern standard of living in farming. As a long-range solution to poverty among southern farmers, self-sufficiency and diversification offered little in an exchange economy where manufactured goods were playing a growing role in the standard of living.

As a matter of fact, many contemporary Americans never expected that farmers across the cotton belt would ever accumulate much or live very well. This was especially true for blacks. After urging farmers to become more self-sufficient, a writer for *The Nation* said in 1893 that "such a life would not be a full one or a liberal one, but it would be a comfortable one." To cultivate less land and become self-sufficient would provide the kind of home, "lowly though it be . . . it would make life worth the toil," wrote another observer.[50] On the eve of World War I there was little evidence to contradict the assumption that the vast majority of southern farmers would remain backward and poor. Calls for changes and reforms over two decades or more had, for one reason or another, been ignored.

5

Southern Farmers from War to Depression

If any proof was needed to show the slight impact of diversification and the continued importance of cotton on southern farms, one need look only at the 1914 crop year. Southern farmers planted nearly 37 million acres of cotton, about 10 million more than in the 1901-1903 period. Even the ravages of the boll weevil could not curb the expansion of cotton growing in the South as a whole, although, as mentioned earlier, in some areas acreage had leveled off or declined slightly. The Carolinas, Georgia, and Alabama had about 3 million more acres in cotton in 1914 than in 1902, and the acreage was up 4.3 million in Texas alone.[1]

In the summer of 1914 prospects looked rosy for the South's cotton farmers. A huge crop of 16.1 million bales, the largest on record, was about to be harvested and prices were excellent—12 to 13 cents a pound at the gin. Then disaster struck. On July 31 the cotton exchanges closed in response to the outbreak of war in Europe, and panic gripped farmers and all of those businessmen whose income relied so heavily on cotton. If the war should cut off export markets for any length of time, surpluses would depress the domestic markets and huge numbers of southern farmers would face ruin. In 1913 about 9.5 million of the 14.1 million-bale crop had been exported, and cotton provided from 53 to 66 percent of the value of all crops in the states from South Carolina to Texas.[2] No wonder the South was in shock. This seemed to be another instance of farmers having an unusual degree of prosperity within their grasp, only to see it slip away, from causes completely outside their control. One observer wrote that "the South had some nine hundred million dollars almost in its pocket when war suddenly leaned over its shoulder and laid a mailed fist on the pile."[3]

In August 1914, of course, no one knew how long the cotton exchanges would be closed or just what effect the restriction on exports would have on prices. Nevertheless, national leaders moved quickly to try to protect cotton farmers. On August 24-25, Secretary of the Treasury William G. McAdoo, members of the Federal Reserve Board, southern congressmen and senators, and several hundred farmers, merchants, and bankers met in Washington to discuss the cotton crisis. McAdoo said that he was concerned with the "growing feeling of hysteria over the situation regarding cotton." He advised bankers not to force farmers to sell cotton on the depressed market in order to pay their debts, and told manufacturers not to wait to buy cotton "for a panic price." "We must put aside selfish motives," he concluded.[4]

All kinds of proposals were advanced to assist cotton growers. The most popular ideas involved creating state and federal warehouses and making federal loans to farmers against stored cotton. This would enable farmers to keep their cotton off a depressed market and yet give them money to live on and to pay debts. The editor of the *Progressive Farmer* wrote that Congress should provide enough money so that farmers could "carry the crop . . . until conditions become normal again."[5] The Wilson administration, however, rejected this approach to help cotton farmers. Congress did pass a Cotton Warehouse Act late in 1914, but no federal funds were appropriated for cotton loans. A campaign to raise a private loan fund fizzled completely.[6]

Meanwhile, cotton at some interior markets dropped to as low as 5.5 cents a pound. In some cases farmers found no market at all for their crop. In desperation a "buy-a-bale" campaign arose in October in an effort to remove 4 million bales from the market. Signs sprang up in northern cities urging people to buy a bale of cotton at 10 cents a pound to assist the South. To help popularize this idea President Wilson bought two bales. Another proposal to increase demand came from an Atlanta labor union which announced that its members would buy clothing made only of cotton cloth.[7] But none of these schemes had any practical effect in stabilizing the market. As it turned out, cotton growers had to make the best individual arrangements they could. A fellow Georgian wrote to Senator Hoke Smith early in October describing what he considered a critical situation. He explained that cotton was bringing only 6.5 cents a pound in his community, but that farmers had bought fertilizer and supplies the previous spring on the prospect of "13-cent cotton." Creditors were closing in on helpless farmers, he said. Since the farmers were receiving about half of the expected price, they could not pay their debts. "You know," he wrote his senator, "if our cotton don't pay our debts, they [creditors] will take everything the farmer has."[8]

When the cotton exchanges reopened on November 16, cotton prices settled out at a little over 7 cents a pound. The average price received by farmers in 1914 was 7.3 cents, or 40 percent less than the year before. The value of cotton to producers throughout the South dropped from $846 million in 1913 to $563 million in 1914.[9]

Cotton farmers were not alone in their misery. Tobacco growers also depended heavily on foreign sales, and the war temporarily depressed markets for the South's approximately 250,000 tobacco producers. Exports of American tobacco were about 100 million pounds less in 1914 than a year earlier, and the price dropped from an average of 12.8 cents a pound in 1913 to 9.8 cents the following year. Farmers' income from tobacco declined by some $20 million, despite the fact that they produced the second largest crop on record.[10] Income to Louisiana sugar producers was also down in 1914. Sugarcane growers, however, were hurt not so much by the outbreak of war as by government action. The Democratic Underwood-Simmons tariff, passed in 1913, had reduced the duties on raw sugar imports by 0.43 cents a pound for 1914, and all tariff protection was to be lost in 1916.[11] Rice, the South's other staple crop, fared better. In 1914 rice acreage was down slightly, but the price was up so the income of rice growers declined very little. Overall, however, 1914 was a tough year for southern farmers, as they suffered income losses estimated at as high as $300 to $500 million.

While nothing could be done to recoup losses on cotton in 1914, some action seemed absolutely necessary for the following year. Many believed that the main need was to reduce cotton acreage in 1915. Talk of curtailing production had followed previous sharp price declines, and 1914 was no exception. Farm journalists, bankers, and government officials strongly advised farmers to cut their acreage drastically. Secretary of Agriculture David F. Houston of Texas warned farmers that the "acreage devoted to the next cotton crop ought to be greatly reduced." Others suggested a 50 percent reduction. Various methods were suggested to assure lower production. The governor of Texas asked his state's lawmakers to pass legislation limiting cotton acreage, and the legislature in South Carolina considered several ways to reduce plantings. Some writers called for state actions outlawing the use of cotton as security for loans, unless farmers promised to reduce their acreage in 1915. None of these suggestions were implemented, however, and farmers were left to make their own planting adjustments.

Advocates of diversified farming saw the cotton crisis of 1914 as a kind of blessing in disguise. Surely, farmers would now see the need for and desirability of diversification. If the "calamitous consequences" of the war caused southern farmers to grow more food, said one writer, "the conflict in Europe will have accomplished something which continued missionary efforts have failed to achieve."[12]

At planting time in early 1915, cotton prices still hung around 7.5 cents a pound, a figure considered below the cost of production. It was the discouraging circumstances associated with continued low prices rather than any campaign to reduce acreage that caused farmers to cut their plantings by about 5 million acres. Indeed, growers planted only 31.4 million acres in 1915, the lowest since 1909. On the other hand, southern farmers planted a little more corn, wheat, and oats.[13]

As a result of lower acreage and poorer yields, 1915 cotton production was some 5 million bales less than the year before, dropping to 11.2 million bales. With less output, prices recovered considerably by harvest time, averaging 11 cents a pound. This gave cotton farmers about $80 million more than they had received for their huge crop of 1914. Stimulated by growing wartime demand, farmers increased their cotton acreage in 1916 by about 3.5 million acres. A writer for the *New Republic* correctly had written late in 1915 that "the white fiber still holds the imaginations of the South."[14] Despite more acres, the boll weevil and unfavorable weather kept the harvest to about 11.4 million bales, the same size crop as in 1915. But prices shot up to between 19 and 20 cents a pound, by far the highest since immediately after the Civil War. This gave cotton producers their first billion-dollar cotton crop in history.

By the end of 1916 many southern farmers were enjoying the greatest prosperity they had ever experienced. Some lost out to bad weather and boll weevil damage, but the majority were better off than at any time within memory. On November 4, 1916, the *Progressive Farmer* carried a two-part cartoon showing on one side a cotton farmer in 1914 on his knees before a cotton buyer begging "Oh, please buy my cotton," and the fat, cigar-smoking merchant holding up his hand against paying 6 cents a pound. The other half of the cartoon showed a prosperous, well-dressed farmer smiling at a cotton buyer who is now on his knees saying, "Oh, sir! please sell me your cotton." The price sign reads 16 cents a pound. The Winston-Salem (North Carolina) *Journal* said that "we doubt whether the South has ever witnessed such an era of prosperity as now prevails." Farmers were reported to be paying off debts and buying clothes, shoes, furniture, and even automobiles. One newspaper story reported that even tenants, including blacks, in Texas were buying autos. Around Valdosta, Georgia, it was said that farmers were not satisfied with Fords but wanted more expensive cars. The Savannah *Press* exclaimed that "Negro farmers are buying automobiles who were content a year ago to ride in an ox-cart, or, at best, in a new red buggy behind a $150 mule." Another publication announced that southern farmers were "having as good time as if it were Christmas."[15]

While observers commented extensively on the South's rising prosperity, they urged farmers not to let high cotton prices distract them from diversification. Farmers were warned that such high prices would not likely continue and they should grow their own food and feed. The *Progressive Farmer*, the South's most widely circulated agricultural journal, constantly insisted that farmers diversify their operations and rely less on purchased supplies. Governor T.W. Bickett of North Carolina said in his inaugural address early in 1917 that if he were "Czar" instead of governor, he would issue an edict ordering anyone who imported "any corn or meal, wheat or flour, beef or bacon" into North Carolina after five years, to be "hanged without trial by jury and without benefit of clergy." The governor admitted that initially he would be denounced but that after a decade "North Carolina would be the richest state in the Union and people would build a monument to him."[16]

Cotton was again king across the South. Acreage dropped slightly in 1917, and production per acre was down again because of a poor crop season and the boll weevil, but prices jumped to nearly twenty-eight cents a pound, double or triple the price in most years before the war. The next year, 1918, southern farmers again experienced poor yields, but higher acreage and good prices gave producers $1.6 billion for their cotton. By June 1919 cotton rose to 43 cents a pound, and, while it declined to an average of about 35 cents by harvest time, the South had its first $2 billion cotton crop.

Southern farmers, at least those who had good crops, were more prosperous than they had ever been. Nevertheless, many of them were angry as cotton prices weakened just as harvest got under way. On September 8, 1919, some 500 delegates from ten cotton states gathered for the American Cotton Association meeting in New Orleans. The extent to which cotton dominated southern thinking and the southern economy was reflected in the statement of Thomas J. Shackleford of Georgia, chairman of the Association's finance committee. "Whoever solves the problem of a fair price for cotton," Shackleford said, "has solved all the problems of the South." Georgia delegates argued that farmers should hold out for at least 37.5 cents a pound, while Texas spokesmen insisted that 50 cents was a fair price. Addressing the meeting, Senator Hoke Smith said that the South would have been better off if it had never raised "a bale of cotton," and expressed the hope that farmers would quit planting the crop "unless they receive a vastly better price for it." He urged farmers who were then picking cotton to market very gradually so as not to depress prices, and to plant fall grains and raise hogs and cattle. Smith even mentioned a farm strike against growing cotton. But the advice of Smith, J.S. Wannamaker, president of the association, and other leaders had no influence on farmers' production plans. Although they may have complained about 35-cent cotton, that figure was enough to stimulate the planting of another large acreage in 1920.[17]

Producers of the South's other staple crops also did well during the war years. Tobacco that had brought between 9 and 10 cents a pound in 1914 and 1915 commanded 28 and 29 cents respectively in 1918 and 1919. Production was also up significantly. From an output of about a billion pounds annually in 1914 and 1915, production reached 1.5 billion pounds in 1919. Sharply higher prices and production increased the value of tobacco about five times during the war years. Rice prices and production also rose substantially. Growers in Arkansas, Louisiana, and Texas saw the value of their crops go from about $24 million in 1915 to $88 million in 1919.

Sugar planters in Louisiana produced less raw sugar at the end of World War I than in the prewar years, but a good crop in 1916 and higher prices produced relatively good times for cane growers during the war period. Raw sugar brought 5.5 cents a pound in 1916, the best price since 1889. Because of the need for sugar in the war effort, the United States Equalization Board was established in June 1918 and set prices for raw sugar at 7.2 cents a pound to encourage greater output. Although cane acreage varied considerably during the war years, it did not show overall expansion. Higher prices more than made up for stable or declining acreage and cane production. By 1919 raw sugar shot up for a time to 24 cents a pound.[18]

Production of the South's principal staple crops—cotton, tobacco, and rice—rose by about 2.5 million acres from 1915 to 1919. At the same time southern farmers increased their acreage of grains and the number of livestock. Corn showed the greatest gain between 1914 and 1919 with the addition of 3.5 million acres in the Carolinas, Georgia, Alabama, Mississippi, Tennessee, Arkansas, Louisiana, and Texas. Wheat and oats acreage also increased. More grain production was a part of the overall expansion in cultivated acreage in the South. There was also a slight increase in milk cows and other cattle during the war period. The nine states mentioned above had 705,000 more milk cows and 625,000 more other cattle in 1919 than when the war broke out five years earlier. Hog numbers rose by about 25 percent.[19]

After about 1909 the USDA and the state experiment stations in the South intensified their efforts to develop a beef cattle industry. The widespread boll weevil attacks provided ideal justification for shifting to cattle raising. Experiment station personnel in Mississippi, Alabama, and other states urged farmers to use purebred bulls and cows, to improve their pastures and feeding methods, and to build barns and silos. As a result of these efforts, hundreds of purebred bulls were sold at public auction in the South between 1914 and 1917. The cooperative extension forces helped to organize baby beef clubs for farm boys and girls between ten and eighteen years of age. Although beef cattle numbers did not increase greatly during the war decade, these early efforts were highly important because they began to improve greatly the quality of many southern herds. Better control over the cattle tick after about 1910 also helped the slowly developing cattle industry.[20]

But talk of diversification far exceeded actual developments on southern farms. This was especially true in relation to expanding livestock production. Livestock and livestock products continued to produce only a small percentage of farm receipts in most southern states. Farm receipts from livestock and their products were only 20 percent of the total in South Carolina and Mississippi and 22 percent in Georgia in the years just before 1920. Farmers continued to depend on crops, mainly cotton, for between 60 and 75 percent of their cash income. Writing about trends in cattle and hog production in the South, specialists in the USDA wrote in 1921 that "the change in number between the last two decades seems disappointing to one who believes that the South would profit by keeping more livestock."[21]

The few farmers who did become successful livestock raisers received considerable attention in the agricultural press and elsewhere. J.C. Travis of Livingston, Alabama, wrote to the *Progressive Farmer* about two farmers in his state who up to 1912 had grown mainly cotton worked by "negro tenants and sharehands." By 1915 most of these workers were gone and cotton had been replaced by herds of purebred Hereford cattle grazing on fine pastures. These farmers also raised grain and hogs. Travis urged his readers to strike for freedom "from the thraldom of all cotton under the negro tenant system" and be saved from "slow but sure financial death." The *Progressive Farmer* also told about a Georgia family who had started out selling a few pounds of butter to earn some "pin money," but then got more cows, bought a cream separator, and in 1916 sold $600 worth of butter. The writer referred to "dairy cows as boll weevil insurance."[22]

While the growth of grain and livestock farming showed substantial percentage gains, the change was much less impressive in absolute terms. When one considered that the nine states in the Deep South had about 2.2 million farms, an increase of 7.5 million acres in grain, 1.3 million more milk cows and other cattle, and 3.6 million hogs seem much less significant. There were still many southern farmers in 1919 who did not have a single milk cow and very little if any other livestock. What happened was that only a portion of the farmers devoted more land and time to grain and livestock farming. Tens of thousands of southern farmers were still locked into cotton and tobacco production.

While farmers received higher prices during the war, increased their production, and were generally better off, they faced some serious problems. The boll weevil was especially destructive in 1915 and

1916, while floods in parts of Alabama and elsewhere destroyed crops
in the latter year. This unusual level of natural hazards caused hardship
for some farmers.

A more serious problem for many landowners was the scarcity of
labor caused by the large migration of blacks out of the region. The drop
in cotton prices in 1914 and the slow recovery in 1915 created special
difficulties for many sharecroppers and tenants. While their income
dropped or remained steady, nonfarm prices rose. Those who existed
on merchant credit were especially hurt. From the viewpoint of many
poor farmers, almost any change appeared to be an improvement.

Coinciding with depressed conditions in the rural South in 1914
and 1915 was the beginning of an industrial resurgence in the North
stimulated by defense and war spending. European immigration drastically declined as a result of the European conflict, leaving the growing
demand for labor unfilled. Employers in Pittsburgh, Cleveland, Chicago, and other cities now turned to the surplus labor of the South. By
1916, under the pull of better economic opportunities, a flood of black
workers streamed northward to the "promised land." Blacks were
attracted most of all by higher wages and better living conditions, but
they also went north in hope of finding better schools and escaping
from racial discrimination and even lynching. The heaviest migration
was from the areas where the one-crop system was most prevalent and
race relations most strained. There were both pull and push factors
working to uproot blacks from their traditional farm homes and life-
styles.

Alarmed at the large numbers of farm and other workers boarding
trains for the North, southerners tried to check the movement. Some
states placed legal restrictions on northern labor agents who were
recruiting black workers. In some cases prospective migrants were
arrested before they could board the train and were forcibly restrained
from leaving the community. More enlightened southerners urged
better treatment and higher pay for blacks as a means of slowing the
northward migration. Consequently, wages were raised. While great
variations existed, it was not uncommon for wages to go up by 50 to 100
percent and sometimes more. Farm wages that had been $8 to $12 a
month before the war rose to $20 to $30 a month after 1916. Nevertheless, between 1915 and 1919 tens of thousands of blacks left southern farm areas as well as towns and cities. This was, of course, not a
new phenomenon. Blacks had migrated to Texas right after the Civil
War, and in 1879 hundreds of blacks had gone to Kansas. Others had
gone north at other times. But the migration during World War I was
unusual because of the large number of persons involved.[23]

However important World War I may have been for the nation's

economic history, it had no noticeable effect on the structure of southern agriculture. When the census takers visited southern farms in 1920,
they found the same trends and conditions as in earlier years. Farms
were small and getting smaller. Average cultivated acreage per operator
was decreasing slightly, and productivity per acre and per farm continued low.

In 1920, for example, there were 2.6 million farms in the eleven
southern states. About half of them were under 50 acres. Approximately 67, 64, and 57 percent of the farms in Mississippi, South
Carolina, and Alabama, respectively, fell in this category. The average
acreage of cropland harvested per farm in North Carolina was only 21
acres, in Mississippi 23 acres, and in Georgia 33 acres. This compared
to 96 acres in Iowa and 132 acres in Kansas. These small farms continued to be the source of low incomes and poverty throughout much
of the South. Only 686,000 of the South's farms, or 26 percent, contained 100 acres or more.[24]

The 881,964 black farmers operated many of the smallest and
poorest farms outside the mountain South. Of this number only
197,774, or 22 percent, were owners. In the East South Central states
black farms averaged only 39 acres in 1920 compared to 89 acres for
whites. The value of land and buildings of these black farms was small,
ranging from $1,228 in Alabama to $3,009 in North Carolina. This
compared to an average of $2,653 and $4,377 in those same states for
white farmers.[25] Tenancy varied from 50 to 65 percent in the southern
states, but for black farmers the figure went as high as 80 to 90 percent
in some areas.

By the World War I period, the United States Department of
Agriculture and the state experiment stations in the South were engaged in a number of studies which investigated the relationship
between farm size, productivity, and low incomes. The researchers
went into selected farm communities and isolated such variables in
farm success as crop acreage, income, debt structure, return on investment, and even color of operator, and found what operations were
most profitable.

One such study was done in Brooks County in extreme southern
Georgia in 1914. The results were crystal clear. Farmers on larger
acreages had more income than smaller farmers, and whites were
better off than blacks. The earnings of white farmers in the survey
averaged $897 a year compared to $476 for blacks. About half of this
income was the imputed value of supplies produced on the farm. In
fact, black families had an average labor income of only $191 a year. This
approximated their cash or credit income. The white operators had
much more income because they had bigger farms. They averaged 166

acres of cropland, while the blacks averaged only 54 acres. The interesting result of this study was that the return on investment was 6.2 percent for both white and black farmers. The income of black farmers was small because of their meager investment. This was just one of the farm management studies which, the author said, had "uniformly shown that the size of the farm business is probably the most important factor in determining the returns the farmer secures for his year's work."

Furthermore, the larger farms produced more and a greater variety of the family's food. On farms under 50 acres the value of food produced was $84.50 per person compared to $125.60 per person on the farms of 250 acres and more. The USDA researchers concluded that "food supplied by the larger farms furnishes a more varied and better quality of diet than on smaller ones. In other words, the larger farms support a much higher standard of living as well as furnish larger net returns in other forms."[26]

A similar study was done of 112 farms in Anderson County of western South Carolina in 1917 and 1918. The farms varied in size from 15 to 1,400 acres. The one-mule farms of 21 to 25 cultivated acres were found to be much less efficient and profitable than those of 41 to 45 and 61 to 65 acres, which required two and three mules, respectively. Farmers in this survey who tilled 61 to 65 acres, had 48 percent more income than those farming 21 to 25 acres, and their return on investment was more than twice as much. In addition, once a minimal acreage was under cultivation, yield was the greatest single factor in farm success. The combination of enterprises on a farm was responsible for only 16 percent of the success factors. This indicated that diversification was much less important to a farmer's welfare than the size of his operation and the productivity of his land.[27]

While most of the surveys being done before 1920 were in areas of commerical agriculture, studies were also undertaken in the mountain regions of the South from West Virginia through the western Carolinas, eastern Kentucky and Tennessee, and northern Georgia. By the second decade of the twentieth century nothing much had changed in that subregion of the South. "As a rule the small mountain farm does not produce more than a scant living for the farm family," wrote a USDA surveyor in 1918. These farmers produced mainly corn and beans, and they kept a few hogs and sometimes a cow or two. The USDA officials reported that many farmers sold almost nothing, while 100,000 families on those small mountain farms had "average receipts" from farm production of about $100 annually. Looking at a small 88-acre farm in the mountains, the writer concluded that "it is impossible" for the family to have anything "left over for the support of community interests or to educate the children properly."[28] While the cash income of these mountain subsistence farmers was small, they usually had sufficient home-grown food and enough cash for minimal needs. Most of them were not a part of commerical agriculture at all.

It was becoming increasingly clear that southern rural poverty was associated directly with uneconomic farm units. The operations were labor intensive, and production was low because of either meager yields or small acreages or both. Farm management specialists were fully aware of the situation and they publicized the results of their studies in hope of encouraging changes in the structure of southern farming. The farm papers also called for "more per acre on more acres."[29]

Unfortunately, time was not ameliorating the problems associated with small, nonproductive farms in so much of the South. In fact, the situation had become intensified by the end of World War I. From Virginia to Texas large numbers of farmers produced so little income that poverty stalked their dilapidated homes and hammered at their spirits. Most of them had no alternative but to continue the struggle without hope of substantial improvement. Some had escaped to northern industrial jobs or found nonfarm work in the South. But the heavy rural population in the region continued the unfavorable balance between land and people. These poverty-ridden farmers lacked nearly everything required for successful and profitable production—land, capital, operating funds, markets for some crops, and management abilities. As the editor of the *Progressive Farmer* wrote in 1916, the inability of southern farmers to borrow working capital at "a reasonable interest rate has kept hundreds of thousands of farmers from investing in better livestock, better implements, and better buildings."[30]

Most southern farmers were still in no position to take advantage of diversification, scientific agriculture, and the management advice coming from the USDA and the colleges of agriculture. They were caught in a net from which there was no escape short of death or some major outside influences strong enough to shake the system. There were few signs of major changes on southern farms in 1920. In almost every community there were some farmers who had the land, capital, and know-how to improve their operations, but they were a small minority.

The figures on farm facilities offer some insight into the conditions on southern farms at the close of World War I. The census of 1920 showed that southern farmers had hardly begun to enter the age of telephones, automobiles, motor trucks, tractors, and electricity. In the states of the old Confederacy a little less than 15 percent of the farms had a telephone compared to 38.7 percent for the nation's farmers as a whole. Only 5.7 and 6.3 percent of the farms in South Carolina and Louisiana respectively had a telephone. In comparison, 76 and 86 percent of the farmers in Nebraska and Iowa enjoyed such a convenience. Electricity was virtually unknown in the rural South, where only between 1 and 3 percent of farms were electrified. In the West North Central states the figure was around 9 percent. Despite the wartime talk about southern farmers rushing to buy automobiles, very few had acquired a car by 1920. In the eleven states from Virginia to Texas, 12 percent of the farmers had an automobile. In Louisiana, Arkansas, Mississippi, Alabama, and Tennessee the average was only 6.8 percent. These meager figures compared to more than 57 percent of the farms which reported automobiles in the North Central states.

Southern farmers were no better off when it came to adopting tractors or motor trucks to increase their efficiency and productivity. While tractors represented the vanguard of agricultural change and were only beginning to be used on American farms, the South lagged far behind the other major agricultural areas of the country. About 1 percent of southern farmers had tractors compared to 8.4 and 5.1 percent in the North West Central and East North Central sections of the country. There were so few motor trucks on southern farms that they were more of a curiosity than a recognized mode of transport. In most southern states the figure was less than half of 1 percent.[31]

During the better times experienced by southern farmers in the fall of 1916, Clarence Poe warned readers of the *Progressive Farmer* "to put aside something against the day of harder times that is sure to come." During the next few years Poe repeated this theme frequently. While the South was harvesting its $2 billion cotton crop in the fall of 1919, Poe's paper carried a large headline which read: "Save Some Money This Fall." He advised the white tenant farmer to move toward acquiring "a home under his own vine and fig tree." This should take precedence over consumer items. "The automobile, the piano and the talking machine are fine," he added, but they should wait. Money, Poe said, should be invested in land ownership.[32]

Poe advocated savings because of the "rainy day that nearly always comes." But not even Poe anticipated the torrent of troubles that hit American farmers in the fall of 1920. Farm prices began to drop in the spring of 1920 and by harvest time cotton brought only 13 to 15 cents a pound compared to 35 cents a year earlier. Tobacco fell from 39 cents a pound in 1919 to 21 cents in 1920. The prices of other southern crops and livestock also declined dramatically. Southerners, of course, were not alone in feeling the financial blow as staple crop farmers everywhere suffered from the postwar economic slump.

Farmers were not only discouraged over low prices, they were downright angry. Spontaneous outrage erupted in parts of the cotton belt as night riders tried to force farmers to hold their cotton off the market so long as it sold for less than 40 cents a pound. When warnings went unheeded, several gins were burned, presumably by irate farmers. In October 1920, the Earle [Arkansas] Compress Company was burned, destroying the building and 5,600 bales of cotton. Night riders were also active in the tobacco belt.

The main reasons for the drastic decrease of farm prices were not hard to find. With the war ended there was less demand both at home and abroad for American farm products. Cotton exports, for example, were about 1.7 million bales less in 1920 than in 1919. Moreover, foreign competition in world markets hurt American farmers. Industrial stagnation and a postwar recession that lasted at least well into 1922 further depressed farm prices.

As if the relatively low farm prices in the fall of 1920 were not bad enough, the cost of producing the year's crop had been high. Commercial fertilizer, which was such a large factor in the cost of producing cotton and tobacco in the Southeast, had been very expensive in the fall of 1919 and early months of 1920. Labor and feed costs were also high, as were living expenses and interest rates. Heavily in debt, most southern farmers, like those elsewhere, found themselves in a crushing cost-price squeeze by 1920 and 1921. The *Yearbook of Agriculture* stated the situation clearly and succinctly: "Expenses have been high and prices low." If one uses an index figure of 100 as equaling the purchasing power of farm commodities on May 1, 1913, the purchasing power of cotton in May 1921 had dropped to only 48. In practical terms this meant that it took more than twice as much cotton to buy the same quantity of nonfarm goods as it did before the war.[33]

But low prices were not the only tough problem facing southern farmers. Many cotton growers continued to suffer from boll weevil infestations which virtually wiped out the crop in some areas in 1920 and 1921. Farmers in Morgan County, Georgia, for example, produced 35,504 bales of cotton in 1919 but only 7,064 bales in 1920. Neighboring counties also had tremendous losses to boll weevils in 1920, 1921, and 1922. So damaging were the attacks in scattered localities that some farmers, mainly sharecroppers and renters, abandoned the land to try their luck in towns and cities. Land grew up in weeds and brush, farm houses stood empty, and unwilling creditors were left holding property of greatly decreased value. Some creditors recognized that if they foreclosed on land or personal property it would not sell for the amount of the loans, so they let farmers who were broke continue to live on the land.

By 1921 letters were flooding the United States Department of

Agriculture and other agencies describing the depressed condition among farmers. Some of the most pitiful communications were from southern cotton growers. One Georgia sharecropper wrote that his family was "naked and barefooted," while a large landholder explained that the 75 to 100 persons on his farms were hit by the boll weevil and suffered from pellagra. "What this class of people are to do," he wrote, "I cannot see." A Texas farmer with 90 acres of cotton wrote in December 1920 that he was broke and that "thousands and thousands of farmers" would be "driven from the farm this year." J.J. Brown, Georgia's commissioner of agriculture, explained in July 1921 that he had been in close touch with agricultural conditions for thirty-five years, and never before had he seen farmers "so depressed and in such an alarming financial condition as they are today."[34]

As in earlier agricultural crises, farmers were flooded with suggestions that would lead to their salvation. They were urged to bring production in line with market demands and eliminate price-depressing surpluses. In 1920 and early 1921 cotton growers were again urged to cut their acreage for the coming crop year. J.S. Wannamaker, president of the American Cotton Association, advanced one of the boldest schemes to reduce surpluses and raise prices. In August 1920, as cotton prices slid downward, he urged establishing committees in each county and township throughout the cotton belt to "secure legally binding contracts" requiring farmers to reduce their cotton acreage by 50 percent in 1921. To assure compliance, the contract would permit measuring fields to check on overplanting. If a violation was found, the contract would permit "the destruction of his cotton down to 50 percent." Wannamaker urged governors of the cotton states to issue proclamations endorsing this approach.[35] Such a scheme, however, was more than a decade ahead of its time.

Although there was widespread discussion about cutting acreage in order to raise prices in 1921, no significant organized campaign resulted. But farmers did respond to market forces and sharply reduced their acreage. With some 5 million fewer acres of cotton in 1921 than a year earlier, production dropped from 13.4 million to 7.9 million bales. Boll weevils also took their toll in 1921 when, because of the pest, production dropped below the usual yield by as much as 45, 32, and 30 percent respectively in Georgia, Alabama, and Mississippi. Despite a much smaller crop in 1921 because of the boll weevil and fewer acres, the price of cotton recovered to only around 16 to 17 cents a pound at the farm. A heavy carryover from 1920 kept higher prices from being paid for the much smaller output.

Not only were farmers urged to bring supply and demand into better balance, but cotton and tobacco growers were advised to organize marketing cooperatives in order to give them greater bargaining power in the market place. As Clarence Poe wrote, "Organize: together control prices."[36] In late 1920 thousands of tobacco farmers in North Carolina, Tennessee, and Kentucky signed up to market their crop through cooperatives. The Tobacco Growers Cooperative Association was officially launched in 1922. Meanwhile, cotton growers were organizing cooperatives. Following the development of some state organizations, the American Cotton Growers Exchange was formed at a meeting in Oklahoma City in April 1921. By 1923 there were 220,000 farmers selling through their cotton associations, which marketed 937,000 bales that year, or nearly 10 percent of the total crop. Encouraged by the promotional and organizational activities of Aaron Sapiro, the nation's leading promoter of agricultural cooperatives, increasing numbers of cotton, tobacco, peanut, and other southern farmers joined marketing cooperatives in the early 1920s. Representatives of the agricultural colleges, the Cooperative Extension Service, editors of agricultural journals, and others lent support to the cooperative movement among southern producers. The campaign for cooperatives was little short of a crusade across much of the South in 1921 and 1922.[37]

Farmers and their spokesmen also pleaded for more liberal credit. The Georgia legislature passed a resolution in 1921 asking for amendments to the Federal Farm Loan Act which would provide southern banks with additional funds that could be loaned to hard-pressed farmers. Senator William J. Harris of Georgia urged the Federal Reserve Board to lower its discount rates in order to expand credit, and recommended extending repayment of agricultural loans to banks for up to a year.[38]

Several southern senators, including Harris, E.D. Smith of South Carolina, J.T. Heflin of Alabama, and Duncan U. Fletcher of Florida, joined the bipartisan farm bloc organized in Washington in 1921 to work for federal farm relief. As a result of the farm bloc's efforts and the support of the USDA and other forces, a sizable amount of national legislation was passed from 1921 to 1923 to help alleviate distress on the farm.[39] Among the most important measures were the Capper-Volstead Act of 1922, which in most cases exempted farmer cooperatives from the antitrust laws, and the Intermediate Credits Act of 1923.

One of the outcomes of the postwar agricultural depression was a series of studies and conferences dealing with farm problems. Among the most important of these was the National Agricultural Conference which opened in Washington, D.C., on January 23, 1922. A committee of the conference reporting on the cotton situation said that two years of bad conditions "have destroyed a large part of the capital invested in cotton production, have faced a large proportion of the landowners, merchants, and fertilizer companies with bankruptcy, and have left a large proportion of the banks in a position where, but for the support of the Federal Reserve System, the War Finance Corporation, and other outside capital, they would be unable to function." The committee recommended diversification, better farm management, expansion of cooperative marketing, lower transportation rates, and more federal aid to combat the boll weevil. The subcommittee on tobacco urged federal and state agencies to investigate "the most economic methods of producing and marketing tobacco," while another committee said that southern sugarcane growers could be helped with a tariff on raw sugar.[40]

Despite the meetings and conferences which recommended more generous credit, cooperative marketing, and a host of other reforms, none of the actions taken by the state or federal governments, or by organized farmers themselves, had any positive effect on farm conditions. Rather, it was an improvement in general economic conditions that brought a degree of recovery to southern farmers. By 1924 and 1925 the situation among cotton growers had improved considerably.

Even though cotton acreage rose in 1922, production barely exceeded 10 million bales and prices increased to about 23 cents a pound. This price was sufficient to encourage farmers to grow 37.1 million acres in 1923, up another 4 million and the highest on record up to that time. The 10.1 millon-bale crop brought around 30 cents a pound in most farm markets. Other than 1919, this was the best price farmers had received for cotton since the late 1860s. Throwing caution to the wind,they increased their acreage to 41.3 million and harvested 13.6 million bales in 1924. Higher output depressed prices, but cotton still brought an average of 23 cents a pound in the fall of 1924, much above prewar levels.

Better cotton prices resulted from increased demand both at home and abroad. Explaining the situation, the USDA reported that there was "increased cotton-consuming power in Europe, following stabilization of currencies and credit conditions." For example, Americans exported 8.4 million bales in 1924, which was up by more than 2 million bales over 1922 and 1923. There was also improvement in consumption by domestic mills.[41] By the mid-1920s, moreover, farmers had reduced boll weevil damage by poisoning the pest with calcium arsenate and adopting better cultural practices. In 1923 and 1924 cotton farmers realized about $1.5 billion annually from their cotton crops.

Higher cotton prices in the mid-1920s brought another wave of cotton fever among southern farmers. Advice to limit cotton plantings and turn to other crops and livestock fell on deaf ears. With cotton above 20 cents at planting time in 1925, growers raised an additional 5 million acres and harvested a crop of 16.1 million bales. This was the largest annual production since the huge crop of 1914. The price dropped to 18 cents a pound, but this was still high enough to cause farmers to increase their acreage in 1926. With 47 million acres, the highest on record, and a heavy average yield of 182 pounds per acre, cotton farmers harvested nearly 18 million bales.[42]

The huge crop produced calamity throughout the cotton belt. Under pressure from such tremendous supplies, cotton prices fell to around 10 cents a pound. Cotton had dropped that low only four times in the previous twenty years. Farmers received about $500 million less for their cotton crop in 1926 than a year earlier, and unusual hardship stalked the homes of southern farm families. Most farmers in the South never had much margin of economic safety, and 10-cent cotton erased what little security they had.

Growers had been warned after the large crop of 1925 not to go "hog wild" on cotton the next year. Farm journal editors, officials of the agricultural colleges and extension service, and bankers were among those urging farmers to show restraint in their cotton plantings. Baylis E. Harris, a member of a Galveston cotton brokerage firm, raised the question early in 1926 as to whether any "organized effort" was going to be undertaken "to save the cotton farmer of the south from disaster the coming fall." But the price was a more important influence on farmer decisionmaking than advice.[43]

Much of the acreage expansion in the middle 1920s had come in the western cotton belt of Oklahoma and Texas. There farmers had turned to mechanization, which reduced labor costs and gave them a distinct advantage over growers in the Southeast. Moreover, southwestern Olkahoma and western Texas were bothered much less by the boll weevil. While farmers in the Southeast and South Central states had to meet competition from growers in the West, they also increased their cotton acreage. After some reduction in acreage in the early 1920s, producers in Louisiana, Arkansas, Mississippi, Alabama, Georgia, and the Carolinas planted more and more cotton in the middle years of the decade. Georgia farmers raised about 900,000 more acres in 1926 than in 1924, and in South Carolina acreage rose by 600,000 in the same period. Georgia and South Carolina both planted less cotton in 1926 than in 1916, but the rest of the Southeast and South Central sections of the cotton belt had expanded their cotton acreage very substantially in that decade.[44] There were especially large increases on newly drained and cleared lands in the Mississippi-Yazoo Delta and in northeastern Arkansas during the 1920s.

How would farmers and others dependent upon the cotton crop respond to the huge surplus and low prices in the fall of 1926? As usual during times of low cotton prices, there was no lack of advice to farmers. Some businessmen and bankers urged the formation of cotton pools to hold part of the crop off the market until prices recovered. This would require an advance of funds from either the private sector or government. But such removal, the bankers said, must be accompanied by a plan to reduce acreage in 1927. Congressman Edward W. Pou of North Carolina urged President Calvin Coolidge to call a special session of Congress to deal with the cotton situation. Others recommended modifying the "buy-a-bale" campaign of 1914 to "burn-a-bale" as the surest way to eliminate price-depressing surpluses. The old idea that women wear wider and longer cotton skirts was also advanced as a way to increase the demand for cotton.

In the midst of the demoralized cotton market, Governor Henry L. Whitfield of Mississippi called a Southwide meeting to deal with the situation. On October 13 and 14 about 700 planters, bankers, and merchants met in Memphis to sit at "the bedside of ailing King Cotton." Foretelling the main thrust of the conference, many delegates arrived wearing ribbons and buttons inscribed with "Cut cotton production by 50 percent."

While the main business of delegates at the Memphis conference was to find a way to reduce cotton production in 1927, there was sharp disagreement over how best to achieve that goal. Some southern leaders believed that voluntary restriction that had been tried so often in the past would not work. A.G. Little, a Blytheville, Arkansas, planter and lawyer, argued that it was time to invoke legislative restrictions on cotton acreage. Despite support from the western cotton belt, delegates from the Southeast defeated this proposal. Representatives from the older cotton areas resented the great expansion of cotton production in Oklahoma and Texas and believed that most of the reduction should be made in that area. And there was little prospect that all of the cotton states would pass restrictive legislation or, if they did, whether such laws could stand the constitutional test.

Once the idea of some form of compulsory restriction on cotton planting had been rejected, the delegates developed a plan for voluntary reduction. Referred to as a stabilization and acreage reduction plan, bankers, merchants, agricultural officials, editors, writers in farm journals, and others launched a program to persuade farmers to reduce their acreage by 25 percent in 1927. State organizations were active in all of the main cotton states, and activities seemed to be based on the assumption that if farmers were properly informed they would voluntarily cut back their plantings. As the campaign gained momentum the governors of Alabama and Mississippi proclaimed October 30 as the beginning of "Cotton Reduction Week." During that week farmers were urged to sign a pledge to reduce acreage in 1927 by no less than one-fourth.

Despite the hoopla associated with the acreage reduction campaign, not everyone agreed with the idea. Governor Miriam A. Ferguson of Texas said she would not advise farmers to cut their cotton production. Better advice, she believed, was to tell farmers to get "a sow, a cow, and a hen," another way of advocating diversification and self-sufficiency. The urban press also expressed opposition to the plan. Others continued to believe that it would not be effective. Senator Ellison D. Smith of South Carolina proposed that bankers and other suppliers of credit require farmers to sign an acreage reduction pledge before extending a loan for operating or living expenses.

This most intensive campaign ever launched to decrease cotton acreage voluntarily met with slight success. While acreage was down some 12.4 percent in 1927, this was only about the usual drop after a low-price year. Farmers were still acting on their own and in response to price rather than on the basis of outside advice. The editor of the Ada (Oklahoma) *Bulletin* wrote during the campaign: "The usual cry for a reduction of cotton acreage will go up, but experience has proved that this cry will produce no results. Cotton raising is as firmly imbedded in the system of the Southern ruralist as sea-faring is to the coast dweller of New England. . . . There is a fascination about it that only removal from their native land will cure." Planned production was still in the future.[45] The cotton crisis would have to become much more serious than it was in 1926 before such a program could be implemented. As prices recovered in 1928 and 1929, farmers increased their cotton production to over 45 million acres with crops of between 14 and 15 million bales annually. There were few signs in any major part of the cotton belt at the end of the 1920s that cotton was being replaced by other crops or livestock.

In the Southwest, cotton farmers were turning to mechanization to lower costs and increase efficiency. Producers hoped that substituting tractors and other improved machinery for mule power would help them fight the cost-price squeeze. A writer for the *Oklahoma Farmer-Stockman* declared early in 1930 that "the trains go rolling down into southwestern Oklahoma and west Texas carrying carload after carload of tractors designed to list, plant and cultivate two, three, and even four rows at a time. The same trains rolling back carry carload after carload of good mules consigned to markets at Memphis or St. Louis." As will be discussed later, some Texas and Oklahoma farmers in the 1920s were beginning to use the crude mechanical picker known as a cotton sled. Hearing of this device, in 1927 a Mississippi planter wrote to Dean A.H. Leidigh of the College of Agriculture at Texas Tech and declared: "*It*

Looks as if you fellows are going to make us produce cheap cotton or no cotton at all."[46]

While farmers clung to cotton growing, neither cotton farmers nor other staple crop producers could gain control of the marketing process. The farmer-owned cooperatives launched with so much enthusiasm in 1920 and 1921 never achieved much success during the 1920s. By the middle of the decade tobacco cooperatives had failed, and many of those organized by cotton growers met a similar fate. In 1927-1928 marketing cooperatives handled only 8 percent of the cotton while similar associations among tobacco growers were virtually extinct. The reasons for failure were about the same as those which had caused the earlier Grange, Farmers' Alliance, and Farmers' Union cooperatives to fail. Lack of capital, poor management, opposition from cotton and tobacco buyers, and the lack of a genuinely cooperative spirit among farmers combined to spell defeat for most marketing cooperatives. Although there were numerous examples of successful cooperatives in the South, they were unable to gain control over the sales of enough commodities to affect prices. Most of them came to accept orderly marketing as their main goal rather than trying to influence or determine commodity prices.[47]

A growing number of farm and political leaders in the South, however, were coming to the conclusion that farmer cooperatives could become effective price stabilizers if they had some federal financial support. When the McNary-Haugen farm relief bill, the main agricultural legislation advanced in the 1920s, was introduced in 1924, southerners were skeptical of its value to the region's farmers. This plan called for assuring fair prices to producers of certain staple crops by segregating price-depressing surpluses from the domestic market. In the case of wheat, for instance, the surplus above domestic needs would be sold at the world price, while it was believed that the portion used at home would rise to a higher level on home markets behind a tariff wall. It was, in short, a two-price system. The losses on exports would be paid by a tax or equalization fee on each unit of the commodity sold.

While this scheme seemed to be ideally suited to wheat because generally only 15 to 30 percent of the crop was exported, it did not appeal to cotton growers, who normally exported around 50 to 60 percent of their production. Southerners did not want any fee or tax levied on their cotton. They preferred some kind of federal appropriation which would help to fund holding operations by the cotton cooperatives. Up to 1926 midwestern proponents of the McNary-Haugen bill had gained relatively little support in the South. But with the drastic drop in cotton prices in 1926, southerners were anxious to lend their support to some kind of surplus control legislation. By the end of the year a coalition of corn and cotton representatives had been organized in Washington to push the McNary-Haugen bill through Congress. To assure widespread southern support, tobacco and rice were also included in the bill.

Passed in February 1927, the McNary-Haugen bill provided for an appropriation of $250 million to help cooperatives stabilize prices by holding surpluses off the market. An equalization fee was to be collected to provide ongoing funds to assist cotton and other cooperatives. This legislation, however, was killed by a presidential veto. Coolidge also vetoed a revised bill passed in 1928, destroying any hope of effective farm relief in his administration.[48]

While southern farmers continued to concentrate on the production of staples in the 1920s, especially cotton, they raised a wide variety of other crops. Some of these were important income producers for at least a few growers. Citrus production had been increasing in Florida for many years, but expansion greatly accelerated in the postwar decade. By the late 1920s Florida orchardists were shipping millions of boxes of oranges and grapefruit to national markets. The Rio Grande Valley of Texas also expanded citrus production, especially grapefruit. But southerners also grew apples and peaches for the commercial markets. Virginia was a leading apple state and Georgia was second only to California in peach production. The boll weevil invasion caused additional Georgia farmers to plant peach trees in the 1920s, and by 1929 the state had 1,703 commercial peach orchards, principally in the Fort Valley area. Other states also expanded their peach growing with resulting overproduction and low prices. Writing from Fort Valley, Georgia, in 1927, an observer reported that one year peaches were dumped into rivers and creeks to get rid of them. No profitable market existed. By 1930 Georgia produced less than half as many peaches as it had in 1926 or 1928. Small fruits such as strawberries were also important to a few farmers in Texas, Louisiana, Mississippi, Alabama, and Florida. Early shipment strawberries from those states rose from 23,000 to about 43,000 acres between 1923 and 1930.[49]

Truck farmers who had begun supplying northern markets in the 1880s expanded their acreage and output during the following years. Early potatoes, cabbage, watermelons, peppers, green peas, and lettuce were among the fresh commodities shipped to northern markets by southern producers in the 1920s.

Besides producing fruits and vegetables for the growing national market, southern farmers raised a wide variety of nuts, of which pecans and peanuts were the most important. While pecans from native trees had been harvested for sale for many years, the grafting of pecan trees to improve the nut quality and the planting of commercial orchards did not begin until around 1905. By the 1920s pecan groves of scientifically bred trees and more systematic harvesting of nuts from the native trees made pecans an important agricultural activity in a few areas of the South. Texas, Oklahoma, and Georgia led in pecan production. Georgia led in the number of improved trees, but production declined everywhere in the late 1920s, partly because of disease problems.[50]

Alabama, Georgia, North Carolina, Texas, and Virginia produced large quantities of peanuts. While peanuts had become a significant crop in some communities by World War I, boll weevil destruction caused some southern farmers to substitute peanuts for cotton after 1915. There was such a dramatic change from cotton to peanuts in Coffee County, Alabama, that in 1919 residents of Enterprise erected a monument to the boll weevil, which was credited for the abandonment of cotton. Peanut acreage varied considerably in the 1920s, but total land devoted to the crop throughout the South was not much larger in 1929 than in 1920.[51]

A new crop that began to make an appearance in the 1920s was the soybean. As early as 1918 E.F. Cauthen of the Alabama Experiment Station wrote that interest in soybeans was "due largely to a changed system of cotton farming made necessary by the invasion of the boll weevil." Cauthen correctly predicted that soybeans would "become a prominent part of Alabama's cropping system." Farmers in other southern states also tested the new crop. Most of the soybeans grown in the South during the 1920s were raised for hay, but an increasing acreage was devoted to raising soybeans for cash sale. Between 1923 and 1929 production of soybeans raised for beans in the eight southeastern states rose from 178,000 to 241,000 acres. The crop had several advantages. Soybeans took less fertilizer than cotton, markets were generally strong, and the crop could be handled with the available machinery.[52]

There was also slight expansion in the production of another oil crop in the 1920s—tung oil. Looking for a crop that would do well on cut-over timberlands, producers in northern Florida, southern Georgia, Alabama, Mississippi, Louisiana, and Texas increased their tung orchards. Although the greatest growth came in the next decade, the first carload of tung oil was shipped from Gainesville, Florida, in 1928. This was the forerunner of things to come.[53]

Although strong efforts were made to get farmers to raise more livestock, this aspect of diversification lost ground in the 1920s. The slogan of "a cow, a sow and a hen" may have read well in the agricultural journals, but farmers largely ignored the advice. There were nearly a million *fewer* milk cows on southern farms in 1930 than in 1922.

For example, in Alabama and Mississippi the number of milk cows declined from 506,000 to 354,000 and from 541,000 to 410,000 respectively. As authorities on Alabama agriculture wrote: "Alabama was less self-sufficient in regard to livestock production in 1930 than in any other previous census period following the Civil War." Writing about the southeastern Coastal Plain in 1929, USDA experts indicated that the main deterrents to dairy and livestock production among southern farmers still prevailed. They explained that poor pastures, lack of feed, and inadequate care of livestock had "resulted in a prejudice against livestock among both farmers and bankers."

Between 1921-1922 and the end of the decade there was also a dramatic drop in the number of swine. In the Carolinas farmers had 2.1 million hogs in 1921 compared to only 1.2 million in 1930. The production of hogs was closely connected with corn acreage, which in turn varied with the actual or hoped-for profitability of cotton. Following the disastrous cotton crop in 1920, for instance, corn acreage went up in all the southern states, but then it dropped as cotton recovered. By the end of the 1920s corn and hog production were both down compared to 1921.[54] The number of chickens either barely held its own or declined slightly.

A major deterrent to diversification continued to be the lack of reliable markets for vegetable, fruit, poultry, or dairy products. This stemmed from the lack of development of large urban centers in the South and inadequate transportation and marketing facilities for perishable products.[55] Many farmers who tried to market vegetables and fruits often suffered huge losses. As mentioned above, some Georgia peach growers in the 1920s simply had to destroy peaches for which there was no profitable market.

As one viewed southern farming in 1930, it was difficult to find many positive changes during the previous generation. Diversification, scientific farming, and improved efficiency had scarcely scratched the surface among southern operators. The South, from North Carolina to eastern Texas, continued to be dominated by small, one- and two-mule farms. The number of farms under 50 acres actually increased in the 1920s, while those of more than 100 acres declined. Tenancy was increasing at a steady rate. There were slightly fewer black tenants in 1930 than a decade earlier simply because blacks had left the farm, but the number of white tenants had risen by some 200,000. There were 384,541 black and 336,817 white sharecroppers in the region, indicating that this kind of wage labor continued to be no respecter of race. Only 164,810 black farmers owned their land, a mere 19 percent of the black operators. This was down from 22 percent in 1920, or a drop of 32,964 black owners in ten years.

Investment in land, implements, and livestock was still small on southern farms compared to other sections of the country. The average value of land and buildings per farm in the southern states was only $3,525, while the figure was $11,029 per farm in the North. The value of machinery and implements, for example, in North Carolina, South Carolina, Georgia, Alabama, and Mississippi averaged only $134 per farm in 1930. In Kansas and Iowa it was $1,010 and $1,259 respectively. The value of livestock on southern farms averaged between $200 and $300 per farm compared to $1,000 to $2,000 and more on midwestern farms. Barely making a living and without sources of credit, southern farmers lacked capital to invest in productive assets.[56]

Low incomes associated with the entire agricultural sector were intensified in the South by a lack of enough commercial production per man or per farm to provide a decent living standard for millions of farm residents. In 1930 the annual per capita income of the southern farm population varied from $120 in Mississippi to $166 in North Carolina.[57] But averages distort the true picture. Many farm families in the South did not receive as much cash per year as the average per capita income. Tenants and sharecroppers continued to be the worst off and, despite the touted Coolidge prosperity, very few of them ever climbed the agricultural ladder to ownership. And black farmers were generally considerably poorer than whites.

Despite widespread rural poverty throughout the South, farmers were probably somewhat better off in the late 1920s than they had been in the 1890s. A study done of black sharecroppers in the Yazoo-Mississippi Delta in 1928 showed that housing had been improved for this class of farmers and that a few homes had a phonograph, some kind of curtains at the window, and homemade kitchen cabinets. Writing about black sharecroppers in Mississippi in 1928, Dorothy Dickens, an investigator from Mississippi A & M College, explained that "the negroes of today certainly have more to eat than the combination of salt pork, cornmeal and molasses" described in a study among Alabama black farmers in 1895-1896. There was a slight increase, mostly among white farm owners, in the use of electric lights and running water and the employment of tractors and motor trucks. In Georgia and Alabama, for example, 2.1 and 1.7 percent of the farms had tractors in 1930 compared to 1.5 and 1.0 percent respectively a decade earlier. Progress toward mechanization was very slow but made some gains. The biggest change was in automobile ownership. More than one-fourth of the farmers had automobiles by 1930. As would be expected, it was the farm owners and better-off tenants who were most likely to acquire more machinery and better facilities. Modern conveniences, however, were outside the possibility for the great majority of southern farmers.[58]

Weighing cotton in the field as pickers stand by, about 1930.
Georgia Department of Archives and History.

A middle-class Georgia farm home of the 1890s.
Georgia Department of Archives and History.

The cabin of a black sharecropper or a poor tenant, about 1900.
Georgia Department of Archives and History.

Preparing land for cotton planting in the 1890s.
Georgia Department of Archives and History.

A black midwife making a home call in 1941, much as in earlier decades.
Georgia Department of Archives and History.

Hog butchering on a southern farm, about 1890.
University of Georgia, College of Agriculture.

One of the better country schools in Georgia, about 1890.
Georgia Department of Archives and History.

Above, hauling cotton bales to market with a four-mule team early in the twentieth century. *Below*, dinner on the grounds, an important part of the social life of southern farmers, about 1900. Georgia Department of Archives and History.

Damaging soil erosion in Tennessee in the 1930s was typical of many parts of the South. Tennessee Valley Authority.

The development of better pastures and improved cattle breeds has given the South a prosperous livestock industry since World War II. Tennessee Valley Authority.

A tobacco harvester which permitted pickers to ride through the field, pick leaves, and rack them preparatory to placing the racks in bulk curing barns. This machine was replaced on larger tobacco farms by the tobacco combine in the 1970s. University of Georgia, College of Agriculture.

Below, digging and turning peanuts so they will dry and be ready for combining, 1970s. University of Georgia, College of Agriculture. *Right,*confined poultry operations for both laying hens and broilers became common throughout the South after 1950. Tennessee Valley Authority.

Spraying fruit trees from an airplane in Florida. This method of fighting insects and plant diseases has been widely used also by cotton and grain farmers since World War II. U.S. Department of Agriculture.

Mechanical cotton pickers, shown in fields near Tunica, Mississippi, had replaced hand pickers on the most modern cotton farms by the 1950s and 1960s. U.S. Department of Agriculture.

Thus, while there was some increase in the standard of living among southern farmers in the early twentieth century, improvements were meager. Living standards of most farm families in the South lagged far behind progress being made by farmers and others elsewhere. They were the people being left behind in a nation experiencing rapid economic development which in turn provided better living conditions for millions of Americans, both rural and urban, in the North and West.

In nearly every southern community there were a few farmers who did well and enjoyed a relatively good living. Some of these were designated as "Master Farmers," and by the late 1920s their successes were being publicized as a means of encouraging others. In January 1928 the *Progressive Farmer* carried a story on the twelve Master Farmers selected in Georgia. They were larger operators with several hundred acres, but none would be considered huge planters. The writer explained that these families were successful because they improved their soil, employed machinery, specialized, adopted the best business and management methods, and maintained more livestock than most of their neighbors. As a result, they enjoyed a reasonably satisfactory standard of living. They resided in fairly comfortable homes surrounded by trees and flowers, and some of them enjoyed automobiles, telephones, and electricity. They represented the farmers who were most likely to utilize the information coming from the colleges of agriculture, the experiment stations, and the USDA. These farmers were the forerunners of fundamental agricultural change in the South.[59]

During the 1920s the USDA, the agricultural experiment stations, and the Cooperative Extension Service expanded their investigations into the southern rural economy and the conditions of farm life. Using the survey method, investigators studied types of farming areas, factors contributing to success on southern farms, income levels, food and nutrition, and other subjects. These studies help provide a clearer picture of what farm life was like and show why farmers continued to wallow in poverty.[60]

Surveys by home economists in South Carolina, Georgia, and Mississippi, for example, showed that farm families throughout the South ate about the same unbalanced and nutritionally deficient diets in the 1920s as they had a generation earlier. While the diets of landowners were usually better than those of tenants and sharecroppers because the farmer kept more livestock and raised more garden produce, most southern farm families continued to eat too much fat and too many cereals and sweets. Diets were deficient in protein and especially so in iron. Studying the diets of children under six years of age in four areas of South Carolina in 1928, Mary E. Frayser found that 41 percent of the white and 71 percent of the black children had what were considered deficient diets. Eleven percent of the white children and 22 percent of the blacks did not have three meals a day. Typical menus among Yazoo-Mississippi sharecroppers included fried eggs or salt pork, biscuit, and sorghum for breakfast, although sometimes there were only biscuits and sorghum. For dinner at noon, peas and cornbread and salt pork, and occasionally milk or biscuit pudding were served, and for supper sausage or salt pork, rice, sorghum, some vegetables, and perhaps tomato pie in season. But many black sharecroppers, according to one investigator, made "their supper off of cornbread and buttermilk."[61]

While most authorities agreed that foods eaten by both black and white farmers were somewhat better than in the 1890s, diets were still poor and were commonly unbalanced and lacked nutritional value. This situation contributed to poor health among rural residents in many communities. Dorothy Dickens, who studied the diets of black sharecroppers in Mississippi, found members of the farm family frequently ill, less resistant to pellagra and other diseases, lacking in energy, and experiencing a higher death rate. While the effect of these conditions on work efficiency cannot be quantified, such poor health surely affected productivity to some extent.

One thing that researchers discovered in the 1920s was that rural southerners were producing a high percentage of their food on the farm. Food self-sufficiency was a message being preached to the converted. E.L. Kirkpatrick of the USDA, who sampled white farmers in South Carolina and Alabama in 1926, found that farmers raised about 75 percent of their food, compared to some 64 percent for those surveyed in Kansas and Nebraska. One hundred representative white farm families in two areas of Mississippi reported in 1927 that they produced 76 percent of their food on the farm. A similar survey in the Yazoo-Mississippi Delta revealed, however, that black sharecroppers raised only 44 percent of their own food.[62]

In light of these and other studies it is clear that diversification had little to offer if it was designed to make farmers more self-sufficient in food. White families were already producing three-fourths or more of the family table needs. Many southern farmers could raise a better and greater variety of food, but they could never become 100 percent self-sufficient if they used coffee, tea, salt, and other products that they could not produce at home. The farmers who needed to raise more of their food were the black and white sharecroppers, and they were the very farmers who were too often discouraged or actually forbidden to use cotton land for vegetables or other food crops.

In their economic and farm management studies, researchers from the federal and state agricultural agencies continued to emphasize that the main difficulties facing southern farmers were poor yields and small farms. Those farms with 20 to 35 acres of cropland simply could not produce enough income to provide a modern standard of living. In study after study they showed the relationship between larger acreages and higher returns, and between better management and increased productivity. For example, a study done of 369 farms over four years, 1925-1928, in eastern South Carolina showed a vast gulf between the earnings of the top 25 percent and the lowest 25 percent of the farmers. The highest one-fourth had average earnings of $3,916 compared to $285 for the lowest 25 percent. The more efficient farmers cultivated more total acres and more acres per mule; they got higher yields of cotton, tobacco, and corn, and produced more of their food and feed on the farm.[63]

It was important that the farm provide full-time employment and utilize mule and horse power and equipment efficiently. One study revealed that on small Arkansas farms of 40 to 80 acres, the operator and his family were occupied productively less than half the time. With such information available, farmers were urged to change. In March 1928 the editor of the *Progressive Farmer* declared that a "direct ratio" existed between income per farm worker and horsepower. To be successful, the editor wrote, farmers needed to utilize power and machinery intelligently and not "do farm work by main strength and awkwardness." Not only would machines save labor that was getting increasingly expensive, they would do the work better and more quickly. The editor was advancing the modern concept to timeliness in farm work as having an important relationship to income and profits.[64]

While the agricultural experts urged farmers to diversify, produce more, and increase their efficiency, they did not often recommend that farmers abandon cotton. Ward C. Jensen, an agricultural economist at Clemson Agricultural College, wrote in 1926 that "nothing has been found to take the place of cotton on an extensive scale that would make the farmers as much money one year with another." Jensen had verified this conclusion by analyzing the cost and income accounts of fifty-seven farmers in a portion of South Carolina's Piedmont. Studies in other states confirmed this conclusion. W.J. Spillman, an economist in the USDA, wrote in 1923 that there was no possibility of substituting truck crops for cotton over "any large area" in the South.[65]

By the end of the 1920s more sophisticated studies showed clearly the fundamental problems facing so many southern farmers. Share-croppers, however, whether white or black, were in no position to change their condition so long as they lived on the land. As has been mentioned repeatedly, they were in reality farm laborers paid with a share of the cotton crop. They were caught in a web of debt, their independence and choice of actions were severely limited, and the black sharecroppers suffered from the social and community controls associated with racism.

Outside of the few larger and more progressive farmers scattered throughout the region, the barriers between most farmers and a better living included small acreages, underemployment, inefficient production, lack of capital, declining soil fertility, ignorance, and tradition. On top of all of these factors was the low return to agricultural labor and investment in general.

In fact, the entire economic and social infrastructure in the South was weak. Roads, transportation facilities, markets for some crops, alternate employment opportunities, availability of capital, and education were all inadequate to provide the needed assistance in agricultural modernization. The situation appeared so grim to President Andrew M. Soule of the Georgia College of Agriculture in the 1920s that he believed little could be done for middle-aged farmers and their wives. He could only hope that agricultural change would come in time to make a better life for the next generation.

In speeches delivered throughout the Southeast during the postwar decade, Soule called for changes that would strengthen the weak economic infrastructure. He urged farmers to use more machinery and equipment, which meant that somehow they must increase farm capitalization. He advocated conserving the soil to make it more productive, and applying better management. Soule accused southern landowners of understanding and appreciating modern farming methods in about the same way that a six-year-old child understood Latin and Greek. Farmers, he insisted, must be more business-oriented, join cooperatives, and work for marketing improvements. Soule repeated what the researchers in his college and elsewhere had shown so clearly. "Production per man has been too low," he argued in one talk, adding that "we are not using enough power and enough equipment." "The farm unit," he maintained, "is too small to function efficiently."[66]

While the relationship between education and economic development cannot be measured precisely, many economists as well as others have held that educational improvement is a vital factor in economic growth. As early as 1915 a writer in the *New Republic* argued that the low standard of education for both whites and blacks in the South was "the chief drawback to its steady and rapid progress toward better agriculture."[67] Andrew Soule surely believed this. Speaking to audience after audience, he argued that the South must upgrade its education if farming was to become profitable. On one occasion he declared that the "one-horse, one-teacher, isolated, run-down, unkempt, and impossible rural schools" were a great deterrent to agricultural progress. The schools, he said, should be consolidated and competent teachers should be hired. With proper education, Soule believed, "a new generation of farmers" would "restore the agriculture of the South to the prestige it once enjoyed and again make of it a profitable and inspiring business."

But there were few signs on the eve of the Great Depression that southern farmers would ever enjoy "a profitable and inspiring business." Small, inefficient, nonproductive farms were the norm throughout much of the South, with accompanying poverty and destitution. And conditions would get much worse before they got better. It was out of the travail of the 1930s that fundamental change would begin to shake the old agricultural South, change that would usher modern farming into the region.

6

The Great Depression Strikes

In 1930 hundreds of thousands of southern farmers began to skid from normal hard times to disastrous depression. If observers believed that life could not get worse than it already was for millions of rural residents in the South, they were badly mistaken. A decade of depression was beginning which forced living standards down well below the poverty levels experienced for years by many southern farm families.

In 1929 farmers planted more than 45 million acres of cotton, produced a crop of 14.8 million bales, and received an average price of more than 16 cents a pound. Tobacco plantings reached nearly 2 million acres, the highest on record up to that time, and season prices averaged about 18.6 cents a pound. Other crops and livestock also brought reasonable prices. But it was a different story in 1930. Reeling under the effect of a weakening domestic and world economy, a slightly smaller cotton crop brought only between 9 and 10 cents a pound and produced an income of $659 million, about half as much as in 1929. Returns from tobacco and other crops were also down sharply. Income from farm production in the ten main cotton states dropped from $2.4 billion in 1929 to only $929 million in 1932. And the problem was not confined to declining agricultural prices. Such farm expenses as interest and taxes, as well as the prices of industrial goods, did not decline anywhere near as much as farm prices. This placed farmers in a vicious cost-price squeeze. Considering the purchase price of cotton as equaling 100 in the period from 1909 to 1914, by 1932 it was only 58.[1] Such a large drop in income and the disparity between farm and nonfarm prices were devastating to people who were already poor.

Southern farmers were, of course, accustomed to some unusually bad years, but 1930 ushered in a decade of depression. Making things even more difficult, large areas of the South suffered from severe drought that year. Indeed, drought produced more hardship in some farm communities than low cotton prices. By January 1931, Red Cross visitors in one Arkansas community found both white and black farmers with only two days' food supply on hand, and some had no food whatever.[2]

To add to the problems of southern farmers, people who had left the farms for industrial or other employment began to drift back to their old homes and communities as they lost their nonfarm jobs. The total farm population in the southern states declined slightly between 1920 and 1930, but in five states—North Carolina, Alabama, Mississippi, Louisiana, and Texas—farm population actually increased. The pressure of population on land resources thus continued heavy. Between April 1, 1929, and March 31, 1930, for instance, there was a positive movement of people from towns and cities to southern farms in eight southern states, instead of the outward flow seen earlier. In that twelve-month period some 17,581 persons returned to the farm in Alabama, while only 7,836 left. Thus, while some southerners continued to leave the farm during the Great Depression, about one-third of the back-to-the-land migrants settled in the South. Between 1930 and 1935 the southern farm population actually increased by some 1.3 million people.[3]

The meager standard of living already experienced by so many southern farmers dropped even further. The proverbial fat pork, meal, and molasses became scarce in many farm homes, clothing became little more than rags, and bad housing deteriorated to the point in some communities that farmers lived outside most of the year. In 1931 Charles S. Johnson of Fisk University did an economic and sociological study of 612 black families in rural Macon County in Alabama's black belt. About 10 percent owned their own farms, some were day laborers, while the majority were sharecroppers and tenants. More than half of the farmers lived in one- and two-room weatherworn shacks that had not been whitewashed or painted for many years, if ever. Many of these houses had holes in the roof, walls, and floor. They leaked when it rained and in winter cold winds howled through the rooms. Windows were broken, doors hung ajar, porch steps were rotted, and chimneys were falling down. One tenant was asked if her house leaked when it rained. "No, it don't leak in here, it jest rains in here and leaks outdoors." Another tenant reported that the landlord had promised five years earlier to fix up his old, dilapidated house, but "all he's give us since then is a few planks to fix the porch. It's nothing doin'. We jest living outdoors." Arthur Raper found in Greene and Macon counties, Georgia, in 1934 that about two-thirds "of the houses occupied by Negroes and one-fourth of those occupied by whites have leaky roofs."

The black farmers surveyed by Johnson reported eating salt pork and bread made of corn or wheat flour when they could get it, and perhaps some syrup or molasses. At certain times of the year they had a few vegetables. One farm wife reported that "we ought to have oatmeal, grits, and things like that to eat but we can't get it," while another told the interviewer that "the baby have to eat what we have and ain't much. I got one old rooster. I wanted to kill him but I ain't got no grease to cook him wid."[4] Nothing had really changed for this class of farmers since the 1890s.

Johnson found a few families among those interviewed who were getting along reasonably well by Depression standards. They lived in five- and six-room houses, had a few head of livestock, sold three or four bales of cotton, raised some corn, and had gardens. Yet their debts wiped out most of their income and some owners found they were little better off than the tenants and sharecroppers. Southern farmers outside the black belt were usually not quite as poor, but almost. Poverty was all pervasive.

By 1931 many larger farm owners saw their farms lost through foreclosure. Even ownership of a large farm provided no safety. A study of loans to 4,750 farmers in southeastern Alabama between 1917 and 1931 found that 30 percent of the operators with 300 to 459 acres and 39 percent of those with 780 to 1,319 acres had been foreclosed on by 1931. In Macon County, Georgia, between 1928 and 1932, loan companies had foreclosed on four farms of between 500 and 1,000 acres and eight containing over 1,000 acres. One of the problems for larger farmers was that they were unable to reduce the cost of sharecropper and hired labor as fast as income declined. In the spring of 1930, for instance, many landlords made advances to tenants when prices were fairly high. By harvest time the low prices could not produce enough income to repay the debt.[5]

Meanwhile, the federal government was struggling to check the decline in farm prices. In June 1929 Congress had enacted the Agricultural Marketing Act, which sought to help farmers obtain better prices through orderly marketing. The law established the Federal Farm Board and appropriated $500 million to provide money to extend loans to approved farmer cooperatives to assist them in holding their wheat, cotton, and other crops off a depressed market. Early in 1930 the American Cotton Cooperative Association was formed, and affiliated cotton cooperatives were permitted to borrow up to 16 cents a pound on cotton bought from farmer members. This maintained an artificial price under cotton for a time, but with declining domestic and foreign demand, prices dropped to 13 cents a pound early in 1930 and continued downward. Having received more than this figure in loans, the cotton cooperatives were facing bankruptcy. To stave off that eventuality, the Federal Farm Board organized the Cotton Stabilization Corporation in June 1930. This agency took over cotton held by the cooperatives and also directly entered the market to support prices. However, in 1931 the Board ceased making advances to the cooperatives and abandoned efforts to support cotton prices directly. Other southern crops, including tobacco, rice, and pecans, also received temporary help from the Farm Board through their cooperatives.[6]

The Federal Farm Board warned that no agency could maintain prices in the face of such overwhelming production coming from American farms. Prices were bound to drop, officials argued, when output so far exceeded domestic and foreign demand. By late 1930 there was a carryover of 4.5 million bales, nearly double that of the previous season, hanging like a sword over any price increases.[7] In light of the large surpluses of cotton and wheat, Alex Legge, chairman of the Board, said early in 1930 that control of production by farmers was absolutely essential. At about the same time the American Cotton Cooperative Association distributed circulars urging cotton growers to cut their plantings in the coming season.

As had been true on earlier occasions when farmers had been advised to cut production, growers paid little attention to the campaign for acreage reduction. While they did show some restraint, they still grew over 45 million acres of cotton in 1930 and seemed determined to plant another large crop in 1931. A writer for the *New Republic* visited an Alabama tenant in the spring of 1931 and found him plowing energetically and getting ready to plant more cotton, even though much of last year's crop was still on hand. "Some of the men who are plowing are hungry. They don't have enough to eat," wrote the visitor. "And with hunger gnawing at their vitals they plow in earnest, because they are in a desperate situation and they exist in terrible anxiety. So they plow hard." The writer explained that cotton farmers needed something with which to buy food and clothing for their families, and "they think cotton is the only thing left."[8]

Just as farmers were about to begin picking the big crop of 1931, which turned out to be more than 17 million bales, the second highest on record, the Federal Farm Board wired the governors of fourteen southern states, asking them to lead a movement to abandon one-third of the current cotton crop. The board wanted state officials to "induce immediate plowing under of every third row of cotton now growing." Stressing that the board's efforts to keep prices from declining had "been outweighed by continued excess production and continually increasing surpluses," the board promised to hold cotton acquired by the Cotton Stabilization Corporation off the market until July 1932. The idea of plowing under every third row of maturing cotton was considered wasteful and impractical. The editor of the *New York Times* called it "blundering absurdity" and "one of the maddest things that ever came from an official body." Members of the New Orleans Cotton Exchange called the Board's suggestion "silly," "impractical," and "ridiculous." Farmers, their spokesmen, and southern political leaders also found the Farm Board proposal highly objectionable and refused to give it serious consideration.[9]

While the Farm Board was urging southern governors to consider rather drastic methods of forcing prices upward, Governor Huey P. Long of Louisiana had his own relief program to redeem southern cotton farmers. With cotton heading toward 5 cents a pound it seemed as though some kind of dramatic action was essential. In calling for a conference to meet in New Orleans on August 21, Long told governors of other southern states that the legislature in each cotton-producing state should pass a law prohibiting the growing of *any* cotton in 1932. The way to raise cotton prices, Long said, was to organize a cotton holiday movement, or "drop-a-crop." The mere commitment to such a program, Long and others believed, would cause cotton prices to rise. In any event, the proposals of the Farm Board and Long certainly reflected desperation among cotton producers and their spokesmen.

While replies from the southern governors were noncommital, representatives from each major cotton state did attend the New Orleans conference. After considerable discussion, the conferees overwhelmingly endorsed the Long plan. But the prohibition against cotton growing would not become effective in any state until the states producing three-fourths of the total crop had passed such legislation. This provision was to keep farmers in states that passed such laws from being penalized in case most other states refused to go along.

Shortly after the New Orleans meeting the Louisiana legislature passed a law that prohibited the "planting, gathering, and ginning of cotton in 1932." A provision was included, however, that permitted Governor Long to suspend the legislation if states producing 75 percent of the South's cotton had not enacted similar measures by January 15, 1932. Long pressed hard to get other states to pass similar laws. Although many farmers were attracted to the idea, other producers, both large and small, opposed this approach to raising prices. Some farmers protested that cotton was their only source of cash to buy certain necessities. As one Georgian wrote, "We have to raise a little cotton to buy sugar, coffee, salt, pepper and such things that we can't raise ourselves."[10]

As other states considered legislation restricting cotton acreage, strong opposition developed from political leaders and economic interests, such as ginners and commission agents, who depended on cotton for a livelihood. Critics argued that textile workers and businesses in the towns would suffer, and that if America stopped producing cotton, even for one year, foreign growers would move in and take an even larger share of the world market. Many also expressed doubt that state governments had the constitutional right to prohibit cotton growing.

The key to success for the entire cotton holiday movement rested with Texas, which produced nearly one-third of the total supply. Without Texas cooperation the proposal was bound to fail. Although Governor R.S. Sterling of Texas opposed the Long plan, and the legislature defeated a bill calling for no cotton planting in 1932, Texas lawmakers did pass a measure restricting cotton acreage in 1932 and 1933 to 30 percent of the acreage grown in 1931. Arkansas, Mississippi, and South Carolina also passed some kind of restrictive laws. The entire holiday movement collapsed, however, when Governor Long, seeing that his program lacked sufficient support, repealed the Louisiana law by executive proclamation on January 28, 1932. Three days later a judge in Texas ruled that to require farmers to reduce acreage by 30 percent was unconstitutional.[11]

Meanwhile, farmers were becoming increasingly desperate. During the discussion over legislative acreage reduction in the late summer of 1931, R.B. Snowden of Arkansas wrote to Farm Board officials that farmers would sign contracts to limit production or do "anything" because "they are today congregating in little wandering groups, hoping, looking, praying for some one to step up with some practical drastic action which will save them quickly from inevitable three and four cent cotton." But neither hoping nor praying helped. Cotton continued its downward slide. When farmers planted their crop in 1931, cotton was bringing 9 to 10 cents a pound. When they began to harvest in August it was about 6.3 cents, and by October, 5.3 cents a pound. In some local markets it was less.[12] The thousands of southern farmers raising tobacco also suffered dramatic price and income declines. Flue-cured tobacco dropped from nearly 15 cents a pound in 1930 to 8 cents a year later.

As the farm depression deepened, the worst features of the southern tenant and sharecrop systems were intensified. With so little money to distribute, relations between landlords and tenants became more strained, race relations more ugly. Black sharecroppers and tenants believed they were being mistreated when landlords and merchants cut off or reduced merchandise or cash credit because they feared the crop would not cover the amount advanced. Sharecroppers commonly complained to Charles S. Johnson and his survey team in 1931 that they could not get credit advances as they had done in better times. One sharecropper asked his landlord to "vance me jest nuff for a pair of overalls. He tells me he needs overalls hisself" and refused, Johnson wrote. Resentments by blacks against white landowners and merchants who cheated them at settlement time also increased. Under pressure to survive, blacks sometimes protested or argued over their accounts, only to be menaced physically or threatened by removal from the land. If relations between tenant and landowner were not outwardly tense, there was an underlying smoldering of distrust and resentment on both sides. Before the Depression was over this would break out into violence in some places.[13]

With cotton prices hovering around 5 cents a pound at planting time in 1932, and the equivalent of two years' supply on hand, it might have been expected that farmers would throw up their hands and abandon the crop. Such was not the case, however. There was a small reduction in acreage, but in the face of disastrous prices farmers still planted more than 38 million acres compared to 41 million in 1931. Why did farmers persist in producing a crop for which there was no profitable market? The answer is not hard to find. For most commercial farmers there was no satisfactory alternative crop. At least cotton would bring in some money. It always had. Furthermore, production of other crops offered no relief because the prices of all crops and livestock were extremely depressed. By 1932 dairymen and other farmers in the Midwest were protesting low prices by threatening a farm strike.

Cutting production to bring supply and demand into better balance was only one method advanced to help depressed southern farmers. Some leaders recommended that the federal government set prices at the cost of production, while others suggested more liberal credit and a moratorium on farm foreclosures. There were those advocating that surplus farm commodities be distributed to the needy and that people use more cotton manufactures. Although in 1931 and 1932 there was little agreement in farm circles or in Washington on how best to solve farm problems, one thing was becoming increasingly clear. Farmers could not lift themselves out of their poverty by their own bootstraps. The old panaceas of diversified farming, cooperatives, and more liberal credit had little relevance to the overwhelming problems growing out of world and national depression. Many producers did grow more food and feed crops after the Depression set in, but this was a move for survival and not a solution to their basic difficulties. Moreover, this kind of self-sufficiency hardly touched the black sharecroppers in the plantation areas who were most needful of home-grown food.

Most farmers had only a faint understanding of the relationship between their condition and what was happening in the rest of the world. The major cotton growers, of course, knew that much of their production was exported and that the position of the American textile industry affected raw material prices. But the relationships were a mystery to the average farmer out in the cotton patch. Under the influence of a strong agrarian tradition which held that agriculture was the basic foundation of the economy, many farmers and their spokesmen believed that unless farmers were prosperous other sectors of the economy would suffer. The cities, as William Jennings Bryan had said in the 1890s, could not exist except on the foundation of the farms. During the 1920s many farm leaders had predicted that unless farmers got a fair share of the national wealth and income, the whole economy would fall. When the Great Depression struck, farm spokesmen proclaimed that one of the major reasons the economy had finally collapsed was because of low incomes and purchasing power by farmers since the end of World War I.

This view was challenged, however, especially during the Depression. Other observers, rather than arguing that farm purchasing power held the key to national prosperity, declared that farmers could not be prosperous unless business and industry were expanding and workers had jobs and money to buy farm products. Farmers, in other words, were dependent upon industrial prosperity and full employment. But most farmers and their representatives continued to believe that agriculture was the most important factor in national prosperity. This being the case, they insisted that the federal government had a responsibility to restore prosperity on the farms.[14] This would help not only individual farmers but the entire economy. With the failure of the Federal Farm Board and the deepening of the Depression in 1932, there were increasingly strong demands from rural America for the federal government to do something to save the farmers. Southerners were in the forefront of this demand and they enthusiastically backed Franklin D. Roosevelt for president.

The victory of the Democrats in 1932 and the election of Roosevelt as president assured farmers that the federal government would at last initiate some kind of bold farm relief program. While he had been purposely vague during the campaign, Roosevelt had promised action on the farm issue. Moreover, Democratic control of Congress had brought southerners into key places of power in Washington. It seemed certain that whatever kind of federal aid Congress approved would include something for producers of the South's major crops.

After the Democrats won control of the House of Representatives in 1930, Marvin Jones of Texas became chairman of the House Agriculture Committee. Born on a cotton farm, Jones had escaped the poverty of the farm by studying law and going into politics, but he never lost his deep and compassionate concern for farmers who, he thought, were getting a "raw deal." In 1933 another southerner, Ellison D. "Cotton Ed" Smith, assumed the chairmanship of the Agriculture Committee in the Senate. Smith was the son of a South Carolina minister, but from the time he entered politics in 1896 he was a strong advocate of helping cotton farmers. Although he became a bitter critic of Roosevelt and much of the New Deal, he was a staunch supporter of legislation that would help cotton and tobacco growers. Another powerful southerner vitally interested in farm welfare was Senator

John H. Bankhead of Alabama. A lawyer and planter, Bankhead was elected to the Senate in 1930 and became an early supporter of Roosevelt. Besides serving on the Senate Agriculture Committee, he was also named to the important Banking and Currency Committee. The southern position was further strengthened in 1931 when Edward A. O'Neal, a northern Alabama planter, was elected president of the American Farm Bureau Federation, the nation's most powerful farm organization. O'Neal had worked actively and successfully to build a political coalition between southern cotton interests and midwestern corn and wheat producers in the 1920s. He knew his way around Washington and commanded great respect in the House and Senate.[15]

It was in an atmosphere of national crisis that the 73d Congress began wrestling with problems of bank failures, unemployment, business closings, agricultural depression, and other problems. Doing something for farmers had a high priority in Congress, partly at least because of the widespread belief stated in the Agricultural Adjustment Act that "a severe and increasing disparity between the prices of agricultural and other commodities" had seriously destroyed "the purchasing power of farmers for industrial products." In short, depression and lack of purchasing power by farmers had brought hard times to the entire economy. Many responsible officials believed that if farm income could be improved, general economic recovery would follow.[16]

Officials in the USDA, now headed by Secretary Henry A. Wallace of Iowa, quickly prepared a far-reaching farm relief bill. It whizzed through Congress and became law on May 12. The Agricultural Adjustment Act sought to get parity prices for basic farm commodities by reducing production and bringing supply and demand into better balance. Parity in this case meant raising prices to a point where farm products would have the same purchasing power they had had in the years 1909-1914, a period when agricultural commodities presumably had a fair exchange value with nonfarm goods. In order to encourage farmers to reduce their output, the law permitted direct government payments to farmers who reduced their acreage. These were known as rental or benefit payments. Farmers, it was thought, would profit in two ways. Reduced production would cut surpluses and encourage higher market prices, and in return for keeping part of their land idle farmers would get a cash payment directly from the federal government. Funds to pay farmers for taking land out of production were to come from special taxes on the processors of certain agricultural products.

In the 1920s the McNary-Haugenites had suggested that surplus farm commodities should be dumped abroad. But framers of the AAA argued that large surpluses should not be produced in the first place.

The world economy was in such a depressed state that foreigners could not absorb, even at low prices, enough of America's agricultural production to remove the price-depressing surpluses found in major crops such as cotton and wheat. Therefore, production must be adjusted to the domestic market and to what export markets could be found.

The law's benefits were initially extended only to seven basic commodities on the theory that if the prices of major commodities were raised, others would follow along in the upward surge. Three of these basic commodities—cotton, tobacco, and rice—were among the South's major commercial crops. While many officials did not consider tobacco a basic commodity, it was included in the bill because of strong political pressure from tobacco-state congressmen. Tobacco representatives also won an unusual concession for their constituents. They were successful in getting the years 1919-1929 as the base from which to calculate parity prices, rather than 1909-1914, used as the base period for other crops. This raised the parity price for tobacco by some 60 percent over what it would have been if the earlier base period had been used. Representatives from the South's peanut districts made a strong effort to have peanuts added to the list of basic crops, but their initial efforts failed.[17]

By the time the AAA became law in the spring of 1933, southern farmers had already planted their cotton, tobacco, and rice. The prospects for cotton prices looked especially bleak, since growers had planted nearly 40.1 million acres. Despite the fact that at planting time cotton prices hovered at around 5 cents a pound, this acreage was an increase over the 36 million acres harvested in 1932. Agricultural observers were forecasting a huge crop. To make matters worse, the carryover in the United States from 1932 was between 12 and 13 million bales, three or four times the usual amount. Low prices and huge supplies simply had not deterred cotton growers from planting an excessive acreage. As officials in the USDA explained the situation: "Growers felt driven, despite the disastrously low price of their staple crop, to increase the acreage devoted to it. They had no other cash crops to which they could profitably turn, and necessity to grow something for revenue was compelling."[18]

How could cotton farmers be paid for producing less when crops were already in the ground? The idea of plowing up cotton had been suggested by the Federal Farm Board in 1931, but then it had not been considered a practical or rational approach to solving the cotton surplus problem. By the spring of 1933, however, farmers were so desperate and the need to get money into the rural communities so essential that the irrationality of destroying growing cotton took on a sudden rationality. Secretary Wallace wrote that "to have to destroy a growing crop is a shocking commentary on our civilization. I could tolerate it only as a cleaning up of the wreckage from the old days of unbalanced production."[19]

Under the best of circumstances it would be a formidable task to persuade approximately 1 million farmers that they should sign contracts to plow up a part of their cotton. But officials were up to the challenge. Working through the agricultural extension services, especially the county agents, and local committees, officials organized a publicity campaign throughout the cotton belt urging farmers to sign contracts reducing acreage from 25 to 50 percent in exchange for cash benefit payments. There was strong pressure on farmers who hesitated or refused to sign. Farmers were to receive from $7 to $20 for each acre plowed under, depending on their estimated yield. They also had the choice of taking a smaller cash payment plus an option on the amount of cotton destroyed at 6 cents a pound. It was believed that prices would rise and farmers would make a profit on their option cotton which had accumulated under the Federal Farm Board program. Farmers had until July 12 to sign an acreage reduction contract.

Following the sign-up program, the next step was for farmers to return to the field and plow up a portion of their growing crop. This occurred in late June and July. It was said that where single-mule plows were used, farmers had a difficult time getting the animals to walk on the row. A *New York Times* editor wrote that mules were being punished "for refusing to trample down the stalks" which they had been "taught to revere."[20]

Destruction of even part of a growing crop brought cries of disbelief and opposition from many quarters. Just before the AAA passed Congress, W.L. Clayton of Anderson, Clayton, and Company, a major cotton broker of Houston, Texas, wrote that he was "decidedly against" the idea of destroying growing cotton. "Public opinion in this country," he wrote, "will always be overwhelmingly opposed to the destruction of surpluses of non-perishable raw materials for food and clothing, whether before or after harvest, for the purpose of raising the price of the remainder."[21] Consumers who feared higher prices, some political conservatives, businessmen, and even ministers who believed that to destroy a maturing crop was contrary to God's will, denounced the action. But, as one observer wrote, "as between the future prospect of hell fire and hell-on-earth of another year of 5-cent cotton, the farmer cheerfully risked his salvation." In Greene County, Georgia, one tenant remarked when told to destroy his cotton: "You know, I ain't never pulled up no cotton stalks befo', and somehow I don't like the idea," to which a friend added, "I been feelin' sorter funeral-like all afternoon." Another farmer said to his neighbor: "Let's swap work that day; you plow up mine, and I'll plow up yours."[22] By late July the freshly turned earth on farm after farm indicated that the plow-up had been successful.

Finally, officials had to make certain that farmers had complied with their acreage reduction contracts. Each cotton field was checked to confirm that the proper amount of each producer's crop had been plowed under. When the "performance and certification" form had been approved in Washington, payment could be made. By summer's end in 1933, the AAA had approved 1,032,000 contracts which removed 10,497,000 acres of cotton from production. Farmers received $116 million in benefit payments, plus additional millions in profit on their cotton options. By fall, government checks were being delivered to hundreds of thousands of rural mailboxes. Moreover, the price of cotton rose to about 10 cents a pound, nearly double what it had been in 1932. Total cash receipts from cotton in the 1933-1934 marketing year reached $896 million, nearly twice the figure received a year earlier. About 20 percent of that came from the government. The program of sign up, plow up, check up, and pay up seemed to be a solid success. In any event, nothing like it had ever happened before in American history. Writing under the title "King Cotton's New Adventure," Charles McD. Puckette of Greenville, South Carolina, declared that it was the "most gigantic agricultural mass movement ever undertaken" among farmers.[23]

While tobacco was included as a basic crop in the AAA, bringing relief to producers was complicated by the production of different kinds of tobacco. Furthermore, many tobacco growers had reduced their acreage voluntarily in 1932 under the influence of low prices, making it more difficult in 1933 to approach the tobacco problem only from the viewpoint of acreage restriction. Some contracts to cut acreage were made, but the main help extended to large numbers of flue-cured and burley producers was through marketing agreements in return for promises to reduce future plantings.

By the summer of 1933 a much larger tobacco crop than had been anticipated was nearly ready for harvest. Prices softened in early August, about the time Georgia and South Carolina producers began to sell. They complained bitterly over the declining market. When eastern North Carolina markets opened on August 29 at even lower figures, producers in that state expressed such outrage that the markets were closed in response to pleas by the governors of North Carolina and South Carolina. Over the next few weeks, AAA officials worked out an agreement with the tobacco companies which resulted in a promise to pay an average price of about 17 cents a pound for flue-cured tobacco. As a part of the agreement, however, farmers had to sign contracts which called for reducing their acreage by not more than 30 percent in 1934 and 1935. Similar agreements were made between the companies and farmers in the burley tobacco areas of Kentucky and Tennessee. As a result of the various programs and agreements, growers received about twice as much money from their tobacco as they had in 1932.[24]

Rice farmers in Arkansas, Louisiana, and Texas had suffered from extremely low prices as a result of surplus production. Agricultural Adjustment Administration officials negotiated marketing agreements in 1933 to raise prices and to bring supply and demand into better balance. Early in 1935 Congress provided for benefit payments and acreage restriction to stabilize the production and incomes of rice growers.[25]

In addition to providing cash benefit payments for cooperating cotton producers, the federal government established the Commodity Credit Corporation in October 1933 to provide price supports. This agency was authorized initially to advance or guarantee nonrecourse loans to farmers on cotton and corn, and later on many other crops. Borrowing from the CCC was highly attractive to farmers. If the price of cotton, for instance, advanced above the loan level, a producer could sell his cotton and take the profit; if it dropped below the loan figure he could forfeit the crop and let the government absorb the loss. On September 18, 1933, some 200 cotton farmers and their spokesmen met in Washington and asked President Roosevelt to guarantee 20 cents a pound for 1933 cotton. After some deliberation, the president announced that the government would lend 10 cents a pound, which was slightly above the going market price. It was subsequent loans by the CCC which stabilized cotton prices for the 1933-1934 crop year. The president insisted, however, that price supports of this kind must be tied to acreage restriction in 1934 and 1935.[26]

A problem that quickly confronted agricultural planners was how to deny benefits of the production control program to farmers who refused to reduce their acreage. While noncooperators could not receive cash benefits or get loans from the CCC, government actions did hold prices up and permit nonsigners to produce as much as they pleased and enjoy the higher price. It seemed unfair that farmers outside the program should benefit. By late 1933 there were strong moves to substitute compulsory for voluntary control.

In the cotton belt, demand for compulsory controls came from the grassroots. The legislative leader of the action was Senator Bankhead of Alabama. In April 1934, Congress passed the Bankhead Cotton Control Act, which provided for limiting the amount of cotton a farmer could market without suffering a stiff penalty. Each cotton farmer was to be given a sales quota based on his production history over recent years, and he received enough tax-exempt certificates to cover that amount. If he marketed more than his quota, he would be taxed enough to make such sales unprofitable. The taxing power used to keep production down, and price support loans from the Commodity Credit Corporation, were the means to bring all cotton farmers into the program. Taxes on excessive marketings also discouraged farmers from improving their production on the fewer acres by applying more fertilizer and utilizing better farming practices. Also in 1934 Congress passed the Kerr-Smith Tobacco Marketing Control Act. This law sought to force farmers to produce only within certain marketing allotments by taxing them on any sales in excess of their quotas. In December 1934, cotton and tobacco farmers voted overwhelmingly to continue the restrictive programs another year.[27]

From the beginning of the New Deal farm relief program, there was political pressure to add other crops to the basic list so they could qualify for special government benefits. In April 1934, peanuts, a southern crop of growing commercial importance, was added to the group of basic commodities. The next month sugarcane was included. In return for cutting acreage, peanut growers received benefit payments of $8 per ton, plus some land diversion payments, in 1934. About four-fifths of the peanut farmers contracted to reduce acreage in 1935. As a result of higher prices and greater production, income to peanut growers in 1935 was about equal to that of 1928. Sugarcane growers were given tonnage allotments in 1934 in return for reducing acreage, then they received benefit and other payments. The income of Louisiana sugarcane producers advanced considerably under the program.[28]

By 1934 federal agricultural programs were funneling help to more than a million southern farmers. Besides higher cotton prices, cash benefit payments from the AAA totaled $296 million during the first two years of the New Deal. But even this improvement brought income from cotton in 1934 only up to 45 percent of what it had been in 1929. Returns from tobacco under the marketing agreements were more than twice as much in 1934 as they had been at the depths of the Depression in 1932. Sugarcane growers received $8.9 million in government payments by 1934. After two years of AAA and related programs, gross income from farm production in the ten southern states (omitting Florida) had risen from $1.1 to $1.9 billion, an advance of about $800 million.[29]

Tobacco growers in North Carolina showed the best gains as that state's farmers more than doubled their farm production income between 1932 and 1934. By late 1934 tobacco growers were actually enjoying a little prosperity, which was felt in the business communities as well as on the farms. One farmer reported that in 1933 five acres of flue-cured tobacco had brought him only $480; in 1934, even after he reduced his acreage, he realized $1,472 for his crop. Late in 1934 the

Kinston *Daily Free Press* reported general prosperity throughout the
region because of much better tobacco prices. Least gains were made
among Florida farmers, who had only a small amount of production
that qualified for benefit payments or price supports under the CCC.[30]

Acreage restrictions, marketing agreements, and price supports
did not exhaust the assistance to farmers provided by the early New
Deal. The Farm Credit Administration reorganized the farm credit
agencies of the federal government and supplied additional credit for
long-term loans, for cooperatives, and for production expenses. By the
end of 1934 the Federal Land Banks and the Land Bank commissioner
had extended around $574 million of mortgage credit to about 290,000
farmers in the ten southern states from North Carolina to Texas. Nearly
80 percent of this money was used to refinance existing farm mortgages
at lower interest rates. The formation of more than 200 Production
Credit Associations throughout the South provided additional sources
of operating funds. The federal government also advanced about $58
million to some 735,000 southern farmers in emergency crop and feed
loans in 1933 and 1934. Credit provided by various agencies of the Farm
Credit Administration was most helpful to farmers and planters who
could provide some type of security and who had the prospect of
economic success on the farm.[31]

Congress also established the Soil Erosion Service in 1933, later
named the Soil Conservation Service, which offered assistance to farmers trying to rebuild their soil fertility. One of the great problems on
thousands of southern farms was poor productivity resulting from soil
erosion, soil depletion, and generally poor farming practices.

Despite noticeable income improvement in some parts of the South
during 1933 and 1934, the amount was insufficient to have much effect
on the standard of living of most farmers. Moreover, the increase was
unequally distributed, going mainly to landowners and cash or share
tenants. Poor tenants and sharecroppers continued in the most dire
economic straits. In a survey of sharecroppers and tenants on 646
plantations in the Southeast, it was found that in 1934 sharecropper
families had an average net cash income of $122 per family, or $28 for
each individual per year; for other share tenants it was $44 a year per
capita. In some areas of the South cash income to people on farms
dropped to as low as $10 to $20 a year.[32]

Untold numbers of farmers and their families eked out an existence
in their constantly deteriorating, weather-beaten, and leaky shacks,
eating mainly fat meat, cornmeal, and molasses—the three M's—and
wearing patched and ragged clothes. Black farmers suffered most, but
poverty gnawed ever deeper into the lives of many white producers as
well. Renwick C. Kennedy of Camden, Alabama, who had lived in the
South all his life, wrote early in 1934 that he had "never seen poverty so

desperate among tenant farmers, white and Negro, as during the last twelve months." Continuing, he wrote: "Homes without a match or a cake of soap, men too weak from hunger to work, naked children, people taking their meals from blackberry bushes and plum thickets, tattered cotton rags for winter clothing."[33] Lethargic because of dietary diseases and ground down by current and future hopelessness, millions of southern farm people did not have a living but a mere subsistence. One contemporary observer referred to conditions as "approaching the level of bare animal existence." For these poverty-stricken rural people there was little or nothing new about the New Deal.[34]

At the depth of the hard times after 1931, many planters and smaller landlords were simply unable to provide credit or "furnish" to their sharecroppers or tenants as they had in the past. Consequently, the amount of cash or credit advanced was reduced to only five or six months a year, or in a growing number of cases tenants were displaced altogether. A study of conditions in three North Carolina cotton and tobacco counties showed that 154 tenants were displaced in 1931 and 181 in 1932. This same survey revealed that of 753 tenants, most of whom were displaced between 1930 and 1934, some 157 lost their farms because the landlord could no longer afford to finance them. Thousands of tenants were thus set adrift during the Depression well before passage of the AAA and the acreage restriction program.[35]

The foreclosure of farm mortgages by banks and insurance companies left many independent farmers nearly as badly off as their former tenants. During the period after 1930 farm foreclosures rose dramatically. When new corporate owners took over, they tended to rent only to farmers who could somehow finance a crop, and many former sharecroppers fell to the position of day laborers who had work only during the busy seasons. This was more economical for the landlord, who had wage payments only during the period of actual employment.[36] In a survey of the eastern cotton belt it was found that between 1930 and 1935 the number of farm wage-earner families increased 19.5 percent, while the number of sharecropper families grew by only 1.4 percent. In the Upper Piedmont the number of sharecroppers actually declined by 12 percent, while wage hand families increased 38 percent.

Many farm families had to turn to relief, at least during part of the year, in order to survive. In October 1933 a little over 12 percent of the farm families in the eastern cotton belt were getting some kind of relief. The figure was 16.5 percent in the Appalachia-Ozark region.[37] Many of these relief recipients were people who had been shifted out of tenancy to casual employment. Help usually came only intermittently, depending on the funding of federal programs, such as the Federal Emergency

Relief Administration, or the need for local labor. Some landlords helped their sharecroppers and tenants get on relief rolls in order to avoid the responsibility of supporting them throughout the year. In effect the landowners shifted part of the cost of producing a crop to the relief agencies. But not all landlords or political leaders wanted the labor force, especially blacks, to receive relief. Federal relief was threatening to employers because it was an open challenge to the terribly low wage scales in agriculture. In a study of 809 Alabama planters, surveyors found that 40 percent of them opposed giving federal relief to sharecroppers and tenants. Landlords feared that such payments might increase the independence of their workers.[38] Governor Eugene Talmadge of Georgia declared late in 1933 that direct and work relief for Negro tenants was "utterly ruining" that "type of farmer." Such workers, Talmadge said, would not "toil ten, twelve or fourteen hours a day in the field" if they could get three times what they could earn "either working for the government or merely drawing relief funds and relief goods." Governed by that thinking, many southern community relief offices were closed during cotton picking season in order to force workers into the field.[39]

While all relief payments were small, black farm families received considerably less than their white neighbors. The prevailing attitude throughout the South held that blacks could live on less than whites, and, as one authority wrote, "the cast system makes equal relief grants psychologically impossible in many parts of the South." Thus blacks usually had to be in considerably worse circumstances than whites before they could even get on the relief rolls. In June 1935 rural white sharecropper families on relief in the eastern cotton belt received an average of $10.49 a month while blacks got only $8.69. For all rural families in the open country, the difference was larger, with white recipients getting an average of $12 a month and blacks only $8. When work relief was provided by the Civil Works Administration between November 1933 and April 1934, white families averaged $130.80 for the period compared to only $70.00 for black workers.[40]

Under the impact of shrinking agricultural income, rural institutions suffered heavily during the Great Depression. Money-starved schools were hit especially hard. The increasing farm population and declining income left many school districts strapped for funds. In 1930 the southern farm population had 17.2 percent of the school age children but only 3.4 percent of the national income. And things got worse as the Depression deepened.[41] The commissioner of education in Georgia wrote in 1932 that "the majority of our 2,595 one-teacher schools for Negroes are housed in dwellings, lodges, churches, and log cabins that are terrible beyond description in regard to structure, equipment, light and sanitation."[42] Most of the children had no textbooks and many teachers had only a seventh-grade education.

But poor educational facilities were not confined to destitute black families. A study in the mid-1930s of ten school districts in Pickens County in Western South Carolina showed that white farm children were denied a decent education as well. The region surveyed consisted of 827 white families of whom 376 were farm owners and 451 were tenants. According to the researchers, only one of the eleven elementary schools could be "classed as satisfactory." The buildings were badly lighted, filled with "old and badly used double desks," some of which were falling apart, and there was no "teaching or instructional material" in any of the schools. Daily absenteeism averaged 33 percent among children from tenant homes, who attended only an average of 107 days per year. The two main causes for keeping pupils out of school were the need for them to work on the farm, and illness and poor health. Some parents reported not sending their children to school because they did not have proper clothing or textbooks.

Many pupils were also undernourished, reflecting the emphasis upon cash crops. Some 75 percent of the tenant families in the South Carolina study did not produce enough milk or butter for home use, and 23 percent of those families had no cow, hog, or garden. As one housewife said: "We eat whatever we can scrape up." Families who did raise a few chickens and produce some eggs often sold them to get a little cash. This was not unlike many midwestern farmers who lived mainly on egg and cream checks during the Depression. Most of the children from white tenant families dropped out of school before finishing the seventh grade. Since the proportion of youth was high in the community—125 people under twenty-one as compared to 100 over that age—the area was becoming increasingly populated with young, poor, uneducated persons. Indeed, this situation was true throughout much of the South.[43]

Other studies showed that the better educated young people and those from families with higher incomes were more likely to leave. As Carl F. Reuss put it after studying Richmond County, Virginia, the "lower class" was increasing, while the county's "better population" was leaving. This situation was bound to have an adverse effect on community social institutions. Wilson Gee, an authority in agricultural economics, studied population trends in Santuc Township of Union County in northwestern South Carolina in 1933. He reported that in the years before 1930 migration had caused "a severe depletion" of the "upper class." If not somehow checked, he wrote, the "large loss of the leading stock of the community would lower the level of rural life." He believed that the depletion of the upper class had already damaged the community's cultural development. Poorer whites and blacks were also leaving.[44]

Rural health, always bad throughout much of the rural South, grew worse during the Depression. In most southern farm communities there were few if any public health services to help retard the spread of communicable diseases, and many farm families had no access to a doctor. Of seventy-three farm families studied in Lee County, South Carolina, in 1929 and 1930, forty-four had bad health, particularly pellagra. There was an especially high incidence of this disease among women, "usually mothers of families." Landowners and tenants alike suffered from the difficulty. In the coastal area of South Carolina, as well as elsewhere, malaria and hookworm were also common maladies.[45]

It was clear enough by 1935 that two years of New Deal efforts had not touched the basic problems facing so many southern farm families. It was true that thousands had been helped temporarily by the direct and work relief programs. Others had received cash benefit payments flowing from Washington. But most sharecropper and tenant families found that nothing much had changed as they struggled to make a living from the land. If anything, their condition was becoming worse and their future was hopeless. Photographs taken by Eudora Welty in Mississippi, and those taken by Dorothea Lange throughout several parts of the old cotton belt, revealed gaunt, poverty-ridden, and desperate people somehow contending with their stark deprivation.[46]

Many of these farm families were only faintly aware of the economic and technological developments which were in the process of changing the demand for agricultural labor so drastically that many of them would become superfluous. The implementation of acreage restriction, benefit payments, credit help, aid for soil conservation, and growing farm mechanization were about to converge in a way that would revolutionize the Cotton South. These developments, as will be seen later, were intimately related. As the modernization of southern agriculture began to emerge in the 1930s, its initial impact on the surplus farm population was devastating. The "Cry from the Cotton," as one writer entitled his book dealing with dispossessed sharecroppers in the 1930s, was loud and pathetic.[47]

7

Crisis, Frustration, and Change in the Late 1930s

It soon became evident that farmers who had larger land holdings and substantial production would be the principal beneficiaries of the New Deal agricultural legislation. Any program that tied benefits to acres of land taken out of cultivation and price supports on production would inevitably be most helpful to those who possessed property. Payments for acreage reduction could mean little to those farmers with 15 to 30 acres who produced only a few bales of cotton. If a producer had 20 acres of cotton and plowed up 5 acres in 1933, he would receive as little as $35 or as much as $100 from AAA payments, depending on his production. A sharecropper or tenant was to get the same proportion of the payment as he did of the harvested crop, which was customarily one-half or one-third. In this illustration, a sharecropper would get somewhere between $17.50 and $50 in acreage reduction payments, plus perhaps a few dollars more from his option cotton. Small operators in the South could expect little from Uncle Sam.

On the other hand, owners and operators of larger farms and huge plantations would be eligible for hundreds or even thousands of federal dollars. A cash tenant with 30 acres of cotton who plowed up 10 acres could receive as much as $110 if his earlier production had averaged from 150 to 174 pounds per acre. A 1934 study of 645 plantations with five or more tenant or labor resident families, including the owner, reported an average AAA payment of $822.[1] But some landlords and planters received huge payments from the government.

In April 1936 the Senate passed a resolution directing the secretary of agriculture to report on all producers who had been paid $10,000 or more under the AAA programs. Of the cotton farmers in 1933, 307 landholders contracted with the AAA to remove 182,792 acres from production and received $4,671,949 in cash benefit and cotton option payments. This was an average for large producers of about $15,500 each. In 1934 and 1935 there were 160 and 186 cotton planters respectively who were beneficiaries of payments of $10,000 or more. Some corporations received very large amounts. The Delta and Pine Land Company of Washington County, Mississippi, was paid $114,840 for 1933 crop reductions, while the Banks and Danner Company of Crittenden County, Arkansas, received $80,000. Such large payments, however, were quite unusual. Most of those getting $10,000 or more from the federal government commonly received between $10,000 and $20,000. These large recipients got 2.6 percent of the total payments made to cotton growers in 1933. Part of the payments to big landowners presumably went to the sharecroppers and tenants, reducing somewhat the total going to owners.[2]

While cotton growers received most of the large government payments, a few producers of other basic crops in the South also received cash benefits exceeding $10,000. In 1935, 42 rice planters in Arkansas, Louisiana, and Texas shared $960,522 in government payments. The Louisiana Irrigation and Mill Company, with land spread over two counties, was paid $73,659 for adjusting production. There were 102 Louisiana sugarcane producers who received more than $10,000 each in 1934. On the other hand, only 4 out of 112,801 flue-cured tobacco growers received such large payments that year, and in 1935 none of the 88,000 commercial peanut farmers were in that category. As would be expected under the program, where land was concentrated in the hands of large individual owners and corporations the number of operators receiving huge payments was highest.[3]

The question arose almost immediately as to why a cap was not placed on the amount of direct payment any farmer could receive. Why were the benefits not tailored or programmed specifically to the ordinary family farmer about which there was so much oratorical concern? Policymakers in Washington did consider the idea of a maximum payment. However, the basic objective of the AAA was to reduce surpluses and to raise prices. Unless the big landowners were permitted to get their proportionate share of the cash benefits, they would not likely join the reduction program. If this important group did not sign up, surpluses could not be controlled. At least, that was the argument advanced by those who opposed placing a lid on payments. Cooperation of the large operators was considered absolutely essential to the success of production control and higher prices for all farmers. Moreover, the larger farmers had greater political influence.

A much more important problem emerged in connection with the distribution of benefits to landlords and tenants. Cash benefits from the plow-up in 1933 were to be divided between landowner and tenant on the basis of how the crop had customarily been distributed. If a sharecropper received half of the crop, he was supposed to get half of the payment from the acreage he removed from production. Except for certain classes of cash and share tenants, however, contracts were made with landlords who were entrusted to give the tenant his share. Agricultural Adjustment Administration officials adopted this policy for at least two reasons. To have made contracts with every sharecropper and poor tenant would have greatly increased the administrative load. But more important was the opposition of landlords, particularly in plantation areas. For the federal government to operate between the landlords and sharecroppers and poorer tenants would threaten the traditional condition of sharecropper dependence. Such a development, landlords claimed, would increase worker independence and weaken the planters' hold over their labor supply. Landlords opposed anything that would disturb the historic relationship between owner and worker, and that would free the labor supply from the local "furnish" and credit system. As one contemporary wrote, "The economic aspects of the situation are decidedly complex but the human relations are even more so."[4]

When the first government checks were distributed in the fall of 1933, thousands of sharecroppers received little or nothing. In many cases landlords just applied the sharecropper's part of the payment to his debts. The payments were a god-send to landlords who had extended credit for supplies, but sharecroppers often realized nothing. "In 1933 we plowed up our cotton," said a group of Alabama sharecroppers, "and on many plantations we received no benefit whatever for this. When payments were allowed us—we were forced to allow it to be applied on our accounts." The government program put money into the pockets of the landlords and even reduced cropper obligations, but all too often it had no effect on improving the life of poor sharecroppers or share tenants. Complaints or appeals by sharecroppers who believed they had been cheated scarcely ever brought any change. The local committees that administered the AAA program usually consisted of larger landowners who had little sympathy with croppers or lower-class tenants. Under these conditions, by 1934 there was widespread criticism by social reformers, by some government officials, as well as by sharecroppers, of the AAA and its policy of distributing benefits in the South. The authors of the book *The Collapse of Cotton Tenancy* wrote: "It is but the blunt truth to say that under the present system the landowner is more and more protected from risk by government activity, while the tenant is left open to risks on every side."[5]

Assuming that individuals act on the basis of self-interest in a private enterprise system, it is not surprising that the landlords tried to maximize their income under the AAA. Not only did they manage to obtain more than their fair share of government payments, they were quick to see that by reducing acreage they did not need so many sharecroppers. If they could rid themselves of surplus croppers, they would receive *all* of the land diversion payments. From the planters' viewpoint, it made economic sense to reduce the number of sharecroppers and employ day labor during periods of peak labor demand. By turning to wage labor, planters could cut the cost of having to support croppers throughout the year. What the workers would do to support themselves and their families when agricultural work was unavailable did not concern most big farmers, especially corporate operators. While many landowners sympathized with the plight of their sharecroppers, turning a profit usually had priority over social responsibility to their farm workers. Family farmers who only had three or four sharecroppers were much more likely to be fair and helpful in dealing with their tenants. But on the large plantations, when labor was not needed in the fields, former sharecroppers would have to seek odd jobs in the rural community or nearby town, or perhaps get on federal relief. Throughout the winter of 1933-1934 an increasing number of sharecroppers and tenants were forced off the farms, mainly in the cotton regions.[6] The future for landless sharecroppers and tenants became even grimmer as the federal programs became a fixed part of American agriculture.

Administrators in the AAA made some half-hearted efforts to keep sharecroppers and tenants from being shoved off the land and to see that benefit payments were divided fairly, but the agency's timid action failed completely. Moreover, there was really little they could do under the law as it was officially interpreted. The 1934 cotton reduction contracts required producers, "insofar as possible," to maintain the same number of tenants on their farms. But there was no real attempt to enforce a provision which was full of loopholes. Furthermore, it was difficult to determine whether a landlord dismissed a tenant because of the acreage reduction program or for some other reason.

So far as assuring that sharecroppers and tenants would receive their fair share of cash payments, AAA officials were either unable or unwilling to challenge the traditional relationships between landlord and tenant. And, as Theodore Saloutos emphasized, "even if these payments had been shared fairly, sharecroppers and tenants would not have experienced significant economic progress." In 1938 nearly half the farmers received less than $40 a year in benefit payments. A larger share of the payments would have given these farmers a little more money for consumer goods, but "it would not have helped their basic position or given them capital to become successful farmers." So, as Saloutos concluded, "there was little in the program, fraud or no fraud on the part of landlords, that would have encouraged poorer farmers to remain on the land if they had alternatives to farming."[7] In any event, partly as a result of acreage restriction and the shifting of sharecroppers to wage labor, the number of sharecroppers in the South declined sharply after 1933.

By 1935, after three years of the AAA, it was clear that the program was run by and for landowners and better-off commercial farmers. This continued to be the case after the AAA was declared unconstitutional in 1936 and Congress passed the Soil Conservation and Domestic Allotment Act. The benefits were programmed to go to farmers with acreage and production; others would have to look elsewhere for help.

What were the practical alternatives for poor southern farmers? What prospects were there for small, largely self-sufficient farmers in the southern Appalachians, the displaced black and white sharecroppers, and thousands of small producers who had neither the land nor the capital to establish a successful commercial farm? The best opportunity open to many sharecroppers was part-time wage labor coupled with some federal relief. Industry had little to offer at a time when more than 8 million people were unemployed. The southern Appalachian farmers continued to eke out an existence on their small, largely self-sufficient acreages, and supplemented their poverty with direct or work relief. Some of the poorest farmers moved to submarginal lands and tried to scratch out a living. But everywhere one looked the prospects for large numbers of farm people in the South were grim.

What made the situation doubly discouraging was that answers to the condition of farm poverty could not be found within the agricultural sector. To really solve the problem of rural poverty required reducing the number of people in the South who depended on agriculture for a living. What was needed was to establish a better balance between farm population and agricultural resources. This problem went back at least two generations in the South, but the Great Depression had intensified the imbalance between land and people. In the past, industry had drawn off millions of surplus agricultural workers nationwide, but off-farm employment dried up in the 1930s and reduced the out-migration flow to a mere trickle. The result was excessive unemployment and underemployment in agriculture. Secretary of Agriculture Wallace explained to Mrs. Roosevelt in 1939 that without more nonfarm jobs or new lands to settle, there was a "damming up on the farms of millions of people who normally would have been taken care of elsewhere." The surplus farm population, he wrote, could "not hope to find a place on the land." The secretary saw the solution not "in making more farms and more farmers, but in making more city employment."[8] While Wallace was describing the national situation, conditions in the South were doubly bad.

Nevertheless, New Deal officials did make some modest efforts to help poor farmers and unemployed urban families who might wish to return to the land. An amendment to the National Industrial Recovery Act of 1933 provided $25 million to aid "in the redistribution of the overbalance of population in industrial centers."[9] The president established a Division of Subsistence Homesteads, which funded the purchase of small farms, usually not more than 5 or 10 acres, near towns where subsistence farmers might supplement their farm production with off-farm employment. These projects had a spotty record. While some participants improved their situations, in general subsistence farms provided no lasting benefit to either poor farmers or unemployed city people.

The Federal Emergency Relief Administration also developed a program early in 1934 to rehabilitate some of the poorest farmers. The Rural Rehabilitation Division within FERA directed state relief administrators to find unused land and relocate landless farmers on small acreages. The FERA provided credit for living and operating expenses. In effect the agency took over the furnishing function of landlords and also arranged for close supervision of the clients. These were to be strictly subsistence operations. The newly financed farmers were not to grow commercial crops because this would add to surpluses and defeat the objectives of the AAA.[10]

Once a farmer qualified for a FERA rehabilitation loan, he could borrow small sums for food, clothing, fuel, tools, and work animals. The average credit extended to clients in Alabama in the spring of 1934 was $94.11. Not many loans were made to the poorest farmers. Supervisors of the program tended to approve the best risks, and most of those receiving help had been small landowners or better-off tenants. As one investigator wrote: "Those families who were presumably in a better financial situation . . . were more often taken on the . . . program than were croppers and farm laborers."[11]

Secretary Wallace, most state agricultural officials, and relief administrators were not enthusiastic about locating people on subsistence farms. Unless such a farmer could find off-farm employment or produce a commercial crop, there would be no way ever to acquire cash to purchase a farm. Subsistence farming was only another way of committing those farmers to permanent want and poverty in a commercial and industrial society. In any event, by February 1935 FERA had made rehabilitation loans to 87,350 families of whom about 93 percent were in the South.

As the New Deal nibbled around the edge of the problem of southern rural poverty, it became increasingly clear that something more drastic must be done if the needs of poor, landless farmers were to be met. Scholars and agricultural administrators alike were saying that the old system of tenancy and sharecropping was collapsing. What was needed, they said, was a federal program to encourage small farm ownership. Frank Tannenbaum, a well known historian of Latin American peasantry, was among those who recommended that the national government acquire land and sell it to poor farmers on credit. After viewing the South's tenancy system, he remarked: "The system is over. It's gone. It's collapsed. . . . The New Deal will have to do something about it."[12] He also believed that the government should provide capital for livestock and equipment and, initially, even money for living expenses. Furthermore, Tannenbaum and others insisted that this type of borrower be given close managerial supervision. The advancing of credit for land and operations, he believed, would put many of the poorer farmers on the road to ownership and reverse the trend of more and more farmers becoming landless.[13] Not only did this seem to be a humanitarian approach to the problems facing small farmers; it also supported the strong family farm tradition. In the minds of an increasing number of economic planners, small farm ownership had become a major goal by the mid-1930s.

The formation of the Southern Tenant Farmers' Union in Arkansas in July 1934 emphasized the need to do something more for poor, landless tenants. Organized by H.L. Mitchell, a former sharecropper and operator of a small cleaning business in Tyronza, Arkansas, and Henry Clay East, another Tyronza resident, the STFU sought to organize sharecroppers for protection against landlords. The union resisted sharecropper evictions, AAA contract violations, and general tenant mistreatment. The idea of an organization among the share-croppers, especially an interracial union, aroused strong opposition among planters and local law enforcement officials. In late 1934 and early 1935 union members were threatened, beaten, and arrested. These violent activities were soon receiving national publicity and bringing embarrassment to the AAA. Through newspaper and magazine accounts, many Americans for the first time gained some insight into the plight of the poorest of southern farmers. After traveling throughout the South, Hugh R. Fraser, a writer for the Scripps-Howard newspaper chain, wrote in February 1935 that he had seen "thousands" of sharecroppers "along the highways and byways of Dixie . . . lonely figures without money, without homes, and without hope."[14]

After much discussion of what might be done to help the most needy farmers, on May 1, 1935, President Roosevelt by executive action established the Resettlement Administration. Funded from the Federal Emergency Relief Act of 1935, the RA was to buy land, resell it to small farmers, provide operating credit, and start landless families on the road to farm ownership. The agency also set up some model cooperative communities, organized purchasing and marketing cooperatives, built houses and other buildings, and engaged in a number of other activities designed to help poor, landless farmers. The RA also took

over the rural rehabilitation programs of the FERA, and by June 1936 it
was helping about 536,300 client farm families with small loans and
grants, most of them in the South.[15]

While the Resettlement Administration provided a fresh start for
some southern farmers, most aspects of the program failed. The agency found that often farmers did not want to leave their eroded acres and
be resettled elsewhere, many lacked the cooperative spirit required in
some projects, while others rejected the close supervision by RA
agents. There was also political opposition to the RA. Congressmen
and senators complained that the agency lacked legislative authority to
engage in certain activities, and believed some features of the program
were radical, collectivist, and even un-American. There was especially
sharp criticism of the cooperative and community-type projects. Hoping to reduce some of the controversy, on December 31, 1936, the
president transferred the RA's programs to the USDA.[16]

Meanwhile, Senator Bankhead of Alabama was pushing a bill in
Congress that would provide legislative authority and direct federal
appropriations to help disadvantaged farmers. When it became evident that lawmakers in Washington would not pass the Bankhead
measure in 1936, President Roosevelt in November appointed a special
committee to study the problem of farm tenancy and to recommend a
program to help landless farmers. In February 1937 the President's
Committee on Tenancy issued a report describing conditions and
including suggestions for congressional action. The committee said
that "farm-home ownership has been approved throughout American
history as a primary means of attaining security." But, the committee
added, in recent years movement on the agricultural ladder had been
"from rung to rung" downward. Indeed, the rungs of the ladder had
"become bars—forcing imprisonment in a fixed social status which it is
increasingly difficult to escape."[17]

To change the situation, the committee recommended long-term
government loans to help tenants buy land and to protect those who
owned farms against loss to creditors. Recipients of federal credit
should be selected on the basis of "reputation for integrity, industry,
thrift, necessary experience, health, and other qualities." The aim was
to establish more family-size farms. The committee also urged the
formation of marketing and purchasing cooperatives, the cooperative
ownership of machinery and equipment, aid to part-time farmers, and
the retirement of submarginal lands. At the base of all the recommendations was the belief that the American land-tenure system needed to
be altered to limit abuses to land and people.[18]

In July 1937, a few months after the President's Special Committee
on Farm Tenancy made its report, Congress passed the Bankhead-
Jones Act. This law established the Farm Security Administration and

initially appropriated $10 million for farm purchase loans. The FSA also took over the Resettlement Administration programs, including some of the community enterprises, which were gradually phased out. The main purpose of the FSA was to loan money to farmers who did not qualify for other types of credit for both land and operating expenses. It was based on the idea that poor farmers could become successful owners if they had credit and supervision.[19]

As had been true of the FERA and Resettlement rehabilitation loans, the FSA usually advanced money to those who had the best chance to succeed. This meant farmers who could make a down payment on land and who had some equipment. Such a policy made business sense, but it offered nothing to the poorest classes of share-croppers and tenants. This group of farmers received small loans and grants which helped solve their immediate needs for food, clothing, and some operating expenses, but the assistance brought little basic change in their condition. Between 1934 and June 30, 1941, loans and grants were made to 606,345 farm families in the states of the old Confederacy. On the other hand, there were only a few loans for farm purchases. During the three years from 1938 through 1940, the FSA made only 8,045 loans to southern tenants to purchase land. Such feeble efforts could not possibly make any noticeable impact on the problem of tenancy in the South.[20]

Officials of the Southern Tenant Farmers Union and some friends of poor farmers in the USDA were highly critical of the FSA. They believed that even if successful, small-farm ownership was no answer to the problem of widespread rural poverty in the South. Gardner Jackson, director of the National Committee on Rural Social Planning, argued that placing people on small farms would "anchor millions of our rural people to a subsistence or a near subsistence level" because they could not produce enough for a decent standard of living. Jackson and others of a more radical bent insisted that the poorest farm people could only be helped by collective land ownership and some kind of a communal agricultural system.[21]

Between 1933 and 1937 the federal government inaugurated a series of programs to rehabilitate poor landless farmers in the South, as well as elsewhere. The prevalent view was that somehow agriculture's poor could be helped by giving them a new relationship to the land. To a considerable extent the ideas and programs reflected the "40 acres and a mule" idea of the post-Civil War years. The few who advocated radical and collectivist approaches to land reform received scant attention. Majority opinion among government and other policymakers held that individual family farm ownership was the key to economic success and security. To achieve that end, the principal role of government should be to supply capital and operating loans and to provide business supervision for farm clients. Almost everyone agreed that many poor farmers in the South, both black and white, lacked the management skills necessary to operate a profitable farm.[22]

While the main thrust of government policy was to transform landless tenants into independent family farmers, an increasing number of observers had little faith in such an approach. This kind of farm relief program, they argued, would not make successful commercial farmers out of the poorest farm residents, and subsistence production held out no hope of ever achieving a modern standard of living. The President's Committee on Farm Tenancy itself declared in one part of its report that "the ignorance, poverty, malnutrition, morbidity and social discriminations by which many farm tenant families are handicapped can not be eliminated by converting tenants into farm owners under some system of easy credit." Henry C. Taylor, an agricultural economist in the USDA explained that some of the ideas being advanced by the President's Committee on Farm Tenancy would actually be harmful if they encouraged people to farm when really they "should enter other occupations." Taylor believed that influences that caused more people to enter farming would "make it all the more difficult to secure parity incomes for farmers." The North Carolina sociologist Rupert B. Vance wrote that with surplus rural population and high birth rates there "was not sufficient demand for farm products nor sufficient land, good, poor, and indifferent, to provide for the farm [population] surplus if migration were cut off." Agriculture, in other words, simply could not absorb so many people and provide an adequate standard of living for them.[23]

The inability of a revived commercial agriculture to provide farm opportunities for the growing number of farm people, and the lack of nonfarm jobs, created a huge rural relief problem in the South. In some cases policies to encourage farmers to become independent commercial operators became confused with those designed mainly to provide relief. Henry C. Taylor warned that "a clear line" should be drawn between "a farm tenancy policy and poor relief policy," and advocated that they be administered separately. There should be, Taylor argued, a distinction between farm policy and social welfare.[24]

A federal program designed to bring permanent help to a substantial number of southern farmers was the Tennessee Valley Authority, established by Congress in 1933. The TVA's major objectives were soil conservation, reforestation, flood control, and improvement in agricultural practices. In addition, by constructing a series of dams on the Tennessee and Cumberland rivers and their tributaries, federal planners hoped to provide cheap hydroelectric power for both farm and industrial use. Low-cost electricity, it was believed, would not only improve farm efficiency but also draw industry to the region, which would supply badly needed nonfarm jobs for the surplus rural population.

When the TVA began to build dams, it had to move people out of the river valleys that would soon be flooded. Data gathered on these farm families by agency representatives further emphasized the destitution and privation on farms in the region. While a few farmers nestled in the Tennessee River Valley had yearly incomes of from $300 to $600, many of the families had less than $150 a year. A fifty-one-year-old black sharecropper with three children near Guntersville, Alabama, farmed 17 acres in 1937 and earned $100. A young white farmer in the same community made about the same from farming, but he had another $100 from day labor. Investigators found a few families living in tents and others with no cash income at all.

The TVA eventually helped to bring about major changes in agriculture and farm life in the Tennessee Valley. It produced cheaper fertilizers, cooperated with farmers to control soil erosion, encouraged the planting of soil conserving crops, and showed farmers how to improve their production methods. Electricity flowed to many southern farms from the TVA generating plants. Farmers also benefited greatly from the Rural Electrification Administration established in 1935. When Congress appropriated $100 million to get the program under way, the editor of the *Progressive Farmer* wrote that it marked the beginning of a movement that would be as influential and beneficial as the free rural delivery of mail or federal aid for road building.[25] But the results of the TVA and REA were really not felt in a major way in the South until after World War II.

The attack on southern rural poverty by government policymakers and social reformers gained widespread public attention in the 1930s. The major forces which were slowly beginning to reshape southern farming, however, were to be found in the growing application of technology and science to agricultural operations. The use of more inanimate power on southern farms, increasing productivity through better application of commercial fertilizers, improved control of crop-destroying insects with chemicals, and better breeding and care of livestock combined to initiate fundamental changes in southern farming. While still lagging behind the other major agricultural regions of the United States, by the late 1930s the South was at last beginning to join the rest of the nation in developing a modernized agriculture.

It had been recognized for many years that a direct relationship existed between meager personal incomes and low productivity on southern farms. Most southern farmers simply did not use land and labor very efficiently. Too much of the work was done by hand with simple tools, or with one or two mules and primitive machinery. A writer for the Commission on Interracial Cooperation exaggerated only slightly when he declared as late as 1937: "Moses and Hammurabi would have been at home with the tools and implements of the tenant farmer. There is nothing complicated about one-horse gears, single-stock plows, long-handled hoes, double-blade axes, and a long sack to drag through the field at picking time."[26] To be sure, southern farmers had used animals and machines to cut the man-hours necessary to produce cotton and other crops, but the reduction had been small compared to that of farmers raising wheat and corn. Between 1855 and 1930 farmers in the corn belt had reduced the man-hours necessary to produce an acre of corn (about 40 bushels) from 33.6 to 6.9 hours. Even the most efficient cotton growers in Texas, who used more and bigger machinery, had only cut the man-hours for an acre of cotton from 148 to 72 in the same period. Thus, while corn growers had reduced man-hours by nearly four-fifths, cotton farmers had cut the needed labor by only one-half. And most cotton growers in the Southeast had not done nearly that well.

To look at the problem another way, the average investment in machinery per farm worker in Iowa and Kansas in 1930 was $1,089 and $920 respectively, while it was a mere $142 and $144 in Alabama and Mississippi. In 1929 a farm worker in Georgia harvested an average of 19.7 acres compared to 70 acres in Iowa and 106 in Kansas. Using more and better machinery to farm more acres was reflected in gross incomes per farm worker. In 1930 average gross income of farm workers was $2,176 in Iowa and $2,204 in Nebraska; the figures were $493 in Alabama and $498 in Mississippi. The highest for any southeastern state was $736 in North Carolina.[27]

Several factors accounted for the slow progress of mechanization on southern farms. In the first place, the large supply of cheap labor discouraged the purchase of machines. So long as there was a surplus of farm workers the economic advantage of investing in machinery was minimal. Most southern farms were too small and the fields too irregular to use tractors and larger plows and tilling equipment efficiently. Even farmers who saw advantages in mechanization found that well up into the 1920s they could not obtain the capital necessary for such an investment. Of 382 operators reporting in one survey, 119 listed the problem of financing machinery as the main factor retarding mechanization.[28] And most lending agencies in the South were not accustomed to making loans for machinery and equipment.

Another strong deterrent to mechanizing farm production in the South was the lack of a machine to weed and pick cotton. Discussing farm mechanization in the South in 1932, L.A. Reynoldson and B.H. Thibodeaux of the USDA wrote that without a mechanical picker "the situation in much of the cotton country remains static." They continued: "Planters in many sections are faced with the necessity of maintaining throughout the year a labor force sufficient to pick the crop, and extensive mechanization would result in piling up many idle hours for the croppers waiting for harvest time." Thus farmers were discouraged from adopting the latest machines to prepare the soil and to plant and cultivate if they had to maintain hand labor for harvesting. To assure an adequate labor supply for picking, many planters considered it economically beneficial to employ workers throughout the year.[29]

Nevertheless, during the 1930s an increasing minority of southern farmers turned to improved machinery as a way to reduce costs and improve their efficiency. They were encouraged in this development by engineers and scientists in the USDA, by the agricultural colleges and experiment stations, by editors of farm papers, and by others.

At the Delta Experiment Station at Stoneville, Mississippi, M.G. Vaiden and his associates published a bulletin in June 1932 entitled *Making Cotton Cheaper*. After carrying on experiments on five Delta plantations, they concluded that production costs could be greatly reduced by using machinery and improving the efficiency of labor. The reason farm incomes were so low compared to industrial wages, they wrote, was because factory workers used machines while much of the farm work was done by hand. They argued that farms must be mechanized as rapidly as possible in order to make labor more productive and to provide a better income for the farmer. Looking at the situation on Delta plantations, Vaiden explained that the policy of paying sharecroppers through advances was most inefficient. "A way must be found," he wrote, "to pay plantation labor after, rather than before, the labor is performed." Vaiden recommended placing labor on a daily cash basis which, he said, "will increase its efficiency 50 to 100%."

Vaiden's main pitch, however, was to get farmers to mechanize. "The replacement of nonessential labor with tractors, 4-mule cultivators, or other large mechanical units tends to stabilize operations at lower cost," he wrote, "and to enable retained farm labor to earn a better living." He predicted that mechanical cotton pickers would be available within a few years which would make possible "maximum, economical use of much more production machinery and will greatly accelerate its improvement." In other words, the mechanical picker would open the way for completely mechanizing the cotton crop, which had historically required intensive hand labor. "Soap box orators," he continued, "may decry cotton pickers, tractors, two and four mule machinery but they and other modern farm machines are just as essential to farmers who expect to earn decent livings and fair returns on investment" as to manufacturers and other businessmen.

Vaiden showed how cotton production costs could be lowered with machinery, and struck hard at the small, poverty-stricken farm operations. Associating these conditions with lack of productivity, he wrote: "Fifteen acre-per-family units can never again be profitable on the average, even in the Delta. Neither labor nor operator will ever be satisfied again with living standards possible under a system requiring so much overhead and the support of so many human beings per unit area. Human demands will continue to exceed possible income. Part of the power now supplied by man must be replaced by mules and machines which are less expensive per unit of power."[30] The one-mule farm simply did not have enough wealth-producing potential to make it a satisfactory family farm unit. One farmer wrote that "it takes money to make money. Now I can never get ahead because my farm is too durn small."[31]

The Mississippi researchers frankly admitted that modern farm machinery would greatly cut manpower needs in southern agriculture. Some readers may have been shocked to read Vaiden's statement that farm labor must be reduced 30 to 50 percent on Delta farms in order to achieve a "decent" standard of living for those remaining. Machines had always reduced human labor, Vaiden explained, and "Americans will not go backward." Recognizing that there was excessive population in agriculture, Vaiden declared that American farms should not be expected to absorb the surplus farm labor, "even at pauper wages." If peasantry was to be avoided, he wrote, "American genius must find other fields for replaced labor" currently present in both the agricultural and the industrial sectors.

Vaiden and his associates at the Delta Experiment Station were offering their advice mainly to planters and large landowners. They gave no consideration to what would happen to the displaced sharecroppers and day laborers when full mechanization occurred. They did, however, see the heart of the small farmer's problem when they explained that the ordinary operator of a few acres would never be able to make a modern living from so little land. While these scholars were thinking in economic rather than social or humanitarian terms, they argued correctly that agriculture in the South could not be expected to absorb the surplus farm population. The solution to the ills of people in southern farming would have to be found outside of agriculture.

Mechanization meant much more, of course, than simply buying two-row or four-row equipment, or purchasing a tractor. To mechanize southern agricultural production meant reorganizing farm operations and changing the relationship between land and people. It meant the organization of larger farms, the increased use of capital, and a different utilization of labor. Mechanization also called for the use of more nonfarm inputs, such as the purchase of gasoline for tractors rather than the raising of corn or hay on the farm to feed mules. Furthermore, mechanized farming required better management and business skills to make a satisfactory return on increased capitalization. While most farmers in the South were too poor, ignorant, and nonproductive to have a choice of continuing in their current condition or adopting new methods, a growing number of middle-class farmers and larger planters were in a position to break from the old patterns.[32]

The New Deal agricultural programs were very helpful to southern farmers who wanted to modernize. Price supports for cotton and other southern crops gave them a fairly dependable and stable income. Their risks, except for the weather, had been greatly reduced. Government lending agencies provided a source of cheap credit for both capital outlays and operating expenses. Indeed, the federal farm credit programs in the 1930s greatly lowered the cost of money and gave progressive landowners an opportunity to change their operations. What happened was that as the cost of credit declined in relation to the cost of labor, farmers turned to machines. It did not make economic sense for many farmers to continue the old labor-intensive system of employing sharecroppers and tenants when cheaper capital would permit them to mechanize and increase their overall efficiency. In the 1930s, for the first time since the Civil War, a growing number of southern farmers had a practical choice of turning to mechanization by substituting capital for labor on a broad scale. Overall throughout the South this trend developed slowly, and mechanization grew at different rates in different parts of the region, but by the late 1930s a more highly capitalized agriculture was beginning to take shape in some parts of the South.

As would be expected, it was the larger farmers who turned first to mechanization. But even farmers who had several hundred acres or more did not mechanize all at once. It was a gradual process for most operators. In a study of planters in three Arkansas Delta counties covering the period 1932 to 1938, it was found that tractors were used most commonly for plowing, disking, and cutting cotton stalks. That is, tractors and other machines were confined mainly to seedbed preparation. Weed control by mechanical cultivating and planting with tractor power came much more slowly. The fact that 57 percent of the planting was done with one-horse equipment on a large cross-section of plantations as late as 1937 indicates the continuing use of draft animals and small equipment. Machine cotton picking, except on a very limited basis, had to wait until after the production of a spindle-type picker in 1941. Nevertheless, the longer farmers had tractors, the more use they made of them. The improvement of the all-purpose tractor and the addition of pneumatic tires in the 1930s also encouraged wider tractor use.[33]

Between 1930 and 1940 farmers and planters in the South acquired 96,645 additional tractors. While the percentage of operators using tractors throughout the South in 1940 was still small, only 2.7 percent in Mississippi and 4.3 percent in North Carolina compared to 55.3 and 53.6 percent in Iowa and Kansas respectively, the number of tractors per 1,000 acres of cropland harvested doubled in some southern states during the 1930s. At the same time horse and mule numbers declined. In Mississippi there were 71.6 horses and mules per 1,000 acres of cropland harvested in 1930 compared to 64.1 a decade later. In three Delta counties in Arkansas the number of tractors per 10,000 acres of cropland harvested increased from 12 in 1932 to 29 in 1938. On the other hand, in some poorer, hilly northern counties there were less than 25 tractors in 1940.[34]

B.O. Williams, a professor of rural sociology at Clemson University, wrote in 1939 that mechanization of agriculture would reshape the "character of the farm population of the South."[35] That was an accurate observation. When farmers increased their investment in machinery, the demand for sharecropper and share tenant labor declined. It was usually more efficient for the landowner to hire wage workers than to maintain resident sharecroppers. Many day laborers continued to live in houses on the plantations, but they were only paid when they were working. There was no annual commitment to them as there had been under the old furnish system. In a study of 246 plantations located in nine areas of the South, the number of crop acres farmed by wage laborers rose 5.1 percent between 1934 and 1937, while croppers farmed about the same percent of crop acreage in both years. It was the share tenants who lost out heavily.[36]

A detailed survey of Arkansas plantations published in 1937 showed the extent to which sharecroppers were being replaced in some areas. On plantations in nine counties, the number of wage hands increased from 225 to 277 between 1930 and 1935, while sharecropper families dropped from 1,396 to 1,294. Farms located closest to cities such as Memphis and Little Rock used the most wage labor because of its cheapness and easy availability. In viewing this changing situation, Paul S. Taylor reported that on a Saturday morning in June 1937, trucks hauled from 1,000 to 1,500 laborers from Memphis across the Mississippi River to plantations in Arkansas. As many as 40 to 50 workers in each truck rode that morning from 35 to 50 miles to the fields and then, after a hard day's work, back to Memphis in the evening. With better machinery the Arkansas planters were cultivating more and more of their land with wage workers. In the 1910 census on plantations the average planter worked only about 60 acres with wage hands, but by 1934 in Arkansas the figure was 282 acres. Conversely, while planters were farming more of their land with wage labor, the average acreage cultivated by sharecroppers and share tenants declined from about 25 to 18 acres in that same period. As the author of the Arkansas study concluded: "The development of superior implements and the in-creased use of machinery on wage crops account in part for the land-lord's increasing portion [of land operated] as compared to the tenant's, who did not commonly utilize these improved methods of produc-tion."[37]

A study of Washington County, Mississippi, provides further evi-dence of changes in the Delta region. The number of tractors increased from 285 to 784 between 1930 and 1935, or 175 percent, while the number of farms declined by 13.9 percent. Total farm population dropped 10.2 percent in the county as the size of farms rose 25.1 percent. Some other Delta counties also saw dramatic increases in the number of tractors. In Mississippi County in eastern Arkansas, plan-ters operated 1,052 tractors in 1940 compared to only 151 ten years earlier.[38]

Sharecroppers and tenants were also threatened by other develop-ments. When cotton acreage was reduced under the federal crop control programs, corn was most commonly substituted for cotton on the diverted acres. In the rolling, upland counties of the Piedmont, hay and other feed grains were planted. The crops that were substituted for cotton took less labor and thereby reduced the economic opportunity for sharecroppers and share tenants. The combination of mechaniza-tion, federal programs, and a different crop mix had a devastating effect on farmers who depended on sharecropping for a living. In 1930 the ten southern states from North Carolina to Texas reported 716,452 sharecroppers. By 1935 the figure showed a modest decline to 659,949, with the largest decreases in Arkansas, Georgia, and Texas. As mecha-nization advanced in the late 1930s, the number of sharecroppers dropped much more dramatically. By 1940 the census reported only 506,407 sharecroppers in the ten southern states, or a decline of some 29 percent in a decade. There was an especially sharp drop in white sharecroppers, but blacks also left the old system in large numbers. In Georgia, for example, white and black sharecroppers declined by about 20,000 for each group in the 1930s, while in Alabama the drop was 15,526 for white sharecroppers and 8,238 for blacks. Among the most dramatic episodes associated with sharecroppers and the surplus farm labor situation in parts of the South were the roadside demonstra-tions in southeastern Missouri in January 1939. More than 1,000 land-less, destitute people camped along highways 61 and 60 in protest of their desperate plight.[39]

But protests and threats of strikes from time to time in the 1930s failed to alter or ameliorate conditions among the South's rural poor. The forces of the marketplace, supported by government policies and technology, erected a cruel but effective winnowing process in south-ern agriculture. Many people suffered greatly before industrialization and war absorbed many of the surplus farmers. The federal government might have eased the necessary transition out of agriculture and reduced the terrible privation, but the dominating economic and political views of the time precluded any such massive governmental assistance that might have eased the shift of people out of agriculture.

Of all classes of farmers it was the blacks who were moving most rapidly out of southern agriculture during the 1930s. A decline in the number of black farmers had begun in the 1920s, but the trend gained momentum during the pre-World War II decade. In 1930 the South had 840,088 black farmers, but by 1940 the figure had dropped to 652,333. Of this number only 159,624, or about 24 percent, were owners who, for the most part, had small acreages.[40] An especially rapid exodus of blacks from southern farms occurred in the late 1930s. Some were "tractored" off the land, but a much larger number left in hope of finding better economic opportunities in the towns and cities. They also hoped to escape discrimination.

Some black leaders were distressed at the movement of blacks out of agriculture. Kelly Miller, former dean of Howard University, wrote to Congressman Arthur W. Mitchell, the only black representative in Congress, in January 1939, urging Mitchell to use his influence to stem the tide. Miller reminded Mitchell that Booker T. Washington had "urged his race to seek their future on the farm rather than to be beguiled by the glitter and glamour of city life." He added that a black family rooted in Alabama's agricultural life had a "much more promising prospect than if transferred to the sidewalks of New York." Indicating that the small-farm philosophy still held sway, Miller suggested that "any ordinary Negro family can take 40 acres and a mule and extract a livelihood from the soil." Congressman Mitchell was less enthusiastic about the rural ideal. While admitting that he viewed blacks leaving southern farms "with great alarm," he understood that oppression and lack of opportunity had been responsible for the exodus. Until those conditions changed, blacks would continue to leave and southern agriculture would become increasingly controlled and worked by whites.[41]

By the late 1930s, mechanization of southern agriculture was making important but spotty advances on a few plantations and farms even without a successful mechanical cotton picker. Planters, smaller landowners, and even better-off tenants were using machines to increase efficiency and to lower production costs. They gradually discarded the old mule-drawn equipment originally hitched to most tractors, and purchased larger plows and disks specifically designed for tractor power. New detachable planters and cultivators also became available. On the larger farms and plantations, mechanical insecticide dusters came into use, and starting in 1924 there was some airborne cropdusting of chemicals to fight insects. An interbureau committee on technology set up by the USDA reported in 1940 that mechanization was already reshaping "the traditional plantation and sharecropper system of farm organization in parts of the South."[42]

Farmers still had to wait, however, to clear out the bottlenecks that would open the way for complete mechanization of cotton production—machines for weeding, thinning, and picking. Inventors had been trying to develop a mechanical cotton picker ever since the 1870s, but none of the machines had proven practical. A machine that stripped the entire boll from the cotton stalk had been in use in parts of Texas since the 1920s. But the stripper collected so much dirt and trash with the cotton that lint quality dropped by one or two grades at most gins. Nevertheless, farmers in West Texas, where the cotton plant was small and where early frost caused the leaves to drop off, found the cotton stripper an important labor saver.

From 1924 onward intensive efforts were made to invent a spindle-type picker that would carefully remove the lint from the boll in the manner of hand picking. That year International Harvester Company bought the rights to a picker built by Angus Campbell and Theodore H. Price. By the 1930s International Harvester and individual inventors like John and Mack Rust experimented regularly with spindle-type machines. A few Rust machines were sold during the decade, but it was not until 1941 that International Harvester perfected and manufactured a one-row, high-drum picker for commercial sale. The entry of the United States into World War II, however, curtailed production of these revolutionary machines.[43]

Engineers were also busy trying to perfect a machine that would thin the cotton with rotating blades. By 1937 the Dixie Cotton Chopper Company of Dallas, Texas, had both one-row and two-row machines on the market. While a worker with a hoe could thin about one acre a day, the two-row machine pulled by a tractor was capable of thinning four acres an hour. The company reported selling 403 one-row mechanical choppers in 1937.[44]

Closely associated with the beginning of modern farm mechanization during the 1930s was the declining number and increase in size of farms. Except for Georgia, South Carolina, Tennessee, and Virginia, the number of farms in the southern states crawled upward after 1920 and, except in Georgia and Mississippi, continued to rise in the early 1930s. After 1935, however, as mechanization advanced and farm people found more off-farm jobs or went on relief, the number of farms in every southern state dropped significantly. The region of the old Confederacy had 346,533 fewer farms in 1940 than five years earlier.

The acreage harvested per farm was still small, but changes in the number and size of farms provided strong signals on the coming structural changes in southern agriculture.[45]

Surely one of the most important developments in the 1930s was the drastic drop in cotton acreage. Land planted to cotton declined from 37.8 million acres in 1929 to about 20 million in 1939. With much less cotton, farmers began devoting more acres to other crops and to hay and forage to meet the demands of a growing livestock industry. Acreage planted to corn and oats in 1939 was up substantially over a decade earlier, as was land in pasture and hay. In some areas soybeans were being substituted for cotton as a cash crop. North Carolina, Arkansas, Mississippi, and Alabama combined had more than one million acres in soybeans by 1939. More and more of the soybeans were being raised for beans rather than for hay, as had been common earlier. Georgia and Alabama farmers also greatly expanded their peanut plantings during the decade.[46]

Despite sharp acreage cutbacks in 1934, tobacco continued to be the major cash crop in North Carolina, Virginia, Tennessee, and Kentucky. The number of farmers raising tobacco increased in South Carolina, and rose rather sharply in Georgia from about 18,000 in 1934 to 34,000 in 1939. The Agricultural Adjustment Act of 1938 provided price supports and marketing quotas, rather than acreage allotments, for tobacco growers. North Carolina was the premier tobacco state, with about half of the state's 288,000 farmers raising the crop in 1939. The acreage and production of rice, another important commercial crop, showed a modest rise in the late 1930s as producers in Arkansas, Louisiana, and Texas planted better seed and used improved machinery and methods of irrigation.[47]

Truck crop and fruit tree acreage also rose in the 1930s. A great vegetable and fruit belt expanded from Florida across the Gulf coast to the Rio Grande Valley of southern Texas. Orange growers in Florida increased their shipments from 32,550 to 52,908 car lots between 1928 and 1938. But it was in southern Texas that citrus production exploded. From only 33 car lots of oranges and 1,617 car lots of grapefruit shipped in 1928, sales in 1938 were 1,167 and 14,636 car lots respectively. Demands for fresh fruits and vegetables the year around by a growing number of Americans, improved refrigeration, and better transportation assured more reliable markets for southern growers.[48] From time to time, however, surpluses and low prices hurt the producers of fruit and vegetables. Markets were not yet dependable enough to provide reliable sales. Stories were common in the 1930s of farmers who shipped loads of watermelons and other commodities to northern markets and received less than the cost of transportation.

Whether it was in response to advice from the agricultural specialists or simply the prospect of more profit is unknown, but an increasing number of southern farmers turned more and more of their attention to livestock enterprises. Between 1930 and 1935 cattle numbers rose substantially, but then declined again so that total cattle on farms was not greatly different at the end of the decade than in 1930. The biggest percentage increase was in Florida. Overall in the South, farms with cattle rose nearly 10 percent during the 1930s. There was an increase in both milk cows and beef cattle. The number of milk cows in both Arkansas and Mississippi, for example, increased by more than 100,000 head. In some regions commercial dairying expanded very significantly. Examples of such areas were south-central Tennessee and east-central Mississippi. In the latter the number of milk cows on farms increased 49 percent between 1928 and 1939. To feed these cows, much more land was planted to pasture, hay, and corn. A major factor in encouraging dairying was the establishment of creameries and dairy plants which provided markets. Other dairies developed near the larger cities such as Nashville and Atlanta to meet the demand for fresh milk. Cattlemen and dairymen were helped by scientists who brought Texas fever under control, as well as other cattle diseases such as anthrax, a very old and destructive cattle disease.[49]

The number of hogs and the percentage of farmers raising hogs rose slightly in the 1930s, but only in a few southern states was the increase substantial. In South Carolina, for instance, 76 percent of the farmers had hogs in 1940 compared to 61 percent a decade earlier. The increase throughout most of the South, however, was much more modest. There was a slight increase in chickens during the 1930s, but poultry had not yet become a significant commercial product.[50] As had been true for many years, farmers kept a few chickens to provide the family with eggs and with meat for Sunday dinner. While southern farming was becoming considerably more diversified in the 1930s, the diversification was directed more toward producing a greater variety of commercial products, rather than toward self-sufficiency.

Mechanization and other modern developments that were beginning to change farming in the South aroused criticism as well as support. Agricultural fundamentalists who held tightly to the agrarian tradition believed that modernized commercial agriculture would destroy farming as a way of life in the South. From the days of Thomas Jefferson, southerners, like most other Americans, believed there was something special about agriculture and rural living. Jeffersonian agrarianism had been advanced mostly by people who did not have to make a living on the farm—politicians, editors, writers, and others—but the praise of agriculture had become deeply imbedded in American culture. Southerners took special pride in their ruralness, and the accompanying social stability.

In 1930 a group of southern writers and scholars, sometimes known as the Nashville agrarians, published a book entitled *I'll Take My Stand*. These writers sharply criticized industrialism and defended the small farm. Herman C. Nixon called growing industrial development in the region "deplorable" because it was overwhelming the South's "agricultural philosophy." He favored small, self-sufficient farms and urged southerners not to sell their souls "for a mess of industrial pottage." Andrew Nelson Lytle criticized those who said, "Industrialize the farm; be progressive; drop old fashioned ways and adopt scientific methods." Lytle urged farmers to turn a deaf ear to those voices calling for progressive agriculture and to reject the idea that farm families deserve "motor-cars, picture shows, chainstore dresses for the women-folk, and all the articles in Sears-Roebuck catalogues." Do not listen to the false prophets from the cities, he warned. Trying to make money on the farm, Lytle wrote, "means the end of farming as a way of life." He was critical of tractors, trucks, and other modern equipment.

While the Nashville agrarians and other writers repeated these themes throughout the 1930s, the transformation of southern agriculture, as well as other aspects of southern life, could not be stopped. Sometimes referred to as "typewriter agrarians," they could no more hold back the changes occurring on southern farms than King Canute could hold back the sea. This did not mean that agrarianism as an ideal lacked support. Indeed, agricultural fundamentalism and the family farm concept provided much of the intellectual justification for price supports, acreage restrictions, credit, resettlement, and other New Deal legislation. But these programs were designed mainly to help commercial farmers become more successful. No amount of agrarian thinking or rhetoric could result in policies that would tie people to small self-sufficient farms in an industrialized, modernized America. Southern farmers like other Americans wanted money to buy the automobiles, "chainstore dresses," and other industrial goods that the Nashville agrarians warned them against. To have a better standard of living, then, meant either to change agriculture or to leave it.[51]

Although fundamental changes in southern agriculture were in the offing by the end of the 1930s, the region still remained remarkably the same. Change was spotty and very limited. Hundreds of thousands of one-mule and two-mule farms dotted the landscape from southern Virginia to eastern Texas. Most farmers still worked only a few acres of land. In 1939 the average cropland harvested was less than 30 acres for farmers in nine southern states from North Carolina to Louisiana. Only 7.9 percent of farmers in the South had tractors and about 9 percent owned motor trucks in 1940. Less than 3 percent of the farmers in Alabama and Mississippi did tractor farming. The great majority of southern farmers continued to live in shabby houses, they suffered from poor health associated with insufficient and unbalanced diets, and their children were denied adequate education. Income came mainly from crops, as had been the case for two generations, indicating only a small shift to livestock farming. In North Carolina, for example, only 12.9 percent of the value of farm products in 1939 came from livestock; in Georgia the figure was 19.8 percent.

Few southern farmers enjoyed modern living. An average of only 3.5 percent of the farmers in the Carolinas, Georgia, Alabama, and Mississippi had telephones in 1940, while only 18.3 percent of the farmers in those same southeastern states had electricity.[52]

Like their parents a generation before, most farmers never went far from home. A trip to Memphis, Atlanta, or Charlotte was most unusual and a subject for lifelong memories and conversation. Many farm folk in the 1930s still never went beyond one of the local towns or villages where they shopped and traded. They generally traveled in wagons pulled by mules, and gathered on the dusty streets on Saturday afternoons to socialize and exchange gossip. Most rural communities did not have paved roads before World War II, and a smaller percentage of southern farmers owned automobiles in 1940 than a decade earlier. Being confined largely to their own community, southern farmers had a strong sense of place. They also recognized a well established social and economic hierarchy. People knew their place in society, especially blacks, and few farmers or their children experienced upward mobility.[53]

The lack of any meaningful progress in living standards continued to be associated with low productivity and subsistence incomes. The average value of farm commodities produced by Alabama and North Carolina farmers in 1939 was only $57 per capita for people on farms. The figure was $89 in Georgia and $84 in Tennessee. By contrast, in Nebraska the value of farm products per capita was $385.[54]

As D.W. Brooks was organizing farmer cooperatives in the 1930s, he told farmers that they must change their methods. "You must get more production," he admonished backward producers, "by using better fertilizer, the right variety of seeds and more effective insecticides." In other words, farmers should apply science to their agricultural operations. Brooks often shocked farm audiences by saying, "The way you farm, you are getting exactly what you deserve."[55] Others were saying the same thing, with about the same negative results.

The New Deal programs, along with the application of technology and science to agriculture, had begun to shake up the old system of farming in the South. But the problem of surplus farm population still prevailed. The farm population in ten southern states dropped only

41,224 between 1930 and 1940, compared to a decline of slightly over a million in the 1920s. Population pressures on the South's agricultural resources thus remained very heavy. Viewing the region in July 1938, President Roosevelt wrote that "the South presents right now the Nation's No. 1 economic problem." Much of that problem was on southern farms. A few weeks later the National Emergency Council reported on the economic situation in the South, outlining problems of employment in both agriculture and industry, and showing how low incomes affected health, housing, and other aspects of life.[56] But it was not discussions by councils or committees that opened the floodgate of change in the rural South. Rather, it was the outbreak of war in Europe and the subsequent involvement of the United States. At last there was a strong national and international demand for farm products and industrial expansion that could use the labor of millions of unneeded farmers.

8

Southern Farmers
and World War II

When *Fortune* magazine wanted to picture a progressive southern farmer for its urban audience in October 1941, only a few weeks before the Japanese attack on Pearl Harbor, the editor sent a reporter to visit with H.L. Wingate in southern Georgia. Wingate, head of the Georgia Farm Bureau, was portrayed as an agricultural "revolutionary." His farm covered 600 acres in Mitchell County and his labor force consisted of an overseer who farmed 90 acres on his own and supervised five black sharecropper families and two black tenants. Despite his portrayal as a highly progressive farmer, Wingate did not yet own a tractor. Fifteen mules furnished the power for his farm. Since 1928, when he took over the farm, Wingate had gradually shifted production away from cotton, peanuts, and tobacco and turned to corn, vegetables, pasture, and livestock. Locally he was known as the "tomato king" because of his large tomato production. As a result of his diversified output, Wingate had raised his family's net cash income to $1,500 a year and in addition produced about $500 worth of food.[1]

There was really nothing very revolutionary about the farming of Harry Wingate. While he had diversified his cash crops, he still used sharecropper labor and was not in the vanguard of mechanization. Nevertheless, Wingate and others like him throughout the South were gradually bringing about fundamental changes in southern agriculture. World War II greatly assisted in this transformation. The increased demand for farm products, rising prices, and the scarcity of labor which encouraged mechanization all combined to hasten the changes that were beginning to emerge in the late 1930s. No revolution occurred on southern farms even in the 1940s, but evolutionary changes surely picked up speed.

When war broke out in Europe in September 1939, most southern farmers had not yet come out of the Depression. Prices of all major farm products were still low. Cotton brought only about 9.9 cents a pound, which was a mere 66 percent of parity; peanuts sold for between 3 and 4 cents a pound, and sugarcane for only $2.85 a ton, which was even lower than in 1932. Tobacco prices were the lowest since 1933, averaging about 15 cents a pound to producers. Cash income from farm marketings in the ten states from North Carolina to Texas totaled $1.6 billion in 1939. This was nearly $200 million *less* than farmers had received in 1936. But between 1936 and 1939 government payments to farmers in those ten southern states rose from about $70 million to $304 million.[2] Indeed, if it had not been for federal payments, southern farmers would have been worse off financially in 1939 than three years earlier. While there were occasional signs that pointed to improved conditions among farmers, they were not at all clear to the men in the cotton or tobacco patches in early 1940.

Cotton, the South's leading cash crop, seemed to be in especially deep trouble in 1939 and 1940. Huge surpluses filled government warehouses. At the end of the 1939 crop year some 12 million bales, about a full year's supply, were being carried over. Fortunately, the effect of the European war was not felt in the cotton markets, and the United States exported about 6.5 million bales in 1939. The following year, however, Britain and other European countries virtually stopped buying American cotton. In 1940 exports reached only 1.2 million bales. Besides the disrupting effects of war, price supports made American cotton uncompetitive in world markets. Throughout the rest of the war only a little more than a million bales of American cotton were exported each year.

The only thing that saved southern cotton growers was the tremendous increase in wartime demand by American mills. Requirements were so heavy that in 1943 the government removed acreage allotments on cotton. Meanwhile prices rose dramatically to an average of about 20 cents a pound during the war years, double the prices in 1939 and 1940. Despite higher prices and freedom from acreage controls, farmers reduced rather than expanded their plantings. Labor shortages and more profitable alternative crops encouraged farmers to place less emphasis on cotton. Only where mechanization was well advanced could cotton acreage be expanded after allotments were abandoned. By 1945 cotton growers harvested around 17 million acres compared to 23.8 million in 1940.[3] But even with this much acreage reduction and expanded demand, the annual carryover during the war years never dropped to less than 10.5 million bales. Surpluses would not go away. Another important development affecting growers in the old cotton belt was the shifting of cotton acreage westward to the irrigated and highly mechanized farms of western Texas, Arizona, and California. This interregional competition posed serious problems for growers in the Southeast.

To replace cotton, farmers responded to the government's demand for oil crops and rapidly increased their acreages of peanuts and soybeans. On the eve of the war there was a surplus of peanuts. In 1941 Congress amended the AAA of 1938 to provide marketing quotas which assessed penalties for marketing peanuts in excess of a farmer's allotment. With the increased demand for oil-producing crops in 1942, the government urged peanut farmers to expand their production to 5 million acres, a jump of 155 percent. As an enticement to enlarge their acreages, producers were at first promised prices equalling 85 and later 90 percent of parity. Even these price incentives, however, were not enough to get farmers to meet government production goals. Nevertheless, in 1942 farmers harvested 3.4 million acres of peanuts compared to 1.9 million in 1941. During the remainder of the war, acreage stood at a little over 3 million. Georgia, Texas, and Alabama farmers, in that order, were the biggest producers. Prices rose from 3.3 cents a pound in 1940 to 6.0 cents in 1942 and to 8.3 cents in 1945. Commercial peanut growers had never had it so good.[4]

Wartime agencies also urged farmers to plant more soybeans. Up to 1941 soybeans had been grown mainly for forage and green manure. But as one authority said, the "sudden wartime increase in demand supplied the catalytic price and marketing conditions which touched off the principal expansion." Southern farmers helped the government to exceed its goals for that important oil crop by 1942. To achieve this objective, however, the price support level had to be lifted. In 1943 price supports were at 114 percent of parity, and they were raised to about 125 percent in 1944 and 1945.[5] With soybeans bringing from $2.00 to $4.00 a bushel, farmers in some parts of the South increased their harvested acreage dramatically. Soybeans were popular not only because of a strong demand and high prices, but also because they could be raised by machine. Moreover, like cotton, soybeans could not be pilfered by sharecroppers or tenants, since they had to be sold to a commercial dealer or a large processing company. The biggest acreage diverted to soybeans occurred in Arkansas, Mississippi, Tennessee, and North Carolina, where they were in some cases substituted for cotton. Those four states harvested only 281,000 acres of soybeans in 1940, but by 1943 the figure had risen to a wartime high of 739,000 acres.[6] The limited acreage diverted from cotton to soybeans during World War II, especially in Arkansas and Louisiana, was only the beginning of a much more widespread trend in the postwar years.

There was also a substantial expansion of other southern staple crops after 1940. The amount of sugarcane in Louisiana and Florida rose from 240,000 acres in 1940 to a high of 290,000 acres in 1942. Throughout the rest of the war, acreage declined slightly but still remained above the prewar years. But production jumped sharply, and prices per ton about doubled. Wartime rationing of sugar lowered demand, but the cut-off of supplies from the Philippines helped American producers. Rice, a major commercial crop in Arkansas, Louisiana, and Texas, experienced strong gains during wartime. Between 1939 and 1944 rice production in those states increased by more than 428,000 acres.[7]

The South's thousands of tobacco growers were especially hard hit by the outbreak of war in 1939. Prices dropped sharply when British buyers did not come into the market. For a time tobacco markets actually closed. To meet what seemed to be a serious crisis, tobacco farmers and their spokesmen moved quickly to get production under control and to achieve higher government price supports. On October 6, 1939, a referendum was held among tobacco growers, at which time nearly 90 percent of them voted for acreage restrictions. In July 1940 another vote was taken which extended crop controls and marketing quotas for three years. Besides restricting acreage and marketings, the tobacco interests in Congress got legislation to change the time period on which parity prices were figured. The new law enacted late in 1940 replaced 1919-1929 with 1934-1938 as the base period. This was very favorable to growers, for it raised the parity price substantially.

Tobacco farmers established themselves in a highly favorable position early in the war, and jealously guarded it in the following years. They had restrictions on marketing which not only aimed to keep price-depressing surpluses off the market, but also made it virtually impossible for new growers to enter tobacco farming. Furthermore, farmers enjoyed favorable parity prices. By 1941 markets had recovered and producers were receiving the best prices in years. From a depressing 16 cents a pound in 1940, tobacco jumped to 26.4 cents in 1941, and by 1944 the seasonal average received by farmers reached 41 cents. A huge crop in 1944 and high prices brought growers $814.9 million, 350 percent more than in 1940. Never had tobacco farmers known such prosperity.[8]

Besides permitting farmers full production and assuring them profitable prices for basic crops, federal officials urged producers to expand dairy and livestock production. In some parts of the South there was a major shift of land use from crops to pasture and forage to take care of greater livestock numbers. This occurred, for example, in the black belt of Alabama and Mississippi, areas of Louisiana and Tennessee, counties in the Georgia Piedmont, and elsewhere. Expanding markets created by growing industrialization and urbanization in the South, together with good prices, encouraged farmers to take up livestock enterprises. Most of the commercial dairies had been established fairly near the major southern cities, such as Atlanta and Birmingham, where large wholesale markets had been developing. Of 119 dairy farmers surveyed in twenty-three counties of Alabama in 1945, 90 were selling to wholesale plants and only 29 directly to homes and stores.[9]

Overall progress in southern dairying, however, was small and spotty during the war years. There were actually about 30,000 fewer cows milked in the eleven southern states in 1944 than in 1939. The largest increases were in Tennessee, but farmers in both the Carolinas, Alabama, and Mississippi also milked more cows at the war's end. The biggest decline in number of milk cows was in Texas. The total number of cattle, however, made fairly good gains during the war. In fact, every southern state had more cattle and calves in 1945 than in 1940.[10]

Although the government urged greater pork production during the war, most southern farmers did not turn to commercial hog raising on any substantial scale. A higher percentage of farmers had hogs in 1945 than in 1940, but the numbers were small.[11] A shortage of feed continued to be a major factor in discouraging hog numbers in the South. But there was a substantial increase in poultry production.

Despite the government's wartime push to produce more livestock products, southern farmers as a whole made little change in the balance between livestock and crops. In 1939, for instance, crops made up about 70 percent of the value of all farm products sold in the eleven southern states, while the figure for livestock and livestock products was about 26 percent; in 1944 the percentage produced by crops had even risen slightly, to 72 percent.[12]

Averages, however, fail to give an accurate picture of what was happening throughout the South. While there was virtually no increase in the importance of livestock as producers of income in the Carolinas, the value of livestock and livestock products in Georgia rose, between 1939 and 1944 from 19.8 to 24 percent of the value of all farm products sold. Some local areas in other states saw significant increases in livestock, even though statewide income from that source did not show noticeable advances. For example, in Montgomery County, Alabama, part of the old black belt, farmers received 57 percent of their income from livestock and livestock products in 1944 and only 22 percent from cotton. This trend toward livestock had been developing earlier but was intensified during the war. At the same time there were 125 commercial dairies in Putnam County in Georgia's Piedmont, where cotton had reigned only a few years before. The increase in livestock raising and dairying was spotty rather than general, however, and depended on markets and developing local land-use patterns. In Texas and Florida, livestock became relatively less important in the total value of farm products sold during war as farmers turned more to crops made unusually profitable by wartime demand.[13]

Since the late nineteenth century the South had produced large quantities of specialty crops. The war created an unusual demand for truck crops, fruits, tung oil, and other commodities. In Chatham County, Georgia, where Savannah was located, only 113 farmers produced vegetables for sale in 1939; by 1945 the number was 420. There was also a large increase in Fulton County, Georgia, to supply the Atlanta market. Peach production in South Carolina rose rapidly just before World War II, but by 1945 the state produced 5.7 million bushels compared to 4.1 million in 1941. Georgia also grew more peaches during the war. The value of Florida's fruits and nuts marketed rose during the war years from 42 to 59 percent of the value of all crops sold by the state's farmers.[14]

Southern farmers increased their output of crops and livestock during World War II on about the same amount of cropland as they had farmed in 1940. Good crop years, some improved methods, including mechanization and better fertilization, combined to keep production relatively high. In the case of cotton, farmers raised 600,000 more bales on nearly 4 million fewer acres of land in 1945 than in 1940. When labor shortages threatened the cotton harvest, pickers worked longer hours, women, children, and townspeople were called into service, and in some areas war prisoners were ordered to the cotton fields.[15]

With labor in short supply and wages high from the producer's point of view, farmers turned increasingly to machines. During the war years they more than doubled the number of tractors in use and bought additional grain combines, hay balers, peanut harvesters, milking machines, and other labor-saving equipment. Wage rates more than tripled in some areas between 1940 and 1945, which encouraged a growing number of southern farmers to buy machinery. A planter in the Mississippi Delta reported in 1944 that he planned to meet the labor shortage by turning to machines. "I have twenty tractors now," he said, "and will continue to mechanize. We are not buying any more mules." A study done of 479 farms in northern Alabama near the end of the war in 1945 showed that farmers had moved rapidly toward mechanization in that area. Tractor power was being used exclusively on 112 of these farms, while tractors and mules together were used on 197, and workstock only on 170 farms. In some cases labor shortages caused producers to shift their efforts to less labor-intensive operations.[16]

Machines were needed to take the place of a rapidly departing labor force. Many young men were drafted for military service, but even larger numbers left southern farms to take jobs in plants and factories. The wartime industrial boom with its demand for workers finally began to provide an outlet for the surplus farm population. Between 1940 and 1945, the South's farm population dropped some 3 million, or about 22 percent. In some parts of the region the decline was even greater. In a thirteen-county area of North Carolina's Piedmont, for example, the farm population dropped 24 percent in those years. A similar decline occurred in six counties of the Georgia Piedmont. The average family size on North Carolina farms fell from 5.9 to 4.56 between 1940 and 1945; in Alabama the drop was from 5.8 to 4.5.[17] The economic impact of fewer farm people was probably greater than the numbers alone would imply because most of those who left southern farms were in the most vigorous and productive age groups.

Despite a large drop in total farm population in the South, the number of farms in the region did not shrink significantly by 1945. The decrease in the eleven southern states was only 94,505. In the Carolinas and Georgia the number of farms actually continued to increase during wartime. Most of the increase, however, was in farms of less than 10 acres, many of which were part-time operations. One of the significant wartime developments was the increase in the number of southern farmers who worked 100 days or more a year off the farm. Although the census reported fewer part-time farmers in 1944 than in 1939, those that did have off-farm jobs devoted more days to their nonfarm employment.[18]

The people who migrated to urban and factory jobs in the Southeast were not usually operating farmers who abandoned agriculture, but their sons and daughters, who were unemployed or under-employed on the farm. It was mainly in the areas where cotton production fell that actual operators gave up farming and sought other work. When larger landowners who had used tenant and sharecrop labor abandoned cotton, there was no longer an opportunity for families offering that kind of labor. This was most evident in the Mississippi Delta and parts of the Piedmont.[19]

Most of the farmers who left the land during the war years were white. There were 81,347 fewer farms in the South operated by whites in 1945 than in 1940, compared to a decline of only 13,158 units farmed by blacks. Indeed, in the Carolinas and Georgia there was a substantial increase in the number of black farmers. The largest declines of blacks on farms occurred in Alabama, Mississippi, Arkansas, Louisiana, and Texas. In those states there were 46,367 fewer farms operated by blacks in 1945 than when the war began. These five southern states were the ones in which farm mechanization was most advanced and where further mechanical progress rapidly took place during the war. Nearly 95 percent of the more than 46,000 black farmers who no longer operated farms in 1945 had been sharecroppers.[20]

The decline of sharecroppers was most marked in the plantation areas. In the fall of 1944, for example, some 2,500 people gathered at the Hopson Brothers Plantation near Clarksdale, Mississippi, where cotton production had been completely mechanized. Tractors had furnished the power to prepare the soil for 2,000 acres of cotton, and to plant the crop. Flame weeders, whose intense heat killed the weeds along cotton rows, had been used, and insecticides had been spread from airplanes. Shortly before picking time, airplanes had also showered chemicals over the fields to defoliate the cotton plants. When the large crowd gathered to watch the climax of the year's production, they saw 7 International Harvester mechanical pickers eat their way through the fields, each harvesting about 1,000 pounds of cotton per hour, as compared to 15 to 20 pounds that a man could pick by hand. To raise that much cotton with tenant farmers and mule power would have required about 130 families, or 600 to 700 people. The Hopsons employed only 40 wage workers.[21]

While the Hopson Brothers represented the rare exception, even in the Delta, in 1944 and 1945, planters in that region greatly reduced their need for sharecroppers by mechanizing. There were both "push" and "pull" factors influencing migration away from southern farms. Restricted cotton acreage and increasing mechanization provided the push that forced farmers off the land in the 1930s, and these factors continued to operate in the war period. But in the 1940s there were compelling pull influences that caused both white and black farmers and their children to leave agriculture. The main pull was the availability and attractiveness of either part-time or full-time nonfarm employment. This placed strong pressure on farmers to mechanize in order to stay in business. W.M. Garrard, general manager of the Staple Cotton Cooperative Association of Greenwood, Mississippi, said in 1944 that cotton production must be mechanized. "Our negroes have moved away, and I don't think they will come back unless forced to by economic necessity."[22]

In the early years of the war, most of the opportunities in southern industry were reserved for whites. Nonagricultural production employment had historically been considered work for white men and women. Blacks thus had less opportunity to participate in the burgeoning number of nonfarm jobs unless they left their home region. Although the Fair Employment Practices Committee forbade discrimination in employment on the basis of race among firms with defense contracts, and legislation existed to prohibit discrimination in federally funded training programs, blacks were denied equal opportunities in both training and employment throughout the South. Many southern employers believed they lacked the ability for most assembly-line jobs, and insisted, moreover, that whites would not work side by side with blacks. By not hiring blacks, employers avoided problems that might grow out of integrating the work place. Wartime administrators in charge of training programs were reluctant to provide blacks with job training even though the programs were segregated. Why train blacks, they argued, when industrialists would not hire them except as kitchen help, plant custodians, or unskilled helpers? When defense employers in Georgia were polled regarding jobs for blacks in September 1941, the survey showed that 95 percent of the openings were reserved for whites. Blacks were excluded from all of the 1,117 skilled or semiskilled jobs. Later in the war more jobs opened up for blacks, but discrimination was an important factor in slowing the black farm-to-factory movement from 1940 to 1945. This helps explain why in some parts of the South the number of black farmers actually increased during the war years. The civil rights campaign was not sufficiently strong in the early 1940s to protect blacks who wished to seek skilled and semiskilled jobs in manufacturing.[23]

The war had a dramatic effect on the income of southern farmers. While most of them were still poor when compared to farmers elsewhere, by the war's end in 1945 they were enjoying unprecedented good times. Much higher prices and expanded production combined to make most producers more prosperous than ever before. Between 1940 and 1944 cash income from farm marketings and government payments in eleven southern states more than doubled, jumping from about $2 to $4.7 billion. On a per capita basis, net income rose from $150 to $454. Yet, despite this sharp rise, southern farmers did not keep up with those in the country's other major agricultural regions. Income of persons on farms nationwide in 1944 was $530 per capita.[24]

Rising incomes and a larger number of off-farm jobs finally gave an increasing number of southern farmers a chance to escape from tenancy. The number of sharecroppers and tenants dropped rather sharply after 1940 as some operators left for industrial jobs and others managed to buy a farm. Tenancy decreased during the war years from an average of 49 to 42 percent in the eleven states of the Confederacy. In some states the decline was considerably greater. The drop in Louisiana and Texas was about 10 percent between 1940 and 1945. The smallest decline in tenancy was in the Carolinas, but even in some areas there a significant drop occurred. A study done of thirteen counties in the southern North Carolina Piedmont showed that tenancy dropped from 51 to 36 percent during the five war years.[25]

Not only were thousands of farmers able to become owners or part-owners, but many were able to increase their living standards. Level-of-living studies revealed that farmer operator families in the South made real economic gains between 1940 and 1945. Using the 1930 average as equaling 100, farmer living levels in the South Atlantic states rose from 65 to 87, or 22 percent; in the East South Central states it was 17 percent; and in the West South Central states, 25 percent, which matched the national average. The level of farm living in North Carolina rose by 30 percent during the war years. This was high for the South, but still fell below the gains made by farmers in the Midwest and Pacific Coast states.[26]

Improved living standards were reflected in a variety of ways. Despite wartime restrictions on the manufacture of automobiles and motor trucks, many more southern farmers owned vehicles by the end of the war. The percentage of southern farms reporting electricity rose from 18.6 percent in 1940 to 31.5 percent five years later. At least some southern farmers were getting out of the dark. Also, thousands of farmers from Virginia to Texas installed running water and telephones. Thus, while still lagging behind the rest of the nation's farmers, more southern farmers were beginning to enjoy aspects of modern living.[27]

Southern political and farm leaders did not hesitate to use the war in their effort to strengthen the federal farm programs. By 1940 these programs had become vitally important to most commercial farmers but especially to those in the South. While about 80 percent of the nation's cropland was covered by federal programs in 1939 and 1940, the figure was 90 percent in the South. The level of government price supports for cotton, tobacco, rice, peanuts, and sugarcane, then, was vital to these producers. By the time the United States entered the war, the price of many farm products was nearing, or even exceeding, parity. In 1942 rice, tobacco, peanuts, and soybeans were all above parity. In urging farmers to engage in all-out production, the Department of Agriculture was reversing the scarcity program which had been administered from Washington since 1933. Having gone through two decades of price-depressing surpluses, however, farmers were nervous about shifting from controls to all-out production. In some cases, such as peanuts, they did not meet government goals.

A matter that greatly worried farmers was what might happen when defense and wartime demands for agricultural commodities no longer existed. Would their shift to full production under price incentives and government pleas end up with huge surpluses and low prices, as had been the case after World War I? That had spelled disaster for hundreds of thousands of farmers in 1920 and 1921. The concern about an orderly transition from war to peace and the need for some assurance of price protection for a time after the war was shared by the South's agricultural spokesmen in Washington. These included House members Henry D. Steagall of Alabama, Stephen Pace of Georgia, Henry Fulmer of South Carolina, Harold D. Cooley of North Carolina, and Senators John H. Bankhead of Alabama and Richard B. Russell, Jr., of Georgia. These were all strong and influential leaders. Ed O'Neal of Alabama, president of the American Farm Bureau Federation, was also a powerful spokesman for commercial farmers, especially those who produced the South's staple crops.

Under the Emergency Price Control Act of October 1942, the Commodity Credit Corporation was directed to support the prices of corn, wheat, cotton, rice, tobacco, and peanuts produced by cooperating farmers for two years after the end of the war at 90 percent of parity. This law also included price supports at 90 percent of parity for two years after the war of a group of so-called Steagall commodities, or those for which the government had asked farmers to increase output to meet defense and wartime demands. As it turned out, this law guaranteed 90 percent of parity prices for the South's main commercial crops, plus several commodities that were not so basic, through the 1948 crop year. It was a definite victory for southern political leadership.[28]

Government price supports and growing changes in crop and farm organization patterns seemed to offer pleasing prospects for southern farmers at the close of World War II. The decreasing emphasis on cotton, development of other cash crops, an increase in pasture and forage for more livestock, greater attention to soil conservation, mechanization, larger farms, and the dependence of fewer people on agriculture were all evidence of fundamental change. Agricultural reformers had been preaching these developments since the turn of the century, but wartime conditions had exerted more influence than years of educational effort. The war had shaken up southern agriculture.

But it was easy to exaggerate the amount of change that had occurred in the rural South by 1945. To be sure, there were areas where dramatic signs of a new agriculture were beginning to appear, but the grip of old and established farming practices had only been loosened, not broken. Most of the South's farms were still largely untouched by modern currents. For example, there was no significant decrease in the number nor increase in the size of farms throughout most of the South. In the eleven southern states there were only 94,303 fewer farms in 1945 than in 1940, and the amount of cropland harvested actually averaged less per farm in 1944 than in 1939. In Alabama, for example, the average acreage of cropland harvested dropped from 30.7 to 27.6 acres, and in Georgia it dropped from 40.7 to 34.6 acres.

If one had traveled from Raleigh, North Carolina, through neighboring South Carolina, on through Georgia, Alabama, Mississippi, Louisiana, and as far west as Dallas, Texas, in 1945, he would have observed many more similarities than differences in the rural landscape from any prewar trip. A traveler would have passed poorly fed and poorly clothed people living in unpainted, weather-beaten shacks made worse with age, eroded fields, much idle land grown up in brush and weeds, and other signs of low productivity and poverty. Certainly more tractors and other machinery would have been in evidence than in the 1930s, and greater numbers of livestock could have been seen grazing on improved pastures, but the vast majority of farms in 1945 were still small, inefficient operations powered by mules pulling primitive equipment.

Nonetheless, by the end of World War II the cumulative effects of New Deal programs and wartime prosperity were beginning to bring noticeable changes to the region. Extensive governmental intervention in the agricultural economy in the 1930s and rising farm incomes generated by war made the years from about 1935 to 1945 a crucial turning point in the history of southern farming. These major historical developments, originating outside the region, began to break the bonds that had stifled agricultural change and held so many people in poverty.

The New Deal programs had begun to change southern agriculture by forcing a reduction in cotton acreage, by paying farmers to adopt soil conservation practices, and by urging them to shift to grass and livestock. Congress helped to initiate some of these changes by supporting staple-crop prices and by putting money directly into farm pockets through acreage diversion payments. It might be added that the Agricultural Adjustment Administration and the Soil Conservation Service touched many more farmers than had ever been reached by the agricultural colleges and the experiment stations. Federal lawmakers had even made some feeble attempts to help poorer farmers through the Resettlement Administration and the Farm Security Administration. What the New Deal had been unable to do was to open up opportunities for the South's surplus farm population. Until that problem could be solved, widespread rural poverty would continue.

Then suddenly, after two decades of depression, World War II produced full economic and industrial recovery that extended into the postwar years. Millions of new nonfarm jobs became available both in the South and throughout the nation. Agriculture in the South now began to shed the weight of surplus and unneeded workers. New markets also suddenly appeared. Moreover, wartime prosperity made it possible for farmers to reduce their debts and to increase capital expenditures. Some bought more and better machinery to replace the departing workers, others purchased additional land and enlarged their farms, and some switched to crops other than cotton and purchased livestock. In 1945 any planter or solid commercial family farmer who looked back over the previous decade could plainly see the fundamental influences of the New Deal and the war on his own or his neighbor's operations.

The prosperity of wartime, however, could not dispel the gnawing problems that were so evident in the rural South. Despite some gradual shift away from cotton after 1933, it continued to be the main cash crop for around 1.2 million, or nearly half, of all the South's farmers. The value of cotton and cottonseed exceeded $1.5 billion, or about 50 percent of all farm income in the South. The future of southern agriculture seemed to rest heavily on the economic health of cotton. But cotton's future at the war's end did not appear bright. Indeed, farmers, ginners, bankers, and others who depended on cotton viewed the situation with alarm.

Two key developments hung like a cloud over southern cotton growers. One was the increasing production of cotton in foreign countries, mainly India, Brazil, and China, which competed with the American product in world markets. In 1941 the United States produced only 38 percent of world production compared to 72 percent back in 1911. In addition, the increased production of rayon was eating into the cotton market. Between 1919 and 1943 the share of the fiber market taken over by rayon rose from 0.3 to 10.6 percent. Production of rayon in the United States alone in 1944 was the equivalent of 1.7 million bales of cotton. And rayon prices were dropping significantly, making the synthetic fiber a tough competitor. The effect of changing conditions for American cotton could be seen in the fact that, despite abnormally high wartime demand, annual carryovers in the United States, as mentioned earlier, never dropped below 10.5 million bales between 1940 and 1945.[29]

These were not matters that southern political leaders could ignore. Even before the war ended, Congressman Stephen Pace of Georgia chaired a subcommittee of the House Committee on Agriculture to study the cotton situation. Pace invited producers, processors, bankers, farm organization leaders, USDA officials, and others to meet in Washington on December 4, 1944. Stressing the importance of the problem, he opened the meeting by saying that cotton related "directly to the economic welfare of more people and has greater bearing upon the economy of the Nation than any other crop grown." O.V. Wells, chief of the USDA's Bureau of Agricultural Economics, expressed the same theme. "Any discussion of cotton," Wells testified, "is in fact a discussion of almost the entire agricultural problem of the South."[30]

In a follow-up to the hearings held in Washington, Congressman Pace's subcommittee sponsored a meeting in Memphis in May 1945 to discuss the "postwar agricultural and economic problems of the Cotton Belt." Some forty-five agricultural educators, scientists, economists, and others participated in the conference. One of the main outcomes of the Memphis meeting was to arrange for the preparation of ten studies on aspects of the southern economy. Two of the most important reports dealt with "Agricultural Adjustments toward an Efficient Agriculture in the South" and "Industrialization in the South." Efficiency on the farm and more nonfarm jobs were clearly interrelated and they were consid-

ered by many to be the main foundation for a prosperous southern
agriculture. In any event, these reports were not completed until
1947.[31]

Concern over the plight of cotton at the end of the war intensified
the campaign for increased farm efficiency throughout the South.
Critics of southern farming had for many years been preaching the
need for greater efficiency on the region's farms and plantations. By the
middle and late 1940s, efficiency had become a fetish. The old ways of
farming must go, and the quicker the better. Economists, scientists in
the agricultural colleges and experiment stations, county agents, writers for the farm press, spokesmen for the USDA, and others spoke and
wrote on the subject at every opportunity. In general, efficiency meant
adopting farm practices that would get greater crop production per acre
and per man hour, or, in the case of livestock, produce more pounds of
beef or chicken with less feed, land, and labor. This further implied that
farmers must have full-time, productive employment, working with
the best equipment on good land. To achieve these goals farmers
would require larger farms, mechanization, improved productivity of
land through conservation and fertilization, the adoption of better crop
and livestock breeds, and skilled management. Farm organization
changes would also be needed.

In May 1942, H.N. Young, an agricultural economist at Virginia
Polytechnic Institute, told a House subcommittee that "low per capita
production is the principal factor limiting incomes and, therefore,
lowering standards of living on our southern farms." H.P. Stukey,
director of the Georgia Experiment Station at Griffin, told a writer for
Progressive Farmer that "in the past our production per man or per
family has been too small to provide an adequate living. We should
plan to cultivate our land so that production per family can be increased." Frank J. Welch, dean of the School of Agriculture at Mississippi State College, declared that the "family-sized farm according to
horse-and-buggy standards must give way to family-sized farms using
modern power and equipment." Perhaps William Meek, an agricultural extension worker in Mississippi, put it best when he told a
group at the Delta Branch Experiment Station in 1947: "Gentlemen,
you've just got to bury grandpa. He's dead."[32] In other words, the
current structure of southern agriculture must be changed.

Efficiency in farm operations, however, was only half of the equa-
tion needed for a prosperous agriculture. World War II demonstrated
what some observers had been saying for years. The South's main farm
problems of overpopulation and surplus labor in agriculture could not
be solved strictly within the farm sector. Surely the old ideas of self-
sufficiency and diversification as portrayed in the early twentieth century by the slogan "a cow, a sow and a hen," were passé in a highly

industrialized and commercialized economy. Industrial jobs had drawn away farm workers during wartime, but the period had been too short to bring population and land resources into a significantly better economic balance. Some economists estimated that in 1945 there was still a 50 percent excess of farm population in some parts of the South.

What seemed obvious was the need for continued expansion of industrialization, coupled with increased efficiency expressed in greater productivity and lower labor costs among the remaining farmers. Larger farms and mechanization of cotton production were considered a "must" by most students of southern agriculture. As Secretary of Agriculture Claude Wickard remarked in late 1944, "Even if farmers received parity for every pound of cotton that could be grown in the South, the incomes of a great many of them would be too low to afford an acceptable level of living." Clarence Poe, who had been observing southern agriculture closely since before 1900, wrote in 1945 that low productivity per acre and per farm family, and a kind of crop farming that provided not much more than six months of productive labor a year, were doomed to fail.[33]

Representative Pace called his subcommittee together in July 1947 to hear the reports authorized at the Memphis meeting two years earlier. Dean Welch of Mississippi State College presented the need for southern agricultural adjustment. The entire thrust of Welch's discussions and recommendations concentrated on the need for greater efficiency. In this respect he spoke for all of the farm experts in the agricultural colleges, the USDA, editors of farm journals, and other reformers. Welch explained that southern agriculture had lagged behind in "scientific and technological" progress, and that "per capita production on southern farms is low, physical resources are uneconomically and often unwisely used, and capital equipment is deficient." He argued that too much labor was being used, as "reflected in low per capita incomes." Larger farms, mechanization, and a reduction of the farm labor force were major elements in Welch's solution to southern farm problems. By using more power and machinery and by increasing the volume of production per acre, at least one-third less labor, Welch said, would be needed on southern farms than was found there as late as 1943. The key to improved efficiency was to substitute capital for labor.

Reformers such as Welch emphasized the direct relationship between low income and underemployment. The lack of full-time productive work on many southern farms, especially on cotton farms, had been recognized since the 1870s. There was an "ineffective use of labor." Part of this took the form of actual idleness in slack labor times, or working on jobs that produced little or no income. To correct this situation, farm specialists urged southerners to establish a better combination of crop and livestock enterprises that would occupy family labor more fully and efficiently. As Clarence Poe wrote in the *Progressive Farmer* late in 1945, farmers should have a 50-50 balance between crops and livestock which would give them high production "based on full year around employment."[34]

The changes advocated for southern farms implied that the surplus workers would have to find employment elsewhere. This meant that nonfarm employment alternatives must be provided through industrialization. Factories, it was said, were the answer to many southern farm problems. The authors of a report on "Industrialization and the South" argued that "the most fundamental forces working against the Cotton Belt are tied in with its present agrarianism." There was still widespread belief in the importance and goodness of farmers in society, but in 1947 and 1948 students of problems in the cotton belt did not let agrarian idealism influence their recommendations for the region's future. Larger and fewer farms, employment of more capital, mechanization, a better combination of crops and livestock, the application of science to agriculture, and soil conservation were considered to be the wave of the future. In other words, southern farmers must emulate producers in the Midwest and Great Plains, where modernized agriculture was far advanced. The people who could not participate in these changes must be absorbed by factories and other nonfarm jobs either on a full- or a part-time basis. "The small farmer, with his 40 acres and his mule," wrote one observer, "will be bought or mortgaged out, to become a wage worker on a plantation run like a factory, or he will move to the city, or he will plant something else [other than cotton]."[35]

But what would happen to the people who left southern farms? Could they be absorbed into nonfarm jobs? After visiting a number of farmers and planters in 1944, Frank H. Jeter wrote in the *Farm Journal* that "some people are not worrying much about it, while others are shrugging it off" as "unfortunate but inevitable." A member of the National Cotton Council said that the problem of displaced farmers and farm workers "should not be allowed to stand in the way of progress." E.D. White, assistant to the secretary of agriculture, told an audience at the second Beltwide Cotton Mechanization Conference in 1948 that any farm unemployment created by mechanizing cotton production must be dealt with by "means other than the slowing down of mechanization." White suggested retraining and relocation.[36] He implied that the agricultural sector had no responsibility for absorbing or caring for surplus workers.

While spokesmen for southern agriculture believed they knew what needed to be done to redeem farm prosperity, they recognized that change would come slowly. I.O. Schaub, director of the North Carolina Agricultural Extension Service, told Pace's subcommittee that "getting large masses of people to respond to recommended changes in their habits and practices is relatively slow and sometimes discouraging."[37] Schaub might have added that many southern farmers did not have the freedom of choice that change implied. They did not possess the land, capital, or managerial talents needed for better farming. And tens of thousands of farmers were devoid of hope. Sharecroppers and tenants had struggled against great odds for years. Some had once been owners and had fallen into tenancy; others had worked hard but failed to rise to land ownership. Working year in and year out, they saw little chance to raise their standard of living. It is no wonder that the common attitude of "We can't make nothin' but a livin' nohow" was heard so often among poor farmers.[38] In the 1940s many farmers in the South, both black and white, were moving from place to place each year, much as their grandfathers had done in the 1890s and their fathers in the 1920s. Lack of standardization in the rural schools made it difficult for students who moved frequently, and their education, although improved over the 1920s, was still pitifully inadequate. Overall, there was nothing in the experiences of these farmers and their families to create hope or incentive. Many of them would be the "farmers left behind."

9

Modernization Comes to Southern Farms

By the middle and late 1940s the changes occurring on some southern farms were attracting national attention. Writers for the popular press toured the South and wrote glowing reports on what they saw. The words "revolution" and "New South" appeared in almost every article. "Revolution in Cotton" was the identical title used for an article in *Collier's* in July 1945 and for one in the *New Republic* about a year later. In order to record the changes in 1949, the editor of *Life* sent Margaret Bourke-White, who had pictured the plight of sharecroppers twelve years earlier, to photograph the new agriculture and other aspects of the New South. She pictured large peach orchards growing on contoured land near Spartanburg, South Carolina, cattle grazing on lush pastures in southern Georgia, a mechanical cotton picker operating near Greenville, Mississippi, and other signs of emerging modernization.[1]

The true modernization of farming in the South, as well as elsewhere, depended on a number of interrelated developments, or what economists sometimes call a package of practices. One of the most obvious of these factors was the mechanization of farm production. The tractor and mechanical cotton picker were the most evident symbols of growing change in the effort to save labor costs on southern farms by the late 1940s. But profitable use of the most modern machinery depended on higher-yielding crops, greater soil fertility, better control of weeds and insects, and changes in farm organization. For example, it would not be profitable to use tractor power to raise cotton that made only 150 pounds per acre, or corn that produced only 10 to 20 bushels to the acre, as had been true throughout most of the South up to World War II.

The tractor needed to be employed on properly fertilized land where hybrid corn producing 40 or 50 bushels to the acre would be planted, or cotton that would yield 300 or 400 pounds per acre. The idea was to increase the volume of production and lower the cost per unit. In the case of livestock, it was not profitable to try to raise blooded stock on brushy and weedy pastures. Improved pasture and forage were as necessary as better breeds. Southern farmers, then, needed to combine the latest advances in technology and science. It was necessary to apply the results of work by engineers, chemists, botanists, agronomists, entomologists, and other scientists, as well as farm management experts, in order to solve the problems of low productivity and meager incomes.

One of the greatest deterrents to change in southern agriculture continued to be the lack of capital. Every step taken to improve agricultural output required investment. This included money for machinery, for enlarging acreages, for soil conservation practices and fertilizer, and for better seed and breeds of livestock. Ever since the Civil War most southern farmers had been grossly undercapitalized. Average farm investment per worker in land and buildings in 1944 and 1945 was only $2,212 and $1,923 in the South Atlantic and East South Central states respectively. This compared to $7,668 in the West North Central states and $7,175 in the East North Central states. Average per worker investment in livestock in the South Atlantic states was only $343, and in equipment a meager $187. This compared to $1,592 and $926 invested in livestock and machinery per worker in the North Central states. This low capital investment continued to reflect low production per farm worker in the South. Using 100 as the index figure for average production per farm worker in the United States in 1944, output per worker in the East South Central and South Atlantic states was only 51 and 61 respectively. For farm workers in the North Central states the figure was 168, or around three times higher. Southern farmers simply did not have much to work with.[2]

Fortunately, the situation regarding the scarcity of capital was beginning to change in the 1940s. There were at least three major sources of farm capital. One, of course, was money saved from current production. Since output and incomes had been so low among most southern farmers, capital accumulation had been slow or in many cases nonexistent prior to World War II. Rather than being able to save anything, many farmers went deeper and deeper into debt. But the high prices and good crops during World War II permitted many producers not only to pay off their debts but to have something left over to spend for more land, machinery, livestock, and other income-producing investments. Farm mortgage debt was down in all of the southern states in 1945 compared to 1940.[3] This meant that farmers had to pay less in interest and principal payments and had more left over for new investment.

Secondly, the agencies of the Farm Credit Administration provided both long-term capital and operating funds at low rates of interest for thousands of farmers. Federal Land Bank loans were extended to only 1,723 farmers in the Carolinas, Georgia, Alabama, and Mississippi in the year ending January 1, 1940; the number had risen to 5,590 for fiscal year 1947. This was still a very small number, but was helpful. Southern farmers also borrowed millions of dollars for short-term operating expenses from the Production Credit Associations. These loans usually did not carry interest rates of more than 4.5 percent. In 1939 this source of cheap credit amounted to only about $80 million, but a decade later some 133,000 farmers in eleven southern states had $286.8 million in PCA credit.[4] A few thousand lower-income farmers were getting cheap credit from the Farmers Home Administration in the late 1940s.

Commercial banks provided a third source of credit to farmers for both capital and operating expenses. These institutions had been inadequate in most farm communities before the Great Depression, and the hard times of the 1930s did not encourage local bankers to finance many farmers. The prosperous 1940s, however, brought more commercial bankers back into the farm-loan business. In 1940 farm-mortgage loans extended by insured commercial banks amounted to only around $80 million in the eleven southern states; by 1949 the figure had more than doubled, to $174.8 million. Insurance companies which had suffered substantial losses on their farm loans in the early 1930s did not reenter the business on the same scale as earlier, especially in the East and West South Central states.[5]

It is clear that the sources of capital and credit had greatly improved for southern farmers by the 1940s, and that interest rates were generally low. It was the farmer who operated most profitably who had the easiest access to needed credit. It was a case of "to him who hath it shall be given." The farmer who could show efficient production plans and who had a record of carrying out those plans was considered a good risk and usually had little difficulty of obtaining adequate capital and operating credit. The poorer southern farmer had to hope that the Farmers Home Administration would assist him. The number of small, poor, inefficient farmers was so large, however, that the FHA, with its limited resources, could not even dent the problem. These farmers either quit farming or found part-time off-farm employment.

Access to capital did not assure success in agriculture. A farmer needed the managerial and organizational abilities to put all of the factors of production—land, labor, and capital—together into a profitable operating unit. As capital requirements rose, in fact, a farmer's business practices were all the more important. Once a farmer had invested money in a tractor and related machinery, a beef cattle herd, or a dairy, he had to manage that investment carefully. Such a farmer had a chance to make larger profits, but big losses were also possible. The one- or two-mule farm could never make a family more than a subsistence living, if that, but losses could never be large. Higher capital investments, then, not only increased the possibilities of profits but also increased a farmer's risks. This situation was recognized in the 1940s, but it became increasingly evident to farmers in later years, particularly in the 1970s and early 1980s.

For many years the agricultural colleges and experiment stations in the southern states had been urging farmers to change their farming practices. Engineers and scientists had done research on farm mechanization, fertilization, soil conservation, specialized crops, marketing, improved pastures and livestock breeds, and many other aspects of southern farming. These institutions had also sponsored farm management studies since before World War I. Even though a great amount of information was available to farmers on how they might make their operations more profitable, most southern farmers were unwilling or unable to employ drastically different farming and land-use practices.

The developments that finally brought drastic agricultural change to the South were largely outside the control or influence of the individual farmers to whom the agricultural colleges and experiment stations directed their advice. The powerful influences of high wartime and postwar prices, federal price supports and other government programs, agricultural technology and the work of scientists were determined by international events, domestic politics, and the support given to research by governments and private companies. But once opportunities were present to inaugurate change, it was up to the individual farmer to take every advantage of the information provided on machines, crops, pastures, livestock, marketing, and overall farm organization practices. By the 1940s more and more southern farmers, some of whom had attended the agricultural colleges, were in the vanguard of change. Those who introduced the most drastic changes in their operations were, of course, a small minority. A larger number adopted some changes, while an even greater number continued in the old ways until they went broke or found nonfarm employment. Throughout most of the South, changes developed slowly in the 1940s but gained momentum rapidly in the late 1950s and 1960s. It cannot be overemphasized, however, that change occurred at vastly different rates in different areas and subregions of the South. Nevertheless, when technology and science teamed up with better informed farmers, the old agriculture which had resisted change for three-quarters of a century was doomed to oblivion. It was a revolution which occurred in less than a single generation. The southern Georgia or central

Alabama farmer who began farming on the eve of World War II and continued to farm in the 1970s found his operations as different as day from night.

More than anything else, mechanization was the agent of change on southern farms. The key to mechanized farming was the tractor, which provided a source of power to cultivate more land better and with less labor. By 1950, 23.4 percent of the farmers in eleven southern states operated tractors, compared to only 6.3 percent in 1940 and 11.7 percent in 1945.[6] The growing use of tractors during the 1940s and 1950s was important far beyond just replacing mule and hand power with machines. Tractors were fundamental in stimulating important shifts in crop patterns and in encouraging an increase in all classes of livestock, except for mules and horses. Tractors and related machines were thus a major factor in changing the structure and organization of southern agriculture.

In 1948 and 1949 the Georgia Agricultural Experiment Station published two studies on the use of tractors in the Piedmont and Coastal Plains. By use of survey methods, researchers got information from sixty-eight farmers in five Piedmont counties and sixty-four producers in two Coastal Plains counties. The idea was to compare the operations of those farmers before and after they obtained one or more tractors. These studies showed that similar trends prevailed in the two areas. Tractor farms were larger, they grew relatively less in row crops, such as cotton and corn, and more in small grains, pasture, and forage. The tractor farmers also had more hogs, milk cows, and beef cattle. Some farmers with tractors in this period continued to maintain workstock, although the numbers gradually decreased. The largest farms were those using tractor and mule power. The general pattern was for a farmer to buy a tractor and use it in conjunction with his workstock for several years. But as farmers found that tractors and other machinery could do more and more of the farm work, they gradually sold off their mules. From 1945 to 1955 the number of mules in the Carolinas, Georgia, Alabama, and Mississippi dropped from about 1.3 million to 951,000.[7]

As farms with tractors got bigger—the acreage rose 29 percent in a period of only five or six years in the Piedmont counties surveyed—the number of sharecroppers declined. But when the sharecroppers left, it did not mean that the land was abandoned. The old sharecrop acreage was incorporated into larger, mechanized operations, and the farmer planted more of his land to grains and forage crops. It was the shifting out of cotton that destroyed most opportunities for sharecroppers, and these researchers found that blacks left farms in large numbers "mainly because of the unfavorable cotton situation to seek more favorable employment elsewhere." While sharecropping continued through the

1950s and even into the 1960s, it declined rapidly during those years.

Tractor farmers not only tended to have larger farms, they also cultivated more acres of cropland. In the group studied, the average cropland rose about 65 percent after the arrival of a tractor. The great expansion on those farms was in grain. Average small-grain acreage per farm rose from 21 to 55 acres under tractor power. There was also a substantial increase in the acreage of lespedeza, grass, hay, and forage. This reflected more emphasis on livestock. In the five Georgia Piedmont counties studied, farmers increased their beef cattle numbers by 174 percent. The number of dairy cows rose 52 percent.

When farmers were asked about the advantages of tractors, they emphasized that they could farm more acres and do the work better and faster. They were impressed with the timeliness of getting jobs completed. Farmers found that one of the greatest advantages provided by tractors was that of increased power. This was essential, for instance, for genuine land improvement. Mule power was not sufficient to change cropping patterns from, say, cotton to grass and back to cotton or corn. Farmers reported that the tractor was very important as a tool for soil conservation and to build pastures. "I couldn't have fall and winter pasture without power equipment," one farmer declared in 1945.[8] Mule power was inadequate for deep plowing, good terracing, removing stumps, rocks, and hedge rows, and filling ditches. If farmers were going to enlarge their grain and hay production, they needed enough power to get the required machinery over more acres. By 1946, of the farmers surveyed in the Piedmont of Georgia, about two-thirds of them had mowing machines and grain combines. To improve the quality of plowing and cultivating, they required power beyond what could be furnished by one or two mules. The tractor, then, proved to be a major facilitator of change in southern farming and was the big influence in permitting the modification of land and cropping patterns. The full impact, however, was not felt until the 1950s and later.[9]

For many farmers and planters throughout the South, mechanization of production was among the highest priorities by the late 1940s and early 1950s. As one observer wrote in 1945, farmers had become convinced that "the one-man, one-mule days are definitely over."[10] Cotton growers were especially anxious to reduce labor costs in order to keep cotton competitive with foreign production and synthetic fibers. The greatest advances in mechanization occurred on the large plantations in the Mississippi Delta.

The problem of mechanizing cotton growing had not been fully solved with International Harvester Company's manufacture of a successful spindle-type picker in 1941. Only about 300 of these machines had been produced and sold by 1947. In July 1948 International Harvester opened a new plant at Memphis to manufacture mechanical pickers, and soon hundreds of these machines were available for cotton farmers.[11] Yet by 1950 only about 5 percent of the nation's cotton was picked by machine, and much of that was in Arizona and California. In the Old South, mechanical cotton pickers were confined mainly to the Mississippi Delta.

Before complete mechanization of cotton production could occur, other changes were necessary. It was important, for example, to breed a cotton plant on which the bolls would develop higher on the stalk and open more evenly. With higher and more uniformly opening bolls, operators could keep the machine out of the dirt and harvest the crop in one trip through the field. To reduce trash in machine-picked cotton, chemicals were required to control weeds and to defoliate the cotton plant before harvest, and gins had to be improved so they could properly clean machine-picked cotton and eliminate grade loss. Entomologists and engineers needed to join efforts to develop proper pesticides and get them spread over the crop in the most efficient way. As mentioned earlier, before full mechanization of the cotton crop could be achieved, the combined contributions of engineers, chemists, fertilizer specialists, plant breeders, entomologists, agronomists, and other scientists were necessary. Full mechanization also required some changes in farm organization throughout much of the cotton belt. Tractors and related machines could not be operated efficiently on most of the small farms that had no more than 20 to 50 acres of cropland. Such small acreages could not justify the capital requirements associated with mechanization. For example, in 1945 a cotton picker cost $2,674 and a tractor $1,250.[12] With only slight exaggeration, a South Carolina farmer reported in 1949 that a picker "cost as much as a hundred acres of land."[13] Tractors, pickers, and other machines were simply not feasible for small cotton growers. Mechanization was much more than engineering. It involved a wide and interrelated set of technological, scientific, economic, and social factors.

By the 1940s the importance of agricultural research and experimentation had become increasingly evident if cotton belt farmers were going to mechanize their operations completely. A big boost to research in cotton mechanization came in 1946, when Congress passed the Research and Marketing Act. Prior to this time the most significant work on cotton mechanization in the South had been done at the Mississippi and Texas agricultural experiment stations. But resources had been limited. In 1947 a regional cotton mechanization research project was established at Stoneville, Mississippi, the site of the Mississippi Delta Branch Experiment Station, with federal funding provided under the Research and Marketing Act. Resources were now available to do more extensive research on all phases of cotton mechanization. Early in 1947 the National Cotton Council of America also pledged to support "programs designed to completely mechanize the production of cotton."[14] The first beltwide cotton mechanization conference was held at Stoneville on August 18 and 19, 1947. This was the beginning of an annual meeting on farm mechanization in the South, indicating how important machine production had become in the minds of agricultural scientists and engineers, management specialists, educators, and farmers.

Weed control was one of the most serious obstacles to complete mechanization of cotton production in the humid southeast. Farmers experimented with the rotary hoe, cross cultivation, and flame weeders in an effort to eliminate thinning and weeding by hand. The flame cultivator was designed to shoot a hot flame at the base of the cotton plant, killing the tender young grass and weeds. It showed considerable promise in the late 1940s, when a number of planters used it successfully. When rainy weather kept machines out of the field, however, the weeds and grass grew so large that the flame would not kill them without also destroying the young cotton plants. Neville W. Bennett, a South Carolina farmer, told delegates at the third Beltwide Cotton Mechanization Conference in 1949 that "we can never mechanize completely, anywhere east of the Mississippi River, unless we have some reliable system of weed control." Because of the need to control weeds, he stated, farmers hesitated to put a worker on a tractor to farm 100 acres of land, tear down tenant houses, and rely on machines. Where would the hundreds of cotton choppers come from, Bennett asked, if the machines could not do their job?[15] The problem remained unsolved and retarded cotton mechanization until chemical weed killers, especially the preemergent types, became available in the early 1950s. Within a decade most progressive growers used chemicals to destroy weeds. An Arkansas planter reported in 1962 that "we do not consider planting any cotton without preemergent chemicals."[16]

Because of the many factors and decisions associated with technological advance, mechanization on southern farms moved ahead by fits and starts. Seldom did a farmer or planter mechanize all at once. In 1946, for example, planters in the Mississippi Delta who owned mechanical pickers did not make full use of them. Most producers used hand labor in order to begin picking earlier and to assure a higher quality of cotton. Some planters reported doing the early picking by hand and then bringing in the machines for later harvesting. Nevertheless, planters in the Mississippi Delta were moving rapidly toward full mechanization of cotton growing by 1947 and 1948, partly because of a scarcity of labor, and also because of their desire to reduce production costs. By 1953 about 25 percent of the cotton in Mississippi Delta counties was picked by machine.[17] Texas farmers who used cotton strippers for harvesting were also becoming fully mechanized.

The large number of small farms throughout most of the South was a major deterrent to mechanization. Of approximately 105,000 farmers in North Carolina growing cotton in 1949, for example, about 73 percent had less than 10 acres each. Only 136 had more than 100 acres. Experts estimated that a farmer needed at least 35 to 50 acres of cropland to justify a tractor, and 100 acres or more of cotton to profit from a mechanical cotton picker. It is not surprising, then, that there were only a few mechanical cotton pickers in North Carolina and other states in the early 1950s, while at the same time hundreds of such machines were being used on plantations in the Mississippi Delta. Nevertheless, on September 16, 1953, International Harvester's office at Charlotte, North Carolina, reported that it had shipped 186 mechanical cotton pickers to dealers in the region.[18]

What many farmers in the Southeast needed was not only larger acreages but also smaller and cheaper machines. George B. Nutt, head of the Agricultural Engineering Department at Clemson University, told a conference at Gadsden, Alabama, in October 1953: "Give our farmers low cost, dependable machines, designed to meet the conditions of this area [the Southeast], and rapid progress will be made in mechanizing the cotton harvest."[19] By the late 1950s "progress through machines" was being seen throughout the South's major farming regions. Especially rapid progress occurred in the Mississippi Delta during the 1950s. By 1960 cotton operations in Delta counties of Arkansas, Louisiana, and Mississippi were nearly 100 percent mechanized. In 1963 some 37 percent of the cotton in Alabama and more than half of the crop in Georgia was picked by machine, indicating that smaller commercial farmers as well as planters had at last abandoned the old methods of production. By the 1960s, the great majority of farmers who grew any substantial acreage of cotton were completely mechanized.[20]

Mechanization, especially the cotton picker, was a major factor in transforming the crop mix and labor organization on southern plantations. From shortly after the Civil War until the 1930s, the so-called fragmented plantation had been most common. Plantations were occupied by sharecroppers and tenants, who lived on the land and farmed a few acres, usually cotton, on some kind of share basis. This system was described by geographers as "the fragmented occupance form," where farmers cultivated small patches of land under at least semi-independent conditions. By the 1940s and 1950s this plantation organization was breaking down. W.M. Garrard, general manager of the Staple Cotton Cooperative Association of Greenwood, Mississippi, said in 1944 that "the old plantation system is what we prefer but we are being forced out of it. It has become hopelessly uneconomic." A year later, Frank J. Welch, head of the department of agricultural economics at Mississippi State College, and D. Miley Gray, of the Mississippi

Agricultural Experiment Station, wrote that "mechanization will all but destroy the old plantation system as it has existed since shortly after the Civil War." That destruction was already well under way when these agricultural experts wrote. H.A. Pedersen and Arthur F. Raper observed in 1954 that Delta plantations were in transition. "The old [mule and hand labor] has not yet gone and the new [mechanization] has not fully arrived. The mixture of the old and new is the thing." By the 1960s, however, the transition was virtually complete.[21]

As planters mechanized, they needed larger fields to make the best use of their equipment. The 20- to 40-acre plots farmed by sharecroppers were a hindrance to centralized operations. Planters therefore got rid of their sharecroppers, either by dismissing them or by the workers' finding nonfarm jobs. Then planters consolidated the fields and destroyed the sharecropper shacks. The planter needed labor to run the machines, but rather than dispersing it over the plantation he brought his hired workers into homes around the machine stations. In some cases this created a kind of small plantation village. The planter now used wage labor under central management and supervision. No longer did the landowner have to insist on cotton or some staple crop in order to assure himself of cash income. He could use the machinery to grow soybeans or grain, or to plant grass and forage for livestock. He would be governed by what was most profitable for him under changing agricultural conditions.

To support the needed machinery, planters often rented land in addition to what they owned. In some cases the largest farms had a small ownership base. The Vandiver plantation in northern Alabama covered some 5,000 acres, but the owner-farm consisted of only 160 acres. The rest of the land was rented, and was farmed by twelve wage hands. Between 1944 and 1964 the percentage of land operated by full owners declined as more land was operated by part owners who had a base of their own and rented additional acres. The Vandiver plantation rented land from thirty-four different landlords. The technological revolution had made the ownership of land less important, while capital investment in machinery and management increased in significance. Land units were combined into large, efficient operations through management rather than ownership. Of course, some large farms and plantations fully owned by the operator continued to be common in parts of the South, especially in the Mississippi Delta.

While these changes were most evident on large plantations, landowners with four or five sharecroppers followed a similar pattern. They and their families, with perhaps one hired hand, could do so much more work with a tractor and other modern machinery that there was no need for sharecroppers. On both the family-size farms and the large plantations a "spatial reorganization" had taken place. As geographer James S. Fisher wrote, plantations had developed into "highly organized, highly centralized, and highly rational production systems." The old fragmentation of labor—sharecroppers and tenants—over the plantation disappeared.[22] Other than the increase in trees, nothing so modified the southern rural landscape in the 1960s and 1970s as the destruction of tens of thousands of sharecropper and tenant houses. They had been the symbol of a fragmented agricultural organization and stark signs of southern rural poverty from the 1870s to World War II. While some shacks remained in the 1980s as reflections of an earlier day, their gradual oblivion heralded a new day on southern commercial farms.

While much of the emphasis was placed on mechanizing cotton production after World War II, other crops also succumbed to mechanization on a wide scale. Machines were readily available for improved ground preparation, planting, cultivating, and harvesting of corn, small grains, soybeans, and forage crops. Tobacco and peanuts, like cotton, resisted mechanization.

Up to the end of World War II most aspects of peanut harvesting were done by hand. It was one of the hardest and dirtiest farm jobs. The peanuts were plowed up, shaken by hand, and stacked on poles for drying. After the peanuts dried they were threshed. In the late 1940s the shakerwindrower came into use. This machine dug and lifted the peanuts from the ground, shook them free of dirt and placed them in windrows. Following a few days of drying, they were threshed with a peanut combine that was pulled through the field behind a tractor. To further increase efficiency agricultural engineers in the 1960s developed the two- and four-row peanut inverter which dug the peanuts and turned the vines so the nuts were on top of the windrow. This permitted better drying of the peanuts, which were then threshed by a self-propelled combine. By the 1970s the latest peanut machinery had come into general use on the larger and more efficient peanut farms. These machines drastically reduced labor requirements for peanut production.[23]

Mechanization of the tobacco harvest presented extremely difficult problems. In the first place, strong traditions on how tobacco ought to be handled had to be overcome. Most farmers, as well as tobacco buyers, believed that leaves must be removed from the tobacco plant by hand. They were then fastened together at the base in a hand-sized collection of three to five leaves and tied to a 5-foot 1-inch stick and hung from tier poles in a tobacco barn for curing.

To mechanize the tobacco harvest completely two things were needed. First, there must be a machine that would pull the leaves from the stalk, and then bulk curing must be accepted. This meant that instead of tying tobacco on sticks and hanging it in curing barns, the farmer would place the tobacco in racks and cure it in bulk curing facilities.

The first step toward mechanizing the tobacco harvest came about 1950, when a machine called a riding primer, or picker, was developed. This was a wheeled rig on which pickers rode. As the outfit moved slowly through the field, at first pulled by a tractor but later self-propelled, pickers removed the tobacco leaves, which were then elevated to a platform, where workers tied them on sticks. While those actually removing the tobacco leaves were able to ride rather than walk through the field, hand work still prevailed. Nevertheless, these riding primers were quickly adopted by North Carolina farmers, and the first ones were used in Georgia in 1953.

Meanwhile, research was being done on bulk curing. Experimentation dealt with the kinds of barns to use and the loading and unloading of the racks or frames of tobacco leaves which had to be placed in the barns. The aim was to handle the racks of tightly packed tobacco with hoists or some other mechanical method. The first commercial bulk curing barn was put into use in Robeson County, North Carolina, in 1960. Within two years about 120 North Carolina farmers had bulk curing units. In Georgia, Burnell Gaskins near Willacoochee installed four bulk curing barns in 1961 for use the following year.

Complete mechanization of the flue-cured tobacco harvest came with development of the tobacco combine. As early as 1947, when he went to North Carolina State College, Robert W. Wilson began research on mechanization of the tobacco harvest. A patent for a machine to remove tobacco leaves from the stalk was taken out in 1954, but the machine did not become practical until after bulk curing had developed and marketing regulations were modified. Wilson left North Carolina State College in 1954, but he did not abandon his interest in mechanical harvesting of tobacco. He and other engineers in time developed a self-propelled tobacco combine. This machine removed the tobacco leaves as it moved through the field and elevated them into racks or containers ready for the bulk curing barns. A few combines were in use in the late 1960s, but this machine came into general use among the larger tobacco farmers only in the 1970s. Most authorities believed that a farmer needed at least 40 acres of tobacco to justify a combine. Nevertheless, on a growing number of farms, tobacco production had been mechanized by the 1970s. Progress in mechanization was confined mainly to the flue-cured tobacco region of the Southeast.[24]

Machines were also developed for the specialized crops, such as nuts and fruits. Equipment to shake the nuts from pecan trees onto canvas or plastic aprons where they could be easily loaded on trucks greatly cut the labor demands for pecan growers in Georgia, Alabama, and Texas.

The growing number of tractors, grain and soybean combines, pick-up hay balers, corn pickers, peanut harvesters, tobacco combines, and other modern machines indicated the degree to which southern farms were becoming mechanized. While many small farms continued to keep mules in the 1950s, the agricultural census of 1960 considered them so unimportant that they were not counted separately. Mules could not compete with tractors, which rapidly began to take the place of human and animal power in southern agriculture in the late 1940s, and replaced people and animals on a broad scale a decade later. Only about 11.7 percent of the farms had tractors in 1945, but by 1970 the figure exceeded 73 percent. The number of combines to harvest grain and soybeans more than doubled between 1945 and 1950, and continued to rise in the following decade.[25]

Moreover, larger and more powerful machines were gradually substituted for smaller and less efficient equipment. The early tractors usually pulled two-row planters and cultivators, and combines had only a five- to eight-foot swath. In the 1950s many producers went to four-row equipment and some to six-row. Eight-row machinery was becoming common among larger farmers in the 1960s.

Machinery at last permitted southern farmers to employ better land-use practices and to carry on their operations in a more timely manner. But machinery was only one aspect of the drive to increase efficiency and productivity. It was essential for southern farmers to increase their production per acre. To do this they planted improved seeds, used more scientific applications of fertilizer, and attacked crop-destroying weeds and insects with chemicals. Improved breeds of cotton and better fertilization helped increase the production of cotton from about 200 to 250 pounds per acre in 1940 to around 400 to 450 pounds in 1960. Farmers grew 12.5 million bales on 23.8 million acres in 1940, but in 1960 they produced 14.3 million bales on only 15.3 million acres.[26] While corn acreage dropped throughout the South after World War II, production per acre rose dramatically as farmers began to plant hybrid varieties and applied balanced fertilizer to produce much more abundant crops. Average corn production was only around 15 bushels per acre from 1937 to 1945, but by 1960 it averaged 40 to 50 bushels, and some farmers were making 70, 80, and even 100 bushels of corn. Tobacco production, about 1,000 pounds per acre in 1940, had increased to more than 1,700 pounds in 1960. Peanut yields in Georgia rose about 4.6 times in the quarter century after 1950.[27]

Researchers in the USDA, the agricultural colleges, and the agricultural experiment stations played a major role in advancing productivity. They bred new crop strains, developed advanced machines, and advised farmers on the best use of fertilizer and how best to control weeds and insects. Before World War II the scientists and engineers from these institutions had not much more than prepared the ground-work for later developments. Their impact had been small because only a few farmers responded to their advice. In 1939, J. Phil Campbell of Georgia, who had worked in various USDA agencies for many years, described the situation: "The Colleges of Agriculture have been doing their work for over forty years and farmers' institutes and agricultural papers have been spreading knowledge in every direction, yet less than five per cent of the farmers in some states of the South has accepted any material improvement in their farm operations, and the great masses are as wedded to their old systems as before these educational movements were inaugurated."

From the 1940s onward, however, hundreds of the larger and more efficient farmers worked closely with agronomists, entomologists, biologists, horticulturalists, engineers, and other specialists at the agri-cultural colleges and experiment stations. A Shelby County, Alabama, cotton farmer told a reporter in 1962 that he had been using a pre-emergent herbicide ever "since it was first recommended by Au-burn."[28] Progressive farmers were anxious to use information based on the latest scientific experiments. The old-time reluctance to accept scientific data, or "book farming," as it had been called, evaporated quickly in the postwar years. By the 1950s farmers were sometimes too anxious to try new crop strains, fertilizers, and production methods. Frank P. King, fomer director of the Coastal Plains Agricultural Experi-ment Station at Tifton, Georgia, recalled that "we had to hide things that were very promising" because farmers would want to try them before they had been sufficiently tested by the station's scientists.[29]

A third aspect of the agricultural revolution joined in by southern farmers was the use of chemicals to increase production and to control insects and weeds. Southern farmers had historically been the leading users of fertilizers and chemical powders and sprays to kill insects. Chemicals had been used in the fight against the boll weevil since before World War I. In the post-World War II period a whole range of new pesticides and insecticides with much higher toxicity came on the market. Among the best known and most widely used until it was outlawed in the early 1970s was DDT. Still fighting the boll weevil and other pests, many cotton farmers sprayed their fields, usually from airplanes, with insecticide on a weekly basis to combat all kinds of damaging insects. Herbicides were applied at planting time to destroy weed growth and to reduce the need for cultivation of row crops. By the 1960s the modern southern farmer was growing better crop strains on land that was properly tilled and fertilized, and on which he had applied chemicals to reduce losses from insects and weeds.[30]

All of these changes brought major shifts in land use patterns throughout the South after World War II. One of the most significant changes was the permanent decline of cotton acreage and the final demise of cotton as the South's major cash crop, except in a few areas such as the Mississippi Delta. Between 1950 and 1960, total cotton acreage harvested in South Carolina, Georgia, Alabama, and Mississippi, the heart of the old cotton belt, declined from 5.2 to 3.6 million acres. Part of this drop could be credited to some forced reduction under government price-support policies. For example, as surpluses mounted in 1949 after farmers had planted some 27 million acres of cotton, Congress reduced production to about 21 million acres for the 1950 crop. But farmers did not plant even that much. Increased demand generated by the Korean War encouraged a sharp increase in acreage, but wartime markets did nothing to relieve cotton's chronic surplus problem. In 1954 Congress reimposed controls by setting the limit at about 21 million acres.[31]

Acreage allotments on many southern farms were too small to support a family. In 1955 about 80 percent of the acreage allotments in North Carolina were only six acres or less. Farmers with such small allotments were unable to afford the machinery and to follow advanced production practices to achieve the needed efficiency. About three out of five of these small cotton producers did not even have a tractor in 1954.[32] The gradual reduction of cotton acreage in the South and the expanding allotments to western growers angered southern politicians and farm spokesmen. Senator Richard B. Russell of Georgia made more than one fight to protect his cotton-growing constituents but without much success. As one Georgian wrote Russell in 1954, "Thousands of farmers have had to leave their farms and seek other work because under the present law they can not have enough acreage to make a living."[33]

The deep concern expressed in the 1940s by southern farmers, agricultural leaders, and politicians over the future of southern cotton became even more serious in the 1950s. No satisfactory solution could be found to the problem of maintaining a profitable price for domestic producers and at the same time making cotton competitive in foreign markets or with synthetic fibers. To have permitted domestic prices to fall to world levels would have been disastrous for many producers. But American cotton was not competitive overseas when prices were supported above world levels. Senator Russell and others supported two-price legislation in the 1950s which would have provided higher prices for domestic consumption and a lower price for cotton exported, but Congress in 1956 only agreed to direct the Commodity Credit Corporation to sell its cotton abroad at the world price and absorb the loss. This was not a true two-price system.

It was a difficult dilemma for cotton growers, and one which was not satisfactorily solved in the postwar years. The cotton problem, however, did add greatly to the drive among producers to increase their efficiency and cut production costs. The ultimate effect was to eliminate most of the small growers who could not, for a number of reasons, become large and efficient enough to produce a decent living. There was no practical price-support policy that could save cotton farmers who grew only 5 or 10 acres of cotton, unless they had other resources. Some authorities favored one policy for larger, more productive farmers, where price would allocate resources to the most efficient cotton producers, while small farmers would be assisted by different, more socially-oriented programs. While Congress discussed various approaches, the smaller growers gradually left the farm or turned to other crops. Many others rented their land or leased their allotments to larger operators. By renting land with allotments or leasing allotments from landowners who did not plant any cotton, the larger farmers could put together sufficient acreage to justify the investment in the latest machinery.[34] Southern cotton farmers had, as mentioned earlier, an additional problem, for they had to compete with growers on the rich, irrigated farms of West Texas, New Mexico, Arizona, and California, where large-scale operations were completely mechanized.

More important than government policy, however, was the belief of more and more southern farmers that their land could be more profitably used for other crops or for livestock. By the 1950s many acres that had been in cotton were being planted to soybeans, grains, and grass. In the 1950s the soybean acreage more than doubled in the ten states from Virginia to Texas, rising from about 3 to 6.2 million acres. In 1960 the Carolinas and Arkansas both had much more land devoted to soybeans than to cotton. There was also a major increase in wheat acreage, especially in the lower Mississippi valley. In some areas soybeans followed wheat in a double-cropping operation. The harvested acreage of fifty-two crops in the eleven southern states was about 71.7 million in 1950; by 1960, fifty-nine crops were harvested on only 59 million acres.[35] Most of the land not in crops had gone into grass, legumes, and timber. The trend becomes clearer when one looks at a specific area of change. Between 1953 and 1957 a study was made of forty plantations in the Mississippi Delta where cotton had been the main crop. In 1953 average cotton plantings on those plantations was 718 acres, but by 1957 there was an average of only 407 acres. The diverted land had been put into soybeans, wheat, and oats.[36]

Second in importance only to the decline of cotton was the increase in grass and livestock. The most dramatic change in the rural landscape from Virginia to eastern Texas in the 1950s and 1960s was the millions of acres of grass and forage on which better bred cattle ranged. After crisscrossing the South on a 15,000-mile trip in 1947, a writer for *Farm Journal* wrote that growing beef production was the thing that impressed him most.[37] While there had been a slow growth of livestock farming before World War II, by the 1940s a series of events was finally coming together to make commercial dairying and beef cattle production feasible on a broad scale throughout the region. These factors included the availability of capital generated by high wartime and postwar prices, along with better credit facilities, the development of more productive and nutritious grasses by plant geneticists, tractor power, which was so essential to shift from row crops to grass, adequate medical treatment for animal diseases, and improved marketing facilities.

Apart from scarcity of capital, the major deterrents to increasing dairy and beef production in the South had been the lack of good permanent pasture, the need for breed improvement, and the problem of reducing losses from disease and pests. In some parts of the South, such as southern Georgia, it was essential to abandon the open range and go to fenced pastures. As late as the 1940s large numbers of cattle in the Coastal Plain region ran at large in the woods, where they existed on rough native grasses, weeds, and brush, much as animals had done in the 1870s and 1880s. Consequently, the cattle were small and their meat was tough. Also calf losses were heavy, partly because of weak and undernourished cows. Moreover, these native brood cows would often go a year or more before rebreeding, which reduced the normal number of calves.

For years progressive farmers and agricultural scientists had been preaching the need for better pastures and hay crops. They realized that a thriving livestock industry rested on adequate and nutritious feed. But, except in a few areas, little progress had been made. One Georgian who grew up on a farm in the early twentieth century said that he had never seen an improved pasture until after he graduated from the Agricultural College at Athens in 1923.[38] By the 1920s, however, some serious field research was under way to determine the value of improved pasture at several of the southern agricultural experiment stations. From 1924 to 1926, for example, researchers at Mississippi State College carried on experiments comparing the condition and production of cows fed on good and poor pastures.[39]

A key problem was developing suitable grasses for the southern soils and climate. In the 1930s scientists at the Coastal Plains Experiment Station at Tifton, Georgia, began a concentrated effort to breed grasses that would thrive in the South and lay the foundation for a profitable livestock industry. Nebraskan Glenn W. Burton, agronomist and plant geneticist, joined the research staff at Tifton in 1936 and began working to improve grasses. The idea of planting grass was not initially popular with many farmers. Indeed, native bermuda was the scourge of cotton farmers, who had for years fought it with hoe and plow. They looked askance at anyone who was trying to improve the worst weed they had to contend with in the cotton patch. Recognizing these attitudes, Burton did not publicize his early grass experiments.[40]

In 1943 Burton released his famous coastal bermuda for general farm use. By the late 1940s thousands of acres of the grass were being planted in Georgia, South Carolina, and Alabama. More alta fescue and other grasses were also being grown. As one observer wrote in 1947, "Those old, eroded cotton fields are beginning to look pretty nice with a blanket of lush-growing grass."[41] Unlike the situation in the Midwest and Great Plains, researchers found that it was absolutely necessary to fertilize southern pasture lands to get the needed nutrition and production. Much of the research at the experiment stations dealt with the kind and amounts of fertilizer that would produce the best growth. While more acreage was devoted to pasture, it was the quality of the grass and forage that made such a great difference in the South's livestock and dairy industries.

The federal government through the Soil Conservation Service provided valuable help to farmers who wanted to shift land from cash crops to grass and forage. Taking the four states of Georgia, Florida, Alabama, and Mississippi to illustrate, the SCS provided funds on a cost-sharing basis to seed and reseed 732,000 acres of pasture and to construct 10,382 farm ponds in 1954 alone. The Soil Bank Act of 1956 offered even greater enticement to farmers and landowners to reduce their cultivated cropland. Under this law, entire farms could be taken out of production in return for cash payments. Much of this idled land was subsequently planted to grass and trees. Probably no single thing did so much to change the landscape of the South as the Soil Bank.

Besides better feed, southern livestockmen needed improved breeds. There had been efforts here and there to upgrade the quality of cattle, and there were herds of purebred Herefords, Black Angus, and other breeds scattered across the South prior to World War II. But most southern cattle were small and scrubby. In the late 1940s and early 1950s southeastern farmers imported an increasing number of high-quality bulls to improve their herds, but often cattle from Texas and the Midwest were subject to diseases common in the warmer and more humid southern climate. Consequently, many southerners imported Brahma blood lines from Texas which produced hardier and larger animals which were also more resistant to disease than some other breeds.[42] Florida ranchers were among the leaders in the Southeast to rely heavily upon cross-breeding with Brahmas. A number of farmers also introduced the Charolais breed. Between 1950 and 1980 the number of cattle and calves in eleven southern states rose by nearly 10 million head. The largest increases were in Texas and Florida but most southern states showed major gains.

Diseases and damaging insects had always plagued southern

farmers who engaged in the beef cattle or dairy business. While Texas fever had been largely brought under control by the 1930s, the screw worm became a scourge throughout much of the Southeast after 1934. Effective chemical treatment of the worms that burrowed into animal flesh became available in the 1940s and made it easier for farmers to deal with that problem. Vaccinations for various diseases, and insecticides to kill flies, grubs, and other insects also helped to improve the health of cattle and increased profits for the developing livestock industry.[43]

Improved farm incomes and better credit facilities were highly important in providing the needed capital for livestock expansion following World War II. Lack of capital for cows and equipment had kept many farmers from entering the dairy and beef cattle businesses. A study done of fifty-four dairy farms in northwestern Louisiana in 1946, for example, showed that the average capital investment was $19,894. Farmers in central Texas in the early 1950s found that it took around $12,000 to start a 24-cow dairy operation just for cows and equipment.[44] Capital and credit on that scale was far beyond the reach of most southern farmers at that time.

The southern credit system had never been geared to livestock farming. Crop loans made in the spring and collected in the fall simply were not suitable for financing cattle raising. Cattlemen needed loans that were at least as long as the production cycle, which for cattle extended over at least two to three years. While commercial bankers entered this market cautiously, by the 1950s both banks and government financial agencies were making loans to livestock producers.

Marketing facilities also greatly improved following World War II, making livestock production more attractive. Better roads and the widespread use of trucks to move animals to market gave farmers more sales opportunities than were available in the prewar years. In a study of 606 Alabama farmers, it was found that 52 percent of them had sold livestock in 1950. About 80 percent of the slaughter cattle were sold through auctions, while country buyers, other farmers, and packers purchased the remainder. Most farmers in this study moved their cattle and hogs to market in trucks and indicated that they were quite well satisfied with their marketing arrangements.[45]

Commercial dairying developed rapidly throughout the South after World War II. Growing urban markets for fluid milk made dairying increasingly attractive to farmers in a position to take advantage of that demand. For many years farmers adjacent to the larger cities had specialized in milk production but, except in a few areas, progress had been slow before 1940. Besides the poor pastures and low productivity of southern cows, dairymen had serious marketing problems. They lacked both adequate transportation and refrigeration. Most southern farmers did not have electricity before World War II.

By the 1940s, however, a series of interrelated developments were taking place to make dairying in the South much more feasible. Pasture and feed improvement, availability of capital, better roads, refrigerated milk tanks on farms, refrigerated tank trucks that regularly picked up a farmer's milk, along with the growing town and urban markets, combined to encourage commercial dairying. In the 1940s and 1950s southern dairy farmers also began to import high-producing Holstein cows from Wisconsin and elsewhere. Initially there was some prejudice against Holsteins because many housewives judged milk by the heavy cream line in the top of the milk bottle. Holstein milk contained less butterfat than that of Jerseys and some other breeds and appeared less desirable in the bottle. But when processors began to homogenize milk, the cream line was no longer an issue with consumers. The important thing was to increase output per cow. In 1940 production of milk per cow in Mississippi was only 2,490 pounds a year; in 1960 it was 3,430 pounds, and by 1975 the figure was 7,180. While this was still relatively low compared to most other states, it showed great improvement in efficiency and productivity.[46]

In any event, from World War II onward commercial dairying expanded rapidly in the South. By 1950 there were 62,809 commercial dairy farms in the eleven southern states, farms on which the operator received half or more of his income from sales of dairy products. The number of dairy cows continued upward until the mid-1960s, when a decline set in. The trend was toward fewer and larger dairy operations. Although the number of dairy farms and cows declined after 1965, productivity rose because of better breeding, improved feed rations, and greater management skills by dairymen.

Commercial dairying in the South was confined mainly to regions that had natural geographic advantages. Putnam and Morgan counties east of Atlanta, northeastern Mississippi, and central Tennessee were among the finest dairy regions of the South. Putnam and Morgan counties produced about an eighth of all the milk sold in Georgia in 1970. Most southern dairies produced for the fluid milk markets of growing urban centers. While family-type operations were common, by the 1960s and 1970s there were some large dry-lot dairies in Florida and elsewhere with hundreds of cows. Despite growing dairy operations, however, the South attained only a rough self-sufficiency in fluid milk production.[47]

One of the most notable developments in southern agriculture from the 1930s onward was the growth of the poultry industry. Historically, poultry had been a barnyard business on most southern farms. It was a sideline activity engaged in mainly by farm wives to provide eggs for the table and to earn a little "egg money" for groceries and other things. Chicken was not eaten regularly but was something families ate on Sunday and on special occasions. Chickens were kept mainly for the eggs. Nowhere in the United States did people eat much chicken meat before World War II. In 1935 the average per capita consumption of chicken nationwide was only 15 pounds, compared to 53 pounds of beef and 48 pounds of pork.[48]

Up to the 1930s commercial poultry production had centered largely in New England, the Middle Atlantic states, and the Midwest. Only a few producers grew broilers until the 1920s, when growers in the Delmarva region (Delaware and the eastern shore of Maryland and Virginia) began to specialize in broiler production. By 1934 Delmarva farmers were raising some 7 million birds a year. Producers in that region sold their chickens in the urban markets of Philadelphia, New York, and other northeastern cities.

Some southerners believed that their region offered attractive opportunities for poultry farming. The climate was mild, markets were growing, and labor was cheap and plentiful. A major factor in encouraging broiler production in the South, however, was the desire by small farmers to find a substitute for cotton or some other crop. For example, in northwestern Arkansas, where broiler output rose rapidly in the late 1930s and 1940s, a decline in the apple industry hurt many small farmers. Meager cotton allotments in northern Georgia left farmers there without adequate income and prompted them to seek alternate enterprises. Researchers found in the broiler area of Mississippi that small farmers needed "a suitable enterprise to supplement farm income and utilize surplus labor." Farmers whose operations were not large enough for dairying, beef cattle, or more acreage of row crops saw poultry, especially broilers, as highly attractive.[49]

Also during the 1930s county agents, representatives from the agricultural colleges and experiment stations, farm journal publishers, and others urged farmers to try poultry on a commercial basis. But farmers responded slowly to this advice. They lacked the capital, markets were not well developed in the South, and often they did not know how to operate a profitable chicken farm. Support to farmers who wanted to begin poultry raising came from a rather unexpected source—the feed dealers. These businessmen saw poultry production as an outlet for greater amounts of feed. As early as 1929 and 1930 some feed companies in Arkansas provided chicks and feed on credit to farmers who wanted to raise broilers. The practice grew rapidly in the late 1930s and 1940s. By World War II there was a strong move toward complete vertical integration in the broiler industry.

The man who promoted the expansion of broiler production in

northern Georgia was Jesse Dixon Jewell, a feed dealer in Gainesville. In 1936 he began providing chicks and feed to farmers on credit and then bought back the mature chickens for marketing. Former cotton farmers were familiar with this kind of short-term credit because store-keepers had customarily advanced supplies or cash at the beginning of the growing season in return for a mortgage on the farmer's crop. Gradually, Jewell made arrangements with bigger feed processors to supply him with even larger quantities of feed, which Jewell in turn sold to farmers on credit. He developed a "businessman-farmer team" which, as one authority wrote, grew "into the agribusiness concept as the chicken business interpreted it." Poultry raising was slowly changing in northern Georgia from a sideline activity to a genuine farm business.

Jewell's next step was to establish a hatchery, and in 1940 he built a processing plant at Gainesville where the birds were prepared for market. By World War II Jewell had an integrated operation where he hatched the eggs, contracted with farmers to raise the chicks on feed that he supplied from his mill to growers on credit, and finally processed and marketed the birds. Farmers provided the housing, labor, and management in return for an assured market. Meanwhile, similar developments were occurring in northern Arkansas, eastern Texas, northern Alabama, and North Carolina. Large feed companies such as Ralston Purina got heavily involved in the business, as did many of the farmer cooperatives. One of the largest integrated operations in the Southeast was controlled by Gold Kist, a huge farmer cooperative which handled millions of broilers annually by the 1960s and 1970s.[50]

A variety of arrangements were made between the feed dealers and farm growers. In the early days of integration the dealer usually furnished the chicks, feed, medicine, and some supervision, while the farmer supplied the houses, equipment, and labor. When the chickens were sold by the feed dealer, the farmer's profit was the difference between the sales price and his debt to the dealer. Under the flat-fee plan the farmer received so much per pound of broiler sold in return for use of his production facilities and his labor. In some cases the integrator furnished everything, including housing and equipment, and simply paid the farmer a salary. But whatever plan was agreed upon, the producer lost much of his independence.

Critics of vertical integration charged that poultry farmers were controlled and sometimes exploited by their suppliers; that, in effect, formerly independent farmers became little more than hired hands. There were numerous examples where small growers seemed to have been crowded out of the market and forced into bankruptcy by large producers backed by the feed companies. But that is only one side of the story. Poultry production before integration had been a very risky enterprise. Markets sometimes fluctuated dramatically, and many chicken farmers had gone broke because of poor demand and low prices. Integration reduced the growers' risk to some degree and gave them greater assurance of a steady and dependable income. Actually, an interdependence developed between the growers and those who supplied the inputs. Broiler producers also benefited from the economy of scale. While in the 1940s most farmers did not produce more than 2,000 to 5,000 broilers at a time, by the 1960s operations of 50,000, 100,000, and 200,000 were common. So, while producers lost some independence, they were probably better off as part of an integrated organization. One economist raised the question of whether it was better to take away much of a grower's decision-making and reduce his risk, or to allow him full freedom with the option of going broke. For him, the implication was clear. Farmers' risk reduction was to be preferred.[51]

It was strong consumer demand for chicken that supported such phenomenal increases in the production and sale of poultry and poultry products. Processed and frozen chicken was ideal for sale in the self-service supermarkets that became increasingly popular after World War II. More important was the fact that chicken meat was comparatively cheap. In 1950 chicken averaged 57 cents a pound, while beef and pork cost 70 and 67 cents a pound respectively. As time went on, chicken's price advantage became even more pronounced. By 1965 chicken had dropped to about 39 cents a pound in the supermarket, while beef and pork were higher than fifteen years earlier.[52]

It was the remarkable gains in efficiency by poultry producers in the South that gave them their advantage. Other southern farmers may have lagged behind in increasing their efficiency, but that was not the case on poultry farms. Efficiency was closely associated with the work of poultry scientists in the fields of nutrition, health, and breeding, as well as the technological advances in production. These efforts resulted in faster-growing birds with better meat quality, hens that laid more eggs per year, and a reduction in labor costs associated with automatic feeding, watering, egg gathering, and other tasks. The results were dramatic. From about 1940 onward there was a steady decline in the amount of feed required to produce a pound of chicken. For example, in 1940 it took about 80 days and 4.2 pounds of feed to produce a pound of live-weight broiler; by 1950 it was 3.3 pounds, and by 1963 only 2.5 pounds of feed were required per pound of gain. By 1977 a 4-pound bird could be brought to market in 53 days on 1.9 pounds of feed for each pound of chicken. Faster gains, mechanized facilities, and better housing greatly reduced the labor requirements for broiler production. In 1950-1951 officials estimated that it took 3.1 man-hours to produce 100 pounds of broilers; in 1960-61 it was 1 man-hour. The average number of eggs laid per hen in 1950 was 118 in Georgia, Alabama, Mississippi, and Arkansas, compared to 235 in 1975.[53]

No other aspect of southern agriculture expanded so rapidly after World War II as the poultry industry. By 1950 Georgia had 7,382 commercial poultry farms, while Arkansas reported 6,608 and Texas 9,669. These three states, plus Virginia, produced 185 million broilers. Other southern states also became big broiler producers. Egg production rose sharply, too. Between 1940 and 1960 Georgia flocks increased production from 524 million to 2.2 billion eggs. As in other aspects of agriculture, the trend was toward fewer and larger poultry farms. By 1974 Arkansas's 4,352 producers sold 437 million birds, and Georgia and Alabama were close behind.[54]

An Arkansas farmer who observed the expansion of the poultry industry was reported to have exclaimed, "Who'd a thought that a dad-burned chicken could scratch cotton off the land." Few would have predicted such a development in the 1930s, but by the 1950s the change had occurred in many areas. Within less than a generation the poultry business had become highly capitalized and specialized. D.F. King, director of Georgia's agricultural experiment stations, wrote in the *Progressive Farmer* in 1961 that "the 'pin-money' poultry flock—the backyard biddies—are fast fading from the southern scene. Poultry is big business in the South today." John K. Bettersworth, an official at Mississippi State College, remarked that he knew fundamental change had occurred in southern agriculture when one could drive from Starkville to the Gulf and never run over a chicken. They were all housed.[55]

The South continued to be a major producer of fruits and vegetables. In 1948 Florida producers raised about 58 million boxes of oranges; by 1978 the figure was 164 million. The development of frozen orange concentrate after World War II greatly increased the market for oranges. Florida farmers, as well as those from Virginia to Texas, also grew tomatoes, fresh corn, beans, peas, melons, apples, peaches, strawberries, blueberries, and large quantities of other fruits and vegetables both for the fresh market and for processing. Much of this production was done on a contract basis where farmers signed agreements to deliver their output to handlers and processors. Some farmers sold produce through farmers' markets, such as the large enterprise on Atlanta's south side.[56]

Basic shifts in farm income followed the dramatic changes in southern crop and livestock patterns after World War II. In 1949 the value of crops sold in the eleven southern states was about $3.5 billion, while livestock and livestock products produced only $1.6 billion. Crops were thus responsible for about 70 percent of the value of all agricultural products sold. Cotton and cottonseed alone brought $1.8 billion, or more than half of this value. In the Carolinas, Georgia, Alabama, and Mississippi, crops accounted for from a low of 62.2 percent in Georgia to a high of 81.9 percent in Mississippi. During the 1950s and 1960s, however, income from livestock and livestock products rose sharply, making up about 44 percent of the total cash receipts from farming in 1960. Within another decade cash receipts from livestock and livestock products in the eleven southern states rose to 51.3 percent of the total. Even in Mississippi, where crops had produced the preponderance of farm income for so long, livestock had surpassed crops as a producer of agricultural income by 1970.[57] Truly, it had been a revolution.

A picture of the new agriculture that had emerged throughout the South in the 1960s and 1970s can best be seen by looking at the ranking of farm commodities in relation to cash receipts. In 1978 the leading products from southern farms were cattle and calves, broilers and eggs, soybeans, tobacco, and dairy products. In South Carolina, tobacco, soybeans, cattle and calves, hogs, and eggs ranked in that order. For Georgia, broilers, peanuts, eggs, cattle and calves, and hogs headed the list, while in Florida, oranges, cattle and calves, nursery products, dairy products, and tomatoes were most important. Cotton no longer held first place in any southern state and it ranked second among commodities in producing cash receipts only in Mississippi and Texas. By 1978 soybeans had replaced cotton as the leading income producer in Mississippi, along with cattle and calves, broilers, and dairy products. In Arkansas, broilers ranked first, followed by soybeans, rice, cattle and calves, and cotton. While southern farmers raised the traditional southern crops of cotton, tobacco, peanuts, rice, and sugarcane, the relative importance of these commodities had greatly declined, though they continued to be highly significant in some areas.[58]

The South had developed a highly diversified agriculture, but it was not the old self-sufficient type of diversification that agriculturalists and publicists had urged before World War I. Farmers diversified into a greater variety of cash-producing commodities, such as soybeans, livestock, dairy products, and poultry, and a large number of specialties, such as apples, peaches, citrus, berries, pecans, vegetables, and forest products. Timber also became an important source of income for thousands of southern farmers. Although the acreage of farm-owned woodlands decreased after 1945, farmers sold millions of dollars' worth of trees for saw timber, fence posts, and other purposes, but mainly for pulpwood used by paper manufacturers. In the 1960s the relative importance of farm timber declined slightly, but it continued to be a major source of income for many farmers, especially in

Georgia, Alabama, and the Carolinas.[59] Timber as a farm enterprise
was most significant in Georgia. In 1960 it provided 3.7 percent of the
total farm income in the state, but by 1978 the figure had dropped to
only 2 percent.

The fundamental changes in southern farming could not have
occurred without important developments outside the agricultural
sector. Among the basic problems facing farmers before World War II
were the lack of cash markets for crops other than cotton and tobacco,
and the absence of nonfarm jobs for the surplus farm population.
Rapid industrialization and accompanying urbanization in the South
and throughout the nation were the keys to expanding both jobs and
markets.

Without more off-farm jobs, the relationship between farm population and agricultural resources could not have been brought into better
balance. A study done of the Mississippi uplands in 1955 showed that
"the efficient reshaping of farm resources" would require "a 60 percent
reduction in the number of farm workers." The researchers explained
that any program "to develop and utilize the human resources of
agriculture more fully must anticipate a continuing large-scale movement of people away from the farms or into part-time nonfarm employment."[60] Many rural communities in the South were in that situation.
Fortunately, nonfarm employment opportunities were becoming increasingly available.

In 1950 there were only 2,331,700 jobs in manufacturing in the
eleven southern states; by 1970 the number was 4,251,000, an increase
of more than 80 percent.[61] During the quarter century after World War
II, growing industry, commerce, insurance, banking, transportation,
and other economic activities provided millions of jobs in the towns
and cities of the South. In the 1960s alone some 4 million nonfarm jobs
were added in the eleven southern states.[62] Cities such as Miami,
Atlanta, Birmingham, Nashville, Memphis, New Orleans, Dallas, and
Houston, as well as scores of smaller towns and cities, absorbed much
of the departing farm population. Through the 1960s, at least, other
rural southerners continued to migrate to northern and western urban
centers. Blacks provided one of the largest migration streams out of the
region.

Accompanying the off-farm migration were technological advances in transportation, including the building of good secondary
roads, which had been lacking before 1940, construction of superhigh-
ways, and the use of refrigerated and other trucks to move products
quickly to the growing urban markets. Rising incomes were also important. Not only did the means become available to ship southern
products to local and northern markets, but rising consumer incomes
produced a year-round demand for fruit, vegetables, broilers, and

other commodities produced in the South. A developing national and international market permitted southern farmers to specialize in additional cash and feed crops, as well as in livestock and their products. Thus economic trends, in both the farm and the nonfarm sectors, combined to transform southern agriculture and bring it into the national mainstream. Like other aspects of southern life, southern agriculture lost much of its distinctiveness.

10

Farmers Left Behind

Within a generation after World War II, commercial agriculture in the South had been modernized and restructured. The rural South of the 1970s little resembled the same region in the 1930s or 1940s. The modern commercial farmer in Georgia, Alabama, or Mississippi could not be distinguished from the progressive operator in Illinois, Iowa, or Nebraska, except in some of the crops he raised. Like the rest of American agriculture, southern commercial farms had become highly capitalized, mechanized, and labor efficient.

From the vantage point of the 1970s, statistics clearly showed the changes that had occurred. Between 1950 and 1975 the number of farms in the eleven southern states dropped from about 2.1 million to 722,000 while the average size rose from 142 to 284 acres. If Texas and Florida, which had larger farms, are omitted, the average size of farms grew from 93 to 216 acres in that quarter century. In the same period, investment in land and buildings for southern farms increased from $8,423 per farm in 1950 to $123,871 in 1974. Even considering inflation, this was a dramatic increase.[1]

Not only had the number and size of farms changed dramatically, but modernization had destroyed the old tenure system that had been prevalent throughout so much of the South since the 1880s. By the 1970s the vast majority of southern farms were operated by owners or part-owners, and the old-fashioned tenancy had nearly vanished. For example, in 1950 some 45 percent of South Carolina's farm units were still operated by tenants; in Georgia, Alabama, and Mississippi it was 43, 41, and 51 percent respectively. The census of agriculture of 1974 reported that only 12 percent of the farmers in South Carolina were tenants, while the figure for Georgia, Alabama, and Mississippi was 8 percent or less.[2] Many modern farmers rented additional land from nonoperating landowners, but this practice had no relationship to the old tenancy.

Black farmers were inordinately affected by the changes that had occurred. In 1920 there were 881,964 black farmers in the eleven southern states. During the next twenty years the number dropped by some 229,631, and it continued to decline in the 1940s. In 1950, however, there were still around 536,000 black farmers, of whom 195,000 were share-croppers. There had been a steady movement of blacks out of southern agriculture from the 1920s onward. But after 1950 the exodus was so great that by the 1970s it could be said that blacks had been all but eliminated from farming. Only 55,995 black farmers remained in 1978, and those on farms with sales of $2,500 or more numbered a mere 20,272 in the eleven southern states. Many of these farmed part-time. The agricultural census of 1978 reported only 9,177 black tenants. The census dropped the sharecropper designation after 1959. The institu-tion that had given hundreds of thousands of blacks, and whites as well, a bare existence for nearly a century was gone, if not entirely forgotten. Sharecropping and tenancy had left scars on many souther-ners. Martin Luther King, Sr., better known as "Daddy" King, recalled in his autobiography how, as a boy, he had seen his father agonize and suffer under the system.[3]

Faced with the new developments in agriculture, blacks who oper-ated small units, often on poor land, simply could not compete. This was true of small white farmers as well. Mechanization and grass were the two developments that destroyed the old-fashioned sharecropping system and drove most small southern farmers out of farming as a full-time occupation. To operate machines efficiently it was necessary to enlarge the fields and combine the small acreages that had been farmed by man and mule for nearly three generations. Machines eliminated most hand labor, and much of the farm population became unneces-sary, even irrelevant. Grass and pastureland had a similar effect on small operators. Commercial beef and dairy production required larger acreages but fewer and more specialized workers. Blacks were affected more than whites because a larger percentage of black farmers had been on small acreages.[4] Southern agriculture, in which blacks had played such a prominent role ever since the early settlers entered the region, by the 1960s and 1970s had become a business operated almost entirely by whites.

With opportunities for any kind of agricultural employment shrinking and off-farm jobs increasing, the farm population declined rapidly after 1940. In the 1920s farm population in the eleven southern states dropped by some 465,000 people, or 3.1 percent, but during the Great Depression of the 1930s it remained about constant. In the following decades, however, the number of people on farms fell with increasing speed as millions left their agricultural roots and headed for mill and factory in the region and throughout the nation. In the 1960s alone, farm population in the South dropped by about 50 percent. Between 1940 and 1970 the number of people on southern farms declined from nearly 14 million to only 2.9 million. It was one of the greatest movements of people in history to occur within a single generation.[5] Farmers made up only 6.9 percent of the southern population in 1970, compared to 43.1 percent in 1940. There had been a fundamental readjustment of people to land. Southern rural society had remained relatively static from the 1880s to the 1940s, but science and technology in agriculture, expanding industrialization, and government policies had combined to destroy the old patterns of agriculture and farm life.

The southern farmers who made the agricultural transition successfully produced incomes that gave them a modern standard of living. Net income per farm was only $2,040 in North Carolina, $1,566 in Georgia, and $1,272 in Mississippi in 1950 after nearly a decade of wartime and high postwar prices. A quarter century later the figures were $8,558, $7,640, and $5,472 per farm in those states. Averages are deceiving, however, because the South continued to have a high proportion of small farms. By the 1970s the more successful commercial farmers had incomes many times these amounts. Of the 722,000 farms in the South in 1974, about 90,000 contained 500 acres or more. Among the larger producers were 98,322 who sold products valued at more than $40,000 each.[6]

With greater productivity and rising incomes, tens of thousands of southern farmers built new and thoroughly modern houses which they filled with the latest conveniences. They sent their sons and daughters to college, traveled, ate packaged food, joined civic clubs, and in general adopted a lifestyle not unlike that of the business and professional people in the towns and cities around them.

Many farmers, however, could not adjust to the demands of modernized agriculture. They lacked the land, capital, knowledge, skills, and sometimes the ambition necessary to become successful farmers. And while the postwar economy was expansive, off-farm jobs were not available for all of the poorly educated and ill-trained farmers and agricultural workers who were no longer needed in farming. The South's problem was not how to develop a progressive and productive agriculture but what to do with surplus farmers who had no place in the rapidly changing rural economy.

Many young people on southern farms had for years wanted to escape from what they considered a poor and drab existence. However much southerners had talked and written about the virtues of rural life, many knew that the image was more romantic than real, more fancy than fact. The writers and politicians could repeat all of the Jeffersonian shibboleths, but the boy in the cotton or tobacco patch knew better. J.C. Bonner, who was raised on a farm in western Georgia in the early twentieth century, recalled after retiring from teaching at Georgia

College in Milledgeville that "the monotony of my existence was re-
lieved only by the slow drift of the seasons." His desire to go to college,
he added, was not prompted by any concern for knowledge or understanding, but "it seemed like a good way to escape from a life of hard
drudgery in an agrarian environment." Another older Georgian recalled in 1982 that he left a Washington County farm in 1910 at age
eighteen to go to Athens because "I just wanted a job off the farm."
Martin Luther King, Sr., wrote in his autobiography, "I *hated* farming"
and left as soon as he could manage it.[7]

Thousands of young men and women, then, did leave southern
farms before World War II, but far too few to keep the population and
resources in balance. The general economy did not expand fast enough
to provide jobs for all of those workers unneeded in agriculture.
Writing in September 1945, a southern county agricultural agent wrote
that commerce, transportation, industry, forest products, and "the
professions must gradually take up the displaced southern farmer."[8]
But time soon demonstrated that there were thousands of southern
farm families who were unable to make the transition to either industrial employment or profitable farming. They were the people left
behind.

Just what would happen to the poorer elements in the farm population had been a matter of deep concern ever since the 1930s, when
sharecroppers began to be pushed off the land by developing technology. Jonathan Daniels, an observant and sympathetic southerner,
wrote in 1941 that several thousand families had been "set free from
tenancy, which means they are free to squat in idleness, to stand on
small-town street corners, to hope only for occasional day labor—free
to starve but for the intervention of relief." Daniels recognized that
"farms of adequate size are essential for farmer security, but adequate-
size farms in most southern states are within reach of fewer people than
the Southern land contains." He added that "sharecropping begins to
look like a system of security which white men and black men once had
but now have lost."[9] Indeed, that was the case. Sharecropping and
tenancy had provided a minimal security, if only a bare existence, but
technology and science were, as Daniels wrote, in the process of
destroying the system.

For a time during World War II it seemed as though an expanding
economy would somehow provide for this poor, surplus farm population—that is, that the problem would gradually go away. Secretary of
Agriculture Charles Brannan testified before a Senate subcommittee
late in 1949 that "many believe that all farmers became rich during the
war and that farmers, as a group, profited from the war to a greater
extent than any other segment of our population." But, he added, that
was not so.[10] As mentioned in chapter 8, spokesmen who appeared

Table 1. Farmers by Economic Class, 1950

Class	Value of Farm Products Sold
I	$25,000 or more
II	$10,000 to $24,999
III	$5,000 to $9,999
IV	$2,500 to $4,999
V	$1,200 to $2,499
VI	$250 to $1,199*

* Providing the operator worked less than 100 days a year off the farm.

before congressional committees that dealt with southern agriculture in 1944 and 1947 testified that the South still had a great surplus of workers in agriculture. The agricultural census of 1950 quantified the problems of small farms, lack of productivity, and surplus farm population in the South.

In 1950 the Census Bureau made a detailed study of farmers by economic class. Commercial farms were defined as those with a value of products sold in 1949 of $1,200 or more, where the operator did not work off the farm more than 100 days a year, and where the family's nonfarm income was less than the value of farm products sold. The classification was as shown in Table 1.

According to the Census Bureau, only about 67 percent of all farms in the eleven southern states sold enough products in 1949 to be classified as commercial farms. For example, 62 percent of the farms in Georga were considered commercial operations, compared to 92 percent in Iowa. Of the South's commercial farms, a high percentage were in classes V and VI, which sold between $250 and $2,499 worth of products annually. Most farmers in class VI averaged about $700 worth of farm sales, while those in class V sold products with an average value of between $1,700 and $1,800. Some 73 percent of the commercial farmers in South Carolina, 67.7 percent in Georgia, 75.7 percent in Tennessee, and 85.3 percent in Mississippi were in these two bottom economic classes.

With such meager productivity and incomes, these farmers continued to have a very low standard of living. High wartime and postwar prices meant little to them. They had too little to sell and government price supports and conservation payments were of no help to nonproducers on a few acres of land. Most of these farmers lived in shacks and cabins as their parents had done before them. Modern conveniences had scarcely touched their lives. Only 10 percent of class V and VI commercial farmers in the Carolinas and Georgia had telephones in 1950; in Alabama and Mississippi it was less than 5 percent.

Running water was a rarity. A survey of 269 black farm families in ten Mississippi counties in 1947 revealed that only two of them had water piped into the house; only 18 percent had an automobile. Of all the farmers in the Carolinas, Georgia, Alabama, and Mississippi in 1950, only 30 and 40 percent in class V and VI respectively had automobiles.[11] Although an increasing number of these farmers had electricity, often as many as 50 to 75 percent, electric power was likely to be limited to a single light bulb in each room.

Thus the census of 1950 presented a bleak picture for tens of thousands of southern farmers. Among the 2.1 million farmers in the eleven southern states, 1.3 million were classified as commercial operators. Of that 1.3 million, however, 873,590 were class V and VI farmers whose prospect of ever becoming successful producers in the sense of making a satisfactory living on the land was most unlikely. While the farm population in the South was declining, the number of small, nonproductive farms continued excessively large. What could be done?

Well before the 1950 census data had been released, a few members of Congress began to show increasing concern for the rural poor. Although there were poor farmers in other regions, by far the largest number were in the South. In the summer of 1949 the Senate authorized an investigation into the broad question of low-income families. A subcommittee of the Joint Committee on the Economic Report held hearings from December 12 to 22, 1949. Senator John Sparkman of Alabama chaired the subcommittee and conducted the hearings. While testimony was taken on several aspects of poverty, low-income farm families, especially those in the South, received extensive consideration.

Ernest E. Neal, director of the Rural Life Council at Tuskegee Institute, Secretary of Agriculture Charles F. Brannan, and two of the nation's leading agricultural economists, Theodore W. Schultz and D. Gale Johnson of the University of Chicago, testified on the issue of farm poverty. Neal, who had worked for a decade among poor black farm families, told the senators that "the Old South is in the midst of a Revolution." Emphasizing what was becoming increasingly evident, Neal explained that the old "share-tenant system" was giving way to "grazing cattle, tractors, and cotton pickers." Many families, he continued, had been made useless "by improved farm practices," but they continued to live on the farm, struggling for a bare subsistence. Negro owners and renters alike, Neal said, were operating units too small for modernized farming or livestock production.

Secretary Brannan added that many farmers did "not possess adequate resources for earning an acceptable living. Their farms simply are too small or too poor. Such farms do not provide their operators with enough days of productive work in a year." This was the same theme that farm editors, researchers at the agricultural colleges, economists, and others had been expressing for years. Brannan believed that the Farmers Home Administration needed more money for both operating and land-purchase loans to help those poorer farmers who might continue to farm. He also recommended industrial development to provide off-farm jobs, and programs to help people adjust out of farming. Such measures included job training, helping farmers to move to new locations, and job information services. In other words, the solution to problems facing many low-income farmers was movement away from the farm.

Economists Schultz and Johnson repeated what they and others had argued for some years. Farmers were poor, as Johnson said, because of "excess farm population and an outmoded production technology." Schultz explained that government programs "tended to favor the larger farmers" and that "poor people living in these poor areas have little political influence in making policy." Schultz expressed amazement that no one in policymaking positions of the federal government had been trying to bring relief to low-income farmers. He declared that one of the reasons that poor farmers were being ignored was because the political power structure, including the major farm organizations, had little or no interest in their problems.[12] Indeed, Congress had made it clear in the late 1930s and 1940s that it did not want such matters studied in depth. When Secretary Brannan was asked why the land-grant colleges were not doing more for low-income farmers, he avoided the question by changing the subject. The implication was clear enough. Powerful political interests objected to shifting the activities of agencies traditionally geared to help the more successful commercial farmers to programs designed to assist those at the bottom of the economic ladder. This matter, however, would arise periodically in future years.

On February 23, 1950, Senator Sparkman presented his subcommittee's report to the full Joint Committee on the Economic Report. Part II dealt with low-income farm families. After repeating much of what had come out in the hearings—the problems of surplus farm population, small land holdings, lack of capital, outmoded methods, etc.— Sparkman's subcommittee made several concrete suggestions. First, the subcommittee recommended studies to determine how federal programs affected different farm income groups, and how current and other government actions might make a greater contribution to low-income farmers. The subcommittee also supported larger appropriations for the Farmers Home Administration so it could assist small farmers to obtain larger land holdings and diversify their operations. It also recommended better education for farm youth and part-time off-farm jobs. Poor black farm families, the subcommittee repeated, were a "special problem" within "the larger problem of rural poverty."[13]

About the same time that congressional committees were studying farm poverty, Theodore W. Schultz's article "Reflections on Poverty within Agriculture" appeared in the February 1950 issue of the *Journal of Political Economy*. This piece had already been printed in the subcommittee hearings, but it now received wider attention, at least among scholars and policymakers. Schultz explained that poverty in agriculture had been commonly accepted by an industrial-urban society without much notice or complaint. Farm poverty, he wrote, had become "an acceptable state socially" and was looked upon by many people "as natural." Failure of Congress to come to grips with poverty in the farm sector, he said, indicated that political leaders "do not believe that poverty in agriculture is an important social problem."[14]

One of the things that emerged from the hearings on low-income farmers in 1949, and in the subsequent committee reports, was the absence of serious research on these groups and their special problems. To get additional information, Senator Sparkman assigned two prominent agricultural economists to study the problems of the nation's poorest farmers. He chose Walter W. Wilcox, who had been at the University of Wisconsin before going to the Library of Congress, and W.E. Hendrix, then associated with the Georgia Agricultural Experiment Station and a scholar thoroughly familiar with poverty on southern farms. Early in 1951 Wilcox and Hendrix submitted their findings, entitled *Underemployment of Rural Families*. Included as a part of the report was a map showing that the great majority of low-income, underemployed farmers were in the South.

Wilcox and Hendrix emphasized that throughout the southern states it was not just a matter of a scattering of poor farmers mixed in with more prosperous operators. Rather, farm underemployment and minimal incomes were characteristic of entire communities. Poverty was a "prevailing pattern" throughout many of the southern states, they wrote. To help assess the situation, they had contacted officials in the agricultural colleges and others in a position to know conditions and asked for their explanations as to why such widespread underemployment existed in farming. They received the usual reasons. From Mississippi came the reply: "This is due mainly to high ratios of population to the land supply," along with the absence of capital equipment. Others said that lack of knowledge and a low level of technology were basic factors.

Three main approaches were recommended to solve problems faced by low- income farmers. In the first place, output per worker on small farms must be increased by encouraging farmers to improve their agricultural practices. Secondly, the size of farms must be increased.

This would involve more long-term credit and the provision of technical and management assistance, something that the FHA could provide. Thirdly, federal help should be given to underemployed farmers who wanted to migrate to nonfarm jobs out of the region, and public and private agencies should step up efforts to entice industries into the low-income agricultural areas.

By studying the statistics and inviting agricultural leaders to evaluate current conditions, the Wilcox and Hendrix study showed conclusively that underemployment and poverty in the South were problems that could not be solved by individual farmers. It was not just a matter of providing some additional credit for farm enlargement, the purchase of machines, or loans for operating expenses. Rather, an entire social and economic pattern of poverty would have to be broken. This would involve better education and health care, improved nutrition, vocational training, programs to facilitate mobility away from the farms, and a shift to nonfarm work for large numbers of farm people. The economists estimated that there were at least 390,000 farm families, mostly in the South, who were essentially "welfare problems."[15]

Hearings, congressional reports, and economic studies seemed to have little noticeable effect on policymakers. While the Wilcox and Hendrix study revived some interest in low-income farmers in the USDA and the land-grant universities, neither Congress nor the major farm organizations supported the recommendations arising out of the numerous investigations. For example, almost everyone familiar with rural poverty in the South, and elsewhere, recommended that more credit be made available to low-income farmers through the Farmers Home Administration. But these pleas fell on deaf congressional ears. In fiscal 1951 the FHA had only enough funds to make 1,674 farm ownership loans in the eleven southern states. Two years later the figure was only 930. This was clear evidence that Congress was not much concerned with poor farmers, to say nothing of the poorest, who could not qualify for FHA loans.

Moreover, the agricultural power structure had relatively little interest in those marginal and submarginal farmers who were barely eking out an existence. At its annual convention in 1950 the American Farm Bureau Federation recognized the importance of rural living and the farm home, but resolved that a good farm life depended mainly on "individual effort rather than on the assistance of government."[16] The main political battles surrounding agriculture in the 1950s dealt with the level of price supports, not how to help poor farmers. Economist Theodore Schultz was absolutely correct when he wrote in 1950 that poverty among tens of thousands of farmers was socially acceptable and programs to deal with the problem had no significant standing among national priorities.

Nevertheless, discussion of farm poverty continued. In January 1954 President Dwight D. Eisenhower called for a study of small, low-income farmers. After more than a year, Secretary of Agriculture Ezra Taft Benson presented a USDA report entitled *Development of Agriculture's Human Resources*. In submitting the report, Benson wrote that he hoped it would stimulate "study and action." He told the president that "a broad, aggressive, well-coordinated assault is urgently needed."

The report's authors stated in the preface that "an important part of the solution to the problems of farmers with low earnings lies outside commercial agriculture." This is what economists and farm management experts had been repeating for years. If that was the case, other major departments of government such as Labor and Health, Education and Welfare, as well as the USDA, must contribute to the solutions. Several elements of government must be organized to deal with the problems of low-income farm families. Expansion of vocational training, strengthening of the employment service, adaptation of agricultural extension work to poor families, and encouragement of rural industry were among the recommendations. Congress, the report added, should expand FHA loans to part-time farmers, grant special funds outside of the current agricultural extension programs to administer certain activities, and make greater appropriations for soil conservation and farm loans. Utilizing all of these approaches, it was recommended that 50 to 100 pilot programs be set up in low-income farm counties to deliver services and provide help.[17]

Later in 1955 more congressional hearings were held on the problems facing low-income farmers. Among the leading experts to testify on southern farm poverty were William H. Nicholls, professor of economics at Vanderbilt University, a widely respected authority on southern farm poverty, and Frank J. Welch, dean of the University of Kentucky's College of Agriculture. These and other authorities strongly indicated the need for major adjustments that were beyond the ability of individual farmers. Nicholls repeated that low-income farm families earned "little because they produce little; and they produce little primarily because they have too little farmland and farm capital to work with." Things would have been even worse, he said, if the "safety-valve of outmigration" had not occurred. But that had not been enough. Nicholls explained that public policy should not be to "eliminate farmers" but to "give low income farmers the opportunity to eliminate themselves by helping them to find better nonfarm job alternatives."

Dean Welch, who had observed poverty on Mississippi farms before he went to Kentucky, told lawmakers that farm poverty could not be cured just by creating larger farms. There must be a "package policy," he argued, involving education, health care, help for out-migration, job training, and other types of assistance. He believed that education was the "primary need." Welch concluded that low-income farm families could be greatly helped if Congress could develop programs in employment, education, social security, health, credit, research, and extension.[18]

Concern with conditions among the poorest farmers was not confined to special studies by scholars and administrators. When the Subcommittee on Family Farms of the House Committee on Agriculture held hearings throughout the country in late 1955 and early 1956, the plight of poorer farmers received prominent attention. At hearings in Texas and North Carolina witnesses argued that something special must be done for this group of rural residents. Alonzo C. Edwards, a farmer and member of the North Carolina legislature, emphasized that programs designed for commercial farmers were not suitable for the smaller, poorer farmers. William D. Poe, son of Clarence Poe and associate editor of the *Progressive Farmer,* made one of the strongest appeals for the poorest farmers. He told the visiting congressmen that there were a half million "forsaken and forgotten southern farm families whose plight is a disgrace to a Nation exulting in its greatest boom in history." These families, he continued, were fighting for their very survival. They are not "mere statistics," he said, "they are flesh and blood human beings. They deserve sympathy, respect, and fair treatment."[19]

By the mid-1950s the pitiful conditions among so many southern farm families were well enough known among agricultural and other government officials, including congressmen and senators, but Congress did not take up this challenge. The USDA nevertheless proceeded to establish some rural-development pilot projects in some of the nation's poorest agricultural regions. By 1958 there were thirty-eight of these projects in the eleven southern states. Most of them were confined to a single county in a state. For example, there were four pilot demonstration rural-development programs in Mississippi, five in Arkansas, four in Georgia, and three in South Carolina.

The three major objectives of the pilot programs were to seek an expansion of nonfarm jobs in rural areas, to improve the health, education, and vocational training of farm people, and to develop more efficient family-size commercial farms. The "package policy" recommended by Welch and others was employed, as the Departments of Interior, Commerce, Labor, and HEW, as well as Agriculture, were all involved in providing ideas and services. Congress provided no special funding, however, and the rural development programs had to struggle along on what little money could be squeezed from USDA's regular appropriations. In 1957 the pilot programs nationwide received

$2,490,645, and in 1958, $2,604,399. Such meager expenditures were not enough even to dent the problem of farm poverty in the South or elsewhere.[20]

It is clear that there was no absence of discussion or study of low-income southern farmers in the 1950s. The problems facing those producers were studied and investigated time and again. In the area of public policy, however, there was an unwillingness to face the questions squarely. Consequently, unrestrained economic forces continued to drive thousands of small, poor, inefficient operators out of farming or into part-time agriculture. Like a tide, mechanization, consolidation of acreages, and changing crop and livestock patterns washed away unneeded farmers. It should be remembered, of course, that the 1950s were a difficult time for nearly all farmers in the United States.

Unfortunately, by the 1950s any program for small, poverty-ridden farmers in the South became entangled with the civil rights movement. To help poor farmers throughout the region meant assisting black producers, whose spokesmen and leaders were supporting school integration and other changes which threatened racial segregation. The Supreme Court decision in the Brown case in 1954 alarmed many white southerners and hardened their position against helping blacks. People like Aubrey W. Williams, an old New Dealer and one of the few white southerners who spoke up boldly for the South's poor farmers and for racial integration, came under sharp attack by the southern political and economic power structure.[21] Those trying to help poor southern farmers to make needed adjustments not only had to overcome indifference and opposition by powerful elites, they had to confront racism as well.

Despite some feeble efforts to help small farmers in the South during the 1950s, nothing improved for tens of thousands of low-income farmers. The census of 1960 showed that of the 735,704 commercial farmers in the eleven southern states, 425,446, or about 57 percent, were in classes V and VI. The definition of economic classes had changed from 1950, but still classes V and VI produced less than $5,000 worth of products. Class VI included farmers whose value of products was below $2,500 annually. There were slightly over 200,000 commercial farmers scattered across the South in 1960 who were in the lowest income category. In a decade the number of these two poorest groups of southern farmers had dropped by more than half, from 873,000 to 403,000. The great majority had left agriculture altogether, except perhaps as laborers, or had become part-time farmers.

Between 1950 and 1960 the number of part-time farmers in the eleven southern states increased by about 106,000. For some poor farmers this was a practical alternative. When one or more members of the family could get a job in a nearby factory and the family could continue small agricultural activity and live in the country home, a better family income and standard of living usually resulted. But there were not enough industrial jobs to absorb all of the surplus farm labor. In the 1950s the number of farms in the South dropped by some 843,000, or around 80,000 a year. This meant that only about one out of eight farmers who quit full-time farming shifted to the position of part-time farmer. Between 700,000 and 750,000 simply vanished from agriculture altogether.[22] A few of those people got work as tractor drivers and in other farm-related jobs, some obtained nonfarm employment in the community or region, while others left the South for work in the North and West.

But tens of thousands of these poorest farmers, both black and white, were unable to make a satisfactory adjustment out of agriculture. Many of them continued living in the open country, getting occasional seasonal employment and perhaps some meager public assistance. These families existed in an environment of stark poverty. They lived in delapidated houses without enough food or adequate health care. Education bypassed many of their children. Unneeded any longer in farming and unable to find suitable employment alternatives, they were left as victims of unrestrained economic change to eke out not a living but a mere existence.

Despite all of the congressional hearings, investigations, and studies done in the 1950s, there was no popular concern over the tragic conditions among the rural poor in the South. USDA experts, officials in the agricultural colleges, representatives of certain social agencies, and others understood the conditions well enough. These experts also knew that the problems of poor rural southerners would have to be solved outside the agricultural sector. Poor farm residents had become welfare and public-assistance problems. Those who administered the pilot rural-development programs recognized that a broad attack was needed to help such families, but they could not muster political support for programs which might be truly helpful. The potential beneficiaries of such programs had no real power either in the southern states or in Washington, D.C.

As agricultural change accelerated in the 1950s and 1960s, more and more unneeded farmers faced insurmountable problems of adjustment. It is instructive to look at what was happening in a single state, Mississippi, from 1950 through 1964. In that fifteen-year period about 145,000 farms, or approximately 57 percent of the total, ceased to exist as separate units. In the five years from 1954 to 1959, the number of farms in the state declined by 80,000, or an average of about 16,000 a year. The biggest losses were in the plantation areas and among share-croppers and tenants. Of the 80,000 who gave up farming in that period, about 25,000 were owners and 55,000 were tenants. The nature

of agricultural change was affecting not only the marginal tenant farmers but the small owner enterprises as well. More than 60 percent of the
farmers who left Mississippi farming in those years were blacks. It was,
of course, the blacks and the poorest whites who were being crowded
out of farming, and they were the very ones with the least education,
the least knowledge, and the least training to do much of anything but
the lowest paid unskilled labor, if indeed they could find any employment at all.[23] They had been dispossessed by what one observer called
the "quiet revolution in the old Cotton South, and sank into new
depths of poverty."[24]

It was not until the early 1960s that the nation became fully aware of
the desperate conditions among displaced farmers throughout much
of the South. A few articles and news stories appeared on rural poverty
before 1964, but it was President Lyndon B. Johnson's "war on poverty"
that placed the spotlight on the South's rural poor. It had been easy to
overlook or ignore rural poverty in the southern states because so
many of the victims were invisible to the more prosperous elements of
society. The poor were frequently isolated, stuck off the main roads in
their miserable shacks, out of sight and out of mind. And many of the
poorest rural southerners were blacks who did not generate much
sympathy among community and political leaders in either the South
or the North. Many Americans did not expect rural blacks to have
much more than a mere subsistence.

On January 31, 1964, President Johnson sent a special message to
Congress on agriculture, about one-third of it dealing with rural poverty. The president urged effective programs of rural development and
called on the USDA, other federal agencies, and state and local governments to join the fight on behalf of poor rural residents. Some six
weeks later Johnson launched his "national war on poverty" and specifically mentioned the needs of farm families who had been struggling
"without hope." In May 1964 he spoke before the Georgia legislature in
Atlanta and again talked about the rural poor. Dramatizing his concern, the president said that he kept a picture of the "tiny house where I
was born, the son of a tenant farmer," over his bed in the White House.
This constantly reminded him, he said, "of the people I come from and
the people I serve."[25] Lyndon Johnson had made rural poverty a major
public issue.

Suddenly poor farmers in the South, especially the large number
of blacks who could find no place in modernized agriculture, began to
receive widespread attention. Asher Byrnes wrote in the *New Republic*
in February 1964 that until recently no one had talked much about the
rural poor. It was "a new development," he said.[26] But from 1964 to the
end of the decade scores of articles told how mechanization, chemicals,
and farm reorganization had affected poor farmers, how they were

living on a bare subsistence and suffering from hunger, malnutrition, poor health, and educational deficiencies.[27] "Lord, I'm Hungry," was the title of one *Newsweek* article on July 24, 1967, telling of conditions among the poor and dispossessed across much of the black belt.

Poverty among blacks in the South also drew the attention of civil rights leaders. People who had been leaderless and voiceless found new spokesmen in Martin Luther King, Jr., Bayard Rustin, and other black leaders. In 1965 King urged public works and "other imaginative, job-producing programs" to help poor blacks leave the farm. Rustin declared that machines had become as "great an enemy of the Negro people as segregation and discrimination," and he too supported public jobs for unemployed rural blacks.[28]

As the civil rights movement gained momentum, the attitudes of white landowners toward blacks hardened. Paternalism and the idea of taking care of "my niggers" weakened noticeably. Some sought to replace black farm workers with whites, while others intensified their move to mechanize as a means of eliminating the need for any kind of hired labor, except perhaps for tractor drivers and a few other skilled employees. One black farmer in Alabama declared in 1967 that "them white folks got a lot more interested in machinery after the civil rights bill was passed." Besides mechanical cotton pickers, chemical weed killers eliminated the little hand work that was left in most cotton fields. The occasional protests and attempted strikes by black farm workers in 1965 and 1966, usually encouraged and organized by civil rights activists, simply speeded up mechanization, which eliminated more small farmers and farm workers.[29]

Meanwhile President Johnson was pushing passage of his Economic Opportunity Act of 1964. Title III dealt with rural poverty. While there was still talk about strengthening the family farm and making people independent on the land, it had become clear that most poor farmers had no chance to achieve such a goal. These farmers had no debt-paying power and therefore were ineligible for any kind of loan that required repayment. Therefore the Economic Opportunity Act proposed outright grants of $1,500 to "low-income rural families" who might use the money to improve their farming operations or to finance nonfarm enterprises that would raise the family income. Loans of up to $2,500 for nonagricultural enterprises were also recommended. These grants and loans were designed for farm families who did not qualify for Farmers Home Administration loans, the agency that heretofore had been the lender of last resort.[30]

The House Agriculture Committee held hearings on Title III on April 27, 1964. Howard Bertsch, administrator of the Farmers Home Administration, was the main witness. While Bertsch explained how he thought grants and long- term, low-interest loans would help, there was general skepticism among committee members as to whether such legislation would help the poorest farmers. Democrat Harlan Hagen of California said that poor farmers such as those found in Appalachia could not be assisted by keeping them on the farm. "You are merely putting money down a rathole to do that," he said.[31]

Congress approved the Economic Opportunity Act in August 1964, but it contained no provision for grants to poor farmers, as had been suggested in the president's bill. A $2,500 loan provision was intact, but this was of little practical value since most poor farmers could not qualify for a fifteen-year repayable loan. There was federal support for general rural development, but no one knew how this might help underemployed and unemployed poverty-stricken farmers throughout the South.

The intentions expressed by President Johnson to help poor southern farmers came to naught. Throughout the rest of the Johnson administration and beyond, the South's poorest farm people attracted widespread attention and sympathy from congressional committees, news reporters, and church and civil rights leaders. Television also introduced the extreme poverty, malnutrition, running sores, bloated bellies, and rural slumlike conditions to millions of affluent American homes. But no bold government action resulted from all this publicity. By that time it had become clearer than ever that there was no place for these dispossessed farmers in agriculture, and they slipped out of farming and onto relief and welfare rolls. The unneeded farmers who could not find regular nonfarm jobs existed on food stamps, welfare payments, housing supplements, and other public assistance.

It took nearly a generation for the nation to accept what agricultural specialists had been saying for years—that the problems of many of the people engaged in farming throughout the South must be solved outside of agriculture. It is true that during the 1960s the idea of Operation Homestead kept popping up. The plan called for a government corporation which would buy land and resell it to small, subsistence farmers on a long-term, low-interest basis. But this scheme seemed to represent the last gasp of agrarian rhetoric rather than any practical solution to the problems of the poorest farm families.[32]

Besides having to face the unremitting economic change in agriculture, black farmers carried the burden of segregation and discrimination. Nowhere was this more evident than in the service offered to farmers by the federal agricultural agencies. As the problems of southern farm poverty became better known nationally in the 1960s, the USDA and its various agencies came under increasing attack. Ever since the 1930s, social reformers had complained that in the South local and state white power structures had controlled the county agents, the work of the experiment stations, the committees that administered the

Agricultural Stabilization and Conservation Service, the Soil Conservation Service, and other federal programs. For example, in 1937 the President's Special Committee on Farm Tenancy reported that "the county agent . . . is, generally speaking, the servant of the landowning and business interests from whom he gets a large portion of his pay, rather than the servant of the mass of the people in the farming areas."[33] According to some critics, it was not only blacks but also small white farmers who had no influence in the supposed democratic administration of agricultural policies at the grassroots. Congressman Thomas G. Abernethy of Mississippi told his colleagues in 1956 that small farmers in his state did not have a single representative on the committees allocating cotton acreage. The question of black participation in the various agricultural administrative and policymaking offices in the South, however, did not become a major issue until civil rights activists made it one. Early in 1965 the Civil Rights Commission charged that four federal farm agencies—the Extension Service, the Farmers Home Administration, the ASCS, and the SCS—were discriminating against blacks. A writer in *Farm Journal* said: "One of the hottest potatoes in a long time has surfaced at last."[34] Despite pressure from civil rights groups, very few blacks were ever elected or appointed to serve on the various county and state agricultural committees that governed the agencies dispensing money, information, and services. Failure of the agricultural agencies to truly integrate in the late 1960s led to continued charges that lack of equal rights accelerated the decline of black farmers.[35]

In an article entitled "The Southern Roots of Urban Crisis" appearing in *Fortune* in 1968, Robert Beardwood dealt with the lack of any black power in southern agricultural policy. Beardwood emphasized how the larger and more powerful white farmers had for many years controlled the agricultural programs for their own benefit. When a group of black farmers was asked if the Extension Service did not show them and their wives how to raise vegetables and chickens, one replied: "We don't hardly ever see those fellas from one year to the next." Examples of discrimination in acreage allotments by the ASCS committees were also revealed. A black farmer in Burke County, Georgia, explained that while his cotton allotment had been reduced, acreage of his white neighbor had been increased. When asked if he could not appeal the decision, he replied, "The appeals committee is white, too."

Any modification of the deep racism so prevalent in the rural South came too late to help many poor black farmers. Whites who controlled the politics and economy of the rural South refused to believe that black farmers deserved fair treatment or special help. The manager of the ASCS office in Waynesboro, Georgia, told the *Fortune* reporter, "I'll admit the small farmer is more vulnerable [to economic problems] than the big one." Then he added: "But these minority people who live in these shacks don't want to work. They'd rather go off somewhere and get on relief."[36]

The United States Department of Agriculture never made any hard fight to assist small farmers in the South. Officials of the USDA and associated agencies, as well as the agricultural colleges, never even fired their guns in the war on rural poverty. They especially ignored the needs of poor black farmers.

The reasons for largely ignoring the poor farmers, both black and white, are clear enough. In the first place, the federal and state agricultural agencies were not philosophically attuned to the poor. The main objective of the USDA, the agricultural colleges, the experiment stations, and the state departments of agriculture had been to increase productivity and efficiency. To achieve these worthy goals, officials worked most closely with the largest, most intelligent, and most productive farmers, who could best take advantage of the information and services offered. Outside of the pilot rural development programs inaugurated in the 1950s, the USDA did little to help prepare people for displacement. Indeed, most agricultural officials believed they had no responsibility to deal with the social and human problems associated with agricultural change in the South.

The habits and traditions of working with the more affluent and progressive operators had become so firmly fixed among agricultural administrators and field workers that to get out and work among the poorest farmers required major mental and programmatic adjustment. Most observers agree that attention could have been given to poor farmers by Cooperative Extension Service workers, officials of the ASCS, and other agencies. USDA and experiment station scientists and engineers might have pursued more projects aimed specifically at helping farmers with the lowest incomes. But most agricultural educators, researchers, and demonstrators believed that they lacked both the resources and congressional and state mandates to spend much time or effort on the poorest farmers. Moreover, most of the professional agriculturalists saw no salvation for poor farmers in agriculture. To spend money on plans and programs for farmers who could not become commercial operators was considered a waste of resources. For better or for worse, these public servants saw their main role as one of assisting the more successful commercial farmers.

The attitudes and actions of those working in the agricultural agencies reflected not only a definite philosophy but the political realities as well. Congress, which determined agricultural policies and provided the needed funds, had little interest in the poorest farmers. As federal farm programs expanded in the 1930s, Congress kept a close watch on how the benefits were distributed. Over the years Washington lawmakers had made it abundantly clear that most federal aid should be directed to the better-off commercial farmers. Skimpy appropriations for the FSA and later the Farmers Home Administration, when billions were being made available to support commodity prices and to make conservation payments to larger producers, were clear indications of congressional intent.

Congress responded to the wants and needs of the larger, better organized commercial farmers because these groups had the most political influence. In farm policy matters a poor people's lobby was no match for the American Farm Bureau Federation, the National Cotton Council, or the numerous farm commodity organizations. The benefits of government went to the organized and the strong. Poor southern farmers were weak and disorganized.

From World War II to the 1970s, those thousands of poor southern farmers who could not become a part of modern agriculture struggled to find a place in American society. Despite all of the talk about government help, the transition out of agriculture for most people was unplanned and unassisted. Private economic forces commanded the decisions. As the transition from farming to nonfarm work or welfare was largely completed by the 1970s, the battle of hundreds of thousands of poor people to survive on the land had largely ended. Reactions to a new and different life varied greatly. A black who worked at a Ford plant in Chicago in the early 1970s told Studs Terkel that, while there were things to complain about, "some of the guys who've been on a farm all their life say, 'This is great, the best thing ever happened to me,' " Others missed farming and work on the land. They felt like the character in Erskine Caldwell's *Tobacco Road* who said: "The mills is sort of like automobiles—they're all right to fool around in and have a good time in, but they don't offer no love like the ground does. The ground sort of looks out after people who keeps their feet on it."[37] This sentimental attachment to the soil could no longer have practical meaning to the great majority of southerners, who had been separated from the land by technology, public policy, and economic change.

11

Problems and Prospects in the Agricultural South

In 1909 two agriculturalists in the USDA wrote that "at best the taking up of a new line of farming requires a readjustment of the usual ways of thinking and doing, a thing difficult in itself and requiring considerable time to accomplish."[1] This observation seemed prophetic. It took more than half a century after 1909 before modernized agriculture became prevalent throughout the South.

Modernization, however, did not free farmers from serious problems. While the fewer and larger operators had a modern standard of living, even the most efficient farmers confronted periodic difficulties. Some of the problems were related to production of specific crops and conditions within southern agriculture, while others were inherent in the overall farm economy.

The most difficult problem facing farmers nationwide in the 1950s and 1960s was the cost-price squeeze. This was not a new phenomenon, but one which struck farmers with special severity as they used more and more nonfarm inputs in the production process. With the increased use of machinery, fertilizer, gasoline and diesel fuel, insecticides and fungicides, hybrid seed, and other inputs, the relationship between the cost of these items and the prices of farm commodities became of critical importance. To meet the growing cost of operation, farmers sought to increase their efficiency by producing more units at less cost per unit.

While government price supports were in place for cotton, rice, tobacco, and peanuts, among the South's major cash crops, support prices did not keep up with inflated operating and living expenses. When farmers sought to increase their efficiency they added to the surpluses which in turn tended to depress prices. During the 1950s and 1960s thousands of farmers throughout the South and elsewhere went out of business because they were unable to survive the cost-price crunch. In the late 1960s increasing exports began to help farmers, but it was not until 1972 and 1973 that conditions showed marked improvement.

In the fall of 1972 the Russians quietly entered the American grain market and began to make large purchases. This, along with other exports, drove prices up in late 1972 and 1973 to undreamed-of levels. Cotton jumped from an average of 27 cents a pound in 1972 to 44 cents in 1973; rice from $6.73 to $13.80 per hundredweight, and soybeans from $4.37 a bushel to $5.68. In 1973 some farmers who sold just at the right time received almost $10 a bushel for soybeans. Tobacco and peanut prices also rose in 1973, but the increases were less dramatic than with cotton, rice, and soybeans. In any event, southern farmers were a part of the nation's unparalleled agricultural prosperity which saw net farm income jump from $18 to $33 billion between 1972 and 1973. Net income per farm in Georgia, for example, rose from $6,046 in 1972 to $9,687 in 1973. The increase in Arkansas, where rice was a major cash crop, was from $5,066 to $11,078.[2]

Demand for farm commodities continued strong in 1974 and to a lesser extent in 1975, and farm income remained high. Some observers were predicting that American farm surpluses were a thing of the past and that world needs would provide stable and profitable markets into the indefinite future. Most acreage restrictions were removed in 1973 and government officials urged producers to plant from fencerow to fencerow to meet the demand. Under the influence of high prices and government advice, southern farmers greatly increased their rice acreage and also expanded soybean production. There was also a considerable expansion of tobacco acreage, although peanut allotments kept peanut acreage about steady at 1.5 million acres. Some southern states also increased their production of wheat.

The farm prosperity of 1973 and 1974 produced a high level of optimism among farmers. Many of them bought more land and expensive machinery on credit, believing that high prices and heavy production were the wave of the future. After all, no less an authority than the secretary of agriculture, Earl Butz, predicted continuous expansion of world markets for American farm products. The secretary told delegates to a food conference in July 1975 that, despite the prospects of large harvests in the United States, Americans should not be lulled "into forgetting the 'frightening challenge' to keep expanding food production in a race with world population."[3]

As a result of good prices and a favorable future, land prices shot upward, greatly increasing capital costs. Machines, including tractors, combines, planters, and other equipment, were getting larger and more expensive. With expensive land and machinery, as well as advancing costs for fertilizer, pesticides, fungicides, and fuel, especially after the Arab oil embargo in 1973, farmers found themselves back in a harsh cost-price squeeze by 1976 and 1977 as agricultural prices weakened.

In the giddy days of high prices and maximum production, some farmers had made bad business decisions. They had borrowed too much, expanded too rapidly, and failed to accumulate any reserves for a time when conditions might change. So long as land prices continued to rise, farmers had sufficient equity to borrow and service their debts. Lower commodity prices and stalling increases in land values, however, could spell disaster for many southern farmers and others throughout the nation.

Farmers blamed the government and the growing power of consumers for some of the problems that surfaced in 1975 and 1976. In August 1975, President Gerald Ford restricted grain exports to the Soviet Union until the effect of such sales on domestic supplies and food prices could be determined. Farmers were fighting mad. They declared that consumers, with government support, had become the principal makers of farm policy. They believed that, after urging farmers to grow more to meet domestic and world needs for food, the government had caved in to consumer demands for lower food prices. Many farmers argued that the federal government should support farm commodity prices at a level profitable to producers. Some said the level of supports should be at 100 percent of parity.

Western farmers had been especially hard hit by low cattle and wheat prices in 1976 and 1977. By the late summer of 1977 talk of an agricultural strike began to be heard in southeastern Colorado, western Kansas and Oklahoma, and northwestern Texas. By September the American Agriculture Movement had emerged. These unhappy farmers demanded that government support prices be set at 100 percent of parity. Unless this was done, they said, a farm strike would begin December 14, 1977. By a strike, farmers meant that they would not plant any crops in 1978 or buy any supplies until Congress met their demands for 100 percent of parity.

By October the AAM had spread to the Southeast, where Tommy Kersey, whose family owned several thousand acres around Unadilla, Georgia, headed the strike efforts. To draw attention to their problems farmers began a series of tractor marches. On October 27 farmers staged a massive demonstration in Alma, Georgia, by driving 1,000 tractors through the little town. A local editor said, "this was the biggest thing I've ever seen happen in Bacon County." Farmers throughout the South now began making plans to cooperate with those in the Midwest and Great Plains for a huge tractor march on Washington. This, it was hoped, would get the attention of Congress. Meanwhile, on November 25, farmers staged a nine-mile-long tractorcade through President Jimmy Carter's home town of Plains, Georgia.

This action was only preliminary to a much larger demonstration on December 10, when farmers from all over the Southeast converged on Atlanta with more than 5,000 tractors. A few drove up the state capitol steps and everyone shouted support for parity prices. Southerners then headed toward Washington, where they joined farmers from all over the country for a giant tractorcade in the nation's capital on January 18, 1978. Farmers tied up traffic in Washington and received widespread press and television coverage. But they wanted legislative action. Following several weeks of lobbying, they did get more generous land diversion payments, extended repayment plans from the Farmers Home Administration, and a large emergency loan program. But Congress rejected their demand for 100 percent of parity. Dissatisfied with these results, the AAM sponsored another tractorcade on Washington early in 1979, but that effort brought even fewer results.[4]

While farm prices improved in 1978 and 1979, the cost-price squeeze continued to plague farmers. Just when some relief appeared in the form of increased exports to Russia in 1980, President Carter announced an embargo on extra sales to the Soviet Union in retaliation for the Russian invasion of Afghanistan in December 1979. Again, farmers were dismayed and angered, but they were unable to change the president's policy. They believed they were the main victims in a foreign policy controversy, and that other economic interests did not have to shoulder such burdens.

By the early 1980s thousands of southern farmers were in very difficult financial straits. A Dooly County farmer in south-central Georgia declared in 1982, "I'd rather have two tickets on the Titanic than be farming today." While earlier the Farmers Home Administration had been considered the lender of last resort, during the late 1970s and early 1980s more and more farmers had to turn to the FHA for credit. In 1976, for example, the FHA carried only 2 percent of the farm loans in Georgia; that figure had jumped to 37 percent by 1981.[5] The situation was similar throughout the South. There were 272,460 FHA farm loans outstanding in the eleven southern states at the end of 1981. Some 52,600, or about 19.3 percent, of them were delinquent. The delinquencies ranged from a low of 7 percent in Louisiana to a high of 39 and 34 percent respectively in Florida and Georgia.[6] In many cases farmers' debts exceeded their assets. Some farmers were foreclosed on or declared bankruptcy. The prospects of so many farmers in Georgia losing their farms prompted a group of Georgians early in 1982 to successfully seek an injunction in the United States District Court in Brunswick which prohibited the Farmers Home Administration from foreclosing until its procedures and practices had been examined.

Some southern farmers faced special problems. The anti-smoking campaign of the 1960s and 1970s threatened the demand for tobacco, but that was only one issue that caused concern for producers of the nation's oldest commercial crop. Many congressmen and senators favored eliminating tobacco price supports altogether, arguing that it was inconsistent for the federal government to try to discourage smoking while at the same time supporting tobacco prices. In 1982, after providing federal price supports for nearly a half century, Congress required that future price support programs be self-supporting. Growers were then assessed a fee of 3 cents a pound to build up a fund to support prices. Moreover, since tobacco allotments were tied to ownership, many landowners who had quit farming leased their acreage quotas at ever higher prices to farmers who needed to enlarge their operations. This increased production costs for many producers.[7]

Peanut farmers also experienced some special difficulties. In 1980 the federal program abandoned acreage allotments and adopted a poundage quota. This placed tight restrictions on producers who grew price-supported peanuts, although limits were removed on peanuts grown for export. These so-called surplus peanuts, however, brought low prices compared to those produced under the poundage allotments.[8] Rice farmers and others who depended so heavily on exports experienced a real struggle in 1982 and 1983 as prices sagged under huge surpluses. Thus, southern farmers in the early 1980s not only suffered from the common problems facing most farmers—the cost-price squeeze, surpluses, low prices, and heavy debts—but many producers in the South faced special difficulties.

For nearly three generations after the Civil War, a majority of southern farmers produced cotton, corn, tobacco, peanuts, and a few other crops on small, nonproductive farms. Except in rice production, large amounts of hand labor were required in most farm operations. This meant that productivity in relation to the amount of labor used was extremely low. The result was low incomes and extensive poverty.

Once the structure of small farms and various kinds of tenancy became established in the South, nothing that farmers tried could bring major change except for a few producers. Reformers recommended crop diversification and self-sufficiency, the use of more machinery, more and better fertilizer, and improved management. But the basic structure held on stubbornly throughout most of the South into the 1930s. Besides knowledge and the will to change, southern farming required one basic element—capital—before a new structure could emerge. Machines to replace human labor, farm enlargement, crop diversification, entrance into livestock production, and other changes all took capital. For the most part, southern farmers were too poor to accumulate capital. Moreover, the economic infrastructure for agricultural improvement in the South was weak. Education and health services were poor, while markets, transportation, and banking and credit facilities were inadequate.

Two developments that occurred simultaneously in the 1930s opened up the floodgates of change in the farming South. The New Deal program of restricting cotton acreage in return for cash payments finally broke the hold of cotton on southern farms and encouraged the planting of other crops. And the price support programs for cotton, tobacco, peanuts, and rice assured farmers a more stable cash income. Farmers were also assisted by the federal credit agencies and the cost-sharing conservation programs. Thus the federal government, beginning in the 1930s, helped to underwrite income stability and capital development.

Accompanying helpful government policies were the remarkable developments in farm science and technology. Growing use of tractors led the machinery parade in the 1930s as planters and farmers, with more capital and credit, invested in all kinds of labor-saving machines. Experimentation with mechanical cotton pickers in the 1930s resulted in the manufacture of a successful spindle-type picker in 1941. This opened the way for the complete mechanization of cotton production. With wider use of machinery, farmers did not need so many sharecroppers or tenants. During the generation after 1935 most of these poor farmers were forced off the land or left of their own accord to find nonfarm employment. World War II opened up many jobs for poor southern farm people. The trends toward mechanization, the application of science in farming operations, the greater variation of commercial crops, the raising of more livestock, and larger farms accelerated slowly after about 1935, speeded up during and right after World War II, and reached floodtide proportions in the late 1950s. By the 1960s the transformation of commercial agriculture in the South had been achieved. Changes occurred at different rates and to different degrees in various sections and subsections of the South, but the structure of southern agriculture had been remade. The old structure—small cotton farms worked by people and mules—had been changed to a highly capital-intensive, diversified, mechanized, and labor-efficient agriculture.

Southern farmers faced the same serious problems after modernization as farmers did in other parts of the country. But their problems were different in nature from those experienced by the poor sharecroppers, tenants, and small landowners from the 1870s through the 1930s. Most southern farmers in the 1980s, whatever confronted them, were glad that the agriculture of hoe, mule, and cotton was gone forever.

Appendix: Statistical Data on Southern Agriculture, 1880-1980

Table A1. Farm Population in Eleven Southern States, 1920-1980 (in thousands)

State	1920	1925	1930	1940	1945	1950	1960	1970	1980*
Va.	1,078	1,020	953	986	831	732	467	238	92
N.C.	1,520	1,566	1,604	1,659	1,360	1,377	950	463	155
S.C.	1,088	1,001	919	917	709	701	433	144	54
Ga.	1,706	1,566	1,423	1,368	1,052	962	515	228	121
Fla.	285	286	280	305	253	233	157	113	59
Tenn.	1,290	1,249	1,219	1,276	1,046	1,016	677	384	142
Ala.	1,355	1,343	1,344	1,343	1,068	960	519	216	88
Miss.	1,288	1,322	1,366	1,403	1,119	1,097	680	277	85
Ark.	1,165	1,153	1,122	1,113	798	802	415	228	108
La.	798	823	833	854	608	567	313	160	59
Tex.	2,314	2,363	2,359	2,160	1,520	1,292	806	471	215
Total	13,887	13,692	13,422	13,384	10,390	9,739	5,932	2,922	1,178

*Based on a different definition of farm population from earlier years.

Sources: Figures for 1920-1970 are from *Farm Population Estimates, 1910-70*, Rural Development Service, USDA, Statistical Bulletin 523 (Washington, D.C.: July 1973), pp. 18-25; 1980 figures are from the *1980 Census of Population* 1, chapter C (Washington, D.C., 1983), for the various states.

Table A2. Number of Farms in Eleven Southern States, 1880-1980

State	1880	1890	1900	1910	1920	1930	1940	1950	1960	1970	1980
Va.	118,517	127,600	167,886	184,018	186,242	170,610	174,885	150,997	97,623	64,572	58,000
N.C.	157,609	178,359	224,637	253,725	269,763	279,708	278,276	288,508	190,567	119,386	93,000
S.C.	93,864	115,008	155,355	176,434	192,693	157,931	137,558	139,364	78,172	39,559	35,000
Ga.	138,626	171,071	224,691	291,027	310,732	255,598	216,033	198,191	103,350	67,431	59,000
Fla.	23,438	34,228	40,814	50,016	54,005	58,966	62,248	56,921	45,100	35,586	39,000
Tenn.	165,650	174,412	224,623	246,012	252,774	245,657	247,617	231,631	157,688	121,406	96,000
Ala.	135,864	157,772	223,220	246,901	256,999	257,395	231,746	211,512	115,788	72,491	58,000
Miss.	101,772	144,318	220,803	274,382	272,101	312,663	291,092	251,383	138,142	72,577	55,000
Ark.	94,433	124,760	178,694	214,678	232,604	242,334	216,674	182,429	95,007	60,433	59,000
La.	48,292	69,294	115,969	120,546	135,463	161,445	150,007	124,181	74,438	42,269	37,000
Tex.	174,184	228,126	352,190	417,770	436,033	495,489	418,002	331,567	227,071	213,550	186,000
Total	1,252,349	1,524,948	2,128,882	2,495,509	2,598,509	2,637,796	2,424,138	2,166,684	1,322,946	909,260	775,000

Sources: Calculated from the pertinent Censuses of Agriculture and from *Agricultural Statistics, 1981* (Washington, D.C., 1981).

Table A3. Average Acres of Cropland Harvested per Farm, 1880-1978

State	1880	1890	1900	1910	1920	1930	1940	1950	1960	1970	1978
Va.	32.4	29.6	25.9	23.1	24.6	23.3	22.0	21.9	33.2	42.0	54.7
N.C.	29.4	29.2	25.0	22.6	21.7	20.8	22.0	20.0	26.7	39.9	58.0
S.C.	34.4	33.9	30.4	29.2	28.0	26.2	31.4	28.4	45.2	63.0	97.7
Ga.	46.2	40.4	36.8	33.2	33.7	32.6	40.7	35.8	54.8	77.1	110.5
Fla.	29.2	20.9	25.0	24.5	22.9	24.7	27.0	30.4	52.2	88.8	93.1
Tenn.	33.8	33.1	29.7	25.9	26.9	24.9	24.9	24.1	30.5	35.8	55.3
Ala.	37.2	34.5	30.1	27.4	28.4	27.6	30.7	27.1	37.4	51.6	83.9
Miss.	39.1	33.8	25.2	22.4	23.4	21.1	23.9	24.4	38.6	89.2	150.1
Ark.	29.2	31.9	28.1	25.0	27.8	27.2	30.5	32.5	74.0	166.1	190.8
La.	39.6	35.7	29.4	29.8	29.0	25.2	27.0	25.4	45.8	117.8	182.4
Tex.	30.8	36.8	42.9	44.0	57.4	61.8	62.3	84.8	140.1	154.5	174.0
Kan.*	51.0	87.7	104.4	111.9	132.6	146.4	114.0	163.6	216.1	231.8	286.7
Iowa*	75.4	90.2	96.2	93.9	95.7	103.6	94.0	111.0	141.0	149.7	207.7

* Included for purposes of comparison.

Table A4. Value of Land and Buildings per Farm in Eleven Southern States, 1880-1978

State	1880	1890	1900	1910	1920	1930	1940	1950	1960	1970	1978
Va.	$1,823	$1,994	$1,618	$2,891	$5,501	$5,016	$3,860	$8,458	$18,635	$47,191	$163,918
N.C.	862	1,031	867	1,800	3,990	3,018	2,647	6,605	15,475	35,551	135,072
S.C.	732	862	816	1,887	4,222	2,401	2,461	5,886	15,685	46,171	146,244
Ga.	807	889	816	1,647	3,663	2,259	2,223	5,623	17,944	54,883	181,876
Fla.	866	2,125	1,000	2,362	5,212	7,179	5,211	16,617	73,554	139,818	351,646
Tenn.	1,248	1,392	1,180	1,953	4,055	3,025	2,683	6,182	13,288	33,176	116,883
Ala.	581	704	603	1,096	2,123	1,952	1,764	4,809	12,780	37,596	128,260
Miss.	912	883	688	1,218	2,903	1,818	1,632	4,566	14,292	51,611	173,475
Ark.	786	950	757	1,440	3,238	2,261	2,108	6,225	18,915	67,532	203,014
La.	1,222	1,232	1,217	1,971	3,499	2,590	2,359	7,416	23,719	74,414	246,753
Tex.	979	1,753	1,964	4,412	8,486	7,260	6,196	20,263	51,787	99,133	275,047
Ia.*	3,061	4,247	6,550	15,008	35,616	19,655	12,614	27,105	49,150	93,694	142,629
Ks.*	1,697	3,359	3,718	9,770	17,122	13,738	9,092	24,344	48,084	91,131	313,288

Sources: The figures for 1880 to 1950 are from the 1950 Census of Agriculture, General Report 2 (Washington, D.C., 1952): 53-55; the remaining figures are from subsequent agricultural censuses.

* Included for purposes of comparison.

Table A5. Approximate Value of Farm Products per Farm in Eleven Southern States, 1879-1978

State	1879	1889	1899	1909	1919	1929	1939	1949	1959	1969	1978
Va.	$385	$331	$516	$819	$2,284	$1,252	$713	$2,318	$4,342	$8,832	$22,933
N.C.	328	280	398	694	2,282	1,040	781	2,113	4,183	10,010	33,941
S.C.	437	446	439	886	2,546	935	665	1,686	3,875	9,156	25,959
Ga.	483	487	464	884	2,058	1,011	594	2,084	5,711	15,423	40,807
Fla.	317	353	449	872	1,870	1,696	1,494	6,758	15,532	31,812	69,148
Tenn.	374	316	473	784	1,952	945	471	1,581	3,009	5,132	14,694
Ala.	418	420	409	715	1,496	856	349	1,419	3,578	8,921	27,398
Miss.	625	508	464	628	1,498	910	413	1,442	4,094	9,440	31,611
Ark.	463	426	446	716	1,825	988	581	2,321	6,728	16,097	42,799
La.	888	784	627	750	1,767	1,046	635	2,247	4,499	11,743	31,611
Tex.	374	516	681	1,029	3,140	1,598	1,128	5,672	9,287	23,077	42,829
Ia.*	734	792	1,598	2,759	6,779	3,303	2,486	8,143	13,074	26,044	64,934
Ks.*	376	570	1,213	2,190	5,341	2,850	1,376	5,971	10,645	21,125	64,984

Sources: Figures are from the decennial agricultural censuses. The figures are not strictly comparable because of changing definitions by the Census Bureau. However, they do approximate the actual values of crops and livestock produced, and provide clear trends in the value of farm commodities per farm over a century. All figures represent current dollars.

* Included for purposes of comparison.

Table A6. Number of Black Farmers in Eleven Southern States and Total for the United States, 1900-1978

State	1900	1910	1920	1930	1940	1950	1960	1970	1978
Va.	44,795	48,039	47,690	39,598	35,062	28,527	15,629	5,453	3,978
N.C.	53,996	64,456	74,849	74,636	57,428	69,029	41,023	13,111	9,289
S.C.	85,381	96,772	109,005	77,331	61,204	61,255	30,953	9,535	6,489
Ga.	82,822	122,554	130,176	86,787	59,127	50,352	20,163	5,571	4,551
Fla.	13,521	14,698	12,954	11,010	9,731	7,473	3,664	1,365	2,478
Tenn.	33,883	38,300	38,181	35,123	27,972	24,044	15,018	4,930	2,477
Ala.	94,069	110,387	95,200	93,795	73,338	57,205	29,206	9,873	4,883
Miss.	128,351	164,488	161,001	182,578	159,256	122,709	55,174	17,184	8,887
Ark.	46,978	63,578	72,275	79,556	57,011	40,810	14,654	3,775	2,196
La.	58,096	54,819	62,036	73,734	59,556	40,599	17,686	5,518	3,400
Tex.	65,472	69,816	78,597	85,940	52,648	34,389	15,432	5,375	7,347
Total	707,364	847,907	881,964	840,088	652,333	536,392	258,602	81,690	55,975
Total U.S.	746,715	893,370	925,708	882,850	681,790	559,980	272,541	90,506	79,916

Sources: 1950 Census of Agriculture, General Report 2 (Washington, D.C., 1952): 1026; 1974 Census of Agriculture 1, pt. 51 (Washington, D.C., 1977), individual state tables; and 1978 Census of Agriculture 1, pt. 51 (Washington, D.C., 1981): 2-3

Notes

Chapter 1

1. *Southern Cultivator* 24 (Feb. 1866): 39. Eliza F. Andrews, *The War-Time Journal of a Georgia Girl* (New York: D. Appleton-Century, 1908), entry for May 15, 1865. C. Vann Woodward, in *Origins of the New South, 1877-1913* (Baton Rouge: Louisiana State Univ. Press, 1971), has an excellent chapter on southern agriculture, "The Unredeemed Farmer."

2. Quoted in Steven W. Engerrand, " 'Now Scratch or Die': The Genesis of Capitalistic Agricultural Labor in Georgia, 1865-1880," Ph.D. diss., Univ. of Georgia, 1981, p. 43.

3. Christie Farnham Pope, "Southern Homesteads for Negroes," *Agricultural History* 44 (Apr. 1970): 201-12. Paul W. Gates, "Federal Land Policy in the South," *Journal of Southern History* 6 (Aug. 1940):303-30. On failure to redistribute land, see Kenneth S. Greenberg, "The Civil War and the Redistribution of Land: Adams County, Mississippi, 1860-1870," *Agricultural History* 52 (Apr. 1978): 292-305; Jonathan M. Wiener, "Planter Persistence and Social Change, 1850-1870," *Journal of Interdisciplinary History* 7 (Autumn 1976): 235-60; Claude F. Oubre, *Forty Acres and a Mule: The Freedmen's Bureau and Black Land Ownership* (Baton Rouge: Louisiana State Univ. Press, 1978); chapter 6 of Edward Magdol's *A Right to the Land: Essays on the Freedmen's Community* (Westport, Conn.: Greenwood Press, 1977); LaWanda Cox, "The Promise of Land for the Freedmen," *Mississippi Valley Historical Review* 45 (Dec. 1958): 413-40.

4. *Report of the Commissioner of Agriculture, 1866* (Washington, D.C., 1867), pp. 573-74. See also Robert G. Athearn, *In Search of Canaan: Black Migration to Kansas, 1879-80* (Lawrence: Regents Press of Kansas, 1978).

5. Quoted in W.C. Scroggs, "Inter-State Migration of Negro Population," *Journal of Political Economy* 25 (Dec. 1917): 1034-35.

6. *Southern Cultivator* 25 (Aug. 1867): 251.

7. C.W. Howard, "Conditions and Resources of Georgia," *Report of the Commissioner of Agriculture, 1866* (Washington, D.C., 1867), pp. 573-74. A report from Charleston, South Carolina, in June 1867 said that planters who could afford it were paying monthly wages, but "the greater number were compelled by poverty to adhere to the former plan of allowing negroes half the crop." *New York Times*, June 19, 1867, p. 2.

8. Joel Williamson, *After Slavery: The Negro in South Carolina during Reconstruction, 1861-1877* (Chapel Hill: Univ. of North Carolina Press, 1965), pp. 89-93.

9. Appling v. Odum, 46 *Georgia Reports* 585 (1872). There is a vast literature that deals in some way with sharecropping and tenancy in the South during the late nineteenth century. See Stephen J. DeCanio, *Agriculture in the Postbellum South* (Cambridge: M.I.T. Press, 1974); Jay R. Mandle, *The Roots of Black Poverty: The Southern Plantation Economy after the Civil War* (Durham, N.C.: Duke Univ. Press, 1978); Robert Higgs, *Cooperation and Coercion: Blacks in the American Economy, 1865-1914* (New York: Cambridge Univ. Press, 1977); James L. Roark, *Masters without Slaves: Southern Planters in the Civil War and*

Reconstruction (New York: W. W. Norton, 1977); Roger L. Ransom and Richard Sutch, *One Kind of Freedom: The Economic Consequences of Emancipation* (Cambridge, England: Cambridge Univ. Press, 1977); Jonathan M. Wiener, *Social Origins of the New South: Alabama, 1860-1885* (Baton Rouge: Louisiana State Univ. Press, 1978); Ronald L. Davis, "Good and Faithful Labor: A Study of the Origins, Development, and Economics of Southern Sharecropping, 1860-1880," Ph.D. diss., Univ. of Missouri, 1974; Ralph Shlomowitz, "The Origins of Southern Sharecropping," *Agricultural History* 53 (July 1979): 557-75; Joseph D. Reid, "Sharecropping As an Understandable Market Response: The Post-Bellum South," *Journal of Economic History* 33 (Mar. 1973): 106-28; Bell I. Wiley, "Salient Changes in Southern Agriculture since the Civil War," *Agricultural History* 13 (Apr. 1939): 65-76; Charles L. Flynn, Jr., *White Land, Black Labor, Caste and Class in Late Nineteenth Century Georgia* (Baton Rouge: Louisiana State Univ. Press, 1983).

10. E.A. Boeger and E.A. Goldenweiser, *A Study of the Tenant Systems of Farming in the Yazoo-Mississippi Delta*, USDA Bulletin no. 337 (Washington, D.C., Jan. 13, 1916), p. 6.

11. Harold D. Woodman, "Post-Civil War Southern Agriculture and the Law," *Agricultural History* 53 (Jan. 1979): 319-37.

12. Ibid., p. 325; *Report of the Industrial Commission on Agriculture*, House Doc. no. 180, 57 Cong., 1 sess. (Washington, D.C., 1901) 11:135; Lee J. Alston and Robert Higgs, "Contractual Mix in Southern Agriculture since the Civil War: Facts, Hypotheses, and Texts," *Journal of Economic History* 42 (June 1982): 328-31; Robert Higgs, "Patterns of Farm Rental in the Georgia Cotton Belt, 1880-1900," *Journal of Economic History* 34 (June 1974): 468-80; and Shlomowitz, "Origins of Southern Sharecropping," pp. 557-75.

13. D. Wallace, "Southern Agriculture: Its Condition and Needs," *Popular Science* 64 (Jan. 1904): 248.

14. "Reports on Georgia Plantation Districts, 1911," by R.P. Brooks, Inquiries, I, 1912, Univ. of Georgia Library, Special Collections.

15. *1954 Census of Agriculture, General Report*, 2 (Washington, D.C., 1956): 1046-48.

16. Vernon Burton, "Race and Reconstruction: Edgefield County, South Carolina," in Edward Magdol and Jon L. Wakelyn, *The Southern Common People* (Westport, Conn.: Greenwood Press, 1980), p. 218; Frank J. Welch, *The Plantation Land Tenure System in Mississippi*, Mississippi Agricultural Experiment Station Bulletin 385 (State College, June 1943), pp. 53-54.

17. *Twelfth Census of the United States, 1900, Agriculture*, pt. 2 (Washington, D.C., 1902): 409.

18. *Southern Cultivator* 25 (June 1867): 198; *Report of the Commissioner of Agriculture, 1873* (Washington, D.C., 1874), p. 17.

19. *Yearbook of Agriculture, 1907* (Washington, D.C., 1908), pp. 669-70; Daniel J. Sully, "King Cotton's Impoverished Retinue," *Cosmopolitan* 46 (Feb. 1909): 253-63.

20. *Twelfth Census of the United States, 1900, Agriculture*, pt. 1: 31-45.

21. Clarence H. Poe, "Rich Kingdom of Cotton," *World's Work* 9 (Nov. 1904): 5488-98.

22. *Tenth Census of the United States, 1880, Agriculture*, 3 (Washington, D.C., 1883): 185, 218, 231, and calculations from other pertinent tables; *Twelfth Census of the United States, 1900, Agriculture*, pt. 2: 406. See also Grady McWhiney, "The Revolution in Nineteenth-Century Alabama Agriculture," *Alabama Review* 31 (Jan. 1978): 3-32.

23. *Twelfth Census of the United States, 1900, Agriculture*, pt. 1: clxxv.

24. James C. Bonner, *Georgia's Last Frontier: The Development of Carroll County* (Athens: Univ. of Georgia Press, 1971), p. 142.

25. Georgia Agricultural Society, *Proceedings of the Spring Meeting, February, 1878* (n.p.), pp. 414, 422; J. Crawford King, Jr., "The Closing of the Southern Range: An Exploratory Study," *Journal of Southern History* 48 (Feb. 1982): 53-70; William T. Mealor, Jr., "Open-Range Ranching and Its Contemporary Successors in South Florida," Ph.D. diss., Univ. of Georgia, 1973.

26. *Report of the Committee on Agriculture and Forestry on Condition of Cotton Growers,*

Senate Report 986, 53 Cong., 3 sess., pt. 1 (Washington, D.C., 1895): 335.

27. *Transactions of the Georgia State Agricultural Society* (Atlanta: J.P. Harrison, 1878), p. 468.

28. *Publications of the Georgia State Department of Agriculture,* 12 (Atlanta, 1886): 202.

29. *Report of the Secretary of Agriculture, 1890* (Washington, D.C., 1890), p. 333.

30. United States Census Office, *Cotton Production in the United States, 1880,* pt. 1 (Washington, D.C., 1884): 169.

31. Thomas P. Janes, *Annual Report of the Commissioner of Agriculture, State of Georgia, 1875* (Atlanta: J.H. Estill, 1875), p. 63.

32. U.S. Census Office, *Cotton Production in the United States, 1880,* pt. 1: 185. D.A. Brodie and C.K. McClelland, *Diversified Farming under the Plantation System,* USDA Farmer's Bulletin no. 299 (Washington, D.C., June 18, 1907), p. 9.

33. Charles H. Otken, *The Ills of the South* (New York: Knickerbocker Press, 1894), pp. 57-58.

34. *1950 Census of Agriculture, General Report,* 2 (Washington, D.C., 1952): 634. The best study of tobacco is Nannie May Tilley, *The Bright-Tobacco Industry, 1860-1929* (Chapel Hill: Univ. of North Carolina Press, 1948).

35. Quoted in Anthony J. Badger, *Prosperity Road: The New Deal, Tobacco, and North Carolina* (Chapel Hill: Univ. of North Carolina Press, 1980), p. 4.

36. Henry C. Dethloff, "Rice Revolution in the Southwest, 1880-1910," *Arkansas Historical Quarterly* 29 (Spring 1970): 66-75; *1950 Census of Agriculture, General Report,* 2: 582.

37. J. Carlyle Sitterson, *Sugar Country: The Cane Sugar Industry in the South, 1753-1950* (Lexington: Univ. of Kentucky Press 1953), p. 231.

38. Ibid., p. 262.

39. G.H. Reuss, *The Organization and Financial Returns of 129 Small Sized Louisiana Cane Farms, 1930,* Louisiana Experiment Station Bulletin 224 (Baton Rouge, July 1931), pp. 5-7. See also William R. Johnson, *A Short History of the Sugar Industry in Texas* ([Houston:] Texas Gulf Coast Historical Association, 1961).

40. John L. Winberry, "The Sorghum Syrup Industry, 1854-1975," *Agricultural History* 54 (Apr. 1980): 349-50.

41. Willard Range, *A Century of Georgia Agriculture* (Athens: Univ. of Georgia Press, 1954), pp. 110-11.

42. A. Oemler, "Truck Farming," *Report of the Commissioner of Agriculture, 1885* (Washington, D.C., 1885), pp. 583-627; L.C. Corbett, "Truck Farming in the Atlantic Coast States," *Yearbook of Agriculture, 1907,* pp. 425-34; Seaman A. Knapp, "Causes of Southern Rural Conditions and the Small Farm as an Important Remedy," *Yearbook of Agriculture, 1908* (Washington, D.C., 1909), p. 313; Jay A. Bonsteel, "Truck Soils of the Atlantic Coast Region," *Yearbook of Agriculture, 1912* (Washington, D.C., 1913), pp. 417-20.

43. *Yearbook of Agriculture, 1905* (Washington, D.C., 1906), pp. 196-97.

44. *Publications of the Georgia State Department of Agriculture, 1886,* 12 (Atlanta: Constitution Book and Job Print, 1886): 195, 205-6, 209.

45. S.W. Doty, *Marketing Livestock in the South,* USDA Farmers' Bulletin 809 (Washington, D.C., Apr. 1917), pp. 3-4.

46. *Twelfth Census of the United States, 1900, Agriculture,* pt. 2: 78, 422.

47. *Report of the Commissioner of Agriculture, 1883* (Washington, D.C., 1883), p. 318.

48. *1950 Census of Agriculture, General Report,* 2: 53-55. See also *Report of the Commissioner of Agriculture, 1883,* p. 319.

49. "Microfilm Manuscript Census of Agriculture, 1880," for Harris County, Georgia, Enumeration District 55, p. 8; Laurens County, Georgia, Enumeration District 65, p. 10; Jackson County, Georgia, Enumeration District 58, p. 21. The names in the Agricultural Census were also examined in the population census to determine color of operator, marital status, and size of family.

50. *Twelfth Census of the United States, 1900, Agriculture,* pt. 1:70-71; *Thirteenth Census of the United States, 1910, Agriculture,* 5, *Report by States* (Washington, D.C., 1913): 350-51.

51. *Thirteenth Census of the United States, 1910, Agriculture,* 6: 871-72, 887.

52. Ibid., pp. 588, 598, 607.

53. Ann Malone, "The Wiregrass Area of Georgia," manuscript located at Agrirama, Tifton, Georgia; John H. Goff, "The Great Pine Barrens," *Emory University Quarterly* 5 (Mar. 1949):21-31.

54. *Thirteenth Census of the United States, 1910, Agriculture,* 5, *General Report,* p. 186.

55. Manning Marable, "The Politics of Black Land Tenure, 1877-1915," *Agricultural History* 53 (Jan. 1979): 142-52; Leo McGee and Robert Boone, eds., *The Black Rural Landowner; Endangered Species, Social, Political, and Economic Implications* (Westport, Conn.: Greenwood Press, 1979), chap. 1. An early study of black landholding is that of W.E.B. DuBois, *The Negro Land-holder of Georgia,* Department of Labor Bulletin 35 (Washington, D.C., 1901). See also *Twelfth Census of the United States, 1900, Agriculture,* pt. 1:xciv, civ.

56. *Thirteenth Census of the United States, 1910, Agriculture,* 5, *General Report,* pp. 196-97. See also *1950 Census of Agriculture, General Report,* 2: 1025.

57. *Twelfth Census of the United States, 1900, Agriculture,* pt. 1: civ, cxxxiv.

58. *New York Times,* Apr. 29, 1901, p. 7; U.S. Census Office, *Report on Cotton Production,* pt. 2: 439.

59. U.S. Senate, *Report of the Committee on Agriculture and Forestry on Condition of Cotton Growers in the United States,* Report No. 986, 53 Cong., 3 sess. (Washington, D.C., 1895), pt. 1: 289. Hereafter cited as *Report on Cotton Growers.*

60. U.S. Census Office, *Report on Cotton Production,* pt. 2: 173; pt. 2: 186.

61. George K. Holmes, "Peons of the South," *Annals of the American Academy of Political and Social Science* 4 (Sept. 1893): 71.

62. *American Agriculturalist* 44 (Nov. 1885): 450.

63. Quoted in Steven H. Hahn, *The Roots of Southern Populism: Yeoman Farmers and the Transformation of the Georgia Upcountry, 1850-1890* (New York: Oxford Univ. Press, 1983), p. 159.

64. Janes, *Annual Report of the Commissioner of Agriculture, State of Georgia, 1875,* p. 55.

65. Poe, "Rich Kingdom of Cotton," p. 5493.

66. Holmes, "Peons of the South," p. 68. See also Eugene Lerner, "Southern Output and Agricultural Income, 1860-1880," *Agricultural History* 33 (July 1959): 117-25.

67. *Twelfth Census of the United States, 1900, Agriculture,* pt. 2: 406.

68. Sully, "King Cotton's Impoverished Retinue," p. 260; *Report of the Secretary of Agriculture, 1890,* p. 335.

69. *Annual Report of the Commissioner of Agriculture, State of Georgia, 1875,* p. 43.

70. U.S. Census Office, *Report on Cotton Production,* pt. 1: 279-81.

71. Ibid., 2: 349.

72. W.M. Hurst and L.M. Church, *Power and Machinery in Agriculture,* USDA Miscellaneous Publication 157 (Washington, D.C., Apr. 1933), pp. 2-4.

73. Hahn, *Roots of Southern Populism,* p. 192. On the relative decline of prices see *Twelfth Census of the United States, 1900, Agriculture,* pt. 2: 407.

74. Hahn, *Roots of Southern Populism,* pp. 190-92.

Chapter 2

1. *Thirteenth Census of the United States, 1910, Population* (Washington, D.C., 1913); see also Harold D. Woodman's comments in *King Cotton and His Retainers* (Lexington: University of Kentucky Press, 1968), chap. 25.

2. *Twelfth Census of the United States, 1900, Population* (Washington, D.C., 1902).

3. Rosser Howard Taylor, *Carolina Crossroads: A Study of Rural Life at the End of the Horse-and-Buggy Era* (Murfreesboro, N.C.: Johnson Publishing Co., 1966), p. 4.

4. *Transactions of the Georgia State Agricultural Society: Proceedings of Fall Meeting, 1876* (Atlanta: James P. Harrison, 1878), pp. 77-78; *Progressive Farmer* 1 (June 9, 1886): 4; and *Southern Cultivator & Dixie Farmer* 48 (Dec. 1890): 600; Joseph Hyde Pratt, "Good Roads Movement in the South," *Annals of the American Academy of Political and Social Science* 35 (Jan. 1910): 110-11; see also the comments on roads in Charles S. Johnson, *Shadow of the Plantation* (Chicago: Univ. of Chicago Press, 1934), p. xviii

5. Wayne E. Fuller, "The South and the Rural Free Delivery of Mail," *Journal of Southern History* 25 (Nov. 1959): 499-521; Charles H. Greathouse, "Free Delivery of Rural Mails," *Yearbook of Agriculture, 1900* (Washington, D.C., 1901), pp. 513-28.

6. Boeger and Goldenweiser, *Study of the Tenant Systems*, p. 14; Glenn N. Sisk, "Social Classes in the Alabama Black Belt, 1870-1910," *Alabama Historical Quarterly* 20 (Winter 1958): 653-55. Labor income was defined as the farm income minus earnings on farm capital and interest on land and equipment. It did not include the value of production of items used by the farm family, such as food and fuel.

7. *Thirteenth Census of the United States, 1910, Agriculture*, 5 (Washington, D.C., 1913): 87, 881.

8. *Report on Cotton Growers*, 1: IV. See also George K. Homes, "Tenancy in the United States," *Quarterly Journal of Economics* 10 (October 1895): 46.

9. *1950 Census of Agriculture, General Report*, 2: 924-25.

10. Quoted in W.O. Atwater and Charles D. Woods, *Dietary Studies with Reference to the Food of the Negro in Alabama in 1895 and 1896*, USDA Experiment Station Bulletin 38 (Washington, D.C., 1897), p. 17.

11. Atticus G. Haygood, *Pleas for Progress* (Nashville: Publishing House of the M.E. Church, South, 1895), p. 143.

12. Mary S. Frayser and Ada M. Moser, *Children of Pre-School Age in Selected Areas of South Carolina*, South Carolina Agricultural Experiment Station Bulletin 260 (Clemson, Sept. 1929), pp. 15-23.

13. *Twelfth Census of the United States, 1900, Agriculture*, pt. 2: 299.

14. Atwater and Woods, *Dietary Studies*, p. 21; Joe Gray Taylor, "The Food of the New South," *Georgia Review* 20 (Spring 1966): 9-28; idem, *Eating, Drinking, and Visiting in the South* (Baton Rouge: Louisiana State Univ. Press, 1982), chaps. 8, 9, 10; Theodore Rosengarten, *All God's Dangers: The Life of Nate Shaw* (New York: Alfred A. Knopf, 1974), p. 14.

15. Jane Maguire, *On Shares: Ed Brown's Story* (New York: W. W. Norton, 1975), p. 23.

16. On the Macon County, Alabama, study see Atwater and Woods *Dietary Studies*; and on conditions in South Carolina, consult Frayser and Moser, *Children of Pre-School Age*, p. 51.

17. Elizabeth W. Etheridge, *The Butterfly Cast: A Social History of Pellagra in the South* (Westport, Conn.: Greenwood Publishing Co., 1972), chaps. 1, 2. Marshall Scott Legan, "Mississippi and the Yellow Fever Epidemics of 1878-1879," *Journal of Mississippi History* 33 (Aug. 1971): 199-217.

18. D. Clayton Brown, "Health of Farm Children in the South, 1900-1950," *Agricultural History* 53 (Jan. 1979): 170-87; Glenn N. Sisk, "Diseases in the Alabama Black Belt, 1875-1917," *Alabama Historical Quarterly* 24 (Spring 1962): 52-61; Taylor, *Carolina Crossroads*, pp. 113-24; and Carter G. Woodson, *The Rural Negro* (Washington, D.C.: Association for the Study of Negro Life and History, 1930), pp. 16-18.

19. *Fourth Annual Report of the State School Commissioner, Submitted to the General Assembly of Georgia* (Savannah: J.H. Estill, 1875), pp. 5-6.

20. H. Leon Prather, Sr., *Resurgent Politics and Educational Progressivism in the New South: North Carolina, 1890-1913* (Rutherford, N.J.: Fairleigh Dickinson Univ. Press, 1979),

pp. 73-75; Taylor, *Carolina Crossroads*, p. 118; and Atticus G. Haygood, *The Case of the Negro as to Education in the Southern States* (Atlanta: J.P. Harrison, 1885), pp. 13-14.

21. *Report of the [U.S.] Commissioner of Education, 1896-97* (Washington, D.C., 1898), 2: 2295; *Report of the State School Commissioner of Georgia, 1895* (Atlanta: Franklin Printing and Publishing Co., 1896), p. 27; *Report of the State School Commissioner of Georgia for 1894* (Atlanta: George W. Harrison, 1895), pp. 6-9. Prather, *Resurgent Politics and Educational Progressivism*, pp. 40-41, 44. Governor Joseph M. Terrell of Georgia told the general assembly in 1902 that the country schools were "in a woeful want." *Journal of the House of Representatives, State of Georgia* (Atlanta: Franklin Printing and Publishing Co., 1902), p. 247.

22. *Report of the [U.S.] Commissioner of Education, 1896-97*, 2: 2295.

23. Stephen B. Weeks, *History of Public Education in Alabama*, U.S. Bureau of Education Bulletin 12 (Washington, D.C., 1915), p. 175; *Report of the State School Commissioner of Georgia for 1887* (Atlanta: W.J. Campbell, 1888), p. 35; Julia L. Willard, "Reflections of an Alabama School Teacher, 1875-1950," *Alabama Historical Quarterly* 38 (Winter 1976): 291-304. In Marshall County, Alabama, in 1885 the average school term for white students was eighty-eight days and for blacks, seventy days. White teachers received $22.08 a month and black teachers $14.98.

24. *Report of the [U.S.] Commissioner of Education, 1896-97*, 2: 1355; *Report of the [U.S.] Commissioner of Education, 1898-99* (Washington, D.C., 1900), 2: 2202: *Report of the State School Commissioner of Georgia for 1892* (Atlanta: George W. Harrison, 1893), p. 110. *Report of the State School Commissioner of Georgia, 1895*, p. 543; Edgar Wallace Knight, *Education in the United States*, 3rd ed. (New York: Greenwood Press, 1951), p. 482.

25. Taylor, *Carolina Crossroads*, p. 107.

26. *Report of the State School Commissioner of Georgia for 1892*, p. 31; ibid., *1894*, p. 6; ibid., *1895*, p. 7.

27. See F.T. Carleton, "The South during the Last Decade," *Sewanee Review* 12 (Apr. 1904): 181.

28. See Richard A. Easterlin, "Why Isn't the Whole World Developed?" *Journal of Economic History* 41 (Mar. 1981): 1-17, in which he argues the importance of education as a factor in economic development.

29. U.S. Bureau of the Census, *Religious Bodies, 1916*, pt. 1 (Washington, D.C., 1916): 111-12; *Compendium of the Eleventh Census of the United States, 1890, Vital and Social Statistics*, pt. 2 (Washington, D.C., 1894): 261-310; Jesse Marvin Ormond, *The Country Church in North Carolina* (Durham: Duke Univ. Press, 1931), p. 37; Henry McGilbert Wagstaff, "A Footnote to Social History," *North Carolina Historical Review* 23 (Jan. 1946): 32-46.

30. Benjamin F. Riley, *A Memorial History of the Baptists of Alabama* (Philadelphia: Judson Press, 1923), pp. 220-21.

31. Ibid., p. 225; Ormond, *Country Church*, p. 330.

32. Bureau of the Census, *Religious Bodies, 1916*, pt. 2: 496-97.

33. Glenn N. Sisk, "Churches in the Alabama Black Belt, 1875-1917," *Church History* 23 (June 1954): 163.

34. Maguire, *On Shares*, p. 23; Taylor, *Carolina Crossroads*, pp. 57-73.

35. Quoted in Hahn, *Roots of Southern Populism*, p. 163.

36. Taylor, *Carolina Crossroads*, pp. 125-30; Glenn N. Sisk, "Social Aspects of the Alabama Black Belt, 1875-1917," *Mid-America* 37 (Jan. 1955): 43; *Progressive Farmer* 30 (Sept. 11, 1915): 840.

37. *Progressive Farmer* 30 (Jan. 16, 1915): 31, 53; ibid., 30 (Feb. 12, 1916): 227. On this issue see Jack T. Kirby, "Clarence Poe's Vision of a Segregated 'Great Rural Civilization,' " *South Atlantic Quarterly* 68 (1969): 27-38.

Chapter 3

1. *Proceedings of the Inter-State Convention of Farmers* (Atlanta: James P. Harrison, 1887), p. 2.

2. USDA, *Report of the Commissioner of Agriculture, 1874* (Washington, D.C., 1875), p. 219.

3. *Yearbook of Agriculture, 1919* (Washington, D.C., 1920), p. 590.

4. Theodore Saloutos, *Farmer Movements in the South, 1865-1933* (Berkeley: Univ. of California Press, 1960), chap. 3.

5. See the principles of the Grange as stated in 1874 in *The Patron's Hand-Book* (Topeka: Kansas Farmer, 1874), pp. 3-4.

6. Solon J. Buck, *The Granger Movement* (Cambridge, Mass.: Harvard Univ. Press, 1913), p. 59.

7. Theodore Saloutos, "The Grange in the South, 1870-1877," *Journal of Southern History* 19 (Nov. 1953): 475-76.

8. Buck, *Granger Movement*, pp. 58-59.

9. *Patron's Hand-Book*, pp. 3-4.

10. Daniel R. Randall, "Cooperation in Maryland and the South," in Herbert B. Adams, ed., *History of Cooperation in the United States*, Johns Hopkins University Studies in Historical and Political Science, 6 (Baltimore: Publications Agency of the Johns Hopkins University, 1888), pp. 503-5; D. Sven Nordin, *Rich Harvest: A History of the Grange, 1867-1900* (Jackson: Univ. Press of Mississippi, 1974), p. 142; J.H. Easterby, "The Granger Movement in South Carolina," *Proceedings of the South Carolina Historical Association"* 1 (1931): 21-32; and Ralph A. Smith, "The Grange Movement in Texas, 1873-1900," *Southwestern Historical Quarterly* 42 (Apr. 1939): 297-315.

11. Buck, *Granger Movement*, p. 252.

12. Nordin, *Rich Harvest*, p. 136.

13. Ibid., pp. 146-47.

14. Buck, *Granger Movement*, pp. 264-65, 273; Randall, "Cooperation in Maryland and the South," pp. 503-5.

15. Saloutos, "Grange in the South," p. 485.

16. Stuart Noblin, *Leonidas LaFayette Polk, Agrarian Crusader* (Chapel Hill: Univ. of North Carolina Press, 1949), pp. 103-5.

17. Robert C. McMath, Jr., *Populist Vanguard: A History of the Southern Farmers' Alliance* (Chapel Hill: Univ. of North Carolina Press, 1975), chap. 1; Lawrence Goodwyn, *Democratic Promise: The Populist Movement in America* (New York: Oxford Univ. Press, 1976), pp. 33 ff; R.L. Hunt, *A History of Farmer Movements in the Southwest, 1873-1925* (College Station, Tex.: Agricultural and Mechanical College of Texas, 1935), pp. 27-40. Saloutos, *Farmer Movements in the South*, pp. 75-76; C. Vann Woodward, *Tom Watson, Agrarian Rebel* (New York: Macmillan, 1938). Also providing important insights are Gerald H. Gaither, *Blacks and the Populist Revolt: Ballots and Bigotry in the "New South"* (University: Univ. of Alabama Press, 1977); Bruce Palmer, *"Man over Money": The Southern Populist Critique of American Capitalism* (Chapel Hill: Univ. of North Carolina Press, 1980).

18. McMath, *Populist Vanguard*, p. 29.

19. Quoted in ibid., p. 38.

20. Ibid., p. 46.

21. Michael H. Schwartz, "An Estimate of the Size of the Southern Farmers' Alliance, 1884-1890," *Agricultural History* 51 (Oct. 1977): 765.

22. McMath, *Populist Vanguard*, p. 45. Also see Gaither, *Blacks and the Populist Revolt.*

23. Quoted in Goodwyn, *Democratic Promise*, p. 121. For criticism of Goodwyn see Stanley B. Parsons, et al., "The Role of Cooperatives in the Development of the Movement Culture of Populism," *Journal of American History* 69 (Mar. 1983): 866-85.

24. John D. Hicks, *The Populist Revolt* (Minneapolis: Univ. of Minnesota Press, 1931),

chap. 7; McMath, *Populist Vanguard*, pp. 90-93; Goodwyn, *Democratic Promise*, pp. 166-69. On the question of price and yield instability as a source of farm unrest, see Robert A. McGuire, "Economic Causes of Late-Nineteenth Century Agrarian Unrest: New Evidence," *Journal of Economic History* 41 (Dec. 1981): 835-49.

25. Hicks, *Populist Revolt*, pp. 429-30.

26. McMath, *Populist Vanguard*, pp. 86-89.

27. Noblin, *Leonidas LaFayette Polk*, pp. 259-60.

28. Alex Mathews Arnett, *The Populist Movement in Georgia* (New York: Columbia Univ. Studies, 1922), p. 107.

29. Gaither, *Blacks and the Populist Revolt*, pp. 29-33.

30. Woodward, *Tom Watson*, chap. 10; Goodwyn, *Democratic Promise*, pp. 214-17; McMath, *Populist Vanguard*, pp. 98-100.

31. Quoted in Noblin, *Leonidas LaFayette Polk*, p. 273.

32. Goodwyn, *Democratic Promise*, pp. 269-99.

33. See Robert F. Durden, *The Climax of Populism* (Lexington: Univ. of Kentucky Press, 1965). On the presidential campaigns of 1892 and 1896 consult H. Wayne Morgan, "Election of 1892," and Gilbert C. Fite, "Election of 1896," in Arthur M. Schlesinger, Jr., and Fred L. Israel, eds., *History of American Presidential Elections, 1789-1968*, 2 (New York: Chelsea House, 1971): 1703-32, 1787-1825. See also Gilbert C. Fite, "Republican Strategy and the Farm Vote in the Presidential Campaign of 1896," *American Historical Review* 65 (July 1960): 787-805.

34. *Report on Cotton Growers*, 1, pt. 1:III.

35. Saloutos, *Farmer Movements in the South*, p. 186: Hunt, *History of Farmer Protest Movements*, pp. 44-50.

36. Saloutos, *Farmer Movements in the South*, p. 186.

37. William P. Tucker, "Populism Up-to-Date: The Story of the Farmers' Union," *Agricultural History* 21 (Oct. 1947): 199; Hunt, *History of Farmer Protest Movements*, chaps. 2-6.

38. Saloutos, *Farmer Movements in the South*, pp. 194-97.

39. Robert L. Tontz, "Memberships of General Farm Organizations, United States, 1874-1960," *Agricultural History* 38 (July 1964): 155. Another approach was to try to hold cotton on the farm until prices rose. W.L. Peek, president of the Georgia Farmers Alliance Exchange, urged farmers in September 1890 to hold their cotton until it brought 10 cents a pound. *Southern Cultivator and Dixie Farmer* 48 (Oct. 1890): 504; see also Charles P. Loomis, "The Rise and Decline of the North Carolina Farmers' Union," *North Carolina Historical Review* 7 (July 1930): 305-25; idem, "Activities of the North Carolina Farmers' Union," *North Carolina Historical Review* 7 (Oct. 1930): 443-62.

40. Quoted in Saloutos, *Farmer Movements in the South*, p. 200; Charles S. Barrett, *The Mission, History and Times of the Farmers' Union* (Nashville: Marshall and Bruce, 1909), p. 101.

41. *Progressive Farmer* 13 (Nov. 29, 1898): 1; ibid., 13 (Feb. 8, 1898): 1.

42. *Atlanta Constitution*, Dec. 29, 1904, p. 1; *New York Times*, Dec. 29, 1904, p. 1.

43. Quoted in Saloutos, *Farmer Movements in the South*, p. 198.

44. Ibid., chap. 11; Joseph C. Robert, *The Story of Tobacco in America* (New York: Alfred A. Knopf, 1949), pp. 154-60; Rich Gregory, "Robertson County and the Black Patch War, 1904-1909," *Tennessee Historical Quarterly* 39 (Fall 1980): 341-58.

45. See William F. Holmes, "Whitecapping: Agrarian Violence in Mississippi, 1902-1906," *Journal of Southern History* 35 (May 1969): 165-85, for views of white farmers on blacks.

Chapter 4

1. *Southern Cultivator* 60 (Feb. 1, 1902): 8; *Report of the Commissioner of Agriculture, 1866* (Washington, D.C., 1867), pp. 5, 6, 572. George Washington Carver, "The Need of

Scientific Agriculture in the South," *Review of Reviews* 25 (Mar. 1902): 320-22.

    2. *Report of the Commissioner of Agriculture, 1873* (Washington, D.C., 1874), p. 17. On early soil conservation efforts in the South, see Arthur R. Hall, "Terracing in the Southern Piedmont," *Agricultural History* 23 (Apr. 1949): 96-109.

    3. Seaman A. Knapp, "Causes of Southern Rural Conditions and the Small Farm as an Important Remedy," in *Yearbook of Agriculture, 1908* (Washington, D.C., 1909), pp. 511-20. *Transactions of the Georgia State Agricultural Society, 1876* (Atlanta: James P. Harrison, 1878), p. 29.

    4. Gavin Wright and Howard Kunreuther, "Cotton, Corn and Risk in the Nineteenth Century," *Journal of Economic History* 15 (Sept. 1975): 526-51.

    5. *Southern Cultivator* 28 (Feb. 1870): 43.

    6. David Dickson, *A Practical Treatise on Agriculture* (Macon, Ga.: J.W. Burke and Co., 1870), p. 40. See the comments on farming methods in *Tenth Census, 1880, Cotton Production in the United States,* 1 (Washington, D.C., 1884): 351.

    7. *Report of the Commissioner of Agriculture, 1869* (Washington, D.C., 1870), p. 529. "United States Manuscript Census of Agriculture, 1880," Harris County, Georgia, p. 8; *Twelfth Census of the United States, 1900, Agriculture,* pt. 1 (Washington, D.C., 1902): 144-55.

    8. J.S. Newman, "The One Horse Farm," *South Carolina Agricultural Experiment Station Bulletin* 84 (Clemson, Apr. 1904): 3-4.

    9. *Southern Cultivator* 60 (Jan. 1, 1902): 3.

    10. Ibid., 27 (Jan. 1869): 53; ibid., 28 (Feb. 1870): 43.

    11. Dickson, *Practical Treatise on Agriculture,* p. 17.

    12. Lester D. Stephens, "Farish Furman's Formula: Scientific Farming and the 'New South,'" *Agricultural History* 50 (Apr. 1976): 377-90.

    13. *Transactions of the Georgia State Agricultural Society, 1878,* pp. 470-71, 478-79.

    14. *Patron's Handbook,* pp. 3-4; Noblin, *Leonidas LaFayette Polk,* pp. 154-55; Barrett, *Mission, History and Times of the Farmers' Union,* p. 107; Saloutos, *Farmer Movements in the South,* pp. 206-7.

    15. *Southern Cultivator* 48 (Oct. 1890): 537; ibid., 60 (Jan. 1, 1902): 3.

    16. Joseph A. Cote, "Clarence Hamilton Poe: Crusading Editor," Ph.D. diss., Univ. of Georgia, 1976, chaps. 1 and 2.

    17. *Progressive Farmer* 12 (Mar. 16, 1897): 1, 12; ibid., 12 (Jan. 25, 1898): 1; ibid., 13 (Aug. 16, 1898): 1.

    18. Roy V. Scott, *The Reluctant Farmer: The Rise of Agricultural Extension to 1914* (Urbana: Univ. of Illinois Press, 1970), p. 20.

    19. Quoted in ibid., p. 30.

    20. Henry C. Dethloff, *A Centennial History of Texas A & M University, 1876-1976,* 1 (College Station: Texas A & M Univ. Press, 1975): 73.

    21. Alfred Charles True, *A History of Agricultural Education in the United States, 1785-1925* (Washington, D.C., 1929), pp. 128-29. Jane M. Porter, "Experiment Stations in the South, 1877-1940," *Agricultural History* 53 (Jan. 1979): 84-101.

    22. For a view of the relevant research being done at the experiment stations in the southern states in the late 1880s and 1890s, see the bulletins published in the different states.

    23. D.A. Brodie and C.K. McClelland, *Diversified Farming under the Plantation System,* USDA Farmers' Bulletin 299 (June 18, 1907), pp. 9-14.

    24. On the institute movement see Scott, *Reluctant Farmer,* chaps. 3 and 4; idem, "Farmers' Institutes in Louisiana, 1897-1906," *Journal of Southern History* 25 (Feb. 1959): 73-90; Allen W. Jones, "The South's First Black Farm Agents," *Agricultural History* 50 (Oct. 1976): 636-44. See also Earl W. Crosby, "Building the Country Home: The Black County Agent System, 1906-1940," Ph.D. diss., Miami Univ., 1977; Crosby, "Limited Success against Long Odds: The Black County Agent," *Agricultural History* 57 (July 1983): 277-88;

and E.R. Lloyd, *Farmers Institutes*, Mississippi Agricultural Experiment Station Bulletin 100 (Agricultural College, Miss., Dec. 1906), p. 3.

25. Scott, *Reluctant Farmer*, p. 209.

26. Ibid., p. 235. See Joseph C. Bailey, *Seaman A. Knapp, Schoolmaster of American Agriculture* (New York: Columbia Univ. Press, 1945), chaps. 6-11. A contemporary account of Knapp's work can be found in "Teaching Farmers to Farm," by W.H.P., in *World's Work* 14 (June 1907): 8987-89. See also Charles S. Davis, "Early Agricultural Demonstration Work in Alabama," *Alabama Review* 2 (July 1949): 176 ff.

27. Bailey, *Seaman A. Knapp*, pp. 214-21.

28. J. Douglas Helms, "Just Lookin' for a Home: The Cotton Boll Weevil and the South," Ph.D. diss., Florida State Univ., 1977. S.M. Tracy, "New Farm Crops for the South," *Annals of the American Academy of Political and Social Science* 35 (Jan. 1910): 52-59; and Frederick W. Williamson, *Origin and Growth of Agricultural Extension in Louisiana, 1860-1948* (Baton Rouge: Louisiana State Univ. Press, 1951), p. 37.

29. True, *History of Agricultural Extension Work*, p. 117.

30. W.J. Spillman, *Soil Conservation*, USDA Farmers' Bulletin 406 (June 16, 1910), p. 14.

31. "The Southern Farmer," *Independent* 63 (Dec. 26, 1907): 1578-79.

32. *Thirteenth Census of the United States, 1910, Agriculture,* see pertinent tables.

33. Ibid.

34. *Fourteenth Census of the United States, 1920, Agriculture* 5, *General Report* (Washington, D.C., 1922), p. 193; see also McGee and Boone, *Black Rural Landowner.*

35. *Transactions of the Georgia State Agricultural Society, 1878,* p. 11; Williamson, *Origins and Growth of Agricultural Extension,* p. 33.

36. W.J. Spillman, "Diversified Farming in the Cotton Belt," *Yearbook of Agriculture, 1905* (Washington, D.C., 1906), p. 194; Scott, *Reluctant Farmer,* p. 115; Frank J. Welch and D. Gray Miley, *Mechanization of the Cotton Harvest*, Mississippi Agricultural Experiment Station Bulletin 420 (State College, Miss., June 1945), p. 20.

37. See a contemporary discussion of the credit problem in B.H. Strong, "Alfalfa in Mississippi," *Mississippi Agricultural Experiment Station Bulletin* 100 (State College, Dec. 1906): 10.

38. F. Lamson-Schiber, *Southern Forage Plants,* in USDA Farmers' Bulletin 102 (Washington, D.C., 1899), pp. 5 ff.

39. D.E. Salmon, "Investigation of Swine Plague, Fowl Cholera, and Southern Cattle Fever," in *Report of the Commissioner of Agriculture, 1881 and 1882* (Washington, D.C., 1882), pp. 258-303; ibid., *1883* (Washington, D.C., 1883), p. 19.

40. See the excellent article by Julius Rubin, "The Limits of Agricultural Progress in the Nineteenth-Century South," *Agricultural History* 49 (Apr. 1975): 362-73, in which he discusses the effect of soil and climate on southern agricultural development. See also D.E. Salmon, "Investigation of Southern Cattle Fever," in *Contagious Diseases of Domesticated Animals*, Department of Agriculture, Special Report 22 (Washington, D.C., 1890), pp. 102-4, 109, 115; W.M. MacKellar, "Cattle Tick Fever," *Yearbook of Agriculture, 1942,* pp. 572-78; and Porter, "Experiment Stations in the South," p. 92. See also Willard Range, *A Century of Georgia Agriculture,* pp. 96-102, for additional discussion of problems relating to diversification.

41. *Yearbook of Agriculture, 1905,* pp. 195-97, 349; *Yearbook of Agriculture, 1907* (Washington, D.C., 1908), p. 434.

42. *Tenth Census of the United States, 1880, Report on Cotton Production in the United States,* pt. 1 (Washington, D.C., 1884): 281.

43. D. Wallace, "Southern Agriculture: Its Condition and Needs," *Popular Science* 64 (Jan. 1904): 245-61.

44. Clarence H. Poe, "Agricultural Revolution a Necessity," *Annals of the American Academy of Political and Social Science* 35 (Jan. 1910): 45.

45. *Progressive Farmer* 30 (Sept. 11, 1915): 846.

46. Ibid., p. 828; Joseph D. Reid, Jr., "Sharecropping in History and Theory," *Agricultural History* 49 (Apr. 1975): 437.

47. Woodman, *King Cotton and His Retainers*, p. 343, chap. 28.

48. James D. Anderson, "The Southern Improvement Company: Northern Reformers' Investment in Negro Cotton Tenancy, 1900-1920," *Agricultural History* 52 (Jan. 1978): 111-31.

49. Seaman A. Knapp, "Causes of Southern Rural Conditions and the Small Farm as an Important Remedy," *Yearbook of Agriculture, 1908*, p. 314.

50. C. Meriwether, "The Southern Farm since the Civil War," *Nation* 57 (Oct. 12, 1893): 264-66; Henry Exall, "Dependence of Agricultural Life upon Conservation of the Soil," *Proceedings, Third Annual Convention, Southern Commercial Congress* (Atlanta: n.p., 1911), pp. 439-40.

Chapter 5

1. *Yearbook of Agriculture, 1907*, p. 666; ibid., *1917* (Washington, D.C., 1918), p. 672.

2. *Yearbook of Agriculture, 1915* (Washington, D.C., 1916), p. 15.

3. "The Plight of King Cotton," *Independent* 80 (Oct. 19, 1914): 108.

4. *Atlanta Journal*, Aug. 24, 1914.

5. Quoted in Congressional Record, 63 Cong., 2 sess., (Oct. 15, 1914), p. 16635.

6. George B. Tindall, *The Emergence of the New South* (Baton Rouge: Louisiana State Univ. Press, 1967), pp. 33-37.

7. *Atlanta Journal*, Aug. 15, 1914.

8. Congressional Record, 63 Cong., 2 sess., (Oct. 12, 1914), p. 16504.

9. *Yearbook of Agriculture, 1915*, p. 13.

10. Ibid., *1916* (Washington, D.C., 1917), p. 631.

11. Sitterson, *Sugar Country*, pp. 548-49.

12. Gilbert C. Fite, "Voluntary Attempts to Reduce Cotton Acreage in the South, 1914-1933," *Journal of Southern History* 14 (Nov. 1948): pp. 83-84. See also C.T. Revere, "Effect of the War on Cotton," *North American Review* 200 (Oct. 1914): 549-58.

13. Revere, "Effect of the War on Cotton," p. 556.

14. "Southern Prosperity," *New Republic* 5 (Dec. 25, 1915): 186-87.

15. "Cotton's Magical Rise Enriching the Nation," *Literary Digest* 53 (Dec. 9, 1916): 1517-22.

16. Quoted in *Outlook* 58 (Feb. 7, 1917): 222. See also O.R. Geyer, "The Agricultural Revolution in the South," *Scientific American* 118 (Apr. 27, 1918): 378, 392.

17. *Atlanta Constitution*, Sept. 9, 1919.

18. Sitterson, *Sugar Country*, pp. 352-55.

19. See the pertinent statistical tables in the *Yearbook of Agriculture*, for 1915, 1916, 1917, 1919, and 1920.

20. F.W. Farley, "Growth of the Beef Cattle Industry in the South," *Yearbook of Agriculture, 1917*, pp. 327-40. See also S.W. Doty, "Marketing Livestock in the South," USDA Farmers' Bulletin 809 (Washington, D.C., Apr. 1917).

21. Report of the Joint Commission of Agricultural Inquiry, *The Agricultural Crisis and Its Causes*, House Report 408, 67 Cong., 1 sess., pt. 1 (Washington, D.C., 1921): 208; *Yearbook of Agriculture, 1921*, p. 338.

22. *Progressive Farmer* 30 (July 3, 1915): 625; ibid., 31 (Nov. 4, 1916): 1292.

23. Emmett J. Scott, *Negro Migration during the War* (New York: Oxford Univ. Press, 1920). See also "Reasons Why Negroes Go North," *Survey* 38 (June 2, 1917): 226-27; George E. Haynes, "Negroes Move North," *Survey* 40 (May 4, 1918): 115-22; Herbert H. Horwill, "A Negro Exodus," *Contemporary Review* 114 (Sept. 1918): 299-305; Percy H.

Stone, "Negro Migration," *Outlook* 116 (Aug. 1, 1917): 520-21; Robert Higgs, "The Boll Weevil, the Cotton Economy, and Black Migration, 1910-1930," *Agricultural History* 50 (Apr. 1976): 335-50. Higgs emphasizes economic opportunity as the main factor that caused blacks to migrate north during World War I. He discounts the effect of the boll weevil and social advantages. See also Florette Henri, *Black Migration: Movement North, 1900-1920* (Garden City, N.Y.: Anchor Press/Doubleday, 1975). There is a good discussion of black migration during the World War I decade in Helms, "Just Lookin' for a Home," chap. 8.

24. *1950 Census of Agriculture, General Report*, 2: 799, 830-31, 837, 838.

25. *Fourteenth Census of the United States, 1920, Agriculture*, 6, pt. 2: 41; pt. 5: 307.

26. E.S. Haskell, *A Farm Management Survey in Brooks County, Georgia*, USDA Bulletin 648 (Washington, D.C., May 1, 1918), pp. 18, 33; H.M. Dixon and H.W. Hawthorne, *An Economic Study of Farming in Sumter County, Georgia*, USDA Bulletin 492 (Washington, D.C., Feb. 10, 1917). The data for Sumter County are for 1913. See also C.L. Goodrich, *Producing Family Farm Supplies on the Cotton Farm*, USDA Farmers' Bulletin 1015 (Washington, D.C., Jan. 1919).

27. A.G. Smith, *A Farm-Management Study in Anderson County, South Carolina*, USDA Bulletin 651 (Washington, D.C., May 8, 1918), pp. 1-19.

28. J.H. Arnold, *Ways of Making Southern Mountain Farms More Productive*, USDA Farmers' Bulletin 905 (Washington, D.C., 1918), pp. 4-14.

29. *Progressive Farmer* 31 (Nov. 11, 1916): 1301.

30. Ibid., p. 1312.

31. Calculated from the *1950 Census of Agriculture, General Report*, 2: 211-34.

32. *Progressive Farmer* 31 (Nov. 25, 1916): 1369; ibid., 34 (Nov. 1, 1919): 1.

33. Gilbert C. Fite, *George N. Peek and the Fight for Farm Parity* (Norman: Univ. of Oklahoma Press, 1954), pp. 19-20; James H. Shideler, *Farm Crisis, 1919-1923* (Berkeley and Los Angeles: Univ. of California Press, 1957); Donald L. Winters, *Henry Cantwell Wallace, As Secretary of Agriculture, 1921-1924* (Urbana: Univ. of Illinois Press, 1970), pp. 65-72. *Yearbook of Agriculture, 1921* (Washington, D.C., 1922), p. 357. The index figures were calculated by economist George F. Warren and were published in the Congressional Record, 67 Cong., 1 sess. (June 21, 1921), p. 2792.

34. Brown's letter was published in the *Congressional Record*, 67 Cong., 1 sess. (July 5, 1921), p. 3332. Other letters are in the files of the secretary of agriculture, Agricultural Situation 1920 and 1921, National Archives, Record Group 16.

35. *Atlanta Constitution*, Aug. 23, 1920.

36. Quoted in Cote, "Clarence Hamilton Poe," p. 46.

37. Joseph G. Knapp, *The Advance of American Cooperative Enterprise, 1920-1945* (Danville, Ill.: Interstate Printers, 1973), pp. 40, 54-60.

38. *Congressional Record*, 67 Cong., 1 sess. (June 29, 1921), p. 3189-90.

39. Arthur Capper, *The Agricultural Bloc* (New York: Harcourt, Brace, 1922), p. 11.

40. *Report of the National Agricultural Conference*, House Doc. 195, 67 Cong., 2 sess., (Washington, D.C., 1922), pp. 150-53, 160.

41. *Yearbook of Agriculture, 1925* (Washington, D.C., 1926), pp. 7, 952.

42. Ibid., *1927* (Washington, D.C., 1928), p. 912.

43. *Oklahoma Cotton Grower*, Mar. 25, 1926.

44. *Yearbook of Agriculture, 1927*, p. 913.

45. Quoted in Fite, "Voluntary Attempts to Reduce Cotton Acreage," pp. 486ff.

46. L.E. Childers, "Tractors Are Moving in as Mules Move Out," *Oklahoma Farmer-Stockman* 43 (Mar. 1, 1930): 179, 199; Gilbert C. Fite, "Recent Progress in the Mechanization of Cotton Production in the United States," *Agricultural History* 24 (Jan. 1950): 24; Leidigh is quoted in Donald E. Green, *Fifty Years of Service to West Texas Agriculture: A History of Texas Tech University's College of Agricultural Sciences, 1925-1975* (Lubbock: Texas Tech Press, 1977), p. 30.

47. Knapp, *Advance of American Cooperative Enterprise*, p. 208.

48. Fite, *George N. Peek*, pp. 151 ff. See also "Why an Equalization Fee Is Necessary," *Progressive Farmer* 43 (Aug. 18, 1928): 856A. See also Philip A. Grant, Jr., "Southern Congressmen and Agriculture, 1921-1932," *Agricultural History* 53 (Jan. 1979): 338-51.

49. Willard Range, *A Century of Georgia Agriculture, 1850-1950* (Athens: Univ. of Georgia Press, 1954), pp. 191-93; *Yearbook of Agriculture, 1931* (Washington, D.C., 1932), pp. 736, 741; and *Macon Telegraph*, July 9, 1927.

50. *Yearbook of Agriculture, 1925*, pp. 286-88; ibid., *1931*, p. 746.

51. Ibid., *1921*, p. 645; ibid., *1931*, p. 816.

52. Ibid., *1924* (Washington, D.C., 1925), p. 742; ibid., *1930* (Washington, D.C., 1930), p. 796.

53. Paul D. Travis, "History of the Timber Industry in Pearl River County, Mississippi," manuscript, Center for the Study of Southern Culture, Univ. of Mississippi, Oxford.

54. See pertinent tables in *Yearbook of Agriculture, 1922* and *1931*. Also consult Marvin Guin, *An Economic Study of Hog Production and Marketing in South Carolina*, South Carolina Agricultural Experiment Station Bulletin 305 (Clemson, Apr. 1936); Ben F. Alvord and M.S. Crosby, *Factors Influencing Alabama Agriculture, Its Characteristics and Farming Areas*, Alabama Experiment Station Bulletin 250 (Auburn, Apr. 1941), p. 42; R.D. Jennings and M.A. Crosby, *An Economic Study of Livestock Possibilities in the Southeastern Coastal Plain*, USDA Technical Bulletin 127 (Washington, D.C., July 1929), pp. 2, 9, 71.

55. Rupert B. Vance, *Human Factors in Cotton Culture* (Chapel Hill: Univ. of North Carolina Press, 1929), p. 234.

56. *Fifteenth Census of the United States, 1930, Agriculture*, 2, pt. 2 (Washington, D.C., 1932): 35; pt. 4, *General Report*, pp. 40, 73.

57. Howard W. Odum, *Southern Regions of the United States* (Chapel Hill: Univ. of North Carolina Press, 1936), p. 402.

58. Dorothy Dickens, *A Nutritional Investigation of Negro Tenants in the Yazoo-Mississippi Delta*, Mississippi Agricultural Experiment Station Bulletin 254 (A & M, Aug. 1928), pp. 5, 9. *Fifteenth Census of the United States, 1930, Agriculture*, 2, pt. 2:54.

59. *Progressive Farmer*, Georgia-Alabama ed., 43 (Jan. 28, 1928): 95.

60. For a good example see T.D. Johnson et al., *An Economic Study of the Columbia Farm Trade Area*, South Carolina Agricultural Experiment Station Bulletin 243 (Clemson, Dec. 1927).

61. Dorothy Dickens, *A Study of Food Habits in Two Contrasting Areas of Mississippi*, Mississippi Agricultural Experiment Station Bulletin 245 (Agricultural College, Nov. 1927); Dickens, *Nutritional Investigation*, p. 35; Frayser and Moser, *Children of Pre-School Age*; Susan J. Mathews, *Food Habits of Georgia Rural People*, Georgia Agricultural Experiment Station Bulletin 159 (Experiment, May 1929).

62. E.L. Kirkpatrick, *The Farmer's Standard of Living: A Socio-Economic Study of 2886 White Farm Families of Selected Localities in 11 States*, USDA Department Bulletin 1466 (Washington, D.C., Nov. 1926), p. 17; Dickens, *Nutritional Investigation*, p. 43.

63. W.C. Jensen and B.A. Russell, *Pee Dee Farm Management Studies, 1925-1930*, South Carolina Agricultural Experiment Station Bulletin 269 (Clemson, Jan. 1931), p. 42. See also C.G. Garner, *Factors Related to Income and Costs of Production on Farms in Marshall and Dekalb Counties, Alabama, 1927-1929*, Alabama Experiment Station Bulletin 236 (Auburn, July 1932); J.T. Sanders, *Farm Ownership and Tenancy in the Black Prairie of Texas*, USDA Bulletin 1068 (Washington, D.C., May 12, 1922); and C.L. Goodrich, *Factors That Make for Success in Farming in the South*, USDA Farmers' Bulletin 1121 (Washington, D.C., Sept. 1927).

64. J.A. Dickey, *Three-Years Study of Farm Management and Income in a Typical Upland Section of Arkansas*, Arkansas Agricultural Experiment Station Bulletin 262 (Fayetteville, May 1931); *Progressive Farmer* 43 (Mar. 10, 1928): 298; ibid., 43 (Feb. 4, 1928): 124.

65. W.C. Jensen, *Farming for Profits: Anderson and Similar Areas of South Carolina*, South

Carolina Agricultural Experiment Station Bulletin 230 (Clemson, June 1926), p. 19. W.J. Spillman, *Distribution of Types of Farming in the United States*, USDA Farmers' Bulletin 1289 (Washington, D.C., May 1923), pp. 14-15.

66. Undated speeches, Soule Papers, Box 11, University Archives, Univ. of Georgia Library.

67. "Southern Prosperity," *New Republic* 5 (Dec. 25, 1915): 186-87.

Chapter 6

1. *Yearbook of Agriculture, 1932* (Washington, D.C., 1932), pp. 659, 686; Henry I. Richards, *Cotton and the AAA* (Washington: Brookings Institution, 1936), p. 13.

2. Tindall, *Emergence of the New South*, p. 355.

3. *Fifteenth Census of the United States, 1930, Agriculture*, 2, pt. 2: 22; Carl C. Taylor, "Constructive Measures for Dealing with the South's Population Problems," *Rural Sociology* 3 (Sept. 1938): 239-57. Conrad Taeuber gives the increase in the farm population in the South between 1930 and 1935 as 612,000. See Taeuber, "The Movement to Southern Farms, 1930-1935," *Rural Sociology* 3 (Mar. 1938): 71. Figures used in the text are from the *Census of Agriculture, 1935, General Report*, 3 (Washington, D.C., 1937), p. 146.

4. Johnson, *Shadow of the Plantation*, pp. 99-101. See also Arthur F. Raper, *Preface to Peasantry: A Tale of Two Black Counties* (Chapel Hill: Univ. of North Carolina Press, 1936), p. 65.

5. E.H. Mereness, *Farm Loan Experience in Southeast Alabama*, Alabama Agricultural Experiment Station Bulletin 242 (Auburn, Jan. 1935), p. 13; and Raper, *Preface to Peasantry*, p. 231.

6. Theodore Norman, "The Federal Farm Board," Ph.D. diss., Harvard Univ., 1939, pp. 260 ff.

7. *Agricultural Statistics, 1936* (Washington, D.C., 1936), p. 80.

8. James Edward Rice, "On a Tenant Farm," *New Republic* 66 (Apr. 15, 1931): 234.

9. "Farm Board's Proposal Rejected," *Commerce and Finance* 20 (Aug. 19, 1931): 1228; *New York Times*, Aug. 13, 1931, p. 1; ibid., Aug. 14, pp. 9, 16.

10. The cotton holiday movement has been best treated by Robert E. Snyder in *Cotton Crisis* (Chapel Hill: Univ. of North Carolina Press, 1984).

11. Ibid., pp. 113, 126.

12. R.B. Snowden to Federal Farm Board, Aug. 22, 1931; section correspondence, Cotton, Jan.-Oct., National Archives, Record Group 16. *Yearbook of Agriculture, 1933* (Washington, D.C., 1933), p. 478.

13. Johnson, *Shadow of the Plantation*, p. 110. See also Pete Daniel, *The Shadow of Slavery: Peonage in the South, 1901-1969* (Urbana: Univ. of Illinois Press, 1972).

14. See Gilbert C. Fite, *American Farmers: The New Minority* (Bloomington: Indiana Univ. Press, 1981), pp. 49-50.

15. Irvin M. May, Jr., *Marvin Jones: The Public Life of an Agrarian Advocate* (College Station: Texas A & M Press, 1980); Christiana M. Campbell, *The Farm Bureau and the New Deal* (Urbana: Univ. of Illinois Press, 1962), p. 59.

16. Edwin G. Nourse, Joseph S. Davis, and John D. Black, *Three Years of the Agricultural Adjustment Administration* (Washington: Brookings Institution, 1937), pp. 19-20.

17. Nourse, Davis, and Black, cited above, provide the details of the Agricultural Adjustment Act of 1933. See also Van L. Perkins, *Crisis in Agriculture: The Agricultural Adjustment Administration and the New Deal, 1933* (Berkeley and Los Angeles: Univ. of California Press, 1969): and C.T. Schmidt, *American Farmers in the World Crisis* (New York: Oxford Univ. Press, 1941), chap. 6. On tobacco see Badger, *Prosperity Road;* and consult Richards, *Cotton and the AAA*, for the cotton situation.

18. *Yearbook of Agriculture, 1934* (Washington, D .C., 1934), p. 28.

19. Henry A. Wallace, *New Frontiers* (New York: Reynal and Hitchcock, 1934), pp. 174-75.

20. *New York Times*, Aug. 10, 1933, p. 3; ibid., Aug. 11, p. 14.

21. Will Clayton to George N. Peek, May 7, 1933, Peek Papers, Univ. of Missouri Library, Columbia.

22. *New York Times*, Aug. 27, 1933, sec. 6, p. 1; and Raper, *Preface to Peasantry*, p. 245.

23. *New York Times*, Aug. 27, 1933, sec. 6, p. 1. See also *Yearbook of Agriculture, 1934*, pp. 28-30; Murray R. Benedict and Oscar C. Stine, *The Agricultural Commodity Programs: Two Decades of Experience* (New York: Twentieth Century Fund, 1956), pp. 3-17.

24. Badger, *Prosperity Road*, pp. 54-65; *Yearbook of Agriculture, 1934*, p. 47; Benedict and Stine, *Agricultural Commodity Programs*, pp. 50-62.

25. Benedict and Stine, *Agricultural Commodity Programs*, pp. 138-40.

26. Richards, *Cotton and the AAA*, pp. 212-20; *New York Times*, Sept. 19, 1933, p. 1; ibid., Sept. 23, p. 1.

27. Richards, *Cotton and the AAA*, chap. 10; Harold B. Rowe, *Tobacco under the AAA* (Washington, D.C.: Brookings Institution, 1935), chaps. 4, 5; Badger, *Prosperity Road*, chap. 3.

28. Benedict and Stine, *Agricultural Commodity Programs*, pp. 147-50; Nourse, Davis, and Black, *Three Years of the AAA*, pp. 112-13; Sitterson, *Sugar Country*, pp. 382-84.

29. *Agricultural Statistics, 1936*, p. 335. *Statistics on Cotton and Related Data, 1920-1956*, USDA Statistical Bulletin 99 (Washington, D.C., Nov. 1957), p. 216. *Yearbook of Agriculture, 1936* (Washington, D.C., 1936), p. 1147.

30. Badger, *Prosperity Road*, p. 95.

31. *Second Annual Report of the Farm Credit Administration, 1934* (Washington, D.C., 1935), pp. 95-97, 150-51, 164-65.

32. T.J. Woofter, Jr., *Landlord and Tenant on the Cotton Plantation* (Washington, D.C.: Works Progress Administration, 1936), pp. 85, 220.

33. Renwick C. Kennedy, "What's Happening in the Cotton Belt," *New Republic* 78 (Apr. 18, 1934): 266-68.

34. Charles S. Johnson, Edwin R. Embree, and W.W. Alexander, *The Collapse of Cotton Tenancy* (Chapel Hill: Univ. of North Carolina Press, 1935), p. 14.

35. Gordon W. Blackwell, "The Displaced Tenant Farm Family in North Carolina," *Journal of Social Forces* 13 (Oct. 1934): 68-69. This question is discussed more fully in chapter 7.

36. Woofter, *Landlord and Tenant*, pp. 155-56.

37. Carle C. Zimmerman and Nathan L. Whetten, *Rural Families on Relief*, WPA Monograph 17 (Washington, D.C., 1938), p. 113.

38. David E. Conrad, *The Forgotten Farmers* (Urbana: Univ. of Illinois Press, 1965), pp. 52-53.

39. *New York Times*, Nov. 5, 1933, sec. 4, p. 6.

40. Thomas C. McCormick, *Comparative Study of Rural Relief and Non-Relief Households*, WPA, Division of Social Research, Research Monograph 2 (Washington, D.C., 1935; reprint: New York: Da Capo Press, 1971). The study dealt with the situation in October 1933. For the quote on the cast system see Zimmerman and Whetten, *Rural Families on Relief*, p. 80. See also Raper, *Preface to Peasantry*, p. 260.

41. William C. Holley, Ellen Winston, and T.J. Woofter, Jr., *The Plantation South, 1934-1937* (Freeport, N.Y.: Books for Libraries Press, 1971 [1940]), pp. 63-64. This study contains material on rural health, education, and other conditions of life in the mid-1930s.

42. *Sixtieth and Sixty-First Annual Reports of the Department of Education, State of Georgia, for the Biennium Ending June 30, 1932* (n.p., n.d.), pp. 43-44.

43. Henry L. Fulmer, *An Analytical Study of a Rural School Area*, South Carolina Experiment Station Bulletin 320 (Clemson, June 1939).

44. Carl F. Reuss, "A Qualitative Study of Depopulation in a Remote Rural District, 1900-1930," *Rural Sociology* 2 (Mar. 1937): 66-75. See also Wilson Gee, *The Qualitative Nature of Rural Depopulation in Santuc Township, South Carolina, 1900-1930*, South Carolina Agricultural Experiment Station Bulletin 287 (Clemson, Jan. 1933).

45. Hazel K. Stiebeling and Hazel E. Munsell, *Food Supply and Pellagra Incidence in South Carolina Farm Families*, USDA Technical Bulletin 333 (Washington, D.C., Oct. 1932), pp. 2-8; Ada M. Moser, *Farm Family Diets in the Lower Coastal Plains of South Carolina*, South Carolina Agricultural Experiment Station Bulletin 319 (Clemson, June 1939). On conditions in the late 1930s see, *Such As Us: Southern Voices of the Thirties*, edited by Tom E. Terrill and Jerrold Hirsch (Chapel Hill: Univ. of North Carolina Press, 1978).

46. Eudora Welty, *One Time, One Place: Mississippi in the Depression* (New York: Random House, 1971); Dorothea Lange and Paul S. Taylor, *An American Exodus* (New York: Reynal and Hitchcock, 1939).

47. Donald H. Grubbs, *Cry from the Cotton: The Southern Tenant Farmers' Union and the New Deal* (Chapel Hill: Univ. of North Carolina Press, 1971).

Chapter 7

1. Woofter, *Landlord and Tenant*, p. 66.

2. *Payments Made under the Agricultural Adjustment Program*, Sen. Doc. 274, 74 Cong., 2 sess. (Washington, D.C., 1936), pp. 22-23, 34-40. Lawrence J. Nelson, "Oscar Johnston, the New Deal and the Cotton Subsidy Payments Controversy, 1936-1937," *Journal of Southern History* 40 (Aug. 1974): 399-416.

3. *Payments Made under the Agricultural Adjustment Program*, pp. 67, 70-71, 76, 102, 117.

4. Harold Hoffsommer, "The AAA and the Cropper," *Social Forces* 13 (May 1935): 495-96.

5. David E. Conrad, *The Forgotten Farmers: The Story of the Sharecroppers in the New Deal* (Urbana: Univ. of Illinois Press, 1965), p. 65; Johnson, Embree, and Alexander, *Collapse of Cotton Tenancy*, p. 51.

6. Badger, *Prosperity Road*, pp. 201-4. Relatively few tobacco farmers were displaced after 1933. There had been a substantial decline of tenants in eastern North Carolina before the New Deal program began, and these farmers were unable to return to tobacco farming after 1933 because they could not obtain an acreage allotment.

7. The best account of tenant and sharecropper problems can be found in: Conrad, *Forgotten Farmers*; Paul E. Mertz, *New Deal Policy and Southern Rural Poverty* (Baton Rouge: Louisiana State Univ. Press, 1978); Donald Holley, *Uncle Sam's Farmers: The New Deal Communities in the Lower Mississippi Valley* (Urbana: Univ. of Illinois Press, 1975); and Louis Cantor, *A Prologue to the Protest Movement: The Missouri Sharecropper Roadside Demonstrations of 1939* (Durham, N.C.: Duke Univ. Press, 1969). Theodore Saloutos, *The American Farmer and the New Deal* (Ames: Iowa State Univ. Press, 1982), p. 265.

8. Quoted in Cantor, *Prologue to the Protest Movement*, p. 156.

9. Quoted in Holley, *Uncle Sam's Farmers*, p. 26.

10. Ibid.

11. Quoted in Mertz, *New Deal Policy*, pp. 88-89; see also p. 85.

12. Quoted in Sidney Baldwin, *Poverty and Politics* (Chapel Hill: Univ. of North Carolina Press, 1968), p. 128.

13. Mertz, *New Deal Policy*, chap. 4.

14. Conrad, *Forgotten Farmers*, quote from p. 167; J. Clark Waldron, "King Cotton and His Slaves," *Nation* 138 (June 20, 1934): 703-5, describes poor farm families in Arkansas. See also H.L. Mitchell, *Mean Things Happening in This Land* (Montclair, N.J.: Allanheld, Osmun, 1979).

15. Baldwin, *Poverty and Politics*, p. 108. See also W.W. Alexander, "Overcrowded Farms," *Yearbook of Agriculture, 1940* (Washington, D.C., 1940), pp. 870-88.

16. Mertz, *New Deal Policy*, p. 164; Baldwin, *Poverty and Politics*, pp. 110-22.

17. President's Special Committee on Farm Tenancy, *Farm Tenancy*, House Doc. No. 149, 75 Cong., 1 sess. (Washington, D.C., 1937), pp. 3, 5.

18. Ibid, pp. 10-15.

19. Mertz, *New Deal Policy*, pp. 187-89; Baldwin, *Poverty and Politics*, pp. 167-92.

20. *Report of the Administrator of the Farm Security Administration, 1941* (Washington, D.C., 1942), pp. 28-29, 31-32.

21. Mertz, *New Deal Policy*, pp. 169-75.

22. Ibid., pp. 176-78; President's Special Committee, *Farm Tenancy*, p. 16.

23. Rupert B. Vance, *All These People: The Nation's Human Resources in the South* (Chapel Hill: Univ. of North Carolina Press, 1945), p. 138. Letter from Taylor to L.C. Gray, printed in President's Special Committee, *Farm Tenancy*, pp. 28-29.

24. *Farm Tenancy*, p. 28.

25. *Progressive Farmer* 50 (May 1935): 5. See TVA Relocation Records, Box 44, National Archives and Records Service, East Point, Georgia. Michael J. McDonald and John Muldowny, *TVA and the Dispossessed: The Resettlement of Population in the Norris Dam Area* (Knoxville: Univ. of Tennessee Press, 1982). On the broader aspects of the TVA see Joseph S. Ransmeier, *The Tennessee Valley Authority: A Case Study in the Economics of Multiple Purpose Stream Planning* (Nashville: Vanderbilt Univ. Press, 1942); Norman I. Wengert, *Valley of Tomorrow: The TVA and Agriculture* (Knoxville: Bureau of Public Administration, Univ. of Tennessee, 1952); D. Clayton Brown, *Electricity for Rural America: The Fight for the REA* (Westport, Conn.: Greenwood Press, 1980); and Marquis W. Childs, *The Farmer Takes a Hand: The Electric Power Revolution in Rural America* (Garden City, N.Y.: Doubleday, 1952), chap. 7.

26. Commission on Interracial Cooperation, *The South's Landless Farmers* (Atlanta: Commission on Interracial Cooperation, 1937), no pagination.

27. W.M. Hurst and L.M. Church, *Power and Machinery In Agriculture*, USDA Miscellaneous Bulletin 157 (Washington, D.C., Apr. 1933), pp. 2-21. See also Martin R. Cooper, Glen T. Barton, and Albert P. Brodell, *Progress of Farm Mechanization*, USDA Miscellaneous Publication 630 (Washington, D.C., Oct. 1947).

28. Holley, Winston, and Woofter, *Plantation South*, p. 20. Interview with Luther Spooner of Donalsonville, Ga., Feb. 24, 1982.

29. *Yearbook of Agriculture, 1932* (Washington, D.C., 1932), pp. 430-31.

30. M.G. Vaiden, J.O. Smith, and W.E. Ayres, *Making Cotton Cheaper*, Delta Experiment Station Bulletin 298 (State College, Miss., June 1932), pp. 2, 9. Vaiden had been a plantation bookkeeper for nine years in 1931. In 1931 the same authors did a similar study which was published as Delta Experiment Station Bulletin 290 (A & M College, Miss., Feb. 1931).

31. *Yearbook of Agriculture, 1940* (Washington, D.C., 1940), p. 893; *Progressive Farmer* 54 (Oct. 1939): 5.

32. See Moses S. Musoke, "Technical Change in Cotton Production in the United States, 1925-1960," Ph.D. diss., Univ. of Wisconsin-Madison, 1976.

33. Holley, Winston, and Woofter, *Plantation South*, p. 19; Paul S. Taylor, "Power Farming and Labor Displacement in the Cotton Belt, 1937," *Monthly Labor Review* 46 (Mar. 1938): 601.

34. J.G. McNeely and Glen T. Barton, *Land Tenure in Arkansas: Change in Labor Organization on Cotton Farms*, Arkansas Agricultural Experiment Station Bulletin 397 (Fayetteville, June 1940), p. 17; *1950 Census of Agriculture, General Report*, 2: 226-27.

35. B.O. Williams, "The Impact of Mechanization of Agriculture on the Farm Population of the South," *Rural Sociology* 4 (Sept. 1939): 300-314. See also Harold Hoffsommer, "Social Aspects of Farm Labor in the South," *Rural Sociology* 3 (Dec. 1938): 434-45; C. Horace Hamilton, "The Social Effects of Recent Trends in the Mechanization of Agriculture," *Rural Sociology* 4 (Mar. 1939): 3-25; and Homer L. Hitt, *Recent Migration into and*

within the Upper Mississippi Delta of Louisiana, Louisiana Agricultural Experiment Station Bulletin 364 (Baton Rouge, June 1943).

36. Holley, Winston, and Woofter, *Plantation South,* p. 6.

37. H.W. Blalock, *Plantation Operations of Landlords and Tenants in Arkansas,* Arkansas Agricultural Experiment Station Bulletin 339 (Fayetteville, 1937), pp. 6, 19; Taylor, "Power Farming and Labor Displacement in the Cotton Belt, 1937," *Monthly Labor Review* 46 (April 1938): 862.

38. For changes and developments on plantations in the Yazoo-Mississippi Delta see E.L. Langsford and B.H. Thibodeaux, *Plantation Organization and Operation in the Yazoo-Mississippi Delta Area,* USDA Technical Bulletin 682 (Washington, D.C., May 1939); *Fifteenth Census of the United States, 1930, Agriculture,* 1, pt. 2: 151; *Sixteenth Census of the United States, 1940, Agriculture,* 1 (Washington, D.C., 1942): 83.

39. *United States Census of Agriculture, 1935, General Report,* 3 (Washington, D.C., 1937): 118-22; *Sixteenth Census of the United States, 1940, Agriculture, General Report,* 3 (Washington, D.C., 1943): 376. For the situation in Missouri's bootheel see Cantor, *Prologue to the Protest Movement,* chaps. 5 and 6. See also Howard Kester, *Revolt among the Sharecroppers* (New York: Covici, Friede, 1936).

40. *1950 Census of Agriculture, General Report,* 2:1025.

41. *Congressional Record,* 76 Cong., 1 sess., 1939, appendix, pp. 488-90. The best bibliographical treatment of black migration is that by Jack Temple Kirby, "The Southern Exodus, 1910-1960: A Primer for Historians," *Journal of Southern History* 49 (Nov. 1983): 585-600. See also Neil Fligstein, *Going North: Migration of Blacks and Whites from the South, 1900-1950* (New York: Academic Press, 1981).

42. *Technology on the Farm: A Special Report by an Interbureau Committee and the Bureau of Agricultural Economics of the USDA* (Washington, D.C., Aug. 1940), p. 63.

43. Fite, "Recent Progress in the Mechanization of Cotton Production," pp. 24-25.

44. *Time* 31 (March 7, 1938): 57.

45. *1950 Census of Agriculture, General Report,* 2: 52-55.

46. Ibid., pp. 584, 594.

47. Ibid., pp. 582, 634; Benedict and Stine, *Agricultural Commodity Programs,* pp. 65-68.

48. *Agricultural Statistics, 1940* (Washington, D.C., 1940), pp. 210-11.

49. *1950 Census of Agriculture, General Report,* 2: 400-401; *Yearbook of Agriculture, 1943-47* (Washington, D.C., 1947), pp. 85-86; W.F. Finner and R.L. Mighell, *Trends in Dairying by Major Type-of-Farming Regions,* USDA Technical Bulletin 751 (Washington, D.C., Jan. 1941), pp. 16-17; C.W. Summerour, "Georgia's Fat Stock Shows Picture Beef Possibilities," *Progressive Farmer* 50 (May 1935): 12. In April 1933 fat cattle shows at Savannah and Albany, Georgia, caused observers to remark that there was "the dawn of a new day in Georgia's agriculture."

50. *1950 Census of Agriculture, General Report,* 2: 424, 446.

51. Twelve Southerners, *I'll Take My Stand: The South and the Agrarian Tradition* (New York: Harper and Bros., 1930), pp. 176-245. See also John Albert Jenkins, "To Find a Land: The Modern South and the Agrarian Tradition," Ph.D. diss., Indiana Univ., 1965; and Jess Gilbert and Steve Brown, "Alternative Land Reform Proposals in the 1930s: The Nashville Agrarians and the Southern Tenant Farmers' Union," *Agricultural History* 55 (Oct. 1981): 351-69.

52. *1950 Census of Agriculture, General Report,* 2:44, 226, 848-49.

53. Merle C. Prunty, "Two American Souths: The Past and the Future," *Southeastern Geographer* 17 (May 1977): 1-2.

54. *1950 Census of Agriculture, General Report,* 2:66.

55. Interview with D.W. Brooks in Atlanta, July 20, 1981.

56. The National Emergency Council, *Report on the Economic Conditions of the South* (Washington, D.C., 1938).

Chapter 8

1. "H.L. Wingate, Revolutionary," *Fortune* 24 (Oct. 1941): 72-77.

2. *Agricultural Statistics, 1940*, pp. 547-48.

3. Ibid., *1945* (Washington, D.C., 1945), p. 70.

4. Ibid., p. 125; Walter W. Wilcox, *The Farmer in the Second World War* (Ames: Iowa State Univ. Press, 1947), pp. 184-88; Benedict and Stine, *Agricultural Commodity Programs*, pp. 152-53.

5. Benedict and Stine, *Agricultural Commodity Programs*, p. 172.

6. *Agricultural Statistics, 1945*, p. 131; ibid., *1942*, pp. 104, 197.

7. Ibid., *1951* (Washington, D.C., 1951), p. 88; *1950 Census of Agriculture, General Report*, 2:582.

8. Badger, *Prosperity Road*, chap. 7; *Agricultural Statistics, 1945*, p. 105.

9. James H. Street, *The New Revolution in the Cotton Economy* (Chapel Hill: Univ. of North Carolina Press, 1957), pp. 72-74; J. Homer Blackstone, *Cost of Producing Fluid Milk in Alabama*, Alabama Agricultural Experiment Station Bulletin 265 (Auburn, 1948), pp. 4-8.

10. *1950 Census of Agriculture, General Report*, 2:401.

11. Ibid., 425.

12. *United States Census of Agriculture, 1945*, 1, pt. 17, *Georgia* (Washington, D.C., 1946): 193, 196; T.L. Senn and J. Sam Taylor, *The Commercial Peach Industry in South Carolina*, South Carolina Experiment Station Bulletin 393 (Clemson, June 1951), pp. 14-17; *1950 Census of Agriculture, General Report*, 2: 695.

13. *1950 Census of Agriculture, General Report*, 2: 754.

14. J. Allen Tower, "Alabama's Shifting Cotton Belt," *Alabama Review* 1 (Jan. 1948): 36; James S. Fisher, "The Modification of Rural Land Occupance Systems: The Central Georgia Piedmont," Ph.D. diss., Univ. of Georgia, 1967, p. 179; *1950 Census of Agriculture, General Report*, 2: 695.

15. "It Will Be Picked," *Business Week*, Oct. 21, 1944, pp. 52-53.

16. Street, *New Revolution in the Cotton Economy*, pp. 194, 204; Frank H. Jeter, "Post-War Fight for Cotton," *Farm Journal* 68 (Nov. 1944): 22; Ben T. Lanham, Jr. *Farm Power Costs and Equipment Costs in Northern Alabama*, Alabama Experiment Station Bulletin 260 (Auburn, Mar. 1947), pp. 6, 22; Wilcox, *Farmer in the Second World War*, p. 67.

17. W.W. McPherson, W.H. Pierce, and R.E.L. Greene, *Opportunities for Adjustment in Farming Systems, Southern Piedmont Area, North Carolina*, North Carolina Experiment Station Technical Bulletin 87 (Raleigh, Sept. 1949), p. 12; *1950 Census of Agriculture, General Report*, 2: 66.

18. *1950 Census of Agriculture, General Report*, 2: 30, 178-79.

19. J.C. Elrod and W.T. Fullilove, *Cost and Utilization of Tractor Power and Equipment on Farms in the Lower Piedmont*, Georgia Experiment Station Bulletin 256 (Experiment, Jan. 1948).

20. *1950 Census of Agriculture, General Report*, 2: 974-80.

21. J.D. Ratcliff, "Revolution in Cotton," *Collier's* 116 (July 21, 1945): 24.

22. Street, *New Revolution in the Cotton Economy*, chap. 9. On this point Merle C. Prunty, Jr., has written that as late as 1960 the pull forces were "erected by factory and city." "Some Contemporary Myths and Challenges in Southern Rural Land Utilization," *Southeastern Geographer* 10 (Nov. 1970): 3.

23. The question of industrial training and jobs for blacks has been discussed by Todd L. Butler in a paper written at the University of Georgia: "Farm Poverty and the Industrial Alternative, 1940-45; The Black Experience in Georgia"; in author's possession.

24. John Leonard Fulmer, *Agricultural Progress in the Cotton Belt since 1920* (Chapel Hill: Univ. of North Carolina Press, 1950), pp. 150-51. Income figures were calculated from *Agricultural Statistics, 1947* (Washington, D.C., 1948), p. 538.

25. *1950 Census of Agriculture, General Report*, 2: 997-98; McPherson, Pierce, and Greene, *Opportunities for Adjustment in Farming Systems*, p. 12.

26. Selz C. Mayo and Robert Bobbitt, *Rural Organization: A Restudy of Locality Groups in Wake County, North Carolina*, North Carolina Agricultural Experiment Station Technical Bulletin 95 (Raleigh, Sept. 1951), p. 14; House Committee on Agriculture, *Long-Range Agricultural Policy*, 80 Cong., 2 sess. (Washington, D.C., Mar. 10, 1948), p. 69.

27. *1950 Census of Agriculture, General Report*, 2: 212.

28. Fite, *American Farmers*, pp. 85-86; Wilcox, *Farmer and the Second World War*, pp. 243-46.

29. Street, *New Revolution in the Cotton Economy*, chap. 4.

30. See the discussion in *Cotton: Hearings before the Subcommittee of the Committee on Agriculture, House of Representatives*, 78 Cong., 2 sess. (Washington, D.C., Dec. 4-9, 1944), pp. 27, 845.

31. Ibid., pp. 36, 43.

32. *A Study of Agricultural and Economic Problems of the Cotton Belt: Hearings before Special Subcommittee on Cotton of the Committee on Agriculture, House of Representatives*, 80 Cong., 1 sess. (Washington, D.C., July 7-8, 1947), pp. 17 ff.

33. *National Defense Migration: Hearings before the Select Subcommittee Investigating National Defense Migration, House of Representatives*, 77 Cong., 2 sess. (Washington, D.C., May 7-8, 1942) pt. 32:12171; Walter S. Brown, "Georgia Farm Leaders Face the Future," *Progressive Farmer* 60 (Apr. 1945): 14; *Study of Agricultural and Economic Problems*, p. 9; Robert C. McManus, "King Cotton Puts Up a Fight," *Farm Journal* 71 (Mar. 1947): 28.

34. *Cotton: Hearings*, p. 95; "The South Must Claim Its Share of American Markets," *Progressive Farmer* 60 (Oct. 1945): 42.

35. J. Mitchell Morse, "Revolution in Cotton," *New Republic* 119 (Aug. 19, 1946): 193; *Study of Agricultural and Economic Problems*, pp. 17 ff.

36. Jeter, "Post-War Fight for Cotton," p. 22; *Progress through Machines: Proceedings of the Second Annual Beltwide Mechanization Conference* (Memphis: National Cotton Council, 1948), p. 8.

37. *Study of Agricultural and Economic Problems*, p. 1152.

38. Ibid., p. 710.

Chapter 9

1. J.D. Ratcliff, "Revolution in Cotton," *Collier's* 116 (July 21, 1945): 24; J. Mitchell Morse, "Revolution in Cotton," *New Republic* 115 (Aug. 19, 1946): 192-94; "The New South, Its Farms, Factories and Folkways Show Exciting Changes," *Life* 27 (Oct. 31, 1949): 79-90. See also the excellent article by Pete Daniel, "The Transformation of the Rural South, 1930 to the Present," *Agricultural History* 55 (July 1981): 231-48.

2. Martin R. Cooper, Glen T. Barton, and Albert P. Brodell, *Progress of Farm Mechanization*, USDA Miscellaneous Publication 630 (Washington, D.C., Oct. 1947), p. 12.

3. *Agricultural Statistics, 1949* (Washington, D.C.,), p. 665.

4. Ibid., *1940* (Washington, D.C., 1940), p. 603; *Fourteenth Annual Report of the Farm Credit Administration, 1946-47* (Washington, D.C., 1947), p. 69; *Annual Report of the Farm Credit Administration, 1948-49* (Washington, D.C., 1949), p. 112.

5. *Agricultural Statistics, 1940*, pp. 599, 613; *Agricultural Statistics, 1949*, pp. 674, 666.

6. *1950 Census of Agriculture, General Report*, 2:226.

7. Ibid., p. 383; *Agricultural Statistics, 1955* (Washington, D.C., 1956), p. 361.

8. W.C. Lassetter, "Machinery Is Remodeling Southern Agriculture," *Progressive Farmer* 60 (Mar. 1945): 14.

9. J.C. Elrod and W.T. Fullilove, *Cost and Utilization of Tractor Power and Equipment on Farms in the Lower Piedmont*, Georgia Agricultural Experiment Station Bulletin 256 (Experiment, Jan. 1948); J.C. Elrod, *Cost and Utilization of Tractor Power and Equipment on Farms in the Coastal Plain*, Georgia Agricultural Experiment Station Bulletin 260 (Experiment, June

1949); Oscar Steanson and Joe F. Davis, *Electricity on Farms in the Upper Piedmont of Georgia,* Georgia Agricultural Experiment Station Bulletin 263 (Experiment, June 1950).

10. Frank H. Jeter, "Give Up Cotton?" *Farm Journal* 69 (Feb. 1945): 22.

11. Fite, "Recent Progress in the Mechanization of Cotton Production," pp. 25-26; idem, "Mechanization of Cotton Production since World War II," *Agricultural History* 54 (Jan. 1980): 198-204.

12. Frank J. Welch and D. Gray Miley, *Mechanization of the Cotton Harvest,* Mississippi Agricultural Experiment Station Bulletin 420 (State College, June 1945).

13. *Progress through Machines: Report of the Proceedings of the Third Annual Beltwide Cotton Mechanization Conference, 1949* (Memphis: National Cotton Council, 1949), p. 64.

14. *Report of the Proceedings of the Beltwide Cotton Mechanization Conference* (Memphis: National Cotton Council, 1947), quote from preface; mimeographed.

15. *Progress through Machines, 1949,* pp. 63-64.

16. *Cotton Production-Mechanization: Summary-Proceedings, 1962 Beltwide Cotton Production-Mechanization Conference* (Memphis: National Cotton Council, 1962), p. 7.

17. Fite, "Mechanization of Cotton Production," p. 203.

18. George B. Nutt, "Progress and Problems in Mechanizing Southeastern Agriculture," *Cotton Mechanization: Proceedings, Seventh Annual Cotton Mechanization Conference* (Memphis: National Cotton Council, 1953), p. 14.

19. Ibid.

20. USDA, *Agricultural Situation* 48 (Washington, D.C., Aug. 1964): 9.

21. Merle Prunty, Jr., "The Renaissance of the Southern Plantation," *Geographical Review* 45 (Oct. 1955): 459-91; Charles S. Aiken, "The Fragmented Neoplantation: A New Type of Farm Operation in the Southeast," *Southeastern Geographer* 11 (Apr. 1971): 43-51; Jeter, "Post-War Fight for Cotton," p. 22; Harald A. Pedersen and Arthur F. Raper, *The Cotton Plantation in Transition,* Mississippi Agricultural Experiment Station Bulletin 508 (State College, Jan. 1954), pp. 3-26.

22. Aiken, "Fragmented Neoplantation," p. 50; Fisher, "Modification of Rural Land Occupance Systems," p. 153.

23. James C. Fortson, *Break-Even Points for Harvesting Machines,* Georgia Agricultural Experiment Station Bulletin, N.S. 66 (Athens, Dec. 1959), pp. 44-61; *Thirtieth Annual Report, 1949-50,* Georgia Coastal Experiment Station Bulletin 49 (Tifton, July 1950), pp. 11-16. See also "Combines and Shakers Brought New Era to Peanut Harvesting," *Southeastern Peanut Farmer* 14 (July 1976): 12.

24. For a discussion of tobacco harvesting see Robert W. Wilson, "Mechanizing Flue-Cured Tobacco Harvest," *Agricultural Engineering* 37 (June 1956): 407; G.L. Bradford et al., *Economic Considerations of Bulk Curing,* Department of Agricultural Economics, North Carolina State College Information Series 102 (Raleigh, May 1963); Charles R. Pugh, "The Structure of Flue-Cured Tobacco Farms," in *Farm Structure: A Historical Perspective on Changes in the Number and Size of Farms,* Senate Committee on Agriculture, Nutrition, and Forestry, 96 Cong., 2 sess., (Washington, D.C., Apr. 1980), pp. 354-55; Verner N. Grise, *Trends in Flue-Cured Tobacco Farming,* USDA, Economics and Statistics Service, Agricultural Economic Report 470 (Washington, D.C., June 1981); Charles Kellogg Mann, *Tobacco: The Ants and the Elephants* (Salt Lake City: Olympus Publishing Co., 1975); interviews with Robert W. Wilson and Burnell Gaskins, Oct. 16, 1982.

25. *1950 Census of Agriculture, General Report,* 2: 226, 222.

26. *Agricultural Statistics, 1942,* p. 104; ibid., *1962* (Washington, D.C., 1962), p. 76.

27. Glenn W. Burton, "Our Role in Feeding the World," College of Agriculture, University of Georgia (Athens, 1976), p. 5.

28. Harold Benford, "Complete Cotton Mechanization Is Here," *Progressive Farmer* 78 (Mar. 1963): 29. The Campbell quote is from a manuscript in the possession of his son, J. Phil Campbell, of Watkinsville, Ga.

29. Interviews with Frank P. King, former director of the Coastal Plains Agricultural Experiment Station, Tifton, Georgia, June 14, 1982; and Glenn W. Burton, June 14, 1982.

30. Thomas R. Dunlap, *DDT, Scientists, Citizens and Public Policy* (Princeton: Princeton Univ. Press, 1981).

31. See *Agricultural Statistics, 1955* (Washington, D.C., 1956), p. 55; *Congress and the Nation, 1945-1964* (Washington, D.C.,: Congressional Quarterly Service, 1965), p. 700.

32. H. Brooks James, "Human Side of Cotton Production," in *Cotton Production: Summary-Proceedings, Third Annual Beltwide Cotton Production Conference* (Memphis: National Cotton Council, 1957), p. 4.

33. J.E. Carter to Richard B. Russell, Jan. 26, 1954, Russell Papers, Russell Library, Univ. of Georgia, IX, B, Box 31.

34. James, "Human Side of Cotton Production," p. 4; James S. Fisher, "Federal Crop Allotment Programs and Responses by Individual Farm Operators," *Southeastern Geographer* 10 (Nov. 1970): 47 ff; Aiken, "Fragmented Neoplantation," pp. 43-51.

35. *Agricultural Statistics, 1951* (Washington, D.C., 1951), pp. 137, 547; ibid., *1962*, pp. 164, 533.

36. Nelson LeRay, Jr., and Grady B. Crowe, *Labor and Technology on Selected Cotton Plantations in the Delta Area of Mississippi, 1953-1957*, Mississippi Agricultural Experiment Station Bulletin 575 (State College, Apr. 1959).

37. J.J. Inskeep, "Grass Boom in Dixie," *Farm Journal* 71 (Sept. 1947): 58.

38. Interview with B.L. Southwell, Tifton, Ga., June 14, 1982.

39. D.W. Skelton, comp., *Improving Pastures in Mississippi,* Mississippi Agricultural Experiment Station Bulletin 419 (State College, June 1945).

40. Interview with Glenn W. Burton, June 14, 1982.

41. Inskeep, "Grass Boom in Dixie," p. 58. See also Alexander Nunn, "Beef Progress Just Begun," *Progressive Farmer* 76 (July 1961): 21; Clarence Poe, "Why the South Turns to Livestock," *Progressive Farmer* 63 (Aug. 1948): 90; Charles E. Ball, "Big Feed Lots Come to the South," *Farm Journal* 83 (Apr. 1959): 37.

42. Ray H. Means, E.B. Ferris, and S.P. Crockett, *Beef Calf Production in Mississippi,* Mississippi Agricultural Experiment Station Bulletin 412 (State College, Jan. 1945).

43. E.C. Cushing and D.C. Parman, "The Screwworm and Blowfly Problem," *Yearbook of Agriculture, 1942* (Washington, D.C., 1942), pp. 313-22. The problems of livestock diseases, cross-breeding, and other matters relating to livestock production are discussed by J. Allen Tower in "The New South: An Old and a New Frontier," *Education* (Jan. 1943).

44. Frank D. Barlow, Jr., and Morris L. McGough, *Dairy Farming in the North Louisiana Upland Cotton Area,* Louisiana Agricultural Experiment Station Bulletin 435 (Baton Rouge, Oct. 1948), p. 6; "How Much to Start Dairying?" in *Farm Family* (published by Humble Oil Company), May 1954, p. 7; J. Homer Blackstone, *Cost of Producing Fluid Milk in Alabama,* Alabama Agricultural Experiment Station Bulletin 265 (Auburn, 1948); Sheldon W. Williams, *Supplies and Use of Milk in Alabama,* Alabama Agricultural Experiment Station Bulletin 282 (Auburn, June 1952).

45. M.J. Danner, "How Alabama Farmers Buy and Sell Livestock," Alabama Agricultural Experiment Station Bulletin 281 (Auburn, Mar. 1952), pp. 31-34.

46. *Agricultural Statistics, 1942,* p. 465; ibid., *1962,* p. 450; ibid., *1976,* p. 366.

47. Lloyd Durand, Jr., "Dairying in the South," *Southeastern Geographer* 10 (Nov. 1970): 29 ff. See also H.B. Henderson, "A History of the Dairy Industry in Georgia," 1981, manuscript copy in the University of Georgia Archives.

48. James R. Anderson, "Specialized Agriculture in the South," *Southeastern Geographer* 10 (Nov. 1970): 21; *Agricultural Statistics, 1940,* p. 413.

49. C. Curtis Cable, Jr., *Growth of the Arkansas Broiler Industry,* Arkansas Agricultural Experiment Station Bulletin 520 (Fayetteville, Apr. 1952), pp. 8 ff; W.E. Christian, Jr., and

Paul T. Blair, *Broiler Production, Financing and Marketing in Mississippi*, Mississippi Agricultural Experiment Station Bulletin 514 (State College, Mar. 1954), p. 7; O.C. Hester and W.W. Harper, *The Function of Feed-Dealer Suppliers in Marketing Georgia Broilers*, Georgia Agricultural Experiment Station Bulletin 283 (Experiment, Aug. 1953), pp. 5 ff.

50. Gordon Sawyer, *The Agribusiness Poultry Industry: A History of Its Development* (New York: Exposition Press, 1971), has a chapter on Jewell. See also Bernard F. Tobin and Henry B. Arthur, *Dynamics of Adjustment in the Broiler Industry* (Boston: Division of Research, Graduate School of Business Administration, Harvard Univ., 1964).

51. Stanley K. Seaver, "An Appraisal of Vertical Integration in the Broiler Industry," *Journal of Farm Economics* 39 (Dec. 1957): 1487-97. See also J.R. Bowring's comments on p. 1499.

52. Edward J. Smith, "Technology in Broiler Production," USDA, Economic Research Service, ERS-246 (Washington, D.C., Aug. 1965), p. 3; *Agricultural Statistics, 1951*, p. 457; ibid., *1976*, p. 411.

53. *Agricultural Statistics, 1942*, p. 527; ibid., *1962*, p. 503. *1950 Census of Agriculture, General Report*, 2:1234; *1974 Census of Agriculture*, 1, pt. 51 (Washington, D.C., 1977), Table 15, p. II-30.

54. *Agricultural Statistics, 1942*, p. 527; ibid., *1962*, p. 503. *1950 Census of Agriculture, General Report*, 2:1234; *1974 Census of Agriculture*, 1, pt. 51, Table 15, p. II-30.

55. D.F. King, "Poultry: South's Golden Nest Egg," *Progressive Farmer* 76 (Feb. 1961): 128. John K. Bettersworth, " 'The Cow in the Front Yard,' " *Agricultural History* 53 (Jan. 1979): 70.

56. Paul W. Chapman, "New $100,000,000 Citrus Industry," *Progressive Farmer* 65 (Apr. 1950): 15; Ronald L. Mighell et al., *Contract Production of Truck Crops, 12 Selected Areas*, USDA, Economic Research Service, ERS-152 (Washington, D.C., Mar. 1964). See also *Agricultural Statistics* for pertinent years.

57. Calculated from tables in USDA, Economic Research Service, *Farm Income, State Estimates, 1959-72* (Washington, D.C., Aug. 1973).

58. *State Farm Income Statistics: Supplement to Statistical Bulletin 627*, USDA, Economics, Statistics and Cooperatives Service (Washington, D.C., Jan. 1980), p. 10.

59. Ibid., and the same for 1949-1962. *The South's Third Forest: A Report of the Southern Forest Resource Analysis Committee, 1969* (n.p., n.d.), pp. 10-11. On soybeans see Harry D. Fornari, "The Big Change: Cotton to Soybeans," *Agricultural History* 53 (Jan. 1979): 245-53.

60. *Development of Agriculture's Human Resources*, House Doc. 149, 84 Cong., 1 sess. (Apr. 1955), pp. 2, 25.

61. *Statistical Abstract of the United States, 1951* (Washington, D.C., 1951), pp. 176; ibid., *1971* (Washington, D.C., 1971), p. 221.

62. Ibid., *1961* (Washington, D.C., 1961), p. 211; ibid., *1971*, p. 218.

Chapter 10

1. *1950 Census of Agriculture, General Report*, 2: 53; *1974 Census of Agriculture, United States Summary and State Data*, 1, pt. 51, Table 1, p. 11-2.

2. *1950 Census of Agriculture, General Report*, 2:997-98; *1974 Census of Agriculture*, 1 pt. 51, Table 4, p. 11-6.

3. *1950 Census of Agriculture, General Report*, 2: 992, 1026; *1978 Census of Agriculture, United States Summary and State Data*, 1, pt. 51, Tables 41, 52, pp. 208-9. Reverend Martin Luther King, Sr., with Clayton Riley, *Daddy King: An Autobiography* (New York: William Morrow, 1980), pp. 24-25.

4. For an early discussion of the decline of black farmers see Ernest E. Neal and Lewis W. Jones, "The Place of the Negro Farmer in the Changing Economy of the Cotton South," *Rural Sociology* 15 (Mar. 1950), p. 37; and James S. Fisher, "Negro Farm Ownership

in the South," *Annals of the Association of American Geographers* 63 (Dec. 1973): 487-88. See also *New York Times,* Dec. 7, 1972, p. 39.

5. Vera J. Banks and Calvin L. Beale, *Farm Population Estimates, 1910-1970,* USDA Statistical Bulletin 523 (Washington, D.C., July 1973); see appropriate tables.

6. USDA Economic Research Service, Series FIS-195 Supplement, *Farm Income: State Estimates, 1949-1963* (Washington, D.C., Aug. 1964), p. 10; USDA, Economic Research Service, *State Farm Statistics,* p. 16; *1974 Census of Agriculture,* 1, pt. 51, Table 3, p. IV-20.

7. J.C. Bonner manuscript, copy in author's possession; *Athens Banner-Herald,* Sept. 12, 1982; *Daddy King,* p. 31.

8. *Progressive Farmer* 60 (Sept. 1945): 23.

9. Jonathan Daniels, "A Native at Large," *Nation* 152 (Apr. 19, 1941): 474.

10. *Low-Income Families: Hearings before the Subcommittee on Low-Income Families of the Joint Committee on the Economic Report,* 81 Cong., 1 sess., Dec. 12-22, 1949 (Washington, D.C., 1950), p. 252.

11. *1950 Census of Agriculture, General Report,* 2: 1133-34, 1137, 1139, 1146, 1154, 1175. Frank J. Welch, *The Labor Supply and Mechanized Cotton Production,* Mississippi Agricultural Experiment Station Bulletin 463 (State College, June 1949), pp. 7-9.

12. *Low-Income Families: Hearings,* pp. 210-12, 253, 307, 318-19. See also Charles M. Hardin, "The Bureau of Agricultural Economics under Fire: A Study in Valuation Conflicts," *Journal of Farm Economics* 28 (Aug. 1946): 635-38.

13. *Low-Income Families and Economic Stability: Report of the Subcommittee on Low-Income Families of the Joint Committee on the Economic Report,* Senate Doc. 146, 81 Cong., 1 sess., (Washington, D.C., 1950), pp. 4-8.

14. Theodore W. Schultz, "Reflections on Poverty within Agriculture," *Journal of Political Economy* 58 (Feb. 1950): 1-15.

15. *Underemployment of Rural Families: Material Prepared for the Joint Committee on the Economic Report,* 82 Cong., 1 sess. (Washington, D.C., 1951), pp. 1-15. See also William E. Hendrix, "Size and Distribution of the Income of Farm People in Relation to the Low Income Problem," *Journal of Farm Economics* 36 (Dec. 1954): 1134-43; idem, "Relation of Chronic Low Farm Income to Major National Economic Problems," *Journal of Farm Economics* 44 (May 1962): 522-33. Some good material can also be found in Arthur L. Moore, *Underemployment in American Agriculture,* National Planning Association, Planning Pamphlet 77 (Washington, D.C., Jan. 1952).

16. *Nation's Agriculture* 24 (Feb. 1951): 11.

17. *Development of Agriculture's Human Resources,* House Doc. 149, 84 Cong., 1 sess., Apr. 27, 1955.

18. *Low-Income Families: Hearings before the Subcommittee on Low-Income Families of the Joint Committee on the Economic Report,* 84 Cong., 1 sess., Nov. 18-19, 1955, pp. 440-90, 493.

19. *Family-Size Farms: Hearings before the Subcommittee on Family Farms of the Committee on Agriculture, House of Representatives,* 84 Cong., 1 sess., Oct. 7, 8, 10, 11, 13, 1955; ibid., pt. 2, Feb. 3, 18, 19, 1956, pp. 447, 459-63.

20. *President's Farm Message, 1959: Hearings before the Committee on Agriculture and Forestry, U.S. Senate,* 86 Cong., 1 sess., Feb. 16, 17, 1959, pp. 228-32.

21. John Salmond, "Vanguard of the Civil Rights Movement: The Post-New Deal Career of Aubrey Willis Williams," *Historian* 44 (Nov. 1981): 51-68.

22. *1959 Census of Agriculture, General Report,* 2, *Statistics by Subjects* (Washington, D.C., 1962): 1226-31.

23. Ellen S. Bryant and Kit Mui Leung, *Mississippi Farm Trends, 1950-1964,* Mississippi Agricultural Experiment Station Bulletin 754 (State College, Dec. 1967), p. 205. See also Andrew W. Baird and Wilfred C. Bailey, *Farmers Moving Out of Agriculture,* Mississippi Agricultural Experiment Station Bulletin 568 (State College, Oct. 1958); Sheridan T. Maitland and George L. Wilber, *Industrialization in Chickasaw County, Mississippi: A Study*

of Plant Workers, Mississippi Agricultural Experiment Station Bulletin 566 (State College, Sept. 1958).

24. "Poverty: 'Lord I'm Hungry,' " *Newsweek* 70 (July 24, 1967): 22.

25. *New York Times*, Feb. 1, 1964, pp. 1, 10; *Congressional, Record*, 88 Cong., 2 sess. (May 11, 1964), p. 10456; for the March 16 speech, see House Doc. 243, 88 Cong., 2 sess. (1964).

26. Asher Brynes, "LBJ and the Farmers," *New Republic* 150 (Feb. 15, 1964): 15.

27. "Off the Land," *Nation* 204 (Feb. 27, 1967): 261.

28. *New York Times*, July 19, 1965, p. 1.

29. "Poverty: 'Lord I'm Hungry,' " pp. 22-24; "Minorities: DP's in the Delta," *Newsweek* 67 (Feb. 14, 1966): 28-30. See also " 'Secret' Crisis in the Delta," *Newsweek* 67 (Mar. 7, 1966): 28-29; "Mississippi Tent City: The Strike That Failed," *Look* 30 (Mar. 8, 1966): pp. 26-29; *Wall Street Journal*, Jan. 9, 1968, p. 6.

30. *The War on Poverty: The Economic Opportunity Act of 1964*, Senate Doc. 86, 88 Cong., 2 sess. (1964).

31. *Agricultural Aspects of the Economic Opportunity Act of 1964: Hearing before the Committee on Agriculture, House of Representatives*, 88 Cong., 2 sess., April 27, 1964, p. 4. President Johnson appointed a National Advisory Commission on Rural Poverty, which submitted a major study entitled *Rural Poverty in the United States: A Report by the President's National Advisory Commission on Rural Poverty* (Washington, D.C., May 1968). A smaller study, *The People Left Behind*, based on the research incorporated in the larger study, was published in September 1967.

32. *Wall Street Journal*, July 9, 1968, p. 6.

33. President's Special Committee on Farm Tenancy, House Doc. 149, 75 Cong., 1 sess. (Washington, D.C., 1937), p. 25.

34. "Negro Farmers Get Unfair Treatment," *Farm Journal* 89 (Apr. 1965): 70.

35. *New York Times*, July 8, 1969, p. 26; *Wall Street Journal*, Dec. 1, 1969, p. 5; "White Agriculture," *New Republic* 161 (Nov. 29, 1969): 11.

36. Robert Beardwood, "The Southern Roots of Urban Crisis," *Fortune* 78 (Aug. 1968): 80 ff; *Wall Street Journal*, Apr. 9, 1969, p. 1. See also Paul Wieck, "Unrepresented Negro Farmers in the South," *New Republic* 153 (Dec. 25, 1965): 8-9.

37. Studs Terkel, *Working* (New York: Pantheon Books, 1972), p. 168. Erskine Caldwell, *Tobacco Road* (New York: Duell, Sloan and Pearce, 1932), p. 279.

Chapter 11

1. C. Beaman Smith and J.W. Froley, *Replanning a Farm for Profit*, USDA Farmers' Bulletin 370 (Washington, D.C., Sept. 29, 1909), p. 5.

2. Pertinent tables in *Agricultural Statistics, 1976*; and in USDA, Economic Research Service, *Indicators of the Farm Sector: State Income and Balance Sheet Statistics*, Statistical Bulletin 678 (Washington, D.C., 1980).

3. *New York Times*, July 10, 1975, p. 39.

4. See Fite, *American Farmers*, pp. 208-17, for a discussion of the early activities of the American Agriculture Movement.

5. *Athens* (Ga.) *Banner-Herald*, Nov. 8, 1982.

6. Interview for WRFG's series "Plowed Under: The Plight of Georgia's Farmers"; *Agricultural Credit Situation and FmHA Loan Programs: Hearings before the Subcommittee on Conservation, Credit, and Rural Development of the Committee on Agriculture, House of Representatives*, 97 Cong., 2 sess., Feb. 4, 9, 10, 12, 1982, pp. 120-21.

7. *Farmers and Consumers* (Atlanta, Ga.,) Oct. 13, 1982, p. 1; *Atlanta Constitution*, Apr. 14, 1983.

8. *Atlanta Constitution*, Mar. 5, 1983.

Comment on Sources

No attempt will be made here to present a comprehensive bibliography for the history of southern agriculture since the Civil War. Most of the sources used in this book have been cited in the footnotes. Nevertheless, some general comments on sources seem in order as a guide to the kinds and quality of research materials available.

Two bibliographies are of special value for the study of southern agricultural history. The first and most important is "A List of References for the History of Agriculture in the Southern United States, 1865-1900," edited by Helen H. Edwards. This typescript guide, published by the Agricultural History Center at the University of California-Davis in March 1971, is essential for the period covered. Books and articles dealing with blacks in southern agriculture can be found in "A List of References for the History of Black Americans in Agriculture, 1619-1980," edited by Joel Schor and published by the Agricultural History Center in June 1981. Many references to aspects of southern agricultural history are also listed in two other publications by the Agricultural History Center. These are, "A List of References for the History of the Farmers' Alliance and the Populist Party," published in June 1973 and compiled by Henry C. Dethloff; and "A Preliminary List of References for the History of American Agriculture during the New Deal Period, 1932-1940," compiled by Harry C. McDean and published in June 1968.

There are abundant primary and secondary sources for the study of southern agricultural history since 1865. The best statistical sources are the United States censuses of agriculture. The manuscript censuses of 1870 and 1880 permit a detailed look at individual farm operations in the census years of 1869 and 1879. It is regrettable that manuscript census data are not available for later years. The decennial published censuses of agriculture are absolutely basic. They contain basic material on the number and size of farms, on crops and livestock, on the value of products sold, on farm tenure, and a vast amount of other data. Besides tables for various states, much of the information is published for individual counties as well. Beginning in 1925 the Census Bureau took an agricultural census in the middle of the decennial years.

Some special census publications are also of great value. In 1880 the Census Bureau authorized a special investigation of the cotton industry, which was published as *Report on Cotton Production in the United States*, 2 vols. (Washington, D.C., 1884). Besides statistical data on cotton growing in the southern states and counties, comments on soil, labor practices, and living conditions were included. In 1910 the Census Bureau made a special study of large plantations in 325 counties throughout the South. This study, published as chapter 12 in the *Thirteenth Census of the United States, 1910, Agriculture* 5 (Washington, D.C., 1913), contains much valuable information on the size of plantations, the type of tenure, and other important data. Much of this study, plus some additional material, was published by the Census Bureau in 1916 under the title *Plantation Farming in the United States* (Washington, D.C., 1916). In 1892 and 1893 the Senate Committee on Agriculture and Forestry gathered a great deal of information on cotton production and economic conditions among cotton farmers throughout the South. This was published in *Report of the Committee on Agriculture and Forestry on Condition of Cotton Growers in the United States, The Present Prices of Cotton, and the Remedy,* 2 vols. (Washington, D.C., 1895).

The annual report of the United States Department of Agriculture, organized in 1862, includes a wide variety of statistical and literary information on southern farming. First titled *Report of the Commissioner of Agriculture* and later known as *Yearbook of the United States Department of Agriculture,* or more commonly *Yearbook of Agriculture,* these volumes include both articles and statistical tables. Since 1936 the USDA has published annually a volume of *Agricultural Statistics* which contains data on southern farming as well as on the rest of the nation's agriculture. *Historical Statistics of the United States* also includes some important statistical series of use to the student of southern agricultural history.

One of the best sources on southern farming from the 1890s onward is the reports of the state agricultural experiment stations. Researchers at these stations have studied a host of problems and topics related to southern agriculture. These have included studies on soils, fertilizers, breeds of cotton, dairying and cattle raising, fruit growing, credit, the boll weevil, diversification, and many other subjects. Among the most valuable studies conducted by experiment station personnel in the early twentieth century were those dealing with farm structure, income, and standards of living.

A field of southern agricultural history that has received exhaustive study by scholars is the late nineteenth century. Of special interest have been the shift from slave to free labor, sharecropping, cotton, the credit system, the role of blacks, and farm productivity in the South. The new economic historians who used models, sophisticated mathematical and statistical methods, and other research techniques flooded the field with books and articles. Examples of this work are Stephen DeCanio, *Agriculture in the Postbellum South* (Cambridge: M.I.T. Press, 1974); Robert Higgs, *Competition and Coercion: Blacks in the American Economy, 1865-1914* (New York: Cambridge Univ. Press, 1977); Roger Ransom and Richard Sutch, *One Kind of Freedom: The Economic Consequences of Emancipation* (Cambridge, England: Cambridge Univ. Press, 1977) and Gavin Wright, *The Political Economy of the Cotton South* (New York: W.W. Norton, 1978). Articles on aspects of late nineteenth-century southern agriculture also appeared in *The Journal of Economic History, Agricultural History,* and other journals. DeCanio's discussion of "Cotton 'Overproduction' in Late Nineteenth Century Southern Agriculture," which appeared in the *Journal of Economic*

History in September 1973, is an example of the large number of articles written on some phase of southern agricultural history by the new economic historians.

The farmers' protest movements are another area of southern agricultural history that has received much scholarly attention. In 1976 Lawrence Goodwyn published the first comprehensive work on the Populists since John D. Hicks's *The Populist Revolt,* which appeared in 1931. While only part of Goodwyn's book *Democratic Promise: The Populist Moment in America* (New York: Oxford Univ. Press, 1976) treats the South, much of the activity of the Farmers Alliance and cooperatives which he discusses occurred in the southern states. To Goodwyn the most significant part of the farmers' revolt was the vision of cooperation, a new society, held by the protesters. The publication of *Democratic Promise* stimulated a lively academic controversy over the meaning and significance of Populism. The two best works that deal exclusively with southern agrarian protest are Theodore Saloutos, *Farmer Movements in the South, 1865-1933* (Berkeley: Univ. of California Press, 1960), and Robert C. McMath, Jr., *A History of the Southern Farmers' Alliance* (Chapel Hill: Univ. of North Carolina Press, 1975).

The demand of black farmers for land and their condition in freedom have been studied by Edward Magdol in *A Right to the Land: Essays on the Freedmen's Community* (Westport, Conn.: Greenwood Press, 1977); Joel Williamson, *After Slavery: The Negro in South Carolina during Reconstruction, 1861-1877* (Chapel Hill: Univ. of North Carolina Press, 1965); Robert Higgs, *Cooperation and Coercion,* cited earlier; and a host of other studies.

General studies of southern agricultural change and development in the early twentieth century are conspicuously lacking. John L. Fulmer surveyed some of the changes on southern farms from 1920 to 1950 in *Agricultural Progress in the Cotton Belt since 1920* (Chapel Hill: Univ. of North Carolina Press, 1950). For the most part, however, a major gap appears in the South's agricultural history between Populism and the New Deal. Government documents, state experiment station bulletins, and articles in scholarly and popular journals are the best sources.

Historians and other scholars, however, have written widely on southern agriculture during the New Deal. In his book *The American Farmer and the New Deal* (Ames: Iowa State Univ. Press, 1982), Theodore Saloutos included material on southern agriculture, including a chapter on black farmers. Older studies include *Cotton and the AAA* by Henry I. Richards (Washington, D.C.: Brookings Institution, 1936), and Harold B. Howe, *Tobacco under the AAA* (Washington, D.C.: Brookings Institution, 1935).

Much of the writing on southern agriculture during the New Deal period has emphasized the plight of the poorer farmers. Among these books are David E. Conrad, *The Forgotten Farmers: The Story of Sharecroppers in the New Deal* (Urbana: Univ. of Illinois Press, 1965); Donald H. Grubbs, *Cry from the Cotton: The Southern Tenant Farmers' Union and the New Deal* (Chapel Hill: Univ. of North Carolina Press, 1971); Paul E. Mertz, *New Deal Policy and Southern Rural Poverty* (Baton Rouge: Louisiana State Univ. Press, 1978); and Donald Holley, *Uncle Sam's Farmers: The New Deal Communities in the Lower Mississippi Valley* (Urbana: Univ. of Illinois Press, 1975). *Prosperity Road: The New Deal, Tobacco, and North*

Carolina (Chapel Hill: Univ. of North Carolina Press, 1980), by Anthony J. Badger, is an excellent study of one important southern crop and the New Deal policies related to it. Economists Murray R. Benedict and Oscar C. Stine have included some very useful material on cotton, tobacco, and rice in *The Agricultural Commodity Programs: Two Decades of Experience* (New York: Twentieth Century Fund, 1956).

The drive toward the modernization of southern agriculture from the late 1930s onward still awaits full historical treatment. *The New Revolution in the Cotton Economy: Mechanization and Its Consequences* (Chapel Hill: Univ. of North Carolina Press, 1957) only begins to fill the need. Accelerating change on southern farms after World War II can be studied in the proceedings of the annual cotton mechanization conferences first held in Stoneville, Mississippi, in 1947 and sponsored by the National Cotton Council. There are, however, two excellent articles that present an overview of recent agricultural change in the South. Pete Daniel's "The Transformation of the Rural South, 1930 to the Present," *Agricultural History* 55 (July 1981): 231-48; and Jack Temple Kirby's "The Transformation of Southern Plantations, ca. 1920-1960," *Agricultural History* 57 (July 1983): 257-76, are the best summaries of the modernization of southern farming. The only brief summary of southern agricultural history is Gilbert C. Fite's, "Southern Agriculture since the Civil War: An Overview," *Agricultural History* 53 (January 1979): 3-21.

Index

acreage control, 66; for cotton, 93, 104, 108, 123-24, 129-30; for tobacco, 131-32, 166
agrarian revolt, 56-61
agrarian tradition, 159
Agricultural Adjustment Act: provisions of, 128-29; payments under, 139-40; declared unconstitutional, 143
agricultural agencies: advocate changes, 76-78; and blacks 223-24; and poor farmers, 223-24
agricultural colleges: contributions of, 76; urge farming changes, 183; farmers seek advice from, 193; on poverty, 224
agricultural experiment stations, 76-78, 183
agricultural journals: support reform, 75-76; subscribers in South, 76
agricultural reform: publications supporting, 72, 75-76; slow progress of, 173; at end of World War II, 174
agricultural societies; 74
agriculture: condition of in South, 21-22, 34-39, 211-18; infrastructure of, 87, 99, 118, 205, 230; economic importance of, 126-27; modernization of, 149-50, 160-61; recommendations to restructure in 1945, 178. See also farmers; farms
Alabama, 7, 8, 13, 43, 52, 77, 83, 99, 102, 112, 116, 121, 122, 134, 155, 166, 168, 193, 203
American Agriculture Movement, 228-29
American Cotton Association, 95, 104
American Cotton Growers Exchange, 105
American Farm Bureau Federation, 128
Arkansas, 11, 83, 102, 131, 140, 145, 188, 201

Bankhead, John H.: supports farmers, 128, 172; backs farm tenant bill, 146
Bankhead Cotton Control Act, 132

Barrett, Charles S.: president of Farmers' Union, 63, 64; friend of presidents, 65; recommends plowing up cotton, 66
benefit payments, 133; in 1930s, 139-41, 164; controversy over, 142-43
Benson, Ezra Taft, 216
black belt, 5, 18
black families: living standards of, 35-38, 121; relief payments to, 136
black farmers: desire for land, 2; as sharecroppers, 15-18; tenancy among, 19; condition in late nineteenth century, 20-21; progress of, 20-21; numbers of, 20-21, 99, 156, 171, 208; as farm owners, 21, 35, 99, 156; main source of income, 21; living standards of, 35-38, 121; diets of, 37-39, 121-22; failures of, 83, 89, 113; in depression, 125-26; leave agriculture, 156, 208; after World War II, 207-8; treatment of, 222-24
black labor, 86-87
blacks: education of, 39-40; segregation of, 46-47; migration during World War I, 98; exodus from farming, 156, 208. See also black farmers; freedmen
black tenants: in Yazoo County, Miss., 19
boll weevil: encourages diversification, 81; invades U. S., 80-82, 94, 97; in early 1920s, 103; monument to, 112
Bonner, J. C., 209
Brannan, Charles F., 212
broilers, 200-201
Brooks, D. W., 35 161
Brooks County, Georgia: economic study of, 99-100
Burton, Glenn W., 196-97
buy-a-bale campaign, 92

Campbell, J. Phil, 193
Campbell, Thomas M., 79